BUSINESS ORGANIZATIONS

A TRANSACTIONAL PERSPECTIVE

SECOND EDITION

Edited by Donald Scotten
University of Southern California
Gould School of Law

cognella® | ACADEMIC PUBLISHING

Bassim Hamadeh, CEO and Publisher
Carrie Montoya, Manager, Revisions and Author Care
Kaela Martin, Project Editor
Alia Bales, Associate Production Editor
Jess Estrella, Senior Graphic Designer
Natalie Lakosil, Licensing Manager
Natalie Piccotti, Senior Marketing Manager
Kassie Graves, Director of Acquisitions and Sales
Jamie Giganti, Senior Managing Editor

Copyright © 2018 by Cognella, Inc. All rights reserved. No part of this publication may be reprinted, reproduced, transmitted, or utilized in any form or by any electronic, mechanical, or other means, now known or hereafter invented, including photocopying, microfilming, and recording, or in any information retrieval system without the written permission of Cognella, Inc. For inquiries regarding permissions, translations, foreign rights, audio rights, and any other forms of reproduction, please contact the Cognella Licensing Department at rights@cognella.com.

Trademark Notice: Product or corporate names may be trademarks or registered trademarks, and are used only for identification and explanation without intent to infringe.

Cover image copyright © 2016 iStockphoto LP/shironosov.

Printed in the United States of America.

ISBN: 978-1-5165-1363-5 (pbk) / 978-1-5165-1364-2(br)

CONTENTS

PART 4: CORPORATIONS

PART 5: HYBRID ENTITIES

PART 6: TAXATION

INDEX   399

PREFACE

After years of using an assortment of casebooks and materials, I was left unsatisfied with how Business Organizations is taught to students. Instead of focusing on lengthy cases and narration of various rules, I have attempted to compile the most relevant statutory principles into one organized compilation. Combining these statutory sections with relevant introductory business concepts, this text is intended to provide students with working knowledge of the laws surrounding business organizations in order to prepare them for any legal or business career.

I would like to thank my research assistants, Michael Spirtos and Evan Markiles, for contributing their time and energy in the drafting and editing of this book and Chris White for improving this book in innumerable ways in the second edition.

PART 1

Overview

CHAPTER 1

UNDERSTANDING TRANSACTIONAL LAWYERING

This book will teach business organizations from a transactional practice perspective. There is a great difference in the legal world between litigation and transactional practice. While most, if not all, of the first year of law school focuses on litigation, much of law practice takes place in the transactional world. What is transactional law? At its heart, transactional law focuses on deals and contracts. Unlike litigators, whose practice focuses on serving their clients by achieving gains for them in an adversarial context, transactional lawyers work together to produce a mutually beneficial result for their clients and those on the other side of the negotiating table.

A. TRANSACTIONAL LAWYERING

Teaching Business Lawyering in Law Schools

Lawyers need to be exposed to the skills and norms of the transactional side of practice as well as the litigation side because there are real differences between transactional lawyers and litigators. Although my prejudices are painted in broad strokes, in general I believe that litigators are more focused on the battle at hand, while transactional lawyers are more relationship oriented and focused on the larger war that must be won. Litigators fight to assign blame for problems that have already occurred, while transactional lawyers strive to avoid problems in the first place. Litigation is by and large a zero-sum game—the parties are fighting over how to split losses. One party will win and one party will lose. In transactional law, on the other hand, the possibility exists for lawyers to add value to a deal. In transactional practice, it is possible for all the parties to leave the closing feeling like the deal was a great idea

Eric J. Gouvin, *Teaching Business Lawyering in Law Schools: A Candid Assessment of the Challenges and Some Sugges-tions for Moving Ahead*, 78 U. Mo. Kan. City L. Rev. 429, 431–33 (2009). Copyright © 2009 by University of Missouri-Kansas City School of Law. Reprinted with permission.

(probably not something that happens very often at the end of a lawsuit). In short, transactional lawyers have a special set of skills and values that need to be acknowledged and taught.

Where law schools do an acceptable job of acculturating our students to the adversarial, litigation side of the profession, we do a less than satisfactory job in inculcating the skills and values of transactional lawyers, including lawyers with the sensibilities necessary to counsel entrepreneurs. This failure to acculturate our students matters because litigators and transactional lawyers approach the practice of law in fundamentally different ways. As a case in point, I recall a transaction from my own practice experience. My firm was known as a business law firm (although we had an excellent litigation department). We represented a Finnish company that was entering into a joint venture with one of the Maine Indian tribes to produce a proprietary building system, the intellectual property for which being owned by our Finnish client. The Indian tribe was represented by a firm that had won a series of brilliantly litigated cases forcing federal recognition of the Maine tribes and establishing a new order for how the tribes were governed.

I do not want to take anything away from counsel for the tribe—they were outstanding litigators. The problem was they could not hang up their litigator hat when they were in a transactional context. This is not to say that business lawyers need not zealously represent their clients in transactions. It is true that the parties to a transaction are, in some sense, adversarial—they both need to negotiate zealously to make sure they get a good deal. In the end, however, both parties at the table need to recognize their common interest in making the deal succeed so they both can make money. A business deal cannot be adversarial in the same way that litigation is adversarial because otherwise no deal would get done: one party would win, one party would lose, and it would become clear to the loser that the deal made no sense.

Needless to say, the transaction between our Finnish client and its Maine Indian tribe partner failed. It limped along for a couple of years, but the counsel for the tribe always saw issues as "us versus them" (i.e., Indians versus Finns) and never as just a problem affecting the venture and, therefore, in the interest of both parties to address jointly with give and take on both sides. In my estimation, the legal counsel for the tribe was so used to the win/lose mentality of litigation that they could not adjust to the possibility of the win/win outcome that well-lawyered business deals envision.

That is one example, but there are many others. If we keep cranking out new lawyers who see the world as a no-holds-barred battle to ultimate victory or defeat, we are going to have the unintended effect of retarding the development of good business lawyering generally. Aspiring business lawyers trained by litigators using litigation-based teaching materials will enter the profession with the wrong orientation to be effective in the deal-making role. To counteract this tendency, law schools should start introducing law students to the culture of business law, and especially the role of the lawyer in entrepreneurial activity. Despite the pressing need for the transactional perspective in the law curriculum, the legal academy has been slow to integrate the professional skills and values of transactional lawyers into the program of legal instruction.

B. WHAT SKILLS DOES A TRANSACTIONAL LAWYER NEED?

What a Transactional Lawyer Needs to Know: Identifying and Implementing Competencies for Transactional Lawyers

I. History of Transactional Training

For various reasons, law schools emphasize the role of lawyer as litigator and provide legal training accordingly. The casebook method is the primary method of teaching in the first year of law school. That method focuses on appellate court cases in which litigation has already occurred. The casebook method continues as the major teaching method beyond the first-year curriculum. By emphasizing "cases" through the casebook teaching method, law school depicts the typical lawyer as a litigator, rather than as a transactional attorney. Whether the law school subject is a litigation-related subject, such as torts, or a transactional subject, such as contracts, the casebook method is the pedagogy of choice. Legal Writing and Analysis, also a first-year course, focuses primarily on litigation analysis and writing skills. Throughout the three years of law school, course offerings lean primarily toward litigation-oriented subjects. As in the first year of law school, transactional subjects continue to be taught from casebooks. Admittedly, the number of law schools offering contract drafting has risen markedly, as have the transactional clinics and transactional externships; however, most extracurricular and clinical opportunities are litigation oriented.

Thus, while more than half of lawyers likely practice transactional law (and undoubtedly a greater percentage are called upon to use transactional skills at some juncture in their practice), law schools fail to adequately train attorneys for transactional practice. The two challenges for law students, young lawyers, and law firms are identifying minimum competencies for transactional practice and identifying how young lawyers might acquire those competencies.

II. Transactional Competencies

While half of all lawyers will go on to become transactional lawyers, they will engage in widely varied kinds of transactional practices, as well as in many different office sizes, locations, and settings. A transactional attorney may focus on real estate transfers, property management, corporate issues, or deals and buyouts. A transactional attorney may work in a large firm where the deals are complex or may practice in a small town or city as a general practitioner. Setting

Lisa Penland, *What a Transactional Lawyer Needs to Know: Identifying and Implementing Competencies for Transactional Lawyers*, 5 J. Ass'n of Legal Writing Directors 118, 120–127 (2008). Copyright © 2008 by Association of Legal Writing Directors. Reprinted with permission.

minimum competencies is designed not to prepare lawyers for a specific type of transactional practice, but to provide them with the baseline of knowledge for the major areas of transactional practice. Clearly, the transactional attorney will build upon this baseline in the practice of law. Thus, this article introduces minimum transactional competencies for both the "deal" lawyer and for the general practitioner. While this article will address how to achieve these minimal competencies, it is the competencies themselves that will guide law students, young lawyers, and law firms as they prepare for transactional practice.

A. Transactional Competencies for the Deal Lawyer

A lawyer who is an expert in putting together business agreements is often known as a "deal" lawyer. Business agreements are legal contracts, and an appropriately constructed contract "express[es] the parties' business deal." Thus, most of the baseline transactional competencies for deal lawyers are related to acquiring adequate background context for business agreements and acquiring the skills necessary to negotiate and draft a business agreement. As noted by one commentator:

> Your junior transactional attorneys take on tough tasks right away, including drafting contracts and performing due diligence. The big problem? Fed a strict diet of case-method analysis in law school, these new practitioners don't have the necessary background to handle their duties effectively. …

So what do "junior deal lawyers" need to know to hit the ground running in transactional practice? While the following list is fleshed out in more detail below, the essential competencies for a deal lawyer are as follows:

1. The ability to understand business associations, advise about business structures, and draft documents related to business associations.

2. The ability to investigate facts and research the law (with emphasis on due diligence).

3. The ability to draft and negotiate contracts.

4. The ability to identify and address the ethical implications of transactional practice.

1. A Deal Lawyer Must Understand the Structure of Business Associations

At the very least, junior deal lawyers need to understand the various business organizations and the practical and legal implications of each. That is, what are the attributes of a corporation, partnership, limited partnership, agency, or sole proprietorship? The lawyer should know how to create all types of business entities and how each entity is governed. The lawyer should be able to advise a client as to the advantages and disadvantages of doing business as a particular entity. The young lawyer should be able to answer the questions of who is in charge of the entity and who can act on behalf of this entity. She should be able to identify other persons and entities that may do business or enter into deals with business associations, such as trustees and beneficiaries, conservators, personal representatives, business promoters, lenders, borrowers, and the like. Again, the legal and practical implications of the nature of these persons and entities should be known. The young business lawyer should be knowledgeable in basic entity finance, including an understanding of financial statements.

2. A Deal Lawyer Must Know How to Investigate Facts and Research the Law

The young lawyer will need to have investigative and research tools in her bag of competencies. The young lawyer must have an understanding of due diligence. Due diligence is investigation of facts; however, it is a special kind of investigation understood as the "examination of a business or portion thereof in connection with a proposed transaction." The young transactional attorney must understand the potential areas of due diligence, including how to review corporate documents and how to obtain information about capitalization and stockholders, to name only a few. The junior deal lawyer must know how to construct relevant areas of inquiry and formulate questions to uncover facts. The junior attorney must have interviewing and counseling skills that will assist her in obtaining information from clients and other parties. The transactional lawyer must have a basic understanding of legal research and those research resources unique to transactional law.

3. A Deal Lawyer Must Know How to Draft and Negotiate a Contract

The competencies of drafting and negotiation are intertwined skills. A young lawyer must understand drafting in order to better negotiate the business deal. Further, the negotiation and drafting process are recursive; often negotiation continues throughout the drafting process. Before beginning to draft, the transactional lawyer must first understand that writing a contract is not like other types of legal writing. As noted by Charles Fox:

> The writing that we are exposed to on a day-to-day basis (even in law school) is almost entirely expository writing, the goal of which is to persuade or provide information to the reader. A contract is different: the goal of a contract is to describe *with precision* the substance of the meeting of two minds, in language that will be interpreted by each subsequent reader in *exactly the same way*.

Once the transactional lawyer begins drafting, the most important drafting skill is an understanding of the building blocks of a contract. The building blocks of a contract are those components of the contract that are necessary to translate the deal into a legally effective document, including representations and warranties, covenants, rights, conditions, discretionary authority, and declarations. Seasoned drafters understand that a party may lose the negotiated advantage of a contract term by failing to use the appropriate building block. Another required drafting skill is understanding the basic parts of contract, that is, the large-scale structure of a contract (introductory provisions, definitions, action sections, etc.). Further the young lawyer must know and understand the particular language used to memorialize a building block or to signify an organizational component of the contract. Principles of clear and unambiguous drafting must be understood, including format, sentence structure, and tabulation. The young attorney must not only understand how to draft a contract, but also, as a key tool in the negotiation process, how to review and comment on a contract drafted by another lawyer.

4. A Deal Lawyer Must Understand the Ethical Implications of Transactional Practice

Any list of competencies for lawyers must include ethical considerations. In the Carnegie Foundation report, *Educating Lawyers*, the authors urge a more deliberate integration of ethics and professionalism during the education of lawyers, be they transactional lawyers or otherwise. Indeed, the report notes that "[p]rofessional education is … inherently ethical education in the deep and broad sense." The need to integrate ethical considerations into educating lawyers is universal, and some of the ethical considerations that transactional lawyers face are universal practice considerations. However, as one commentator noted, the ABA Model Rules of Professional Conduct, as well as case law and ethical opinions, focus on ethical issues that arise in litigation; thus, the ethical considerations unique to transactional practice may not be as transparent to young lawyers who have been trained using these resources.

The young transactional lawyer must understand how to allocate responsibility between client and attorney. She must have a thorough understanding of the scope of knowledge and experience she should obtain before endeavoring to carry out a particular transaction. The transactional attorney must understand how to interact with third parties and the scope of the attorney's duties to those third parties who may not be clients of the attorney, or even direct beneficiaries of the deal. The ethical parameters of joint representation, a situation allowed in transactional practice, must be clearly understood by the transactional attorney. Finally, the transactional attorney must be aware of the ethical implications of multi-jurisdictional transactions.

CHAPTER 2

INTRODUCING BUSINESS ORGANIZATIONS

A. WHAT ARE BUSINESS ORGANIZATIONS?

Business organizations are the legal structures that people utilize to operate a business. Every day, we each come into contact with business organizations, from purchasing a coffee at Starbucks to checking email on Google. While we are most familiar with business organizations that are multibillion-dollar corporations, any business (no matter how large or small) can operate under a variety of organizational forms. The selection of an organizational form must be made carefully, as the choice will have significant implications for the business. The legal form will determine how a business must be run, the manner in which it is taxed, the personal liability of the owners, the way ownership interests can be transferred, the process for exiting the business, and more. The ultimate decision as to what form is best for a business will depend on the business objectives and the desires of the transactional lawyer's client.

In our study of business organizations, we will examine how these legal entities are formed, operated, and terminated. We will focus on the rights, duties, obligations, and responsibilities of the various actors within business organizations. These actors include the people who own, invest in, or manage a business.

B. WHY FORM A BUSINESS ORGANIZATION?

Before introducing the common types of business organizations from which a client can choose, we should ask a fundamental question: Why do people form business organizations (referred to as "firms" by economists)?

Form and Function in Business Organizations

Why Do People Form Firms?

[There are] at least five general reasons: (i) delegation and specialization, (ii) diversification, (iii) separation and legitimacy, (iv) managing competition, and (v) discipline and incentives. There may be more.

Delegation and Specialization

People often retain agents because they do not have the time or expertise to conduct their own business. In other words, it may be cheaper to hire someone to do some tasks than it is to do them yourself, whether in terms of out-of-pocket expenses or in terms of opportunity costs. And if you need someone to perform a particular task repeatedly, it may be cheaper still to hire one or more employees.

But why would an employee take a job in such a pyramid scheme in which the employer keeps the profits? In theory, the employee could sell his or her services to the firm or its customers and keep the profit. One answer is that a firm may be able to generate more business opportunities than could a self-employed individual. The firm may have some employees who spend their time primarily generating business opportunities—such as a sales staff or rainmaker—while others do the actual work. Moreover, the firm may have other resources or tools that the employee needs in order to do the work—tools that the employee could not afford to acquire individually. Thus, another reason for forming a firm is to facilitate specialization and delegation to achieve economies of scale. This is a fairly simple reason for firms, but there is no doubt some truth in it. Indeed, it is more or less the model that comes to mind when one talks about agency costs.

On the other hand, individuals could in theory rent all of these resources to each other. For example, one person might set up shop as a business-getter and then sell business opportunities to those who specialize in performance. Of course, some customers might object to being sold a product or service by one person, only to have some other person provide the service. Still, some industries are so organized, at least roughly speaking. Indeed, that is the essential idea behind franchising.

The classic response to the question of why people form firms is that markets do not work very well for some (or many) transactions. As Ronald Coase pointed out long ago, this is particularly true when it is difficult to determine the value of a particular input up front or to determine its contribution to return after the fact.

Richard A. Booth, *Form and Function in Business Organizations*, 58 Bus. Law 1433, 1334–39 (2003). Copyright © 2003 by Richard A. Booth. Reprinted with permission.

The classical theory of the firm explanation seems to miss some rather obvious reasons for firm formation. For one, some tasks simply cannot be performed by a single individual acting alone. A Broadway play is a good example. Of course, it may be possible for one of the actors to hire the rest of the cast. But someone still needs to direct the show. Thus, one function of the firm may be to establish lines of authority in the context of an undertaking in which it is important to choose a course of action from among multiple acceptable alternatives. For another, some inputs may not be available for rent. For example, an entrepreneur who needs more capital may not be able to borrow all that he needs. Thus, he may have no choice but to form a corporation and sell shares if he is unwilling to take on a partner.

More importantly, the classical explanation seems to suggest that forming a firm should be more the exception than the rule. That is, it suggests that one would form a firm and submit to it only if necessary. But the opposite seems to be closer to the truth. People seem more inclined to do business in groups than to strike out on their own. Indeed, going into business solo is typically seen as a relatively high-risk strategy. In any event, there would seem to be far more firms in the world than one would expect if forming a firm is, in fact, a last resort.

Diversification

Although delegation and specialization may be sufficient reasons for forming a firm, participants in a firm may also benefit from diversification in a variety of ways. A firm may be able to generate a more regular stream of business opportunities than could an individual. Also, the firm may be able to smooth out the income stream for individuals. For example, a lawyer may join a law firm in order to be assured of a steady income irrespective of whether his or her individual practice is busy or slow during any particular period. Similarly, by joining a firm, one may be able to call on others to fill in if one is too busy or even simply to manage one's schedule and get in a round of golf. A firm may also provide a form of insurance by absorbing the costs of accidents through vicarious liability. These benefits may exist quite independently from economies of scale. For example, a lawyer may bill $500,000 per year on the average by billing $1,000,000 every other year or $2,000,000 every fourth year. If the lawyer joins together with a large enough group of other lawyers with similar billing patterns, everyone in the firm can be paid regularly on the basis of the average. No one in the firm makes any more money (on the average) than he would as a solo practitioner. In other words, there are no economies of scale. Nevertheless, the lawyers in the firm are distinctly better off because they have a regular income. Risk is reduced even though return remains the same.

Separation and Legitimacy

In some cases, people form a firm simply to separate business from self. (Martha Stewart may be the exception that proves the rule.) Of course, one of the primary motivations here is limited liability and the insulation of assets from unrelated liabilities. But limited liability aside, forming a corporation (for example) may give the business more legitimacy than doing business under one's own name as a sole proprietor. It suggests to the world that the business is something more than (and different from) the individual who owns it. Of course, technically, that is true with a corporation. And indeed this separation of business from participants is what allows a corporation to raise equity capital from outside investors. Separation may also be achieved simply by filing an assumed name certificate and calling oneself a company. Thus, to some extent the separation rationale is circular. Forming a company generates legitimacy only because the world associates the word with legitimacy.

A related, but somewhat more substantial reason for forming a firm is that when two or more people have joined together to conduct a business, it suggests that the business may be better thought out and therefore more trustworthy than a business that has been started by a single individual who may have idiosyncratic ideas. Similarly, it may be easier to attract others to join a firm than it is to retain the services of an independent contractor or freelance agent to provide some needed input. Or association with a firm may add value to an agent's contribution. For example, I joined a law faculty in part because it gave my work a legitimacy that would have been difficult to achieve on my own. My basic point here is that there is a tendency to view firms primarily in terms of internal control structure. But external appearance may also matter. To sum up, people sometimes form firms simply to gain status for the enterprise or to define status to the world.

Managing Competition

In some cases, people form firms to reduce competition. In other words, two or more competitors might form a partnership in order to split the available profits, while saving the costs of competing (such as advertising). Of course, by eliminating competition, a firm may also be able to raise prices or restrict output. Although this may be illegal under the antitrust laws for very large businesses, it is fairly clear that it is an important reason for some smaller businesses. Indeed, it has become quite common even for relatively mundane businesses to seek or demand non-competition agreements even from low level employees. (For example, Hank Hill might be asked to agree not to go to work for another propane company in Texas.) Whatever one might think of such tactics, and whether or not such agreements are ultimately enforceable, it is quite clear that non-competition is a motive. Moreover, although one could attempt to negotiate a series of contracts with one's competitors, such tactics would likely be illegal even on the smallest scale. In any event, it is far easier to achieve the same result by forming a firm or by requiring employees to sign a non-competition agreement.

Although it is clear that businesspeople might form a firm to reduce competition, it is also possible that forming a firm may increase competition. In some cases, consumers are more likely to seek out a department store or supermarket than a boutique or specialty shop. Of course, the opposite is true as well. I would never think of going to my car dealer rather than Jiffy Lube or a similar operation for an oil change. The point is that a firm with a wider array of products and services may sometimes be more attractive to consumers. Or the firm may serve to concentrate talent in such a way that it produces a better product. For example, a law firm (or a law faculty for that matter) may produce better services or written product because the various members are able to have their work reviewed, checked, or commented on by others. Again, the outside world may be more inclined to view a group as more legitimate than an individual, but to some extent it may be because the product of the group is superior.

Mixed motives are also possible. For example, a group medical practice may seek out a new partner in order to offer a new area of care or expanded hours. But the group may also worry that the new recruit may use the group as an entrée to the community and then split off to form a new competing practice taking business along.

Discipline and Incentives

One final motivation for forming a firm (or joining one) is that association with a group may generate additional motivation, perhaps particularly for people who are not self-starters. In other words, it may be that people form or join firms to force themselves to work harder or to impose discipline that may be difficult to self impose. For example, securities firms have traditionally been fairly serious about policing themselves (recent events notwithstanding), although one could argue that they do so mostly to avoid punishment or private litigation. Another related reason for forming or joining a firm is to gain the benefits of institutional memory.

To sum up, there are several distinct reasons why people form firms. Curiously, most of those reasons seem to turn more on the relationship of active participants to each other or on the relationship of the firm to various third parties (including creditors), than on the relationship between participants and investors. Of course, investors are interested in how well managers work with each other, but not too interested. A diversified investor cares little about the fortunes of individual companies. It may be, therefore, that we lawyers, judges, and academics have given short shrift to how well the rules work for those who toil day to day in the trenches of partnerships and corporations. Moreover, the recent spate of corporate scandals strongly suggests we should focus more on internal controls than we have in the past, particularly in connection with firms that do not have a large, involved shareholder. External monitors may not be nearly as important as we have made them out to be.

CHAPTER 3

ORGANIZATIONAL FORMS & CONSIDERATIONS

A. CHOOSING A LEGAL STRUCTURE

When a client seeks advice on selecting a legal structure to operate a business, a transactional lawyer should discuss with the client several key factors that vary among legal structures. Based on the client's relative interest in each factor, the lawyer can make a recommendation that will best serve the client. There are five key factors for the client to consider when choosing a legal structure:

1. Taxation
2. Liability and risk
3. Management
4. Continuity and transferability
5. Expense and formality

1. Taxation

A legal structure determines how you or your business is taxed. For four of the common organizational types (sole proprietorship, partnership, LLC, and S-corporation), the business as an entity does not pay taxes. Rather, profits and losses from the business pass through to the owner(s) and are reflected on the personal tax return(s) of the owner(s) (taxes are reported on the owners' tax returns). Only C-corporations as a business entity pay taxes.

Source: Fed. Deposit Ins. Corp. and U.S. Small Bus. Ass'n, *Participant Guide: Organizational Types and Considerations for a Small Business*, Fin. Educ. Curriculum 1, 7–14, http://www.sba.gov/sites/default/files/files/PARTICIPANT_GUIDE_ORGANIZATIONAL_TYPES.pdf (last visited Sep. 26, 2017). Copyright in the Public Domain.

2. Liability and Risk

The liability and risk to which you are exposed when starting a business can generally be categorized as:

- Person or property

- Contractual

The person or property category, also called "tort risk," is defined as intentional or unintentional harm to the person or property of another person. Some examples of tort risk are worker injury, product liability, automobile liability, and general liability, such as when somebody falls on a wet floor. Contractual liability and risk is associated with contract disputes with financers, vendors, and customers.

Legal structures determine who, or what entity, is legally responsible for liability for judgments if there is a successful lawsuit against the business. In particular, judgments against a business could result in the owner being held personally liable to pay for damages; that is, all of the owner's personal assets (including the owner's house) could be seized to pay a judgment. New business owners commonly misunderstand liability factors and assume they always need to incorporate to protect themselves from liability. Insurance and well-written contracts can help manage risks to business owners.

3. Management

Each legal structure has its own decision-making authority.

4. Continuity and Transferability

This factor refers to how a business persists and how the business is sold to new ownership.

5. Expense and Formality

Expenses, complexity, and legal responsibilities differ between the different types of business structures.

B. MENU OF LEGAL STRUCTURES

Depending on a client's weighing of the above factors, different types of legal structures may be more appropriate than others. When considering the variety of legal structures to choose from you must keep in mind two things: 1) the preferences of the client and 2) the goals of the business. For example, a simple Mom & Pop shop may want to form a different legal entity than a group of business school graduates creating the next Google.

Each of the common entity types is described on the following pages using the five selection factors described previously.

1. Sole Proprietorship

A sole proprietorship is a type of business entity that is owned and run by one individual and in which there is no legal distinction between the owner and the business. In other words, the business is one and the same as the owner.

The sole proprietorship is the most common form of operation for small businesses.

a. Taxation

A sole proprietorship has pass-through taxation. The business itself does not file a tax return; rather, the income (or loss) passes through and is reported on the owner's personal tax return. Sole proprietors often need to make quarterly estimated tax payments.

b. Liability and Risk

The owner of a sole proprietorship has unlimited personal liability for any liabilities incurred by the business. You can manage much of this risk with insurance and sound contracts.

c. Management

Control of a sole proprietorship belongs entirely to the owner, who also assumes the full risk of the business.

d. Continuity and Transferability

A sole proprietorship lasts as long as the owner is alive and operating the business or until the business is sold. The owner can also sell business assets as well as transfer the business to a family member, often through the estate planning process.

e. Expense and Formality

The sole proprietorship is the simplest way of doing business. The costs to create a sole proprietorship are very low and very little formality is required. A sole proprietorship may be an appropriate form of business for many small and start-up business ventures.

2. General Partnership

A general partnership is an association between two or more people in business seeking a profit. Like a sole proprietorship, partnerships have pass-through taxation and owners are personally liable for the debts of the business. General partnerships can be created with little formality, but because more than one person is involved, a written contract stipulating the terms of the partnership, called a "partnership agreement," should be created.

a. Taxation

Like a sole proprietorship, a partnership is a tax-reporting entity, not a tax-paying entity. A partnership must file an annual information return with the US Internal Revenue Service (IRS) to report the income and losses from its operations, but it does not pay federal income tax. A partnership "passes through" any profits or losses to its partners, which are divided based on the partnership agreement. Each partner includes his or her share of the partnership's income or loss on his or her tax return and may need to make estimated tax payments quarterly.

b. Liability and Risk

Owners of a general partnership have unlimited personal liability. In general, each partner is jointly [and severally] liable for the partnership's obligations. Joint liability means that each partner can individually be held responsible for the entire amount of an obligation of the partnership. However, as with the sole proprietorship, insurance and quality contract design can protect the partnership against most risks.

c. Management

Partners have equal management rights, unless otherwise stipulated in the partnership agreement.

d. Continuity and Transferability

A partnership exists as long as specified in the partnership agreement. The partnership agreement will determine the consequences of a partner dying or leaving the business. The business could remain in the hands of the remaining partners or be dissolved.

e. Expense and Formality

Again, general partnerships are similar to sole proprietorships in their legal creation and maintenance and thus have low expense and legal formality. New potential partners should create their partnership agreement with the help of an experienced attorney and accountant. Partnership agreements cover topics such as:

- Capital contributions
- Distribution of profits
- Management duties
- Bookkeeping
- Banking
- Termination

3. Corporations

A corporation is a legal entity that is separate and independent from the people who own or run the corporation. This means that the corporation itself, not the shareholders that own it, is held legally liable for the actions and debts incurred by the business. As a corporation, it has privileges such as the ability to enter into contracts but it also has certain responsibilities such as the payment of taxes.

Corporations are more complex than other business structures. There are also potentially costly administrative fees to create and maintain a corporation as well as more complex tax and legal requirements. Most businesses do not need to incorporate. Corporations are generally suggested for established, larger companies with multiple employees or when certain other factors apply, such as a corporation that sells a product or provides a service that could expose the business to sizable liability.

To form a corporation requires the filing of articles of incorporation with your secretary of state or, in some states, your state's corporations division. Filing articles of incorporation will usually cost no more than a few hundred dollars in fees. While the contents of articles of incorporation vary from state to state, most will establish the following:

- Company name
- Company purpose
- Company stock quantity and price
- Resident agent name and address
- Corporate officers names and addresses

Only after the articles of incorporation are filed and accepted by your state, does the corporation acquire legal existence. Once incorporated, the board of directors meets for the first time, followed by at least one annual meeting per year. The board of directors appoints officers who conduct the business of the corporation. Corporate ownership is more complex because a corporation has a legal identity separate from those of its owners. Corporations designate ownership by issuing shares of stock. Thus, owners are shareholders who have received or purchased stock in the corporation.

Shareholders typically have various rights, including the right to do the following:

- Elect directors
- Receive information
- Inspect corporate records
- Vote on fundamental business decisions such as mergers and liquidations
- Share in dividend distributions

a. Taxation

For federal income tax purposes, a C-corporation is recognized as a separate tax paying entity. So, a C-corporation pays corporate income tax on any corporate profits. The individuals who own the corporation will pay personal income tax on the corporate profits distributed by the corporation to the owners. This creates the issue of "double taxation.

By contrast, S-corporations are corporations that elect to pass corporate income, losses, deductions, and credit through to their shareholders for federal tax purposes. Shareholders of S-corporations report the corporation's income and losses on their personal tax returns and are assessed tax at their individual income tax rates. This allows S-corporations to avoid double taxation on the corporate income.

b. Liability and Risk

A corporation is, strictly defined, a legal entity that is "immortal." That is, a corporation does not terminate upon the owner's death. Corporations can enter into and dissolve contracts, incur debts, sue, or be sued, own property, and sell property, as any individual may do. Corporation owners themselves have limited liability. While an individual may own all the shares in a corporation, that owner is not personally responsible for the corporation. With this limited liability, investors cannot lose more money than the amount they have invested in the corporation. Owners are not personally responsible for the debts and obligations of the corporation in the event these are not fulfilled. In other words, if a company with limited liability is sued, then the plaintiffs are suing the company, not its owners, or investors. Care should be taken to not "pierce the corporate veil." Personal checking accounts should not be used for business purposes, and the corporate name should always be used when interacting with customers.

c. Management

A corporation's overall management is vested in the board of directors chosen by the shareholders. The officers handle the business' day-to-day affairs under the board's general direction.

In small corporations, the managers, owners, and the board of directors are often the same people. In larger corporations, those three roles can be held by different people. For example, corporate boards often place day-to-day management decisions in the hands of a chief executive officer (CEO), who may also be the board chairman or president. The CEO supervises other executives, including the following people:

- Vice presidents who oversee various corporate functions
- Chief financial officer (CFO)
- Chief operating officer (COO)
- Chief information officer (CIO)

d. Continuity and Transferability

The independent life of a corporation makes possible its continuation, and the relatively undisturbed continued operation of the business, regardless of incapacity or death of one or more stockholders. The corporation as a separate legal entity does not cease to exist if one or more of its owners die. A business' corporate existence lasts as long as its shareholders decide the corporation should exist. Corporations can last for decades, through multiple generations of owners. Ownership of a corporation can be transferred by sale of the stock. Additional owners can be added either by the corporation selling stock or by current owners selling some of their stock.

e. Expense and Formality

Corporations are more complex entities to create, have more legal and accounting requirements, and are more complex to operate than sole proprietorships, partnerships, or LLCs. Investors are more easily attracted to corporations, but more complex ownership, reporting, and management requirements go along with this advantage. Disadvantages also include having to hold regular meetings of directors, keeping records of corporate activity, and maintaining the corporation's ongoing financial independence.

4. Limited Partnerships and Limited Liability Partnerships

Limited partnerships (LPs) and limited liability partnerships (LLPs) are two other organizational options for two or more people who plan to maintain a business for profit. Some jurisdictions only allow those who are licensed to practice in certain professions, such as law or accounting, to be eligible for the LLP structure.

a. Taxation

The tax treatment for LPs and LLPs is similar to general partnerships as discussed earlier. Profits and losses are passed through to the partners so the partners can reflect them on their individual tax return.

b. Liability and Risk

With the limited partnership structure, liability varies depending on the type of partner:

- A "general partner" has unlimited personal liability. The general partner is responsible for the everyday operations of the business.

- "Limited partners" are personally liable only up to their personal investment in the partnership. The limited partner must maintain a limited role in the day-to-day administration of the business. Legal counsel can advise what, if any, activities are permissible for a limited partner (besides contributing capital) to perform without losing the shield of limited liability.

With a limited liability partnership, personal liability for partners may be limited, but the rules vary considerably from state to state.

c. Management

The general partner in a limited partnership is responsible for the ordinary operations of the business. So, the limited partner does not control how the business will be run. The limited partnership structure generally encourages investors for short term projects, or for investing in capital assets. It is not often used for operating retail or service businesses.

d. Continuity and Transferability

How long a limited partnership exists depends on the partnership agreement. Partnerships may also be terminated if a partner becomes disassociated from the partnership, such as if a partner wants to leave the partnership.

e. Expense and Formality

Unlike a general partnership, the creation of a limited partnership or limited liability partnership requires a filing, possibly including the written partnership agreement, with the state. A limited partnership will likely also be required to include "limited partnership" or "LP" as part of its name, just as limited liability partnerships will be required to include that phrase or LLP in their name.

5. Limited Liability Company (LLC)

An LLC is similar to a corporation in some ways while similar to a general partnership or a sole proprietorship in other ways. An LLC is considered a type of unincorporated association, not a corporation, even though it is a business entity. Similar to a corporation, though, owners have limited personal liability for the debts and actions of the LLC. Other features of LLCs are more like a partnership, including the benefit of pass-through taxation and greater management flexibility in allocating profits.

Owners of an LLC are called members. Since most states do not restrict ownership, members may include individuals, corporations, other LLCs, and foreign entities. An LLC can have any number of members. Most states permit an LLC with only one owner, called a "single member LLC."

To form an LLC, you file paperwork, usually called "articles of organization," with a state agency (often the secretary of state), pay a filing fee, and create an LLC operating agreement which sets out the rights and responsibilities of LLC members.

a. Taxation

Like a sole proprietorship or a partnership, an LLC is not considered separate from its owners for tax purposes. Instead, an LLC is what the IRS calls a "pass-through entity." Business income passes through the business to LLC members, who report their share of profits, or losses, on their individual income tax returns.

b. Liability and Risk

Like owners of a corporation, all LLC owners are protected from personal liability for business debts and claims, a feature known as "limited liability." If a business with limited liability owes money or faces a lawsuit, only the assets of the business itself are at risk. Creditors usually cannot reach the personal assets of the LLC owners, except in cases of fraud or illegality. However, owners of an LLC must take care to not "pierce the corporate veil," which would expose the owners to personal liability. For example, LLC owners should not use a personal checking account for business purposes, and should always use the LLC business name (rather than the owner's individual names) when working with customers.

c. Management

The operating agreement for an LLC sets forth how the business is managed. The owners of most small LLCs participate equally in the management of the business. This type of LLC arrangement is known as a a "member-managed LLC." Alternatively, members can designate one or more owners, or even an outsider, to take responsibility for managing the LLC. This is called a "manager-managed LLC." Non-managing owners, such as family members who have invested in the company, share in LLC profits without participating in the direct management of the LLC.

d. Continuity and Transferability

LLC members, somewhat like partners in a partnership, cannot transfer their ownership. In most circumstances, an LLC does not possess continuity of life and is usually dissolved upon the death or retirement of any member. Some states require an LLC's operating agreement to set the limit of the company's existence to 30 years. Also, states may require majority or even unanimous member consent to transfer ownership to a new member.

e. Expense and Formality

One disadvantage of forming an LLC, instead of a partnership or a sole proprietorship, is that you pay a filing fee (ranging from $100 to $800) when you submit your articles of organization. On the positive side, articles of organization are short, simple documents. You may be able to quickly prepare articles of organization on your own using a form provided by your state's filing office. Even though an operating agreement may not be required by your state law, you should create one anyway. An LLC operating agreement sets out rules for the ownership and operation of the business, much like a partnership agreement or corporate bylaws. A typical operating agreement includes:

- Percent interest in the business for each member
- Member rights and responsibilities
- Member voting power
- Profit and loss allocation
- Management structure
- Rules for meetings and votes

Also included in operating agreements are "buy–sell" provisions, which determine what happens if a member wants to sell an interest in the company or when a member dies or becomes disabled.

C. Comparison of Entity Characteristics

Type	Liability	Management	Transferability	Formation Requirements	Taxation
Sole Proprietorship	Unlimited	Owner manages	Owner can transfer ownership interest at will	None required (may choose a DBA)	Pass-through *or* double tax
General Partnership	Unlimited	Partners manage	Partners cannot transfer their full ownership interest without unanimous consent	Can be formed by oral or written agreement, *or* through conduct	Pass-through *or* double tax
Limited Partnership	GPs: Unlimited LPs: Limited	GPs manage LPs may have certain voting rights	Partners cannot transfer their full ownership interest without unanimous consent	Must file certificate of limited partnership with state	Pass-through *or* double tax
Limited Liability Parnership	Limited	Partners manage	Partners cannot transfer their full ownership interest without unanimous consent	Must file articles of limited liability partnership with state	Pass-through *or* double tax
Limited Liability Company	Limited	Members may manage *or* appoint managers to manage	Members cannot transfer their full ownership without unanimous consent	Must file articles of organization with state	Pass-through *or* double tax
Corporation	Limited	Managed by officers, who are controlled by a board of directors; shareholders have certain voting rights	Shareholders can freely transfer ownership interest	Must file articles of incorporation with state	Double taxation for C-corporations; pass-through for S-corporations

PART 2

Foundational Concepts

CHAPTER 4

AGENCY

Agency is the foundation for business organizations. No organization can act for itself: it acts only through its agents. The law of agency affects, among others, relationships between employers and employees, between partners, and between corporations and officers. Whether an agency relationship exists is central to questions of authority and liability in business organizations.

We will study agency law as described in the Restatement Third of Agency. The Restatement is a treatise on agency law written by the American Law Institute ("ALI"). ALI is an organization in the United States that seeks to clarify, modernize, and improve the law. ALI (made up of 4000 lawyers, judges, and law professors) drafts, discusses, revises, and publishes Restatements of the Law, model statutes, and principles of law that are influential in both courts and legislatures, as well as in legal scholarship and education.

A. RESTATEMENT 3D OF AGENCY

In General

The subject matter of this Restatement, the common law of agency, encompasses the legal consequences of consensual relationships in which one person (the "principal") manifests assent that another person (the "agent") shall, subject to the principal's right of control, have power to affect the principal's legal relations through the agent's acts and on the principal's behalf. Relationships of agency usually contemplate three parties—the agent, the principal, and third parties with whom the agent interacts in some manner. This Restatement also embraces the situation in which the legal consequences of agency apply to a relationship in which an actor appears to third parties to be acting as a person's agent but the relationship between the putative principal and the actor lacks elements of the common-law definition of agency.

Many questions governed by common-law agency doctrines involve the legal consequences of an agent's interactions with third persons. Such

Excerpt from Restatement (Third) of Agency *Introduction* (2006). Copyright © 2006 by American Law Institute. Reprinted with permission.

interactions may create legal rights and duties as between the principal and the third party, the agent and the third party, and the principal and the agent. The common law of agency also governs the legal consequences of the relationship of the agent and the principal with each other, which is in many respects defined and governed by any agreement between them.

Organizations

Doctrines within the common law of agency are formulated without regard to whether a person is an individual or a legal or commercial entity or other legally recognized nonindividual person, including an organization. This Restatement follows this convention, but it also discusses at length the application of agency doctrine to organizations. Many agents hold positions in organizations. This Restatement thus covers applications of agency doctrine to persons who act as representatives of corporations, partnerships, other business organizations, and private not-for-profit entities. In that context, the focal point for the application of agency doctrine is determining either the duties owed the organization by those holding positions within it or the consequences of interactions between actors in positions defined by one organization with individuals external to the organization or with actors who hold positions in another organization.

Common Law and Statutes

Although the subject of this Restatement is the common law of agency, many references are made to statutory material. Modern common-law doctrines operate in the context of statutes. Increasingly, statutes influence common-law development, as explained more fully below. However, despite the significance of all sorts of statutes, the common law of agency retains coherence in two respects. Its basic concepts and doctrines apply in diverse contexts, including those affected by statutes. Agency has also retained structural coherence, despite statutory developments, in large measure because many statutes make implicit or explicit reference to common law or presuppose a background that includes basic common-law doctrines. Statutory developments thus have not transformed the law of agency into a law of agencies.

B. WHAT IS AGENCY?

§ 1.01 Agency Defined

Agency is the fiduciary relationship that arises when one person (a "principal") manifests assent to another person (an "agent") that the agent shall act on the principal's behalf and subject to the principal's control, and the agent manifests assent or otherwise consents so to act.

Source: Restatement (Third) of Agency §§ 1.01-1.04 (2006). Copyright © 2006 by American Law Institute. Reprinted with permission..

Comment:

Elements of agency. As defined by the common law, the concept of agency posits a consensual relationship in which one person as a representative of or otherwise acts on behalf of another person with power to affect the legal rights and duties of the other person. The person represented has a right to control the actions of the agent. Agency thus entails inward-looking consequences, operative as between the agent and the principal, as well as outward-looking consequences, operative as among the agent, the principal, and third parties with whom the agent interacts. Only interactions that are within the scope of an agency relationship affect the principal's legal position.

Agency encompasses a wide and diverse range of relationships and circumstances. The elements of common-law agency are present in the relationships between employer and employee, corporation and officer, client and lawyer, and partnership and general partner. People often retain agents to perform specific services. Agents who lack authority to bind their principals to contracts nevertheless often have authority to negotiate or to transmit or receive information on their behalf. Some common forms of agency have a personal and noncommercial flavor, exemplified by the relationship created by a power of attorney that confers authority to make decisions regarding an individual's health care, place of residence, or other personal matters.

Creation of agency. Under the common-law definition, agency is a consensual relationship. The definition requires that an agent-to-be and a principal-to-be consent to their association with each other. [U]nexpressed reservations or limitations harbored by the principal do not restrict the principal's expression of consent to the agent.

As to the agent, a relationship of agency requires that the agent "manifests assent or otherwise consents so to act" … it is not necessary to the formation of a relationship of agency that the agent manifest assent to the principal, as when the agent performs the service requested by the principal following the principal's manifestation, or when the agent agrees to perform the service but does not so inform the principal and does not perform. It is a question of fact whether the agent has agreed.

Fiduciary character of relationship. If the relationship between two persons is one of agency, the agent owes a fiduciary obligation to the principal. Fiduciary duty does not necessarily extend to all elements of an agency relationship, and does not explain all of the legal consequences that stem from the relationship. Most questions concerning agents' fiduciary duty involve the agent's relationship to property owned by the principal or confidential information concerning the principal, the agent's undisclosed relationship to third parties who compete with or deal with the principal, or the agent's own undisclosed interest in transactions with the principal or competitive activity.

Illustration:

> P, an operatic tenor, employs A as a business manager with author-
> ity to book P's performances. P directs A to book P to perform
> a concert in a particular concert hall owned by T. A knows that
> the acoustic quality of T's concert hall has recently deteriorated
> in quality due to an error made in remodeling. Neither the error
> nor the deterioration is public knowledge, and A has no reason to
> believe P knows of it. A books P to perform in T's concert hall
> without telling P about the acoustic deterioration because A hopes
> to obtain employment with T. A has breached A's fiduciary duty to
> P, even though A carried out P's literal instructions.

Principal's power and right of interim control. An essential element of agency is
the principal's right to control the agent's actions. The power to give interim
instructions distinguishes principals in agency relationships from those who
contract to receive services provided by persons who are not agents. In many
agreements to provide services, the agreement between the service provider
and the recipient specifies terms and conditions creating contractual obligations that, if enforceable, prescribe or delimit the choices that the service provider has the right to make. [S]etting standards in an agreement for acceptable
service quality does not of itself create a right of control.

Illustration:

> *P owns a professional baseball team.* Needing a new general manager,
> P negotiates an agreement with A, a manager. A insists that P pro-
> vide an assurance in A's employment agreement that A will have
> autonomy in running the team. P agrees. Before the start of the sea-
> son, P directs A to schedule no night games on weeknights during
> the school term. It is feasible for A to comply with P's directive. A
> must obey the instruction. Alternatively, A may resign. If A resigns,
> A has a contract claim against P. If A does not resign, A may have
> a contract claim against P, but A's ability to recover on the claim
> would depend, inter alia, on A's ability to show damage.

Acting on behalf of. The common-law definition of agency requires as an
essential element that the agent consent to act on the principal's behalf, as
well as subject to the principal's control. From the standpoint of the principal,
this is the purpose for creating the relationship. The common law of agency
encompasses employment as well as nonemployment relations. Employee
and nonemployee agents who represent their principal in transactions with
third parties act on the principal's account and behalf. By consenting to act on
behalf of the principal, an agent who is an employee consents to do the work
that the employer directs and to do it subject to the employer's instructions.
In either case, actions "on behalf of" a principal do not necessarily entail that
the principal will benefit as a result.

§ 1.02 Parties Labeling and Popular Usage not controlling

An agency relationship arises only when the elements stated in § 1.01 are present. Whether a relationship is characterized as agency in an agreement between parties or in the context of industry or popular usage is not controlling.

Comment:

Whether a relationship is one of agency is a legal conclusion made after an assessment of the facts of the relationship and the application of the law of agency to those facts. Although agency is a consensual relationship, how the parties to any given relationship label it is not dispositive. Nor does party characterization or nonlegal usage control whether an agent has an agency relationship with a particular person as principal. The parties' references to functional characteristics may, however, be relevant to determining whether a relationship of agency exists.

§ 1.03 Manifestation

A person manifests assent or intention through written or spoken words or other conduct.

Comment:

In general. A manifestation is conduct by a person, observable by others, that expresses meaning. It is a broader concept than communication. The relevant state of mind is that of the person who observes or otherwise learns of the manifestation.

Expressive conduct is not limited to spoken or written words, although it often takes those forms. Silence may constitute a manifestation when, in light of all the circumstances, a reasonable person would express dissent to the inference that other persons will draw from silence. Failure then to express dissent will be taken as a manifestation of affirmance.

Manifestations by organizations. [A]n organization manifests its assent to be bound by the acts of individuals through the observable connections between the individual and the organization. An organization manifests assent to an individual by appointing that person to a position defined by the organization. Organizations generally operate by subdividing work or activities into specific functions that are assigned to different people.

Unintended manifestations. If a principal voluntarily manifests assent or intention, the manifestation is effective although it is made negligently or is otherwise in error. The principal's manifestation of assent determines whether a relationship of agency arises, not the principal's unexpressed intention if otherwise unknown to the agent. An agent's reasonable understanding of the principal's intention determines whether the agent has acted with actual authority…

Manifestations understood in context. A manifestation does not occur in a vacuum, and the meaning that may reasonably be inferred from it will reflect the context in which the manifestation is made. Assent and intention may be expressed explicitly, but often they are inferred from surrounding facts and circumstances. For example, if an organization hires a person as its purchasing manager, the organization's act expresses assent that the person undertake the manager's role as defined by the organization. Such assent would be communicated by someone acting and speaking on behalf of the organization. If a person is in a particular industry, industry custom and practice shape how others in that industry will understand manifestations that the person makes. In the absence of manifestations to the contrary, engaging an agent to accomplish an objective that in a particular industry requires that particular actions be taken would manifest assent to those actions.

Between particular persons, prior dealings or an ongoing relationship frame the context in which manifestations are made and understood. For example, an agent may know, based on prior dealings with the principal, that the principal uses language idiosyncratically or that a particular statement by the principal does not accurately reflect the principal's intention. The operative meaning of the principal's manifestation to the agent is that which the agent has reason to know the principal intends.

Illustrations:

> P says to A, "Sell my horse for me." A knows that what P intends to sell is P's cow. A has actual authority to sell only the cow. Whether A has apparent authority to sell the cow, or the horse, or neither, is governed by § 2.03.

> [In contrast,] P, a dealer in used books, retains A to buy books on P's behalf. P directs A to buy only "first editions." A knows that by "first editions," P means first editions published in the United Kingdom. As to A, P has not manifested assent to A's purchase on P's behalf of first editions published outside the United Kingdom.

In some circumstances, a manifestation may be made by conduct alone or by conduct that carries meaning at odds with words expressed previously or simultaneously. For example, if a lawyer accepts a retainer and files a complaint on behalf of a person, a client-lawyer relationship results although the lawyer has disclaimed in writing any intention to have such a relationship. Actions may speak louder than words. Likewise, in some circumstances, failure to object may properly be understood as a manifestation of intention or consent. As between the agent and the principal, an unexplained failure to object may also in appropriate circumstances constitute a manifestation of assent or intention.

§ 1.04 Terminology

(2) Disclosed, undisclosed, and unidentified principals.

(a) Disclosed principal. A principal is disclosed if, when an agent and a third party interact, the third party has notice that the agent is acting for a principal and has notice of the principal's identity.

(b) Undisclosed principal. A principal is undisclosed if, when an agent and a third party interact, the third party has no notice that the agent is acting for a principal.

(c) Unidentified principal. A principal is unidentified if, when an agent and a third party interact, the third party has notice that the agent is acting for a principal but does not have notice of the principal's identity.

(5) Person. A person is (a) an individual; (b) an organization or association that has legal capacity to possess rights and incur obligations; (c) a government, political subdivision, or instrumentality or entity created by government; or (d) any other entity that has legal capacity to possess rights and incur obligations.

Comment:

Disclosed, unidentified, and undisclosed principal. Whether a principal is disclosed, undisclosed, or unidentified depends on the manifestations of the principal and the agent and the notice received by the other party at the time of that party's transaction with the agent. The principal is no longer undisclosed if the agent discloses either the principal's identity or the fact that the agent represents a principal without identifying the principal. The principal is no longer undisclosed even if such disclosure is contrary to the principal's instructions.

Manifestations of a principal or an agent may reasonably indicate to a third party that the agent acts on behalf of a principal and the principal's identity. If so, the principal is disclosed although the third party subjectively believes that the agent acts alone and represents no one. If the third party has notice that an agent acts on behalf of a principal, even though the agent has represented otherwise, the principal is not undisclosed but is either disclosed or unidentified, depending on the facts of which the third party has notice. If manifestations as to the principal's existence or identity are ambiguous, the third party's belief is conclusive if it is reasonable. These distinctions are relevant to whether an agent becomes a party to a contract made on the principal's behalf and to set-off rights.

Illustration:

T owns an auction house through which T, acting as chief auctioneer, sells art objects. A frequently bids at auctions conducted by T. T knows that A owns an art gallery and that A sometimes places objects that A buys at auction for sale in A's gallery. T also knows that A sometimes bids at auctions on behalf of other persons. Before an auction to be conducted by T, A agrees to bid on behalf of P, a collector of paintings. At the auction, A is the highest bidder on a painting. T believes that A's bid is on A's own account. As to T, P is A's undisclosed principal.

C. HOW IS AN AGENCY RELATIONSHIP FORMED?

1. Actual Authority

§ 2.01 Actual Authority

An agent acts with actual authority when, at the time of taking action that has legal consequences for the principal, the agent reasonably believes, in accordance with the principal's manifestations to the agent, that the principal wishes the agent so to act.

Comment:

Rationale. Actual authority is a consequence of a principal's expressive conduct toward an agent, through which the principal manifests assent to be affected by the agent's action, and the agent's reasonable understanding of the principal's manifestation. An agent's actions establish the agent's consent to act on the principal's behalf, as does any separate manifestation of assent by the agent. When an agent acts with actual authority, the agent's power to affect the principal's legal relations with third parties is coextensive with the agent's right to do so, which actual authority creates. In contrast, although an agent who acts with only apparent authority also affects the principal's legal relations, the agent lacks the right to do so, and the agent's act is not rightful as toward the principal. Actual authority often overlaps with the presence of apparent authority.

The focal point for determining whether an agent acted with actual authority is the agent's reasonable understanding at the time the agent takes action. Although it is commonly said that a principal grants or confers actual authority, the principal's initial manifestation to the agent may often be modified or supplemented by subsequent manifestations from the principal and by other developments that the agent should reasonably consider in determining what the principal wishes to be done. A principal's manifestations may reach the agent directly or indirectly. Often a principal's manifestation will state that the agent should refrain from acting in a particular way. In that situation, the agent's failure to act conforms to the principal's expressed wishes. The presence of actual authority requires that an agent's belief be reasonable at the time the agent acts. It is also necessary that the agent in fact believes that the principal desires the action taken by the agent.

Illustrations:

P gives A a power of attorney authorizing A to sell a piece of property owned by P. P subsequently says to A, "Don't sell the property. Lease it instead." After P's statement, A has actual authority only to lease.

Source: Restatement (Third) of Agency §§ 2.01-2.03, 3.01, 3.03, 4.01, 4.02 (2006). Copyright © 2006 by American Law Institute. Reprinted with permission..

Same facts as [above], except that A overhears P say to a third party that P no longer wishes to sell the property and wishes A to lease it. A has actual authority only to lease because A knows P does not wish the property to be sold.

Same facts as [the first illustration], except that, after telling A to lease the property instead of selling it, P tells F that P regrets making this statement and wishes that the property be sold. A is unaware of P's statement to F. A sells the property to T, showing T the power of attorney. T is unaware of P's oral statements to A and F. A did not have actual authority to sell the property. A acted with apparent authority…

Most conferrals of authority combine two elements. The first, always present, is a manifestation, however general or specific, by a principal as to the acts or types of acts the principal wishes to be done. The second, less invariably present, consists of instructions or directives that specify how or within what constraints acts are to be done. A principal's communications to an agent begin with an initial expression granting authority, followed in many instances by instructions or directions that clarify matters, prescribe in more specific terms what the principal wishes the agent to do, or reduce or enlarge the scope of the agent's authority. A principal's manifestations may raise questions—at one end, as to whether the principal wishes the agent to move beyond the acts explicitly specified in order to fulfill the principal's implicit purpose and, at the other end, as to whether implicit restrictions apply in addition to the limits the principal has stated. An agent must interpret the principal's manifestations and determine how to act. The context in which the relationship is situated, including the nature of the principal's objectives and the custom generally followed in such circumstances, affects how the agent should interpret the principal's manifestations.

Organizational principals. When a principal is an organization, the relationship between actual authority and apparent authority may be difficult to untangle due to the significant role of custom and practice. In many organizations, including large and complicated ones, written job descriptions do not exist for many executive and managerial positions.

Actual authority to do an act that is treated as the act of the organization spans its highest levels of hierarchy to its lowest. Executive or managerial capacity is not a sine qua non for the existence of actual authority.

Illustration:

P Corporation employs A as a clerk in its mail room. A's duties include initialing receipts presented by carriers. A initials a receipt for a valuable package shipped by T using C, a carrier. A's action acknowledges receipt by P Corporation.

§ 2.02 Scope of Actual Authority

(1) An agent has actual authority to take action designated or implied in the principal's manifestations to the agent and acts necessary or incidental to achieving the principal's objectives, as the agent reasonably understands the principal's manifestations and objectives when the agent determines how to act.

(2) An agent's interpretation of the principal's manifestations is reasonable if it reflects any meaning known by the agent to be ascribed by the principal and, in the absence of any meaning known to the agent, as a reasonable person in the agent's position would interpret the manifestations in light of the context, including circumstances of which the agent has notice and the agent's fiduciary duty to the principal.

(3) An agent's understanding of the principal's objectives is reasonable if it accords with the principal's manifestations and the inferences that a reasonable person in the agent's position would draw from the circumstances creating the agency.

Comment:

Rationale. Actual authority is an agent's power to affect the principal's legal relations in accord with the agent's reasonable understanding, at the time the agent acts, of the principal's manifestations to the agent. The determination of reasonableness is a question for the trier of fact. If an agent's understanding is reasonable, the agent has actual authority to act in accordance with the understanding, although the principal subsequently establishes that the agent was mistaken. The agent's belief must be grounded in a manifestation of the principal, including but not limited to the principal's written or spoken words. Thus, it is often said that implied authority is actual authority proved circumstantially, which means it is proved on the basis of a principal's conduct other than written or spoken statements that explicitly authorize an action.

Acts necessary or incidental to achieving principal's objectives. If a principal's manifestation to an agent expresses the principal's wish that something be done, it is natural to assume that the principal wishes, as an incidental matter, that the agent take the steps necessary and that the agent proceed in the usual and ordinary way, if such has been established, unless the principal directs otherwise. The underlying assumptions are that the principal does not wish to authorize what cannot be achieved if necessary steps are not taken by the agent, and that the principal's manifestation often will not specify all steps necessary to translate it into action.

Illustrations:

P employs A, an auctioneer, to sell goods owned by P. A has authority to accept bids on P's behalf.

[Alternately,] P, a dealer in antiques, employs A to enter into contracts on P's behalf for the purchase of antiques. A has authority to sign memoranda of sale to satisfy the Statute of Frauds. Separately, a writing may be necessary to establish A's authority.

Agent's reasonable understanding of principal's manifestation. An agent does not have actual authority to do an act if the agent does not reasonably believe that the principal has consented to its commission. Whether an agent's belief is reasonable is determined from the viewpoint of a reasonable person in the agent's situation under all of the circumstances of which the agent has notice. Lack of actual authority is established by showing either that the agent did not believe, or could not reasonably have believed, that the principal's grant of actual authority encompassed the act in question. This standard requires that the agent's belief be reasonable, an objective standard, and that the agent actually hold the belief, a subjective standard.

Illustration:

P, a photographer, employs A as a business manager. P authorizes A to endorse and deposit checks P receives from publishers of photographs taken by P. Based on P's statements to A, A believes A's authority is limited to endorsing and depositing checks and does not include entering into agreements that bind P in other respects. A endorses and deposits a check from T, a magazine publisher, made payable to P. Printed on the back of the check is a legend: "Endorsement constitutes a release of all claims." It is beyond the scope of A's actual authority to release claims that P has against T.

Interpretation by agent. In order to determine with specificity what a principal would wish the agent to do, the agent must interpret the language the principal uses or assess the principal's conduct or the situation in which the principal has placed the agent. An agent's position requires such interpretation regardless of the circumstances under which the principal created actual authority.

A principal may believe when initially giving instructions to the agent that the principal's best interests will be served by investing the agent with a large measure of discretion, a decision later regretted by the principal when reviewing the agent's actual use of discretion. Regardless of any later regret, the principal is bound by the agent's acts so long as the agent's interpretation was reasonable.

Illustrations:

A is the manager of a retail clothing store owned by P, who owns several such stores. P authorizes store managers to buy, from vendors specified by P, inventory of items specified by P for their stores up to limits specified in dollar amount. P identifies "men's dress shirts" as an inventory type that A has authority to buy. A knows that by "dress shirts" P means "shirts suitable for wearing with a tuxedo." A does not have actual authority to buy dress shirts not suitable for tuxedo wear.

Same facts as [above], except that P ascribes no unusual meaning to "men's dress shirts" that is known to A. P provides A with no directions as to the color assortment of shirts. At the time A places the order, a particular color is fashionable and A orders many shirts in that color, believing that the fashion will continue. The shirts fail to sell. A had actual authority to buy the shirts.

Explicit instructions. A principal may direct an agent to do or refrain from doing a specific act. The agent's fiduciary duty to the principal obliges the agent to interpret the principal's instructions so as to infer, in a reasonable manner, what the principal would wish the agent to do in light of the facts of which the agent has notice at the time of acting.

Regardless of the breadth or narrowness with which a principal has conveyed authority to the agent, an agent's actual authority extends only to acts that the agent reasonably believes the principal has authorized or wishes the agent to perform. The fiduciary character of the agency relationship shapes the agent's permissible interpretation of authority, disallowing an interpretation that is inconsistent with interests of the principal that the agent knows or should know.

Consequences of act for principal. Even if a principal's instructions or grant of authority to an agent leave room for the agent to exercise discretion, the consequences that a particular act will impose on the principal may call into question whether the principal has authorized the agent to do such acts.

Three types of acts should lead a reasonable agent to believe that the principal does not intend to authorize the agent to do the act. First are crimes and torts. If a principal authorizes the agent's commission of a crime or an intentional tort, the principal will be subject to liability for the agent's wrongdoing. Second, acts that create no prospect of economic advantage for a principal, such as gifts and uncompensated uses of the principal's property, require specific authorization. This is so even if an agent has notice that the principal acts philanthropically as to matters unconnected to the agency. Third, some acts that are otherwise legal create legal consequences for a principal that are significant and separate from the transaction specifically directed by the principal. A reasonable agent should consider whether the principal intended to authorize the commission of collateral acts fraught with major legal implications for the principal, such as granting a security interest in the principal's property or executing an instrument confessing judgment.

§ 3.01 Creation of Actual Authority

Actual authority, as defined in § 2.01, is created by a principal's manifestation to an agent that, as reasonably understood by the agent, expresses the principal's assent that the agent take action on the principal's behalf.

Comment:

Manifestation an essential requirement. [A]n agent's actual authority originates with expressive conduct by the principal toward the agent by which the principal manifests assent to action by the agent with legal consequences for the principal. A principal's unexpressed willingness that another act as agent does not create actual authority. The principal must make a manifestation… that expresses this willingness. The manifestation may be made directly by the principal to the agent or may reach the agent through a more circuitous route. The principal's unexpressed reservations and qualifications do not reduce the agent's actual authority.

Illustrations:

> P, a producer and bottler of beverages, retains A as P's agent with authority to purchase tea leaves on P's behalf. P executes a power of attorney that authorizes A to purchase ingredients and containers of all kinds. After executing the power, P places it in a desk drawer and does not mention it to A, nor does P in any other way indicate to A that P has expanded A's authority. A enters into a contract that purportedly binds P to purchase bottles from T. A lacks actual authority to make the contract.

> Same facts as [above], except that P, intending to mail the power of attorney to A, misaddresses the envelope to A's friend B. When B opens the envelope, B realizes the error and gives the power of attorney to A. A then enters into the contract purportedly binding P to purchase bottles from T. A has actual authority to make the contract.

Actual authority may exist although there is no contract between a principal and agent; a relationship of agency does not require that the principal or the agent receive consideration from the other. It is not necessary to the existence of actual authority that an actor promise or otherwise undertake to act as agent. However, an actor is not an agent… unless the actor manifests assent or otherwise consents to a relationship of agency. The agent's manifestation need not be made explicitly, nor be made directly to the principal.

A person may request an action from another, indicating that no further communication should precede the action. If the action is taken it is inferred that the actor consented to act as an agent unless the actor manifests a contrary intention or unless the circumstances so indicate. The inference is strengthened if the action is one that only an agent with actual authority could properly do.

Illustrations:

> P, a dealer in used books, writes to A, who purchases books on P's behalf, stating the titles of specific books and telling A to purchase one copy of each and ship it to P immediately. A does as directed. A acts with actual authority.

> Same facts as [above], except that P tells A to draw on P's bank account to pay for the books before shipping them to P. A makes the purchase in A's own name, pays with funds from P's account,

then dies. No other facts demonstrate A's intention. It is inferred that A purchased the books as P's agent.

2. Apparent Authority

§ 2.03 Apparent Authority

Apparent authority is the power held by an agent or other actor to affect a principal's legal relations with third parties when a third party reasonably believes the actor has authority to act on behalf of the principal and that belief is traceable to the principal's manifestations.

Comment:

Rationale. Apparent authority holds a principal accountable for the results of third-party beliefs about an actor's authority to act as an agent when the belief is reasonable and is traceable to a manifestation of the principal. As to the third person, apparent authority when present trumps restrictions that the principal has privately imposed on the agent. The relevant appearance is that the principal has conferred authority on an agent. A principal may not choose to act through agents whom it has clothed with the trappings of authority and then determine at a later time whether the consequences of their acts offer an advantage.

A belief that results solely from the statements or other conduct of the agent, unsupported by any manifestations traceable to the principal, does not create apparent authority unless, as explained below, the agent's conduct has been directed by the principal. An agent's success in misleading the third party as to the existence of actual authority does not in itself make the principal accountable.

Illustration:

> P owns a granary and employs A to manage it. A's employment agreement with P states that A's authority to purchase grain is limited to transactions that do not exceed $5,000; larger purchases require P's express approval. This limit is unusual in the granary business. P directs A to tell T, a seller of grain, that A's unilateral authority to purchase is unlimited because P believes this will induce T to give priority to orders placed by A. A represents to T that A's authority to purchase is unlimited and enters into a contract on P's behalf with T to buy $10,000 of grain. P is bound by the contract with T. A has actual authority to make the representation to T. A has apparent authority to enter into the contract with T because T reasonably believes A has authority to bind P to a contract to buy the grain.

Reasonable belief. It is usually a question for the trier of fact whether a reasonable person in the position of a third party would believe that an agent had the authority or the right to do a particular act. It is a separate but related question of fact whether such a belief is traceable to a manifestation of the principal.

Apparent authority is based on a third party's understanding of signals of all sorts concerning the actor with whom the third party interacts. When the third party knows the actor is an agent and knows the identity of the principal, the presence of apparent authority turns on the tie between these signals and the principal in the mind of the reasonable third party. The third party observes the agent in a particular context, one that may be defined in part by interactions, dealings, or relationships between the principal and the agent that the third party has observed in the past, by an organization, by an industry and its customs; by a type of transaction that is conventionally done in a particular way; or, if in a new context, by reasonable expectations based on analogous situations and other relevant circumstances. Of course, the reasonable third party should also assess the credibility of assertions made directly by the agent. If the agent tells the third party that a transaction is beyond the agent's authority, it is not reasonable for the third party to believe thereafter that the agent has such authority absent a credible change in circumstances that augment the agent's authority.

Illustration:

> P Corporation, a manufacturer of specialty food items, retains A, a commodity food broker, to purchase a large quantity of an expensive commodity, Q, for P Corporation's manufacturing needs. A enters into a contract on P Corporation's behalf to purchase a large quantity of Q from T. P Corporation does not itself communicate directly or indirectly with T concerning A's authority. It is customary in the Q trade for a broker to obtain the principal's consent before fixing a binding contract for Q because its price fluctuates sharply. It is also customary for a third party to confirm with the principal or someone else other than the broker that a broker has the principal's consent. A assures T that it will not be necessary for T to contact P Corporation because A has already done so. A does not have apparent authority to bind P Corporation to the contract, nor is it reasonable for T to believe that A has authority to represent that T has consented to the transaction.

Reliance. Many cases stating that apparent authority requires "reliance" on the part of the plaintiff do not articulate what specifically must be shown. Successful assertions of apparent authority by third parties as the basis on which to bind a principal follow action or forbearance on the part of a third party as a result of the agent's action and the principal's manifestation. Establishing that a plaintiff took an action as a result of the principal's manifestation may also help to establish that the person to whom the manifestation was made believed it to be true.

Undisclosed and unidentified principals. When a third party interacts with an actor known to be someone's agent, but the third party does not know the principal's identity, the third party does not know whom the agent represents and whose legal position the agent's acts may affect. If the agent occupies a position customarily carrying authority to do specific types of acts on behalf of a principal, it is reasonable for the third party to believe that the agent possesses such authority even though the third party does not know the identity of the principal. The principal's identity is irrelevant to the reasonableness of a third party's belief that a principal has consented to be bound by the acts of a conventional type of agent.

§ 3.03 Creation of Apparent Authority

Apparent authority, as defined in § 2.03, is created by a person's manifestation that another has authority to act with legal consequences for the person who makes the manifestation, when a third party reasonably believes the actor to be authorized and the belief is traceable to the manifestation.

Comment:

Manifestation an essential requirement. Apparent authority is present only when a third party's belief is traceable to manifestations of the principal. The fact that one party performs a service that facilitates the other's business does not constitute such a manifestation. For example, by clearing securities trades for another firm, a securities broker does not make a manifestation to customers of the firm sending the orders that it acts with the authority of the clearing firm.

A principal may make manifestations regarding an agent's authority in many ways. In some settings, the principal's acts speak so loudly that explicit verbal communication is unnecessary. Similarly, an indirect route of communication between a principal and third party may suffice, especially when it is consistent with practice in the relevant industry.

Illustration:

> Senior officers of P Corporation have been involved in complicated negotiations for the purchase of custom-designed machinery, to be specially designed by T and manufactured by S Corporation. P Corporation's CEO receives a joint letter from T and the CEO of S Corporation stating that they have scheduled a meeting to finalize terms and that P Corporation should send a representative with authority to commit it. P Corporation's CEO sends A, the Executive Vice President of P Corporation. As to S Corporation and T, P Corporation has manifested that A has authority to commit it to the terms of the transaction.

A principal may also make a manifestation by placing an agent in a defined position in an organization or by placing an agent in charge of a transaction or situation. Third parties who interact with the principal through the agent will naturally and reasonably assume that the agent has authority to do acts consistent with the agent's position or role unless they have notice of facts suggesting that this may not be so. A principal may make an additional manifestation by permitting or requiring the agent to serve as the third party's exclusive channel of communication to the principal.

A principal may also create apparent authority by actually or apparently authorizing an agent to make representations to third parties concerning the agent's own authority or position, even though the agent's representations by themselves would be insufficient. The determinative question is whether a third party can establish a linkage between statements of authority by the agent and a manifestation of assent by the principal to the making of such statements.

A principal's inaction creates apparent authority when it provides a basis for a third party reasonably to believe the principal intentionally acquiesces in the agent's representations or actions. If the third party has observed prior interactions between the agent and the principal, the third party may reasonably believe that a subsequent act or representation by the agent is authorized because it conforms to the prior pattern observed by the third party. The belief is thus traceable to the principal's participation in the pattern and failure to inform the third party that no inferences about the agent's authority should be based upon it.

4. Ratification

§ 4.01 Ratification Defined

(1) Ratification is the affirmance of a prior act done by another, whereby the act is given effect as if done by an agent acting with actual authority.

(2) A person ratifies an act by

   (a) manifesting assent that the act shall affect the person's legal relations, or

   (b) conduct that justifies a reasonable assumption that the person so consents.

Comment:

The nature and effect of ratification. As the term is used in agency law, ratification is both an act and a set of effects.

Ratification often serves the function of clarifying situations of ambiguous or uncertain authority. A principal's ratification confirms or validates an agent's right to have acted as the agent did. That is, an agent's action may have been effective to bind the principal to the third party, and the third party to the principal, because the agent acted with apparent authority. If the principal ratifies the agent's act, it is thereafter not necessary to establish that the agent acted with apparent authority.

The sole requirement for ratification is a manifestation of assent or other conduct indicative of consent by the principal. To be effective as a ratification, the principal's assent need not be communicated to the agent or to third parties whose legal relations will be affected by the ratification.

The effects of the principal's ratification are also fair to the agent because by assenting to the agent's act the principal usually eliminates claims that the principal or the third party might otherwise assert against the agent. Ratification is an all-or-nothing proposition in two basic respects. First, in most cases, by ratifying the principal eliminates claims the principal might otherwise have against the agent for acting without actual authority. Were the doctrine otherwise, the principal could speculate at the agent's expense by ratifying a transaction as against the third party, but holding the agent accountable if, after the time of ratification, the transaction turned out to be a losing proposition for the principal. Second, a principal must ratify a single transaction in its entirety, thereby becoming subject to its burdens as well as enjoying its benefits.

Actions that constitute ratification. Ratification requires an objectively or externally observable indication that a person consents that another's prior act shall affect the person's legal relations. To constitute ratification, the consent need not be communicated to the third party or the agent. This is so because the focal point of ratification is an observable indication that the principal has exercised choice and has consented. In contrast, the principal's manifestation of assent to the agent is essential to the presence of actual authority, and the principal's manifestation to the third party is essential to the presence of apparent authority.

Illustration:

> P, who deals in used cars, employs A as a retail salesperson. A is not authorized to make public statements on behalf of P. A is interviewed on a local television program and, without P's consent, falsely accuses a competitor of P's of engaging in illegal sales practices. A knows these statements to be false. P watches the television program and, the next day, congratulates A on A's television appearance. P has ratified A's tortious conduct.

Failure to act as ratification. A principal may ratify an act by failing to object to it or to repudiate it. Failure to object may constitute... a manifestation when the person has notice that others are likely to draw such an inference from silence.

Illustration:

> Same facts as [above], except that P, who knows of the statement A made during A's television appearance, says nothing to A or anyone else about it. It may be found that P has ratified A's conduct.

§ 4.02 Effect of Ratification

(1) [R]atification retroactively creates the effects of actual authority.
Comment:

Ratification has an immediate effect on legal relations between the principal and agent, the principal and the third party, and the agent and the third party. Ratification recasts those legal relations as they would have been had the agent acted with actual authority. Legal consequences thus "relate back" to the time the agent acted.

D. WHAT ARE AN AGENT'S FIDUCIARY DUTIES?

§ 8.01 General Fiduciary Principle

An agent has a fiduciary duty to act loyally for the principal's benefit in all matters connected with the agency relationship.

Comment:

In general. The relationship between a principal and an agent is a fiduciary relationship. An agent assents to act subject to the principal's control and on the principal's behalf. Although an agent's interests are often concurrent with those of the principal, the general fiduciary principle requires that the agent subordinate the agent's interests to those of the principal and place the principal's interests first as to matters connected with the agency relationship.

The fiduciary principle supplements manifestations that a principal makes to an agent, making it unnecessary for the principal to graft explicit qualifications and prohibitions onto the principal's statements of authorization to the agent.

Illustrations:

P engages A to manage P's business of dealing in property. P furnishes A with a power of attorney that states that A "shall have power to do and perform for me any and all acts that I might do and perform myself if personally present concerning any property, real or personal, in which I might own any interest of any type, including but not limited to the signing and delivery of any and all deeds, deeds of trust, promissory notes, leases and other instruments that I might personally sign and deliver." P makes no other relevant manifestation to A. A executes a deed that conveys Blackacre, owned by P, to A for no consideration. At P's election, A's conveyance of Blackacre is ineffective. A's conveyance of Blackacre to A is inconsistent with A's duty to act loyally for P's benefit.

Same facts as [above], except that A conveys Black-acre to T. Same result. By conveying Blackacre to T without consideration, A has not acted loyally for P's benefit.

The general fiduciary principle complements and facilitates an agent's compliance with duties of performance that the agent owes to the principal. An agent has a duty to the principal to use care in acting on the principal's behalf. An agent also has a duty to use reasonable efforts to provide material information to the principal. An agent's failure to provide material information to the principal may facilitate the agent's breach of the agent's duties of loyalty to the principal.

Source: Restatement (Third) of Agency §§ 8.01, 8.08 (2006). Copyright 2006 by American Law Institute. Reprinted with Permission.

Illustration:

> P, who owns Blackacre, lists it for sale with A. T makes an offer to A to buy Blackacre for $110,000. Unaware of T's offer, and unbeknownst to T, P informs A that P is willing to sell Blackacre for $100,000. A accepts T's offer on P's behalf, remits $100,000 to P, and pockets the extra $10,000. A is subject to liability to P. T's willingness to pay $110,000 for Blackacre is material information that A has a duty to furnish to P as stated in § 8.11. A's retention of $10,000 is also a breach of A's duty to act loyally for P's benefit; A's duty … not to acquire a material benefit from a third party in connection with transactions undertaken on P's behalf; and A's duties … in connection with P's property.

An agent's breach of the agent's fiduciary obligation subjects the agent to liability to the principal. An agent's liability stems from principles of restitution and unjust enrichment, from the agent's duty to account to the principal, and from tort law. The agent's breach subjects the agent to liability to account to the principal. In general, an agent has the burden of explaining to the principal all transactions that the agent has undertaken on the principal's behalf. The agent bears this burden because evidence of dealings and of assets received is more likely to be accessible by the agent than the principal. Tort law subjects the agent to liability to the principal for harm resulting from the breach.

Scope of duty. [A]n agent's fiduciary duties to the principal vary depending on the parties' agreement and the scope of the parties' relationship. The scope of an agency relationship can be analyzed by identifying the parties to the relationship, examining whether particular interactions are as principal and agent, and specifying the duration of the relationship.

In an agency relationship, an agent's fiduciary obligation is owed to the principal. When a principal is an organizational entity, an agent has a fiduciary obligation to the entity. Law distinctive to that form of entity may also subject the agent to fiduciary duties to constituents of the entity, such as shareholders in a corporation. Under contemporary partnership legislation, a partner in a general partnership explicitly owes fiduciary duties of loyalty and care "to the partnership and the other partners…."[1]

§ 8.08 Duty of Care

Subject to any agreement with the principal, an agent has a duty to the principal to act with the care, competence, and diligence normally exercised by agents in similar circumstances. Special skills or knowledge possessed by an agent are circumstances to be taken into account in determining whether the agent acted with due care and diligence. If an agent claims to possess special skills or knowledge, the agent has a duty to the principal to act with the care, competence, and diligence normally exercised by agents with such skills or knowledge.

---

1   Unif. P'ship Act (1997) § 404(a).

Comment:

The duties stated in this section will often overlap with an agent's duties of performance that are express or implied terms of a contract between principal and agent. However, the duties stated in this section are tort-law duties because they "denote the fact that the actor is required to conduct himself in a particular manner at the risk that if he does not do so he becomes subject to liability to another to whom the duty is owed for any injury sustained by such other, of which that actor's conduct is a legal cause."[2] Tort law imposes duties of care on an agent because the agent undertakes to act on behalf of the principal, because the principal's reliance on that undertaking is foreseeable by the agent, and because it is often socially useful that an agent fulfill the agent's undertaking to the principal.

Statutory provisions may also be relevant in determining the duties of care owed by an agent. For example, some organizational statutes establish standards of conduct for officers and others who act on behalf of an organization. Under… the Model Business Corporation Act, an officer must act, in performing the officer's duties, "with the care that a person in like position would reasonably exercise under similar circumstances … ."[3] The Revised Uniform Partnership Act states that a partner owes a duty of care to the partnership and to other partners "in the conduct and winding up of the partnership business" that is limited to "refraining from engaging in grossly negligent or reckless conduct, intentional misconduct, or a knowing violation of law."[4] The Uniform Limited Liability Company Act imposes a comparable standard on an LLC's managers and members who are also managers.[5]

If an agent undertakes to perform services as a practitioner of a trade or profession, the agent "is required to exercise the skill and knowledge normally possessed by members of that profession or trade in good standing in similar communities"[6] unless the agent represents that the agent possesses greater or lesser skill. An agent may reasonably be expected to know at least the basic rules and practices under which the agent's industry or profession operates.

---

2   Restatement (Second) of Torts § 4 (1977).
3   Model Bus. Corp. Act § 8.42(a)(2)
4   Rev. Unif. P'ship Act § 404(c).
5   Unif. Ltd. Liab. Co. Act § 409(c) and (h)(2).
6   Restatement (Second) of Torts § 299A (1977).

E. WHAT LIABILITIES DO PRINCIPALS AND AGENTS HAVE?

1. Contract

§ 6.01 Agent for Disclosed Principal

When an agent acting with actual or apparent authority makes a contract on behalf of a disclosed principal,

(1) the principal and the third party are parties to the contract; and

(2) the agent is not a party to the contract unless the agent and third party agree otherwise.

Comment:

Bases and consequences of contractual liability when agent acts on behalf of disclosed principal. An agent acts on behalf of a disclosed principal when the third party with whom the agent deals has notice that the agent acts for a principal and also has notice of the principal's identity. An agent has power to make contracts on behalf of the agent's principal when the agent acts with actual or apparent authority.

A principal may manifest assent to the agent's power to commit the principal either to the agent or to third parties. If the principal's manifestation is made to the agent and the agent acts reasonably in accordance with the manifestation, the agent acts with actual authority. If the third party reasonably believes that the agent acts with authority and that belief is traceable to a manifestation made by the principal to the third party, the agent acts with apparent authority. Actual authority does not require that apparent authority be present.

Illustration:

> P, a wine merchant, engages A to dispose of portions of P's inventory. P directs A to sell all of P's inventory of French wines to T, another wine merchant. A makes an offer to T on P's behalf. T replies: "I do not believe that you have authority to sell all of P's French wine, but I will chance it and accept the offer." There is a contract between P and T. A had actual authority to bind P, although T doubts whether this is so.

An agent who enters into a contract on behalf of a disclosed principal does not become a party to the contract and is not subject to liability as a guarantor of the principal's performance unless the agent and the third party so agree. Thus, in the absence of such agreement, an agent for a disclosed principal who enters into a contract on the principal's behalf is not subject to liability if the principal fails to perform obligations created by the contract. As a consequence, the agent is not a necessary party to breach-of-contract litigation between a disclosed principal and the third party to a contract made by the agent on the principal's behalf.

Source: Restatement (Third) of Agency §§ 2.04, 6.01-6.03, 6.10, 6.11, 7.01, 7.03, 7.04, 7.07, 7.08 (2006). Coypright 2006 by American Law Institute. Reprinted with permission.

Through ratification, a person may become a party to a contract purportedly made on that person's behalf by another who acted without actual or apparent authority.

A principal who deals with third parties through an agent ordinarily expects to become a party to transactions entered into on the principal's behalf by the agent. When the third party knows the identity of the principal, the third party ordinarily expects that the principal, and not the agent, will become a party to the transaction. This is because third parties do not ordinarily rely on agents' solvency or ability to perform the promises required to consummate a transaction. An agent and a third party, however, may agree otherwise.

Contract made on behalf of a disclosed principal. If an agent makes a contract in the name of a principal or a description in the contract is sufficient to identify the principal, the principal is a disclosed principal and is a party to the contract. When a disclosed principal is a corporation or other organization with separate legal personality, the corporation becomes a party to contracts made on its behalf by its agents. Corporate or other organizational agents, like agents for other disclosed principals, are not parties to a corporate contract unless the agent and the third party so agree.

Illustrations:

P, a farmer, incorporates the farm business under the name "P Farms Corp." P operates the business of P Farms Corp. as its chief executive officer. On behalf of and in the name of P Farms Corp., P purchases supplies on credit from T. P is not a party to, and is not subject to liability on, contracts between P Farms Corp. and T.

Same facts as [above], except that P purchases the supplies for delivery to the farm but does not specify whether P buys them in the name of P Farms Corp. Parol evidence would be necessary to resolve the ambiguity whether P and T intended P personally or P Farms Corp. to be the party to the contract.

Same facts as [the first illustration], except that P does not incorporate the farming business. Instead, P leases the farm land to S, P's son, who operates the farm business using the assumed name "P Farms." P continues to live in a residence on the farm. S purchases supplies for the farm on credit from T, which T delivers to the farm. All of S's purchases are pursuant to orders signed "P Farms—S." P occasionally signs receipts for the supplies when T delivers them. Unless parol evidence so establishes, P is not a party to contracts between S and T. S is a party to contracts with T.

Whether the existence and identity of any principal have been disclosed are questions of fact. The third party with whom an agent deals does not have a burden of inquiry. A third party's failure to inquire whether an agent acts on behalf of a principal is not tantamount to disclosure of the principal's existence and identity. A third party will be treated as having notice of an agency relationship if the third party has actual knowledge of it or reason to know of it or if the third party has been given a notification of it.

If an agent acts with actual or apparent authority in making a contract on behalf of a principal, the principal should be bound by the contract even though the principal claims that maintaining secrecy of the principal's identity was essential to achieving the principal's objectives.

Agreement that agent shall be a party to contract. When an agent enters into a contract on behalf of a disclosed principal, the agent is not a party to the contract unless the agent and the third party so agree. The third party has the burden of showing a manifestation of assent by the agent to such an agreement. Loose usage by an agent of such terms as "I," "me," "mine," "we," or "ours" in referring to a business does not, standing alone, constitute a manifestation of assent to be bound personally but may corroborate other evidence.

Illustrations:

> P, a dealer in rare books, retains A to buy books on P's account. A negotiates to buy a book on P's account from T, who knows that A represents P. A says, "I will buy the book for $200." In the absence of other facts, A is not a party to the contract.

> Same facts as [above], except that in negotiations with A, T is represented by T's agent, B. B says to A, "I warrant that the book is a first edition." In the absence of other facts, neither A nor B is a party to the warranty.

§ 6.02 Agent for Unidentified Principal

When an agent acting with actual or apparent authority makes a contract on behalf of an unidentified principal,

(1) the principal and the third party are parties to the contract; and

(2) the agent is a party to the contract unless the agent and the third party agree otherwise.

Comment:

Bases of contractual liability when agent acts on behalf of unidentified principal. An agent acts on behalf of an unidentified principal when the third party with whom the agent deals has notice that the agent acts on behalf of a principal but does not have notice of the principal's identity. Many cases ... refer to such a principal as a "partially disclosed principal."[7] This Restatement instead uses the term "unidentified principal."

An agent has power to make contracts on behalf of an unidentified principal when the agent acts with actual or apparent authority, just as an agent acting with actual or apparent authority has power to make contracts on behalf of a disclosed principal. If an agent purports to act on behalf of an undisclosed

---

7 *See* Restatement (Second) of Agency § 4(2) (1977).

principal but lacks actual or apparent authority to bind the principal, the agent is subject to liability on the agent's implied warranty of authority.

An agent makes a contract with a third party on behalf of an unidentified principal by manifesting assent to an exchange that constitutes valid consideration. The third party's manifestation of assent is made to the agent, who the third party has notice acts on behalf of a principal. An unidentified principal may also be subject to liability as a consequence of a promise made by an agent that is not supported by consideration but that should reasonably be expected to induce action or forbearance on the part of a third party. In either situation, the third party has notice that the agent acts on behalf of another person. On the other hand, when an agent acts on behalf of an undisclosed principal, the third party lacks notice that it deals with an agent.

Unless the third party and the agent agree otherwise, an agent who makes a contract on behalf of a disclosed principal does not become a party to the contract. In contrast, as stated in subsection (2) of this section, an agent who makes a contract on behalf of an unidentified principal becomes a party to the contract unless the third party and the agent agree otherwise. When a third party has notice that an agent deals on behalf of a principal but does not have notice of the principal's identity, it is not likely that the third party will rely solely on the principal's solvency or ability to perform obligations arising from the contract. Without notice of a principal's identity, a third party will be unable to assess the principal's reputation, assets, and other indicia of creditworthiness and ability to perform duties under the contract. If an agent provides reassurances about the principal's soundness only generally or describes the principal, the third party will be unable to verify such claims without notice of the principal's identity.

Contract made on behalf of unidentified principal. A principal is unidentified when the third party does not have notice of the principal's identity at the time the agent enters into a contract on the principal's behalf. Ordinarily it is the agent who provides notice of the principal's identity. However, the source of the third party's enlightenment is irrelevant to the legal relations among the parties. Regardless of the source of notice of the principal's identity, once the third party has such notice, the third party is in a position to assess the principal's reliability.

Illustrations:

> P, who deals in antiques, retains A to purchase antiques on P's behalf. P directs A not to disclose P's identity to persons with whom A deals. A complies. A contracts to buy an antique clock owned by T, telling T that A is purchasing the clock on behalf of A's principal. P is A's unidentified principal. P and T are parties to the contract for the sale of the clock. A is also a party to the contract unless A and T agree otherwise.

> Same facts [above], except that, prior to contracting to sell the clock, T learns from a friend that A represents P. As to T, P is A's

disclosed principal. T knew P's identity when making the contract with A. P and T are parties to the contract for the sale of the clock. A is not a party unless A and T agree otherwise.

A person who wishes to act as an undisclosed or unidentified principal to a contract may provide instructions to an agent prohibiting disclosure of the principal's existence or identity in the agent's dealings with third parties on the principal's behalf. If the agent then reveals the principal's identity contrary to those instructions, or the third party otherwise learns the principal's identity, the principal nevertheless will be bound by the contract if the agent acted with actual or apparent authority in making it.

Notice of principal's identity and agent's status. A third party has notice of a principal's identity when, regardless of the source, the third party has notice of facts reasonably sufficient to identify the principal. It is a question of fact whether a third party has such notice. It is a presumption that notice of facts that form a basis for further sleuthing by a third party, such as searches in public records, do not constitute reasonably sufficient notice of a principal's identity. In particular, an agent's use of a trade name, which may be traced to its registered user through a search of public filings, is not sufficient to disclose a principal's identity. The presumption may be overcome by evidence of custom in a particular trade or industry. In some circumstances, custom and usage may make it reasonable to expect that third parties will ascertain principals' identities by checking records maintained by others. This may be so in industries where parties regularly deal through intermediaries and information about principals' identities is readily accessible to those who provide services.

Illustration:

> P Corporation owns a restaurant, named The Magic Moment, that A manages. A enters into a contract with T, an interior designer, to refurbish the entrance to the restaurant. A signs the contract "A, The Magic Moment." T, A, and P Corporation are parties to the contract. Depending on what a reasonable person in T's position would understand to be the meaning of "A, The Magic Moment" under the circumstances, P Corporation is either A's unidentified or A's undisclosed principal in A's dealings with T. Both A and P Corporation are subject to liability on the contract with T.

Agent's position as party to contract. In an action by a third party against an agent who has made a contract on behalf of an unidentified principal, the agent may assert all defenses that arise from the transaction itself and defenses available to the agent personally.

§ 6.03 Agent for Undisclosed Principal

When an agent acting with actual authority makes a contract on behalf of an undisclosed principal,

(1) unless excluded by the contract, the principal is a party to the contract;

(2) the agent and the third party are parties to the contract; and

(3) the principal, if a party to the contract, and the third party have the same rights, liabilities, and defenses against each other as if the principal made the contract personally, subject to §§ 6.05–6.09.

Comment:

Rationales for contractual liability. Contemporary contract doctrine requires a manifestation of mutual assent to an exchange and consideration for the formation of a contract. However, when an agent acts on behalf of an undisclosed principal, the third party does not manifest assent to an exchange with the principal and the principal does not make a manifestation of assent to the third party. The third party's manifestation of assent is made to the agent to whom the third party expects to render performance and from whom the third party expects to receive performance. In contrast, when an agent makes a contract on behalf of a disclosed principal, the third party has notice of the principal's existence and identity. When an agent makes a contract on behalf of an unidentified principal, the third party has notice that the agent acts on behalf of a principal but does not have notice of the principal's identity. In both cases, the third party manifests assent to an agent with notice that the agent represents another person who will be a party to the contract.

However, well-settled doctrine treats an undisclosed principal as a party to a contract that an agent makes on behalf of the principal, unless the contract excludes the principal as a party. If an agent acts with actual authority in making a contract on an undisclosed principal's behalf, the basis for treating the principal as a party to the contract is that the agent acted reasonably on the basis of the principal's manifestation of assent to the agent. The principal's liability on the contract is thus consistent with the agent's reasonable understanding of the principal's wishes. The principal has rights under the contract because the agent acted on the principal's behalf in making the contract. A third party, however, may exclude an undisclosed principal as a party to a contract by explicitly so providing in a contract.

Moreover, even if comparable results could be achieved through assignment, it may be commercially more convenient to treat an undisclosed principal as a party to contracts made on the principal's behalf by an agent. It may be advantageous to an undisclosed principal to acquire contractual rights directly through an agent, rather than risk any delay or other slippage that may intervene if the principal may acquire rights only by assignment. It may also be advantageous to an agent to represent principals whose interest is not disclosed. If an agent invests in developing a distribution network, the agent may be concerned that third parties who know the identity of the agent's principals will deal directly with them, bypassing the agent.

An agent who makes a contract on behalf of an undisclosed principal also becomes a party to the contract. The basis for treating the agent as a party to the contract is the expectation of the third party. The agent has dealt with the third party as if the agent were the sole party whose legal relations would be affected as a consequence of making the contract.

Contract made on behalf of undisclosed principal. If an agent acts without actual authority in making a contract on behalf of an undisclosed principal, the principal may be subject to liability... A principal in such a case may acquire rights against the third party by ratifying the agent's conduct... An agent does not act with apparent authority with regard to an undisclosed principal because the principal has made no manifestation requisite for apparent authority.

An undisclosed principal only becomes a party to a contract when an agent acts on the principal's behalf in making the contract. Thus, an undisclosed principal does not become a party to a contract when the agent does not intend to act for the principal. Factual circumstances at the time the agent acts are relevant to proving the agent's intention.

Illustration:

> P authorizes A to buy a particular computer from T in A's name for P and gives A the money necessary for the purchase. Instead, A purchases the computer from T on A's own credit, intending to abscond with both the computer and P's money. P is not liable to T on the contract for the computer. A did not intend to act on P's account in purchasing the computer.

A principal is undisclosed if, at the time a contract is made, the third party with whom the agent deals has no notice that the agent is acting on behalf of a principal. It is a question of fact whether the third party has received sufficient notice that the contract is made with an agent who represents a principal and sufficient notice of that principal's identity. The third party is not subject to a duty to discover the principal's existence or identity; the responsibility is the agent's if the agent wishes to avoid personal liability on the contract. However, a third party may have sufficient notice of the principal's existence or identity from sources apart from the agent.

Illustrations:

> A, the President of P College, hires T, an architect, to prepare plans for a new college building. T has reason to know that A contracts on behalf of P College.

> [In contrast,] A is the President of P Corporation, which owns a large ranch. A hires T to grind stumps on ranch property. T knows that the ranch property is large and that the ranch uses a trade name, "Rocking D Ranch." T's knowledge of these facts does not give T reason to know that A makes the stump-grinding contract on behalf of P Corporation.

§ 6.10 Agent's Implied Warranty of Authority

A person who purports to make a contract, representation, or conveyance to or with a third party on behalf of another person, lacking power to bind that person, gives an implied warranty of authority to the third party and is subject to liability to the third party for damages for loss caused by breach of that warranty, including loss of the benefit expected from performance by the principal, unless

(1) the principal or purported principal ratifies the act as stated in § 4.01; or

(2) the person who purports to make the contract, representation, or conveyance gives notice to the third party that no warranty of authority is given; or

(3) the third party knows that the person who purports to make the contract, representation, or conveyance acts without actual authority.

Comment:

An agent's implied warranty of authority is a solution to a problem otherwise confronted by third parties who deal with persons whom they believe to act as agents with power to bind a principal. Believing that a principal is bound by a contract, representation, or conveyance purportedly made on the principal's behalf, the third party will often rely on receiving performance from the principal, forgoing other opportunities and incurring costs in anticipation of receiving performance from the principal. Unless an agent risks some liability when a third party believes the agent acts with authority to bind the principal, agents may be tempted to act beyond the bounds imposed by the principal's manifestation of assent to the agent, in the hope that, if the transaction turns out to be advantageous for the principal, the principal will ratify what the agent has done.

However, an agent does not become a party to a contract made on behalf of a disclosed principal unless the agent so agrees with the third party. Thus, if the principal on whose behalf the agent purports to act is not bound by a contract because the agent acted without actual or apparent authority, the third party may not subject the agent to liability on the contract unless the agent agreed to become a party. The third party may be able to establish that the person on whose behalf the agent purported to act has ratified the agent's action, thereby creating the effects of actual authority. Alternatively, the third party may be able to establish that the person on whose behalf action was purportedly taken should be estopped to deny the existence of an agency relationship with the actor. If the third party cannot establish ratification or estoppel and the agent has not become a party to the contract, the third party faces the prospect of loss that is unrecoverable from either the agent or the principal on whose behalf the agent purported to act.

A principal may be bound by an agent's action although the agent acted without actual authority if the agent acted with apparent authority. If a principal is bound to a third party on the basis of an agent's apparent authority, the agent is not subject to liability to the third party on the agent's implied warranty of authority, although the agent acted without actual authority.

Illustration:

> A and B are co-owners of property. A executes a lease of the property to T, signing the lease on two separate lines, one below the other: "A; A as agent for B." A had no actual or apparent authority to sign on B's behalf. Unless B ratifies A's action, A is subject to liability to T for loss to T resulting from T's reliance on A's implied representation that A had power to bind B.

§ 6.11 Agent's Representations

(1) When an agent for a disclosed or unidentified principal makes a false representation about the agent's authority to a third party, the principal is not subject to liability unless the agent acted with actual or apparent authority in making the representation and the third party does not have notice that the agent's representation is false.

(2) A representation by an agent made incident to a contract or conveyance is attributed to a disclosed or unidentified principal as if the principal made the representation directly when the agent had actual or apparent authority to make the contract or conveyance unless the third party knew or had reason to know that the representation was untrue or that the agent acted without actual authority in making it.

(3) A representation by an agent made incident to a contract or conveyance is attributed to an undisclosed principal as if the principal made the representation directly when

    (a) the agent acted with actual authority in making the representation, or

    (b) the agent acted without actual authority in making the representation but had actual authority to make true representations about the same matter.

> The agent's representation is not attributed to the principal when the third party knew or had reason to know it was untrue.

Comment:

Agent's representation concerning agent's own authority. An agent's own statements about the nature or extent of the agent's authority to act on behalf of the principal do not create apparent authority by themselves. An agent acts with apparent authority only when a third party's belief that the agent acts with authority is reasonable and is traceable to a manifestation made by the principal. An agent does not act with apparent authority when a third party has reason to know that the agent acts without actual authority, despite protests by the agent to the contrary.

Illustration:

> P, who owns a tree nursery, tells T, who owns a garden center, that A is authorized to sell P's trees only at prices set by P and

communicated by P to T. A tells T that A now has P's authority to set the prices for P's trees. A's statement to T does not by itself create apparent authority to bind P to sell trees to T at prices set by A.

However, a principal's manifestation may invite a third party to deal with the principal on a basis to be stated by the agent. If so, representations made by the agent may create apparent authority when the principal's manifestation incorporates them by reference. The principal may then be subject to liability to the third party, although the agent has falsely represented the agent's authority to the third party, unless the third party had notice that the agent's representation was false. A principal does not invite a third party to deal on a basis to be stated by the agent simply because the agent has access to information about an event that is relevant to whether the agent has actual authority to take action.

Illustrations:

P, who deals in cattle, retains A to buy cattle for P. P tells T, another cattle dealer, that A has authority to buy cattle when the market price of cattle in Mexico reaches a certain point. T makes a contract to sell cattle to A on P's account, relying on A's untruthful statement that the price of cattle in Mexico has reached the point specified by P. P is not subject to liability on the contract. By stating that A's authority to buy cattle was contingent on a price in a particular market, P did not invite T to rely on A's statement whether that contingency had occurred.

Same facts as [above], except that P tells T that A has authority to buy cattle "when the Mexican market hits the right price." T asks what that price might be. P replies: "A will tell you." P has invited T to deal on terms to be stated by A. P is subject to liability on a contract A makes with P even though the price stated by A to be the right price in the Mexican market is not the right price as P defines it.

2. Tort

§ 2.04 Respondeat Superior

An employer is subject to liability for torts committed by employees while acting within the scope of their employment.

Comment:

[This] doctrine establishes a principle of employer liability for the costs that work-related torts impose on third parties. Its scope is limited to the employment relationship and to conduct falling within the scope of that relationship because an employer has the right to control how work is done. This right is more detailed than the right of control possessed by all principals, whether or not employers.

Respondeat superior is inapplicable when a principal does not have the right to control the actions of the agent that makes the relationship between principal and agent performing the service one of employment... In general, employment contemplates a continuing relationship and a continuing set of duties that the employer and employee owe to each other. Agents who are retained as the need arises and who are not otherwise employees of their principal normally operate their own business enterprises and are not, except in limited respects, integrated into the principal's enterprise so that a task may be completed or a specified objective accomplished. Therefore, respondeat superior does not apply.

Respondeat superior assigns responsibility to an employer for the legal consequences that result from employees' errors of judgment and lapses in attentiveness when the acts or omissions are within the scope of employment. A firm or organization that employs individuals usually structures their work to limit the scope of discretion and individual action, thus limiting the occasions when unreasonable decisions are likely to be made. Impulsive conduct is not typical of firms or organizations. The firm as a principal may always act more rationally and reasonably than would most individuals acting by themselves because different individuals are assigned different tasks, often monitoring and checking each other. Respondeat superior creates an incentive for principals to choose employees and structure work within the organization so as to reduce the incidence of tortious conduct. This incentive may reduce the incidence of tortious conduct more effectively than doctrines that impose liability solely on an individual tortfeasor.

§ 7.03 Principal's Liability

(1) A principal is subject to direct liability to a third party harmed by an agent's conduct when

    (a)　as stated in § 7.04, the agent acts with actual authority or the principal ratifies the agent's conduct and

        (i)　the agent's conduct is tortious, or

        (ii)　the agent's conduct, if that of the principal, would subject the principal to tort liability; or

    (b)　as stated in § 7.05, the principal is negligent in selecting, supervising, or otherwise controlling the agent; or

    (c)　as stated in § 7.06, the principal delegates performance of a duty to use care to protect other persons or their property to an agent who fails to perform the duty.

(2) A principal is subject to vicarious liability to a third party harmed by an agent's conduct when

    (a)　as stated in § 7.07, the agent is an employee who commits a tort while acting within the scope of employment; or

(b) as stated in § 7.08, the agent commits a tort when acting with apparent authority in dealing with a third party on or purportedly on behalf of the principal.

Comment:

Liability on basis of principal's own conduct; vicarious liability. A principal's own fault may subject the principal to liability to a third party harmed by an agent's conduct. Often termed "direct liability," such liability stems either from the principal's relationship with an agent whose conduct harms a third party or from the agent's failure to perform a duty owed by the principal to the third party. A principal is subject to liability under § 7.04 when an agent acts with actual authority in committing a tort, that is, when the agent reasonably believes, based on a manifestation of the principal, that the principal wishes the agent so to act. A principal is subject to liability under § 7.05 on the basis of the principal's negligence in selecting, supervising, or otherwise controlling or failing to control the agent. A principal is subject to liability under § 7.06 when the principal owes a duty to protect a third party and an agent to whom the principal has delegated performance of the duty fails to fulfill it.

An agent's tort may, separately, subject a principal to vicarious liability. Under § 7.07, a principal is subject to liability when an agent who is an employee as defined in § 7.07(3) commits a tort while acting within the scope of employment. Under § 7.08, a principal is subject to liability when actions taken by an agent acting with apparent authority constitute a tort or enable the agent to conceal its commission. A principal who is vicariously liable may, additionally, be subject to liability on the basis of the principal's own conduct.

Significant consequences may follow from the distinction between direct and vicarious liability. In particular, a principal's vicarious liability turns on whether the agent is liable. In most cases, direct liability requires fault on the part of the principal whereas vicarious liability does not require that the principal be at fault. The distinction may also be relevant to whether a loss is insurable.

Organizational principals. A principal that is not an individual can take action only through its agents, who typically are individuals. Even when an agent is not an individual, its ability to act derives from its own agents. An organization's tortious conduct consists of conduct by agents of the organization that is attributable to it. An organization may breach a duty of care that it owes to a third party even though the breach cannot be attributed to any single agent of the organization. Thus, an organization's conduct may be tortious when it fails to fulfill a duty that the organization owes to a third party. For example, a custodian owes a duty of reasonable care to third parties with respect to risks created by those in its custody. A custodian that is an organization would breach its duty of reasonable care through the action or inaction of its employees and other agents, including the prescription and enforcement by managerial agents of directives and guidelines to be followed by other agents.

§ 7.04 Agents Acts with Actual Authority

A principal is subject to liability to a third party harmed by an agent's conduct when the agent's conduct is within the scope of the agent's actual authority or ratified by the principal; and

(1) the agent's conduct is tortious, or

(2) the agent's conduct, if that of the principal, would subject the principal to tort liability.

Comment:

In general. When an agent acts with actual authority, the agent reasonably believes, in accordance with manifestations of the principal, that the principal wishes the agent so to act. If a principal ratifies an agent's conduct, the principal assents to be affected by the legal consequences of the action. The legal consequences created by ratification are those of actual authority. If an agent's action within the scope of the agent's actual authority harms a third party, the principal is subject to liability if the agent's conduct is tortious. If the agent's conduct is not tortious, the principal is subject to liability if the same conduct on the part of the principal would have subjected the principal to tort liability. For example, an agent's action may not be tortious because the agent lacks information known to the principal. In either situation, the agent is the instrumentality through which the principal achieves the principal's objective. If the agent uses means other than those intended by the principal, the principal is subject to liability if the agent's choice of means is within the scope of the agent's actual authority.

If a result follows from a directive to engage in tortious conduct and the person who gives the directive intends that result, it is immaterial to the person's liability that the person did not contemplate the particular tortious means through which the result was accomplished.

Illustrations:

P, who publishes a newspaper, engages D to deliver copies of the newspaper to a neighboring community. P directs D to deliver the newspapers in the midst of an ice storm when both P and D know that driving conditions are hazardous, that the vehicle D will use is not equipped for such conditions, and that D lacks experience in driving under such conditions. In the course of making deliveries, D skids on an icy road, injuring T. P is subject to liability to T. P's instruction to D directed D to act in a negligent manner. D is also subject to liability to T.

Same facts as [above], except that P contracts with A Corporation to provide delivery services. D is an employee of A Corporation. D's supervisor, also an employee of A Corporation, relays P's instruction to D. P is subject to liability to T, even if P's contract with A Corporation does not establish a relationship of agency... P's instruction to D, relayed through A Corporation, directed D to act in a negligent manner. D is also subject to liability to T. A Corporation is also subject to liability to T. D acted within the scope of D's employment.

Same facts as [the first illustration], except that S pays F to enter T's apartment and remove and destroy T's personal property. F, P, and S are subject to liability to T. F committed a tort at S's direction. P intended the result that followed from F's conduct, although P did not contemplate that F as opposed to S enter T's apartment.

It may seem problematic to characterize an agent's tortious conduct as falling within the scope of the agent's actual authority because in ordinary usage characterizing an action as "authorized" connotes that it is done rightfully, which is not the case from the perspective of a third party who is harmed by a tort committed by an agent. However, an agent acts with actual authority when the agent reasonably believes, on the basis of a manifestation of the principal, that the principal wishes the agent so to act. Tortious conduct by an agent thus may be consistent with the agent's actual authority. That does not, of course, immunize either the agent or the principal from liability to a third party harmed by the agent's conduct.

§ 7.07 Employee Acting Within Scope of Employment

(1) An employer is subject to vicarious liability for a tort committed by its employee acting within the scope of employment.

(2) An employee acts within the scope of employment when performing work assigned by the employer or engaging in a course of conduct subject to the employer's control. An employee's act is not within the scope of employment when it occurs within an independent course of conduct not intended by the employee to serve any purpose of the employer.

(3) For purposes of this section,

  (a) an employee is an agent whose principal controls or has the right to control the manner and means of the agent's performance of work, and

  (b) the fact that work is performed gratuitously does not relieve a principal of liability.

Comment:

When tortious conduct is within the scope of employment—in general. If an employee commits a tort while performing work assigned by the employer or while acting within a course of conduct subject to the employer's control, the employee's conduct is within the scope of employment unless the employee was engaged in an independent course of conduct not intended to further any purpose of the employer.

[R]espondeat superior subjects an employer to vicarious liability for employee torts committed within the scope of employment, distinct from whether the employer is subject to direct liability. An employer's ability to exercise control over its employees' work-related conduct enables the employer to take measures to reduce the incidence of tortious conduct. It may be difficult, after the fact of an employee's tortious conduct, to identify an instance of negligence on the part of the employer. This may be so even when, before the fact of the employee's tortious conduct, steps were available to the employer that, if taken, would have prevented the tort. In contrast, when an employee's tortious conduct is outside the range of activity that an employer may control, subjecting the employer to liability would not provide incentives for the employer to take measures to reduce the incidence of such tortious conduct. Moreover, for an employer to insure against a risk of liability, whether from third-party sources or its own assets, the risk must be at least to some degree ascertainable and quantifiable.

Under subsection (2), an employee's tortious conduct is outside the scope of employment when the employee is engaged in an independent course of conduct not intended to further any purpose of the employer. An independent course of conduct represents a departure from, not an escalation of, conduct involved in performing assigned work or other conduct that an employer permits or controls. When an employee commits a tort with the sole intention of furthering the employee's own purposes, and not any purpose of the employer, it is neither fair nor true-to-life to characterize the employee's action as that of a representative of the employer. The employee's intention severs the basis for treating the employee's act as that of the employer in the employee's interaction with the third party.

Conduct in the performance of work and scope of employment. An employee's conduct is within the scope of employment when it constitutes performance of work assigned to the employee by the employer. The fact that the employee performs the work carelessly does not take the employee's conduct outside the scope of employment, nor does the fact that the employee otherwise makes a mistake in performing the work. Likewise, conduct is not outside the scope of employment merely because an employee disregards the employer's instructions.

Illustrations:

P, who writes bail bonds, employs A as a bond "runner." A's assigned work is to locate persons for whom P has written bonds who jump bail and return them to custody. P directs A to search for J. A mistakenly identifies T as J, breaks down the door of T's home, and holds T at gunpoint. Under applicable law, A's conduct toward T is tortious. P is subject to liability to T. A's actions constituted performance of work P assigned to A.

Same facts as [above], except that P instructs its runners to contact Ps office prior to attempting a forcible entry into a residence. A neglects to do this before breaking down the door of T's home. Same result.

An employee's failure to take action may also be conduct within the scope of employment. For example, an employee's failure to do work assigned by the employer, when harm to a third party results, under some circumstances may constitute negligence.

The determinative question is whether the course of conduct in which the tort occurred is within the scope of employment. Intentional torts and other intentional wrongdoing may be within the scope of employment. For example, if an employee's job duties include determining the prices at which the employer's output will be sold to customers, the employee's agreement with a competitor to fix prices is within the scope of employment unless circumstances establish a departure from the scope of employment. Likewise, when an employee's job duties include making statements to prospective customers to induce them to buy from the employer, intentional misrepresentations made by the employee are within the scope of employment unless circumstances establish that the employee has departed from it.

Definition of employee. Numerous factual indicia are relevant to whether an agent is an employee. These include: the extent of control that the agent and the principal have agreed the principal may exercise over details of the work; whether the agent is engaged in a distinct occupation or business; whether the type of work done by the agent is customarily done under a principal's direction or without supervision; the skill required in the agent's occupation; whether the agent or the principal supplies the tools and other instrumentalities required for the work and the place in which to perform it; the length of time during which the agent is engaged by a principal; whether the agent is paid by the job or by the time worked; whether the agent's work is part of the principal's regular business; whether the principal and the agent believe that they are creating an employment relationship; and whether the principal is or is not in business. Also relevant is the extent of control that the principal has exercised in practice over the details of the agent's work.

§ 7.08 Agent Acts with Apparent Authority

A principal is subject to vicarious liability for a tort committed by an agent in dealing or communicating with a third party on or purportedly on behalf of the principal when actions taken by the agent with apparent authority constitute the tort or enable the agent to conceal its commission.

Comment:

Connection between apparent authority and agent's tortious conduct. An agent acts with apparent authority with regard to a third party when the third party reasonably believes that the agent or other actor has authority to act on behalf of the principal and that belief is traceable to manifestations made by the principal. When an agent acts with apparent authority, the agent's motivation is immaterial to the legal consequences that the agent's action carries for the principal. Likewise, the fact that an agent's conduct is not in fact beneficial to the principal does not shield the principal from legal consequences. This is because apparent authority holds a principal accountable for the results of third-party beliefs about an actor's authority to act as an agent when the belief is reasonable and is traceable to a manifestation made by the principal. So to charge a principal is fair because it is the principal's manifestation that clothes the agent with the appearance of authority to act on the principal's behalf and that induces the third party reasonably to believe that the agent acts with actual authority.

Apparent-authority … focuses on the reasonable expectations of third parties with whom an agent deals. [A]pparent-authority… [is understood as] a principal's vicarious liability when a third party's reasonable belief in an agent's authority to speak or deal on behalf of a principal stems from a manifestation made by the principal and it is through statements or dealings that the agent acts tortiously.

A principal's liability under the rule stated in this section does not depend on whether the principal benefits from the agent's tortious conduct. A principal is also subject to liability under the rule stated in this section when an agent's tortious conduct leads to physical injury.

Illustrations:

> P Numismatics Company urges its customers to seek investment advice from its retail salespeople, including A. T, who wishes to invest in gold coins, seeks A's advice at an office of P Numismatics Company. A encourages T to purchase a particular set of gold coins, falsely representing material facts relevant to their value. T, reasonably relying on A's representations, purchases the set of coins. P is subject to liability to T. A is also subject to liability to T.

> Same facts as [above], except that A persuades T to pay cash for the coins and to leave the coins with A so that they may be safely stored by P Numismatics Company. A then absconds with both the coins and the cash paid by T. Same results.

> [Another example,] O, who owns an office building, retains P, a construction firm, to renovate the building. T, a prospective tenant, visits the building. T asks P's site manager, A, whether it will be safe for T to inspect a particular group of offices. A tells T to ask G, a security guard in the building, saying "G's our point person for safety." G tells T that the offices in question are safe to visit although G does not know whether this is so. Unbeknownst to T, G is an employee of Guards, Inc., not P. P and Guards, Inc., have instructed A and G never to direct prospective tenants within the building, but T neither knows nor has reason to know this. T reasonably believes that G, to whom A directs T, has authority to answer questions from prospective tenants. T is injured when T falls through the weakened flooring in one of the offices. P is

subject to liability to T. G is also subject to liability. Guards, Inc., is subject to liability as stated in § 7.07.

A principal is not subject to liability under the rule stated in this section unless there is a close link between an agent's tortious conduct and the agent's apparent authority. Thus, a principal is not subject to liability when actions that an agent takes with apparent authority, although connected in some way to the agent's tortious conduct, do not themselves constitute the tort or enable the agent to mask its commission.

Illustration:

P Insurance Company appoints A as an agent with authority to sell policies and collect premiums on its behalf. A writes an insurance policy on the life of T without T's knowledge or consent, forging T's signature on the application and naming B as the policy's beneficiary. A then arranges to have T murdered by B, who obtains and cashes the check issued by P Insurance Company when it receives notice of T's death. P Insurance Company is not subject to liability to T's estate. Neither A nor B acted with apparent authority in committing their wrongful acts against T.

An actor may continue to possess apparent authority although the principal has terminated the actor's actual authority or the agency relationship between them. This is so because a third party may reasonably believe that the actor continues to act as an agent and within the scope of actual authority on the basis of manifestations previously made by the principal. Such a manifestation, once made, remains operative until the third party has notice of circumstances that make it unreasonable to believe that the actor continues to have actual authority.

§ 7.01 Agent's Liability to Third Party

An agent is subject to liability to a third party harmed by the agent's tortious conduct. Unless an applicable statute provides otherwise, an actor remains subject to liability although the actor acts as an agent or an employee, with actual or apparent authority, or within the scope of employment.

Comment:

An agent whose conduct is tortious is subject to liability. This is so whether or not the agent acted with actual authority, with apparent authority, or within the scope of employment.

The justification for this basic rule is that a person is responsible for the legal consequences of torts committed by that person. A tort committed by an agent constitutes a wrong to the tort's victim independently of the capacity in which the agent committed the tort. The injury suffered by the victim of a tort is the same regardless of whether the tortfeasor acted independently or happened to be acting as an agent or employee of another person.

An agent's liability is based on the agent's conduct; the agent's status is, separately, a basis for imposing liability only when a statute, regulation, or ordinance so provides. It is ordinarily immaterial to an agent's liability that the agent's tortious conduct may, additionally, subject the principal to liability.

An agent's individual tort liability extends to negligent acts and omissions as well as to intentional conduct. It is also immaterial to an agent's tort liability to a third party whether the agent benefited personally from the tortious conduct.

Illustrations:

> A is the sole proprietor of a delivery firm doing business as "Ace Trucking." A owns a truck used in Ace Trucking's business. A drives the truck negligently, injuring T, in the course of making a delivery. A is subject to liability to T.

> Same facts as [above], except that A has incorporated A's firm as "Ace Trucking, Inc." and transferred ownership of the truck to it. A is the sole shareholder, officer, and director of Ace Trucking, Inc. A is subject to liability to T. Ace Trucking, Inc., is also subject to liability to T.

> Same facts as [the first illustration], except that the truck is driven by E, an employee of Ace Trucking, Inc. E is subject to liability to T. Ace Trucking, Inc., is also subject to liability to T.

> [In addition,] A is the Chief Financial Officer of P Corporation, engaged in the manufacture of bulk pharmaceuticals. To finance an acquisition, P Corporation enters into a loan agreement with T Bank that requires P Corporation to place all payments from its customers into a special "blocked" bank account to be held in trust for T Bank. Instead, A diverts payments received from P Corporation's customers into other bank accounts for P Corporation's general use. Under applicable law, A's diversion of the payments constitutes conversion of T Bank's property. A is subject to liability to T for the conversion, although A did not derive a direct personal benefit from the converted funds.

F. HOW IS AN AGENCY RELATIONSHIP TERMINATED?

§ 3.06 Termination of Actual Authority

An agent's actual authority may be terminated by:

(1) the agent's death, cessation of existence, or suspension of powers as stated in § 3.07(1) and (3); or

(2) the principal's death, cessation of existence, or suspension of powers as stated in § 3.07(2) and (4); or

(3) the principal's loss of capacity, as stated in § 3.08(1) and (3); or

Source: Restatement (Third) of Agency §§ 3.06, 3.11 (2006). Copyright 2006 by American Law Institute. Reprinted with permission.

(4) an agreement between the agent and the principal or the occurrence of circumstances on the basis of which the agent should reasonably conclude that the principal no longer would assent to the agent's taking action on the principal's behalf, as stated in § 3.09; or

(5) a manifestation of revocation by the principal to the agent, or of renunciation by the agent to the principal, as stated in § 3.10(1); or

(6) the occurrence of circumstances specified by statute.

Comment:

Agreement between principal and agent and changes in circumstances. The basis for actual authority is a manifestation of assent made by a principal to an agent. When the manifestation is embodied in an agreement that specifies circumstances under which the agent's actual authority shall terminate, occurrence of a specified circumstance effects termination of the principal's expressed assent. Regardless of whether the initial agreement contains a termination provision, mutual agreement to terminate the agency relationship is always effective to terminate the agent's actual authority.

Following the principal's manifestation of assent to an agent, circumstances may change such that, at the time the agent takes action, it is not reasonable for the agent to believe that the principal at that time consents to the action being taken on the principal's behalf even though the principal has not manifested dissent to the action by that time. For example, the agent may become insolvent and have notice that it is important to the principal to be represented by a solvent agent. The agent may lose capacity to bind itself by a contract or to become subject to other obligations and have notice that it is important to the principal that the agent retain such capacity. Events that are totally outside the control of the agent or the principal may also make it unreasonable for the agent to believe that the principal consents to the agent's action. For example, if the principal retains the agent to sell goods in a particular geographically defined market, the occurrence of war or widespread civil unrest may so impair the value of the agent's efforts to the principal that the agent would not be reasonable in believing the principal wishes the agent to sell into the territory. The agent then lacks actual authority so to act but would have acted with actual authority had the agent acted prior to the change in circumstances. The focal point for determining whether an agent acted with actual authority is the time of action, not the time of the principal's manifestation, which may be earlier.

Manifestation of dissent—revocation and renunciation. In a relationship of agency, the principal or the agent has power to terminate the agent's actual authority. The power is exercised through a manifestation of dissent to the other through which the principal revokes the agent's authority or the agent renounces it.

Death, cessation of existence, suspension of powers, and loss of capacity. Agency is a relationship between two persons in which one acts on behalf of the other.

This is so even when the principal or the agent, or both, are not individuals. When a principal ceases to exist, the expression of assent in the principal's manifestation to the agent becomes inoperative because it is no longer that of a person, presently in existence, on whose behalf the agent acts. Likewise, when an agent ceases to exist, actual authority terminates because the principal's manifestation of assent was to a particular person who no longer can take action.

§ 3.11 Termination of Apparent Authority

(1) The termination of actual authority does not by itself end any apparent authority held by an agent.

(2) Apparent authority ends when it is no longer reasonable for the third party with whom an agent deals to believe that the agent continues to act with actual authority.

Comment:

Principal's death or loss of capacity. A principal's death or loss of capacity does not by itself or automatically end the agent's apparent authority.

An agent may act with apparent authority following the principal's death or loss of capacity because the basis of apparent authority is a principal's manifestation to third parties, coupled with a third party's reasonable belief that the agent acts with actual authority. Neither element requires that the principal consent or manifest assent at the time the agent takes action. When third parties do not have notice that the principal has died or lost capacity, they may reasonably believe the agent to be authorized.

Lingering apparent authority. An agent's apparent authority may survive or linger after the termination of actual authority because apparent authority is present when a third party reasonably believes that the agent is authorized to take action and the belief is traceable to a manifestation made by the principal. Apparent authority protects third parties who interact with an agent on the basis of the principal's prior manifestation and who lack notice that the agent's actual authority has terminated.

Often termed "lingering authority," the doctrine stated in this section recognizes that it is reasonable for third parties to assume that an agent's actual authority is a continuing or ongoing condition, unless and until a third party has notice of circumstances that make it unreasonable so to assume. These circumstances include notice that the principal has revoked the agent's actual authority, that the agent has renounced it, that the agent's authority was limited in duration or to a specific undertaking, or that circumstances otherwise have changed such that it is no longer reasonable to believe that the principal consents to the agent's act on the principal's behalf.

Illustrations:

P Corporation, in the recycling business, retains A as a purchasing agent to buy recyclable material on its behalf. A is authorized by P Corporation to buy on terms that commit P Corporation to pay for the material when it arrives at P Corporation's recycling facility. A has purchased recyclables many times from T, who is in the business of building demolition. P Corporation terminates A's actual authority. T has no notice of the termination. As to T, A continues for a reasonable period of time to possess apparent authority to purchase from T on terms comparable to those on which A has made prior purchases on P Corporation's behalf.

Same facts as [above], except that the local newspaper publishes a story about A's termination on its front page. As to T, A's apparent authority has ended.

[Another example,] P Corporation, a manufacturer of semiconductors, retains A as a sales representative. A has often sold semiconductors manufactured by P Corporation to T. P Corporation is headquartered in the nation of B, which adopts a regulation prohibiting the export of semiconductors into the nation of C, where T is located. T is aware of the regulation. In all of T's prior dealings with P Corporation, including those through A, P Corporation has meticulously complied with legal regulations, including prior prohibitions on export. Following B's adoption of the export ban and while it is in effect, A does not have apparent authority to bind P Corporation to a contract to sell semiconductors to T.

Same facts as [the proceeding illustration], except that the senior officer of P Corporation tells A to disregard the export ban but, when asked, to deny that such an instruction has been given. Although A lacks apparent authority as to T, A has actual authority to bind P Corporation to a contract with T.

Notice of termination of authority. Apparent authority is not present when a reasonable person in the position of a third party would not believe that the principal consents to the agent's or other actor's conduct. If a third party has notice of facts that call the agent's authority into question, and these facts would prompt a reasonable person to make inquiry of the principal before dealing with the agent, the agent does not act with apparent authority. This general principle is applicable to determining whether and when an agent acts with the lingering appearance of authority after the agent's actual authority has terminated. Lingering authority does not survive a statement that the agent's authority has terminated, made by the principal to the third party with whom the now-former agent deals.

Illustration:

P Corporation, a manufacturer, retains A as its exclusive sales agent for a territory that includes T. P Corporation so notifies T. Later, P Corporation terminates A's authority. P Corporation sends a letter to T's headquarters informing T that A is no longer authorized. The letter arrives at T's headquarters at 9:00 a.m. A's apparent authority ends as soon as T or T's office force has an opportunity to read and act upon the mail.

CHAPTER 5

Accounting Basics

The point of this chapter is simply to make you aware of financial statements, and give you with a basic literacy of the information within them. There is no need to understand the complex details involved in preparing financial statements and calculating various numbers; that is a task for accountants. A basic understanding of financial statements, though, is important for a transactional lawyer. For example, if your client asks for advice about whether the corporation can legally distribute dividends, you may need to review financial statements to provide an answer.

Beginners' Guide to Financial Statements

There are three main financial statements. They are: (1) balance sheets, (2) income statements, and (3) cash flow statements. Balance sheets show what a company owns and what it owes at a fixed point in time. Income statements show how much money a company made and spent over a period of time. Cash flow statements show the exchange of money between a company and the outside world also over a period of time.

Let's look at each of these three financial statements in more detail.

A. Balance Sheets

A balance sheet provides detailed information about a company's assets, liabilities and shareholders' equity.

Assets are things that a company owns that have value. This typically means they can either be sold or used by the company to make products or provide services that can be sold. Assets include physical property, such as plants, trucks, equipment and inventory. It also includes things that can't be

Excerpt from *Beginners' Guide to Financial Statements (sic)*, U.S. Securities and Exchange Commission (Feb. 5, 2017) http://www.sec.gov/investor/pubs/begfinstmtguide.htm. Copyright in the Public Domain.

touched but nevertheless exist and have value, such as trademarks and patents. And cash itself is an asset. So are investments a company makes.

Liabilities are amounts of money that a company owes to others. This can include all kinds of obligations, like money borrowed from a bank to launch a new product, rent for use of a building, money owed to suppliers for materials, payroll a company owes to its employees, environmental cleanup costs, or taxes owed to the government. Liabilities also include obligations to provide goods or services to customers in the future.

Shareholders' equity is sometimes called capital or net worth. It's the money that would be left if a company sold all of its assets and paid off all of its liabilities. This leftover money belongs to the shareholders, or the owners, of the company.

The following formula summarizes what a balance sheet shows:

$$\text{ASSETS} = \text{LIABILITIES} + \text{SHAREHOLDERS' EQUITY}$$

A company's assets have to equal, or "balance," the sum of its liabilities and shareholders' equity.

A company's balance sheet is set up like the basic accounting equation shown above. On the left side of the balance sheet, companies list their assets. On the right side, they list their liabilities and shareholders' equity. Sometimes balance sheets show assets at the top, followed by liabilities, with shareholders' equity at the bottom.

Assets are generally listed based on how quickly they will be converted into cash. Current assets are things a company expects to convert to cash within one year. A good example is inventory. Most companies expect to sell their inventory for cash within one year. Noncurrent assets are things a company does not expect to convert to cash within one year or that would take longer than one year to sell. Noncurrent assets include fixed assets. Fixed assets are those assets used to operate the business but that are not available for sale, such as trucks, office furniture and other property.

Liabilities are generally listed based on their due dates. Liabilities are said to be either current or long-term. Current liabilities are obligations a company expects to pay off within the year. Long-term liabilities are obligations due more than one year away.

Shareholders' equity is the amount owners invested in the company's stock plus or minus the company's earnings or losses since inception. Sometimes companies distribute earnings, instead of retaining them. These distributions are called dividends.

A balance sheet shows a snapshot of a company's assets, liabilities and shareholders' equity at the end of the reporting period. It does not show the flows into and out of the accounts during the period.

Balance Sheet Exemplar (McDonald's Corporation—2012 Annual Report)

Consolidated Balance Sheet

IN MILLIONS, EXCEPT PER SHARE DATA	12/31/2012	2011
ASSETS		
Current assets		
Cash and equivalents	**$2,336.1**	$2,335.7
Accounts and notes receivable	**1,375.3**	1,334.7
Inventories, at cost, not in excess of market	**121.7**	116.8
Prepaid expenses and other current assets	**1,089.0**	615.8
Total current assets	**4,922.1**	4,403.0
Other assets		
Investments in and advances to affiliates	**1,380.5**	1,427.0
Goodwill	**2,804.0**	2,653.2
Miscellaneous	**1,602.7**	1,672.2
Total other assets	**5,787.2**	5,752.4
Property and equipment		
Property and equipment, at cost	**38,491.1**	35,737.6
Accumulated depreciation and amortization	**(13,813.9)**	(12,903.1)
Net property and equipment	**24,677.2**	22,834.5
Total assets	**$35,386.5**	$32,989.9
LIABILITIES AND SHAREHOLDERS' EQUITY		
Current liabilities		
Accounts payable	**$1,141.9**	$961.3
Income taxes	**298.7**	262.2
Other taxes	**370.7**	338.1
Accrued interest	**217.0**	218.2
Accrued payroll and other liabilities	**1,374.8**	1,362.8
Current maturities of long-term debt		366.6
Total current liabilities	**3,403.1**	3,509.2
Long-term debt	**13,632.5**	12,133.8
Other long-term liabilities	**1,526.2**	1,612.6
Deferred income taxes	**1,531.1**	1,344.1
Shareholders' equity		
Preferred stock, no par value; authorized – 165.0 million shares; issued—none		
Common stock, $0.01 par value; authorized: 3.5 billion shares; issued: 1,660.6 million shares	**16.6**	16.6

Source: http://www.sec.gov/Archives/edgar/data/63908/000006390814000019/mcd-12312013x10k.htm, U.S. Securities and Exchange Commission. Copyright in the Public Domain.

Additional paid-in capital	**5,778.9**	5,487.3
Retained earnings	**39,278.0**	36,707.5
Accumulated other comprehensive income	**796.4**	449.7
Common stock in treasury, at cost; 657.9 and 639.2 million shares	**(30,576.3)**	(28,270.9)
Total shareholders' equity	**15,293.6**	14,390.2
Total liabilities and shareholders' equity	**$ 35,386.5**	$ 32,989.9

B. Income Statements

An income statement is a report that shows how much revenue a company earned over a specific time period (usually for a year or some portion of a year). An income statement also shows the costs and expenses associated with earning that revenue. The literal "bottom line" of the statement usually shows the company's net earnings or losses. This tells you how much the company earned or lost over the period.

To understand how income statements are set up, think of them as a set of stairs. You start at the top with the total amount of sales made during the accounting period. Then you go down, one step at a time. At each step, you make a deduction for certain costs or other operating expenses associated with earning the revenue. At the bottom of the stairs, after deducting all of the expenses, you learn how much the company actually earned or lost during the accounting period. People often call this "the bottom line."

At the top of the income statement is the total amount of money brought in from sales of products or services. This top line is often referred to as gross revenues or sales. It's called "gross" because expenses have not been deducted from it yet. So the number is "gross" or unrefined.

The next line is money the company doesn't expect to collect on certain sales. This could be due, for example, to sales discounts or merchandise returns.

When you subtract the returns and allowances from the gross revenues, you arrive at the company's net revenues. It's called "net" because, if you can imagine a net, these revenues are left in the net after the deductions for returns and allowances have come out.

Moving down the stairs from the net revenue line, there are several lines that represent various kinds of operating expenses. Although these lines can be reported in various orders, the next line after net revenues typically shows the costs of the sales. This number tells you the amount of money the company spent to produce the goods or services it sold during the accounting period.

The next line subtracts the costs of sales from the net revenues to arrive at a subtotal called "gross profit" or sometimes "gross margin." It's considered "gross" because there are certain expenses that haven't been deducted from it yet.

The next section deals with operating expenses. These are expenses that go toward supporting a company's operations for a given period—for example, salaries of administrative personnel and costs of researching new products. Marketing expenses are another example. Operating expenses are different from "costs of sales," which were deducted above, because operating expenses cannot be linked directly to the production of the products or services being sold.

Depreciation is also deducted from gross profit. Depreciation takes into account the wear and tear on some assets, such as machinery, tools and furniture, which are used over the long term. Companies spread the cost of these assets over the periods they are used. This process of spreading these costs is called depreciation or amortization. The "charge" for using these assets during the period is a fraction of the original cost of the assets.

After all operating expenses are deducted from gross profit, you arrive at operating profit before interest and income tax expenses. This is often called "income from operations."

Next companies must account for interest income and interest expense. Interest income is the money companies make from keeping their cash in interest-bearing savings accounts, money market funds and the like. On the other hand, interest expense is the money companies paid in interest for money they borrow. Some income statements show interest income and interest expense separately. Some income statements combine the two numbers. The interest income and expense are then added or subtracted from the operating profits to arrive at operating profit before income tax.

Finally, income tax is deducted and you arrive at the bottom line: net profit or net losses. (Net profit is also called net income or net earnings.) This tells you how much the company actually earned or lost during the accounting period. Did the company make a profit or did it lose money?

Income Statement Exemplar (McDonald's Corporation—Annual Report 2012)

Consolidated Statement of Income

IN MILLIONS, EXCEPT PER SHARE DATA	12/31/2012	2011
REVENUES		
Sales by Company-operated restaurants	$ 18,602.5	$ 18,292.8
Revenues from franchised restaurants	8,964.5	8,713.2
Total revenues	27,567.0	27,006.0
OPERATING COSTS AND EXPENSES		
Company-operated restaurant expenses		

Source: http://www.sec.gov/Archives/edgar/data/63908/000006390814000019/mcd-12312013x10k.htm, U.S. Securities and Exchange Commission. Copyright in the Public Domain.

Food & paper	**6,318.2**	6,167.2
Payroll & employee benefits	**4,710.3**	4,606.3
Occupancy & other operating expenses	**4,195.2**	4,064.4
Franchised restaurants-occupancy expenses	**1,527.0**	1,481.5
Selling, general & administrative expenses	**2,455.2**	2,393.7
Impairment and other charges (credits), net	**8.0**	(3.9)
Other operating (income) expense, net	**(251.5)**	(232.9)
Total operating costs and expenses	**18,962.4**	18,476.3
Operating income	**8,604.6**	8,529.7
Interest expense-net of capitalized interest of $15.9, $14.0 and $12.0	**516.6**	492.8
Nonoperating (income) expense, net	**9.0**	24.7
Income before provision for income taxes	**8,079.0**	8,012.2
Provision for income taxes	**2,614.2**	2,509.1
Net income	**$ 5,464.8**	$ 5,503.1
Earnings per common share—basic	**$ 5.41**	$ 5.33
Earnings per common share—diluted	**$ 5.36**	$ 5.27
Dividends declared per common share	**$ 2.87**	$ 2.53
Weighted-average shares outstanding—basic	**1,010.1**	1,032.1
Weighted-average shares outstanding—diluted	**1,020.2**	1,044.9

C. CASH FLOW STATEMENTS

Cash flow statements report a company's inflows and outflows of cash. This is important because a company needs to have enough cash on hand to pay its expenses and purchase assets. While an income statement can tell you whether a company made a profit, a cash flow statement can tell you whether the company generated cash.

A cash flow statement shows changes over time rather than absolute dollar amounts at a point in time. It uses and reorders the information from a company's balance sheet and income statement.

The bottom line of the cash flow statement shows the net increase or decrease in cash for the period. Generally, cash flow statements are divided into three main parts. Each part reviews the cash flow from one of three types of activities: (1) operating activities; (2) investing activities; and (3) financing activities.

Operating Activities

The first part of a cash flow statement analyzes a company's cash flow from net income or losses. For most companies, this section of the cash flow statement reconciles the net income (as shown on the income statement) to the actual cash the company received from or used in its operating activities. To do this, it adjusts net income for any non-cash items (such as adding back depreciation expenses) and adjusts for any cash that was used or provided by other operating assets and liabilities.

Investing Activities

The second part of a cash flow statement shows the cash flow from all investing activities, which generally include purchases or sales of long-term assets, such as property, plant and equipment, as well as investment securities. If a company buys a piece of machinery, the cash flow statement would reflect this activity as a cash outflow from investing activities because it used cash. If the company decided to sell off some investments from an investment portfolio, the proceeds from the sales would show up as a cash inflow from investing activities because it provided cash.

Financing Activities

The third part of a cash flow statement shows the cash flow from all financing activities. Typical sources of cash flow include cash raised by selling stocks and bonds or borrowing from banks. Likewise, paying back a bank loan would show up as a use of cash flow.

Cash Flow Statement Exemplar (McDonald's Corporation—2012 Annual Report)

Consolidated Statement of Cash Flows

IN MILLIONS	*12/31/2012*
Operating activities	
Net income	**$ 5,464.8**
Adjustments to reconcile to cash provided by operations	
Charges and credits:	
Depreciation and amortization	**1,488.5**
Deferred income taxes	**134.5**
Impairment and other charges (credits), net	**8.0**
Share-based compensation	**93.4**
Other	**(100.0)**
Changes in working capital items:	
Accounts receivable	**(29.4)**
Inventories, prepaid expenses and other current assets	**(27.2)**
Accounts payable	**124.1**
Income taxes	**(74.0)**
Other accrued liabilities	**(116.6)**
Cash provided by operations	**6,966.1**

Source: http://www.sec.gov/Archives/edgar/data/63908/000006390814000019/mcd-12312013x10k.htm, U.S. Securities and Exchange Commission. Copyright in the Public Domain.

Investing activities	
Capital expenditures	(3,049.2)
Purchases of restaurant businesses	(158.5)
Sales of restaurant businesses and property	394.7
Other	(354.3)
Cash used for investing activities	(3,167.3)
Financing activities	
Net short-term borrowings	(117.5)
Long-term financing issuances	2,284.9
Long-term financing repayments	(962.8)
Treasury stock purchases	(2,615.1)
Common stock dividends	(2,896.6)
Proceeds from stock option exercises	328.6
Excess tax benefit on share-based compensation	142.3
Other	(13.6)
Cash used for financing activities	(3,849.8)
Effect of exchange rates on cash and equivalents	51.4
Cash and equivalents increase (decrease)	0.4
Cash and equivalents at beginning of year	2,335.7
Cash and equivalents at end of year	$ 2,336.1
Supplemental cash flow disclosures	
Interest paid	$ 533.7
Income taxes paid	2,447.8

D. BRINGING IT ALL TOGETHER

Although this chapter discusses each financial statement separately, keep in mind that they are all related. The changes in assets and liabilities that you see on the balance sheet are also reflected in the revenues and expenses that you see on the income statement, which result in the company's gains or losses. Cash flows provide more information about cash assets listed on a balance sheet and are related, but not equivalent, to net income shown on the income statement. And so on. No one financial statement tells the complete story. But combined, they provide very powerful information for investors. And information is the investor's best tool when it comes to investing wisely.

PART 3

General Partnerships

CHAPTER 6

Introduction to General Partnerships

A. What Is a General Partnership?

The drafters of the Revised Uniform Partnership Act describe a general partnership as follows:

> A partnership is a form of business organization. It exists whenever more than one person associates for the purpose of doing business for profit. The notion is that the partners join their capital and share accordingly in profits and losses. They also share control over the enterprise and subsequent liabilities. Historically, every partner is equally able to transact business on behalf of the partnership. Creditors of the partnership are entitled to rely upon the assets of the partnership and those of every partner in the satisfaction of the partnership's debts. The character of any partnership depends upon the agreement of the partners.
>
> A partnership may be as simple as two people meeting on a street corner and deciding to conduct some business together, arising from no more than verbal agreement and a handshake. A partnership may also be as complex as a large law firm, with tiers of partners and varying rights and obligations, memorialized in extensive written agreements. Partnership law must accommodate them all.

Excerpt from *Partnership Act Summary," Uniform Partnership Act (1994)*. Unif. Law Comm'n, http://www.uniformlaws.org/ActSummary.aspx?title=Partnership%20Act (last visited June 7, 2013). Copyright © 1994 by National Conference of Commissioners on Uniform State Laws. Reprinted with permission.

B. THE UNIFORM PARTNERSHIP ACT

The National Conference of Commissioners on Uniform State Laws (NCCUSL) is an organization that promotes uniformity of state laws. It has operated since 1892 and its members include practitioners, judges, and law professors. NCCUSL promotes uniformity in areas of law where it believes uniformity among the states is desirable. To achieve uniformity, NCCUSL drafts and proposes a statute for adoption by state legislatures. A proposed uniform statute does not become law until it is adopted by a state legislature.

In 1914, NCCUSL proposed the Uniform Partnership Act (UPA) to make uniform the law of partnership. Every state except Louisiana adopted it. In 1997, NCCUSL promulgated a revised partnership statute in order to reflect developments in case law and business practice. The revised partnership act is known as the Revised Uniform Partnership Act (RUPA). Thirty-nine states have adopted RUPA. This is the law we will study here.

CHAPTER 7

Forming General Partnerships

A. Formation

It is important to understand how general partnerships are formed because, unlike other types of business entities such as corporations or limited liability companies, general partnerships can be formed without any of the partners actually intending that result. Transactional lawyers must be able to advise their clients on what steps to take to ensure their general partnership has been formed; or, alternatively, in the event their clients are not interested in forming a general partnership, on which actions to avoid in order to protect themselves from the unlimited liability that general partnerships impose.

Section 202. Formation of Partnership.

(a) Except as otherwise provided in subsection (b), the association of two or more persons to carry on as co-owners a business for profit forms a partnership, whether or not the persons intend to form a partnership.

(c) In determining whether a partnership is formed, the following rules apply:

    (1) Joint tenancy, tenancy in common, tenancy by the entireties, joint property, common property, or part ownership does not by itself establish a partnership, even if the co-owners share profits made by the use of the property.

    (2) [...].

    (3) A person who receives a share of the profits of a business is presumed to be a partner in the business, unless the profits were received in payment:

        (i) of a debt by installments or otherwise;

Source: Rev. Unif. Partnership Act §§ 106, 202 (1994). Copyright © 1994 by National Conference of Commissioners on Uniform State Laws. Reprinted with permission.

(ii) for services as an independent contractor or of wages or other compensation to an employee;

(iii) of rent;

(iv) of an annuity or other retirement or health benefit to a beneficiary, representative, or designee of a deceased or retired partner;

(v) of interest or other charge on a loan, even if the amount of payment varies with the profits of the business; or

(vi) for the sale of the goodwill of a business or other property by installments or otherwise.

Comment

1. [A] partnership is created by the association of persons whose intent is to carry on as co-owners a business for profit, regardless of their subjective intention to be "partners." Indeed, they may inadvertently create a partnership despite their expressed subjective intention not to do so. The new language alerts readers to this possibility.

As under the UPA, the attribute of co-ownership distinguishes a partnership from a mere agency relationship. A business is a series of acts directed toward an end. Ownership involves the power of ultimate control. To state that partners are co-owners of a business is to state that they each have the power of ultimate control. On the other hand, as subsection (c)(1) makes clear, passive co-ownership of property by itself, as distinguished from the carrying on of a business, does not establish a partnership.

3. Subsection (c) provides three rules of construction that apply in determining whether a partnership has been formed under subsection (a). The sharing of profits is recast as a rebuttable presumption of a partnership, a more contemporary construction, rather than as prima facie evidence thereof. The protected categories, in which receipt of a share of the profits is not presumed to create a partnership, apply whether the profit share is a single flat percentage or a ratio which varies, for example, after reaching a dollar floor or different levels of profits.

Like its predecessor, RUPA makes no attempt to answer in every case whether a partnership is formed. Whether a relationship is more properly characterized as that of borrower and lender, employer and employee, or landlord and tenant is left to the trier of fact. As under the UPA, a person may function in both partner and nonpartner capacities.

Section 106. Governing Law.

(a) Except as otherwise provided in subsection (b), the law of the jurisdiction in which a partnership has its chief executive office governs relations among the partners and between the partners and the partnership.

(b) The law of this State governs relations among the partners and between the partners and the partnership and the liability of partners for an obligation of a limited liability partnership.

Comment

RUPA looks to the jurisdiction in which a partnership's chief executive office is located to provide the law governing the internal relations among the partners and between the partners and the partnership. The concept of the partnership's "chief executive office" is drawn from UCC Section 9–103(3)(d). It was chosen in lieu of the State of organization because no filing is necessary to form a general partnership, and thus the situs of its organization is not always clear, unlike a limited partnership, which is organized in the State where its certificate is filed.

The term "chief executive office" is not defined in the Act, nor is it defined in the UCC. Paragraph 5 of the Official Comment to UCC Section 9–103(3)(d) explains:

> "Chief executive office" … means the place from which in fact the debtor manages the main part of his business operations. … Doubt may arise as to which is the "chief executive office" of a multi-state enterprise, but it would be rare that there could be more than two possibilities. … [The rule] will be simple to apply in most cases. …

In the absence of any other clear rule for determining a partnership's legal situs, it seems convenient to use that rule for choice of law purposes as well.

The choice-of-law rule provided by subsection (a) is only a default rule, and the partners may by agreement select the law of another State to govern their internal affairs, subject to generally applicable conflict of laws requirements.

B. Entity vs. Aggregate Theory

Whether a general partnership is viewed as an aggregate of its partners, with no legal distinction from the partners, or as an entity, distinct from its partners, has a number of practical consequences. For instance, whether the partnership can sue or be sued in its own name or whether property is owned by the partnership itself or by the partners collectively. Under UPA, partnerships are viewed as an aggregate of their partners. Under RUPA, partnerships are viewed as separate entities from their partners.

Section 201. Partnership as Entity.

(a) A partnership is an entity distinct from its partners.

Comment

RUPA embraces the entity theory of the partnership ... .

Giving clear expression to the entity nature of a partnership is intended to allay previous concerns stemming from the aggregate theory, such as the necessity of a deed to convey title from the "old" partnership to the "new" partnership every time there is a change of cast among the partners. Under RUPA, there is no "new" partnership just because of membership changes ....

C. PARTNERSHIP AGREEMENT

The uniform acts on general partnerships (either UPA or RUPA) provide a set of default rules that govern partnerships. Partners, however, can contract around these rules by creating a partnership agreement. If a partnership agreement exists, it governs the partnership not the default rules. The default rules would only govern where the partnership agreement is silent. Critically, certain statutory rules cannot be contracted around and will apply to any partnership.

Section 101. Definitions.

In this [Act]:

(7) "Partnership agreement" means the agreement, whether written, oral, or implied, among the partners concerning the partnership, including amendments to the partnership agreement.

Comment

The RUPA definition is intended to include the agreement among the partners, including amendments, concerning either the affairs of the partnership or the conduct of its business. It does not include other agreements between some or all of the partners, such as a lease or loan agreement. The partnership agreement need not be written; it may be oral or inferred from the conduct of the parties.

Section 103. Effect of Partnership Agreement; Nonwaivable Provisions.

(a) Except as otherwise provided in subsection (b), relations among the partners and between the partners and the partnership are governed by the partnership agreement. To the extent the partnership agreement does not otherwise provide, this [Act] governs relations among the partners and between the partners and the partnership.

Source: Rev. Unif. Partnership Act §§ 101, 103, 201 (1994). Copyright © 1994 by National Conference of Commissioners on Uniform State Laws. Reprinted with permission.

(b) The partnership agreement may not:

(1) [...];

(2) unreasonably restrict the right of access to books and records under Section 403(b);

(3) eliminate the duty of loyalty under Section 404(b) or 603(b)(3), but:

   (i) the partnership agreement may identify specific types or categories of activities that do not violate the duty of loyalty, if not manifestly unreasonable; or

   (i) all of the partners or a number or percentage specified in the partnership agreement may authorize or ratify, after full disclosure of all material facts, a specific act or transaction that otherwise would violate the duty of loyalty;

(4) unreasonably reduce the duty of care under Section 404(c) or 603(b)(3);

(5) eliminate the obligation of good faith and fair dealing under Section 404(d), but the partnership agreement may prescribe the standards by which the performance of the obligation is to be measured, if the standards are not manifestly unreasonable;

(6) vary the power to dissociate as a partner under Section 602(a), except to require the notice under Section 601(1) to be in writing;

(7) vary the right of a court to expel a partner in the events specified in Section 601(5); or

(8) vary the requirement to wind up the partnership business in cases specified in Section 801(4), (5), or (6);

(9) [...]; or

(10) restrict rights of third parties under this [Act].

Comment

1. The general rule under Section 103(a) is that relations among the partners and between the partners and the partnership are governed by the partnership agreement. To the extent that the partners fail to agree upon a contrary rule, RUPA provides the default rule. Only the rights and duties listed in Section 103(b), and implicitly the corresponding liabilities and remedies under Section 405, are mandatory and cannot be waived or varied by agreement beyond what is authorized. Those are the only exceptions to the general principle that the provisions of RUPA with respect to the rights of the partners inter se are merely default rules, subject to modification by the partners. All modifications must also, of course, satisfy the general standards of contract validity.

3. Subsection (b)(2) provides that the partnership agreement may not unreasonably restrict a partner or former partner's access rights to books and records under Section 403(b). It is left to the courts to determine what

restrictions are reasonable ... Other information rights in Section 403 can be varied or even eliminated by agreement.

4. Subsections (b)(3) through (5) are intended to ensure a fundamental core of fiduciary responsibility. Neither the fiduciary duties of loyalty or care, nor the obligation of good faith and fair dealing, may be eliminated entirely. However, the statutory requirements of each can be modified by agreement, subject to the limitation stated in subsections (b)(3) through (5).

There has always been a tension regarding the extent to which a partner's fiduciary duty of loyalty can be varied by agreement, as contrasted with the other partners' consent to a particular and known breach of duty. On the one hand, courts have been loathe [sic] to enforce agreements broadly "waiving" in advance a partner's fiduciary duty of loyalty, especially where there is unequal bargaining power, information, or sophistication. For this reason, a very broad provision in a partnership agreement in effect negating any duty of loyalty, such as a provision giving a managing partner complete discretion to manage the business with no liability except for acts and omissions that constitute willful misconduct, will not likely be enforced ... On the other hand, it is clear that the remaining partners can "consent" to a particular conflicting interest transaction or other breach of duty, after the fact, provided there is full disclosure.

RUPA attempts to provide a standard that partners can rely upon in drafting exculpatory agreements. It is not necessary that the agreement be restricted to a particular transaction. That would require bargaining over every transaction or opportunity, which would be excessively burdensome. The agreement may be drafted in terms of types or categories of activities or transactions, but it should be reasonably specific.

A provision in a real estate partnership agreement authorizing a partner who is a real estate agent to retain commissions on partnership property bought and sold by that partner would be an example of a "type or category" of activity that is not manifestly unreasonable and thus should be enforceable under the Act. Likewise, a provision authorizing that partner to buy or sell real property for his own account without prior disclosure to the other partners or without first offering it to the partnership would be enforceable as a valid category of partnership activity.

5. Subsection (b)(3)(i) permits the partners, in their partnership agreement, to identify specific types or categories of partnership activities that do not violate the duty of loyalty. A modification of the statutory standard must not, however, be manifestly unreasonable. This is intended to discourage overreaching by a partner with superior bargaining power since the courts may refuse to enforce an overly broad exculpatory clause.

Subsection (b)(3)(ii) is intended to clarify the right of partners, recognized under general law, to consent to a known past or anticipated violation of duty and to waive their legal remedies for redress of that violation. This is intended to cover situations where the conduct in question is not specifically authorized by the partnership agreement. It can also be used to validate conduct that might otherwise not satisfy the "manifestly unreasonable" standard. Clause (ii) provides that, after full disclosure of all material facts regarding a specific act or transaction that otherwise would violate the duty of loyalty, it may be authorized or ratified by the partners. That authorization or ratification must be unanimous unless a lesser number or percentage is specified for this purpose in the partnership agreement.

6. Under subsection (b)(4), the partners' duty of care may not be unreasonably reduced below the statutory standard set forth in Section 404(d), that is, to refrain from engaging in grossly negligent or reckless conduct, intentional misconduct, or a knowing violation of law.

For example, partnership agreements frequently contain provisions releasing a partner from liability for actions taken in good faith and in the honest belief that the actions are in the best interests of the partnership and indemnifying the partner against any liability incurred in connection with the business of the partnership if the partner acts in a good faith belief that he has authority to act. Many partnership agreements reach this same result by listing various activities and stating that the performance of these activities is deemed not to constitute gross negligence or willful misconduct. These types of provisions are intended to come within the modifications authorized by subsection (b)(4). On the other hand, absolving partners of intentional misconduct is probably unreasonable. As with contractual standards of loyalty, determining the outer limit in reducing the standard of care is left to the courts.

The standard may, of course, be increased by agreement to one of ordinary care or an even higher standard of care.

7. Subsection (b)(5) authorizes the partners to determine the standards by which the performance of the obligation of good faith and fair dealing is to be measured. The language of subsection (b)(5) is based on UCC Section 1-102(3). The partners can negotiate and draft specific contract provisions tailored to their particular needs (e.g., five days notice of a partners' meeting is adequate notice), but blanket waivers of the obligation are unenforceable.

8. Section 602(a) continues the traditional UPA Section 31(2) rule that every partner has the power to withdraw from the partnership at any time, which power cannot be bargained away. Section 103(b)(6) provides that the partnership agreement may not vary the power to dissociate as a partner under Section 602(a), except to require that the notice of withdrawal under Section 601(1) be in writing.

10. Under subsection (b)(8), the partnership agreement may not vary the right of partners to have the partnership dissolved and its business wound up under Section 801(4), (5), or (6). Section 801(4) provides that the partnership must be wound up if its business is unlawful. Section 801(5) provides for judicial winding up in such circumstances as frustration of the firm's economic purpose, partner misconduct, or impracticability. Section 801(6) accords

standing to transferees of an interest in the partnership to seek judicial dissolution of the partnership in specified circumstances.

12. Although stating the obvious, subsection(b)(10) provides expressly that the rights of a third party under the Act may not be restricted by an agreement among the partners to which the third party has not agreed.

CHAPTER 8

OPERATING GENERAL PARTNERSHIPS—PART 1

A. HOW IS A GENERAL PARTNERSHIP MANAGED AND CONTROLLED?

Unlike other business entities, general partnerships have a simple structure: each partner has equal rights in management of the business (unless contracted for otherwise).

Section 401. Partner's Rights and Duties.

(f) Each partner has equal rights in the management and conduct of the partnership business.

(i) A person may become a partner only with the consent of all of the partners.

(j) A difference arising as to a matter in the ordinary course of business of a partnership may be decided by a majority of the partners. An act outside the ordinary course of business of a partnership and an amendment to the partnership agreement may be undertaken only with the consent of all of the partners.

(k) This section does not affect the obligations of a partnership to other persons under Section 301.

Comment

7. Under subsection (f), each partner has equal rights in the management and conduct of the business. It is based on UPA Section 18(e), which has been interpreted broadly to mean that, absent contrary agreement, each partner has a continuing right to participate in the management of the partnership and to be informed about the partnership business, even if his assent to partnership business decisions is not required.

10. Subsection (i) continues the substance of UPA Section 18(g) that no person can become a partner without the consent of all the partners.

Source: Rev. Unif. Partnership Act §§ 401, 403 (1994). Copyright © 1994 by National Conference of Commissioners on Uniform State Laws. Reprinted with permission.

11. Subsection (j) continues with one important clarification the UPA Section 18(h) scheme of allocating management authority among the partners. In the absence of an agreement to the contrary, matters arising in the ordinary course of the business may be decided by a majority of the partners. Amendments to the partnership agreement and matters outside the ordinary course of the partnership business require unanimous consent of the partners.

12. Subsection (k) is new and was added to make it clear that Section 301 governs partners' agency power to bind the partnership to third persons, while Section 401 governs partners' rights among themselves.

Section 403. Partner's Rights and Duties with Respect to Information.

(a) A partnership shall keep its books and records, if any, at its chief executive office

(b) A partnership shall provide partners and their agents and attorneys access to its books and records. It shall provide former partners and their agents and attorneys access to books and records pertaining to the period during which they were partners. The right of access provides the opportunity to inspect and copy books and records during ordinary business hours.

(c) Each partner and the partnership shall furnish to a partner:

   (1) without demand, any information concerning the partnership's business and affairs reasonably required for the proper exercise of the partner's rights and duties under the partnership agreement or this [Act]; and

   (2) on demand, any other information concerning the partnership's business and affairs, except to the extent the demand or the information demanded is unreasonable or otherwise improper under the circumstances.

Comment

1. Since general partnerships are often informal or even inadvertent, no books and records are enumerated as mandatory.

In general, a partnership should, at a minimum, keep those books and records necessary to enable the partners to determine their share of the profits and losses, as well as their rights on withdrawal. An action for an accounting provides an adequate remedy in the event adequate records are not kept. The partnership must also maintain any books and records required by state or federal taxing or other governmental authorities.

2. Under subsection (b), partners are entitled to access to the partnership books and records. Former partners are expressly given a similar right, although limited to the books and records pertaining to the period during which they were partners.

A partner's right to inspect and copy the partnership's books and records is not conditioned on the partner's purpose or motive. Compare RMBCA Section 16.02(c)(l) (shareholder must have proper purpose to inspect certain corporate records). A partner's unlimited personal liability justifies an unqualified right of access to the partnership books and records. An abuse of the right to inspect and copy might constitute a violation of the obligation of good faith and fair dealing for which the other partners would have a remedy.

Under Section 103(b)(2), a partner's right of access to partnership books and records may not be unreasonably restricted by the partnership agreement. Thus, to preserve a partner's core information rights despite unequal bargaining power, an agreement limiting a partner's right to inspect and copy partnership books and records is subject to judicial review.

3. Subsection (c) is a significant revision of UPA Section 20 and provides a more comprehensive, although not exclusive, statement of partners' rights and duties with respect to partnership information other than books and records. Both the partnership and the other partners are obligated to furnish partnership information.

Paragraph (1) is new and imposes an affirmative disclosure obligation on the partnership and partners. Paragraph (1) provides expressly that partners must be furnished, without demand, partnership information reasonably needed for them to exercise their rights and duties as partners. In addition, a disclosure duty may, under some circumstances, also spring from the Section 404(d) obligation of good faith and fair dealing.

Paragraph (2) continues the UPA rule that partners are entitled, on demand, to any other information concerning the partnership's business and affairs. The demand may be refused if either the demand or the information demanded is unreasonable or otherwise improper. That qualification is new to the statutory formulation. The burden is on the partnership or partner from whom the information is requested to show that the demand is unreasonable or improper.

The Section 403(c) information rights can be waived or varied by agreement of the partners, since there is no Section 103(b) limitation on the variation of those rights as there is with respect to the Section 403(b) access rights to books and records.

B. WHO MAY BE LIABLE IN A PARTNERSHIP?

Section 301. Partner Agent of Partnership.

Subject to the effect of a statement of partnership authority under Section 303:

(1) Each partner is an agent of the partnership for the purpose of its business. An act of a partner, including the execution of an instrument in the partnership name, for apparently carrying on in the ordinary course the partnership business or business of the kind carried on by the partnership binds the partnership, unless the partner had no authority to act for the partnership in the particular matter and the person with whom the partner was dealing knew or had received a notification that the partner lacked authority.

(2) An act of a partner which is not apparently for carrying on in the ordinary course the partnership business or business of the kind carried on by the partnership binds the partnership only if the act was authorized by the other partners.

Comment

1. Section 301 sets forth a partner's power, as an agent of the firm, to bind the partnership entity to third parties. The rights of the partners among themselves, including the right to restrict a partner's authority, are governed by the partnership agreement and by Section 401.

2. Section 301(1) retains the basic principles reflected in UPA Section 9(1). It declares that each partner is an agent of the partnership and that, by virtue of partnership status, each partner has apparent authority to bind the partnership in ordinary course transactions. The effect of Section 301(1) is to characterize a partner as a general managerial agent having both actual and apparent authority coextensive in scope with the firm's ordinary business, at least in the absence of a contrary partnership agreement.

Section 301(1) effects two changes from UPA Section 9(1). First, it clarifies that a partner's apparent authority includes acts for carrying on in the ordinary course "business of the kind carried on by the partnership," not just the business of the particular partnership in question.

The other change from the UPA concerns the allocation of risk of a partner's lack of authority. RUPA draws the line somewhat differently from the UPA.

Under UPA Section 9(1) and (4), only a person with knowledge of a restriction on a partner's authority is bound by it. Section 301(1) provides that a person who has received a notification of a partner's lack of authority is also bound. The meaning of "receives a notification" is explained in Section 102(d). Thus, the partnership may protect itself from unauthorized acts by

Source: Rev. Unif. Partnership Act §§ 301, 305–307 (1994). Copyright © 1994 by National Conference of Commissioners on Uniform State Laws. Reprinted with permission.

giving a notification of a restriction on a partner's authority to a person dealing with that partner.

3. Section 301(2) is drawn directly from UPA Section 9(2), with conforming changes to mirror the new language of subsection (1). Subsection (2) makes it clear that the partnership is bound by a partner's actual authority, even if the partner has no apparent authority. Section 401(j) requires the unanimous consent of the partners for a grant of authority outside the ordinary course of business, unless the partnership agreement provides otherwise. Under general agency principles, the partners can subsequently ratify a partner's unauthorized act.

Section 305. Partnership Liable for Partner's Actionable Conduct.

(a) A partnership is liable for loss or injury caused to a person, or for a penalty incurred, as a result of a wrongful act or omission, or other actionable conduct, of a partner acting in the ordinary course of business of the partnership or with authority of the partnership.

(b) If, in the course of the partnership's business or while acting with authority of the partnership, a partner receives or causes the partnership to receive money or property of a person not a partner, and the money or property is misapplied by a partner, the partnership is liable for the loss.

Comment

Section 305(a) imposes liability on the partnership for the wrongful acts of a partner acting in the ordinary course of the partnership's business or otherwise within the partner's authority.

The partnership is liable for the actionable conduct or omission of a partner acting in the ordinary course of its business or "with the authority of the partnership." This is intended to include a partner's apparent, as well as actual, authority, thereby bringing within Section 305(a) the situation covered in UPA Section 14(a).

Section 305(b) is drawn from UPA Section 14(b), but has been edited to improve clarity. It imposes strict liability on the partnership for the misapplication of money or property received by a partner in the course of the partnership's business or otherwise within the scope of the partner's actual authority.

Section 306. Partner's Liability.

(a) Except as otherwise provided in subsections (b) and (c), all partners are liable jointly and severally for all obligations of the partnership unless otherwise agreed by the claimant or provided by law.

(b) A person admitted as a partner into an existing partnership is not personally liable for any partnership obligation incurred before the person's admission as a partner.

Comment

1. Section 306(a) changes the UPA rule by imposing joint and several liability on the partners for all partnership obligations where the partnership is not a limited liability partnership. Under UPA Section 15, partners' liability for torts is joint and several, while their liability for contracts is joint but not several.

Joint and several liability under RUPA differs, however, from the classic model, which permits a judgment creditor to proceed immediately against any of the joint and several judgment debtors. Generally, Section 307(d) requires the judgment creditor to exhaust the partnership's assets before enforcing a judgment against the separate assets of a partner.

2. Subsection (b) eliminates an incoming partner's personal liability for partnership obligations incurred before his admission as a partner. In effect, a new partner has no personal liability to existing creditors of the partnership, and only his investment in the firm is at risk for the satisfaction of existing partnership debts. As under the UPA, a new partner's personal assets are at risk with respect to partnership liabilities incurred after his admission as a partner.

Section 307. Actions By and Against Partnership and Partners.

(a) A partnership may sue and be sued in the name of the partnership.

(b) An action may be brought against the partnership and, to the extent not inconsistent with Section 306, any or all of the partners in the same action or in separate actions.

(c) A judgment against a partnership is not by itself a judgment against a partner. A judgment against a partnership may not be satisfied from a partner's assets unless there is also a judgment against the partner.

(d) A judgment creditor of a partner may not levy execution against the assets of the partner to satisfy a judgment based on a claim against the partnership unless the partner is personally liable for the claim under Section 306 and:

    (1) a judgment based on the same claim has been obtained against the partnership and a writ of execution on the judgment has been returned unsatisfied in whole or in part;

    (2) the partnership is a debtor in bankruptcy;

    (3) the partner has agreed that the creditor need not exhaust partnership assets;

    (4) a court grants permission to the judgment creditor to levy execution against the assets of a partner based on a finding that partnership assets subject to execution are clearly insufficient to satisfy the judgment, that exhaustion of partnership assets is excessively burdensome, or

that the grant of permission is an appropriate exercise of the court's equitable powers; or

(5) liability is imposed on the partner by law or contract independent of the existence of the partnership.

Comment

1. Section 307 is new. Subsection (a) provides that a partnership may sue and be sued in the partnership name. That entity approach is designed to simplify suits by and against a partnership.

At common law, a partnership, not being a legal entity, could not sue or be sued in the firm name. The UPA itself is silent on this point, so in the absence of another enabling statute, it is generally necessary to join all the partners in an action against the partnership.

Most States have statutes or rules authorizing partnerships to sue or be sued in the partnership name. Many of those statutes, however, are found in the state provisions dealing with civil procedure rather than in the partnership act.

2. Subsection (b) provides that suit generally may be brought against the partnership and any or all of the partners in the same action or in separate actions. It is intended to clarify that the partners need not be named in an action against the partnership. In particular, in an action against a partnership, it is not necessary to name a partner individually in addition to the partnership. This will simplify and reduce the cost of litigation, especially in cases of small claims where there are known to be significant partnership assets and thus no necessity to collect the judgment out of the partners' assets.

3. Subsection (c) provides that a judgment against the partnership is not, standing alone, a judgment against the partners, and it cannot be satisfied from a partner's personal assets unless there is a judgment against the partner. Thus, a partner must be individually named and served, either in the action against the partnership or in a later suit, before his personal assets may be subject to levy for a claim against the partnership.

4. Subsection (d) requires partnership creditors to exhaust the partnership's assets before levying on a judgment debtor partner's individual property where the partner is personally liable for the partnership obligation under Section 306. That rule respects the concept of the partnership as an entity and makes partners more in the nature of guarantors than principal debtors on every partnership debt. It is already the law in some States.

Under subsection (d), however, a creditor may proceed directly against the partner's assets if (i) the partnership is a debtor in bankruptcy; (ii) the partner has consented; or (iii) the liability is imposed on the partner independently of the partnership. For example, a judgment creditor may proceed directly against the assets of a partner who is liable independently as the primary tortfeasor, but must exhaust the partnership's assets before proceeding against the separate assets of the other partners who are liable only as partners.

There is also a judicial override provision in subsection (d)(4). A court may authorize execution against the partner's assets on the grounds that (i) the partnership's assets are clearly insufficient; (ii) exhaustion of the partnership's assets would be excessively burdensome; or (iii) it is otherwise equitable to do so. For example, if the partners who are parties to the action have assets located in the forum State, but the partnership does not, a court might find that exhaustion of the partnership's assets would be excessively burdensome.

Summers v. Dooley

94 Idaho 87 (1971)

DONALDSON, Justice.

The pertinent facts leading to this lawsuit are as follows. Summers (plaintiff-appellant) entered a partnership agreement with Dooley (defendant-respondent) in 1958 for the purpose of operating a trash collection business. The business was operated by the two men and when either was unable to work, the non-working partner provided a replacement at his own expense. In July, 1966, Summers approached his partner Dooley regarding the hiring of an additional employee but Dooley refused. Nevertheless, on his own initiative, Summers hired the man and paid him out of his own pocket. Dooley, upon discovering that Summers had hired an additional man, objected, stating that he did not feel additional labor was necessary and refused to pay for the new employee out of the partnership funds. Summers continued to operate the business using the third man and in October of 1967 instituted suit in the district court for $6,000 against his partner, the gravamen of the complaint being that Summers has been required to pay out more than $11,000 in expenses, incurred in the hiring of the additional man, without any reimbursement from either the partnership funds or his partner. After trial before the court, sitting without a jury, Summers was granted only partial relief and he has appealed.

The principal thrust of appellant's contention is that in spite of the fact that one of the two partners refused to consent to the hiring of additional help, nonetheless, the non-consenting partner retained profits earned by the labors of the third man and therefore the non-consenting partner should be estopped from denying the need and value of the employee, and has by his behavior ratified the act of the other partner who hired the additional man.

The issue presented for decision by this appeal is whether an equal partner in a two man partnership has the authority to hire a new employee in disregard of the objection of the other partner and then attempt to charge the dissenting partner with the costs incurred as a result of his unilateral decision.

In the instant case the record indicates that although Summers requested his partner Dooley to agree to the hiring of a third man, such requests were not honored. In fact Dooley made it clear that he was "voting no" with regard to the hiring of an additional employee.

Copyright in the Public Domain.

An application of the relevant statutory provisions and pertinent case law to the factual situation presented by the instant case indicates that the trial court was correct in its disposal of the issue since a majority of the partners did not consent to the hiring of the third man. I.C. § 53–318(8) provides:

> "Any difference arising as to ordinary matters connected with the partnership business may be decided by a *majority of the partners* …" (emphasis supplied)

A noted scholar has dealt precisely with the issue to be decided.

> "… if the partners are equally divided, those who forbid a change must have their way." Walter B. Lindley, A Treatise on the Law of Partnership, Ch. II, § III, ¶ 24–8, p. 403 (1924). See also, W. Shumaker, A Treatise on the Law of Partnership, § 97, p. 266.

In the case at bar one of the partners continually voiced objection to the hiring of the third man. He did not sit idly by and acquiesce in the actions of his partner. Under these circumstances it is manifestly unjust to permit recovery of an expense which was incurred individually and not for the benefit of the partnership but rather for the benefit of one partner.

Judgment affirmed. Costs to respondent.

Nat'l Biscuit Co., Inc. v. Stroud

249 N.C. 467 (1959)

PARKER, Justice.

C. N. Stroud and Earl Freeman entered into a general partnership to sell groceries under the firm name of Stroud's Food Center. There is nothing in the agreed statement of facts to indicate or suggest that Freeman's power and authority as a general partner were in any way restricted or limited by the articles of partnership in respect to the ordinary and legitimate business of the partnership. Certainly, the purchase and sale of bread were ordinary and legitimate business of Stroud's Food Center during its continuance as a going concern.

Several months prior to February 1956 Stroud advised plaintiff that he personally would not be responsible for any additional bread sold by plaintiff to Stroud's Food Center. After such notice to plaintiff, it from 6 February 1956 to 25 February 1956, at the request of Freeman, sold and delivered bread in the amount of $171.04 to Stroud's Food Center.

The General Assembly of North Carolina in 1941 enacted a Uniform Partnership Act, which became effective 15 March 1941. G.S. Ch. 59, Partnership, Art. 2.

Copyright in the Public Domain.

G.S. § 59–39 is entitled "Partner Agent of Partnership as to Partnership Business", and subsection (1) reads: "Every partner is an agent of the partnership for the purpose of its business, and the act of every partner, including the execution in the partnership name of any instrument, for apparently carrying on in the usual way the business of the partnership of which he is a member binds the partnership, unless the partner so acting has in fact no authority to act for the partnership in the particular matter, and the person with whom he is dealing has knowledge of the fact that he has no such authority." G.S. § 59–39(4) states: "No act of a partner in contravention of a restriction on authority shall bind the partnership to persons having knowledge of the restriction."

G.S. § 59–45 provides that "all partners are jointly and severally liable for the acts and obligations of the partnership."

G.S. § 59–48 is captioned "Rules Determining Rights and Duties of Partners." Subsection (e) thereof reads: "All partners have equal rights in the management and conduct of the partnership business." Subsection (h) hereof is as follows: "Any difference arising as to ordinary matters connected with the partnership business may be decided by a majority of the partners; but no act in contravention of any agreement between the partners may be done rightfully without the consent of all the partners."

Freeman as a general partner with Stroud, with no restrictions on his authority to act within the scope of the partnership business so far as the agreed statement of facts shows, had under the Uniform Partnership Act "equal rights in the management and conduct of the partnership business." Under G.S. § 59–48(h) Stroud, his co-partner, could not restrict the power and authority of Freeman to buy bread for the partnership as a going concern, for such a purchase was an "ordinary matter connected with the partnership business," for the purpose of its business and within its scope, because in the very nature of things Stroud was not, and could not be, a majority of the partners. Therefore, Freeman's purchases of bread from plaintiff for Stroud's Food Center as a going concern bound the partnership and his co-partner Stroud.

Sladen, Fakes & Co. v. Lance, 151 N.C. 492, 66 S.E. 449, is distinguishable. That was a case where the terms of the partnership imposed special restrictions on the power of the partner who made the contract.

It would seem a fair inference from the agreed statement of facts that the partnership got the benefit of the bread sold and delivered by plaintiff to Stroud's Food Center, at Freeman's request, from 6 February 1956 to 25 February 1956. But whether it did or not, Freeman's acts, as stated above, bound the partnership and Stroud.

The judgment of the court below is Affirmed.

CHAPTER 9

Operating General Partnerships—Part 2

A. What Fiduciary Duties Do Partners Have?

Simply defined, fiduciary duties are a partner's obligations in a general partnership to act, or refrain from acting, in certain ways. These duties engender a culture of diligence, honesty and trust among partners. Without fiduciary duties, partners would be required to expend potentially limitless resources in monitoring one another to protect against careless or selfish acts by other partners.

Section 404. General Standards of Partner's Conduct.

(a) The only fiduciary duties a partner owes to the partnership and the other partners are the duty of loyalty and the duty of care set forth in subsections (b) and (c).

(b) A partner's duty of loyalty to the partnership and the other partners is limited to the following:

    (1) to account to the partnership and hold as trustee for it any property, profit, or benefit derived by the partner in the conduct and winding up of the partnership business or derived from a use by the partner of partnership property, including the appropriation of a partnership opportunity;

    (2) to refrain from dealing with the partnership in the conduct or winding up of the partnership business as or on behalf of a party having an interest adverse to the partnership; and

    (3) to refrain from competing with the partnership in the conduct of the partnership business before the dissolution of the partnership.

Source: Rev. Unif. Partnership Act § 404 (1994). Copyright © 1994 by National Conference of Commissioners on Uniform State Laws. Reprinted with permission.

(c) A partner's duty of care to the partnership and the other partners in the conduct and winding up of the partnership business is limited to refraining from engaging in grossly negligent or reckless conduct, intentional misconduct, or a knowing violation of law.

(d) A partner shall discharge the duties to the partnership and the other partners under this [Act] or under the partnership agreement and exercise any rights consistently with the obligation of good faith and fair dealing.

(e) A partner does not violate a duty or obligation under this [Act] or under the partnership agreement merely because the partner's conduct furthers the partner's own interest.

(f) A partner may lend money to and transact other business with the partnership, and as to each loan or transaction the rights and obligations of the partner are the same as those of a person who is not a partner, subject to other applicable law.

Comment

1. Section 404 is new. The title, "General Standards of Partner's Conduct," is drawn from RMBCA Section 8.30. Section 404 is both comprehensive and exclusive.

Section 404 begins by stating that the **only** fiduciary duties a partner owes to the partnership and the other partners are the duties of loyalty and care set forth in subsections (b) and (c) of the Act. Those duties may not be waived or eliminated in the partnership agreement, but the agreement may identify activities and determine standards for measuring performance of the duties, if not manifestly unreasonable. *See* Sections 103(b)(3)-(5).

2. Section 404(b) provides three specific rules that comprise a partner's duty of loyalty. Those rules are exclusive and encompass the entire duty of loyalty.

Subsection (b)(l) is based on UPA Section 21(1) and continues the rule that partnership property usurped by a partner, including the misappropriation of a partnership opportunity, is held in trust for the partnership.

Subsection (b)(2) provides that a partner must refrain from dealing with the partnership as or on behalf of a party having an interest adverse to the partnership. This rule is derived from Sections 389 and 391 of the Restatement (Second) of Agency. Comment c to Section 389 explains that the rule is not based upon the harm caused to the principal, but upon avoiding a conflict of opposing interests in the mind of an agent whose duty is to act for the benefit of his principal.

Section (b)(3) provides that a partner must refrain from competing with the partnership in the conduct of its business. This rule is derived from Section 393 of the Restatement (Second) of Agency and is an application of the general duty of an agent to act solely on his principal's behalf.

Under Section 103(b)(3), the partnership agreement may not "eliminate" the duty of loyalty. Section 103(b)(3)(i) expressly empowers the partners, however, to identify specific types or categories of activities that do not violate the duty of loyalty, if not manifestly unreasonable. As under UPA Section 21, the other partners may also consent to a specific act or transaction that otherwise violates one of the rules. For the consent to be effective under Section 103(b)(3)(ii), there must be full disclosure of all material facts regarding the act or transaction and the partner's conflict of interest.

3. Subsection (c) is new and establishes the duty of care that partners owe to the partnership and to the other partners. The standard of care imposed by RUPA is that of gross negligence, which is the standard generally recognized by the courts. Section 103(b)(4) provides that the duty of care may not be eliminated entirely by agreement, but the standard may be reasonably reduced.

4. Subsection (d) is also new. It provides that partners have an obligation of good faith and fair dealing in the discharge of all their duties, including those arising under the Act, such as their fiduciary duties of loyalty and care, and those arising under the partnership agreement. The exercise of any rights by a partner is also subject to the obligation of good faith and fair dealing. The obligation runs to the partnership and to the other partners in all matters related to the conduct and winding up of the partnership business.

The obligation of good faith and fair dealing is a contract concept, imposed on the partners because of the consensual nature of a partnership. See Restatement (Second) of Contracts § 205 (1981). It is not characterized, in RUPA, as a fiduciary duty arising out of the partners' special relationship. Nor is it a separate and independent obligation. It is an ancillary obligation that applies whenever a partner discharges a duty or exercises a right under the partnership agreement or the Act. The meaning of "good faith and fair dealing" is not firmly fixed under present law. "Good faith" clearly suggests a subjective element, while "fair dealing" implies an objective component. It was decided to leave the terms undefined in the Act and allow the courts to develop their meaning based on the experience of real cases. Some commentators, moreover, believe that good faith is more properly understood by what it excludes than by what it includes.

In some situations the obligation of good faith includes a disclosure component. Depending on the circumstances, a partner may have an affirmative disclosure obligation that supplements the Section 403 duty to render information.

Under Section 103(b)(5), the obligation of good faith and fair dealing may not be eliminated by agreement, but the partners by agreement may determine the standards by which the performance of the obligation is to be measured, if the standards are not manifestly unreasonable.

5. Subsection (e) is new and deals expressly with a very basic issue on which the UPA is silent. A partner as such is not a trustee and is not held to the same standards as a trustee. Subsection (e) makes clear that a partner's

conduct is not deemed to be improper merely because it serves the partner's own individual interest.

That admonition has particular application to the duty of loyalty and the obligation of good faith and fair dealing. It underscores the partner's rights as an owner and principal in the enterprise, which must always be balanced against his duties and obligations as an agent and fiduciary. For example, a partner who, with consent, owns a shopping center may, under subsection (e), legitimately vote against a proposal by the partnership to open a competing shopping center.

6. Subsection (f) authorizes partners to lend money to and transact other business with the partnership and, in so doing, to enjoy the same rights and obligations as a nonpartner.

* * *

Meinhard v. Salmon

249 NY 458 (1928)

CARDOZO, Ch. J.

On April 10, 1902, Louisa M. Gerry leased to the defendant Walter J. Salmon the premises known as the Hotel Bristol at the northwest corner of Forty-second street and Fifth avenue in the city of New York. The lease was for a term of twenty years, commencing May 1, 1902, and ending April 30, 1922. The lessee undertook to change the hotel building for use as shops and offices at a cost of $200,000.

Salmon, while in course of treaty with the lessor as to the execution of the lease, was in course of treaty with Meinhard, the plaintiff, for the necessary funds. The result was a joint venture with terms embodied in a writing. Meinhard was to pay to Salmon half of the moneys requisite to reconstruct, alter, manage and operate the property. Salmon was to pay to Meinhard 40 per cent of the net profits for the first five years of the lease and 50 per cent for the years thereafter. If there were losses, each party was to bear them equally. Salmon, however, was to have sole power to "manage, lease, underlet and operate" the building.

The two were coadventurers, subject to fiduciary duties akin to those of partners (*King v. Barnes*, 109 N. Y. 267). As to this we are all agreed. The heavier weight of duty rested, however, upon Salmon. He was a coadventurer with Meinhard, but he was manager as well. During the early years of the enterprise, the building, reconstructed, was operated at a loss. If the relation had then ended, Meinhard as well as Salmon would have carried a heavy burden. Later the profits became large with the result that for each of the investors there came a rich return. For each, the venture had its phases of fair weather and of foul. The two were in it jointly, for better or for worse.

Copyright in the Public Domain.

When the lease was near its end, Elbridge T. Gerry had become the owner of the reversion. He owned much other property in the neighborhood, one lot adjoining the Bristol Building on Fifth avenue and four lots on Forty-second street. He had a plan to lease the entire tract for a long term to someone who would destroy the buildings then existing, and put up another in their place. In the latter part of 1921, he submitted such a project to several capitalists and dealers. He was unable to carry it through with any of them. Then, in January, 1922, with less than four months of the lease to run, he approached the defendant Salmon. The result was a new lease to the Midpoint Realty Company, which is owned and controlled by Salmon, a lease covering the whole tract, and involving a huge outlay. The term is to be twenty years, but successive covenants for renewal will extend it to a maximum of eighty years at the will of either party. The existing buildings may remain unchanged for seven years. They are then to be torn down, and a new building to cost $3,000,000 is to be placed upon the site. The rental, which under the Bristol lease was only $55,000, is to be from $350,000 to $475,000 for the properties so combined. Salmon personally guaranteed the performance by the lessee of the covenants of the new lease until such time as the new building had been completed and fully paid for.

The lease between Gerry and the Midpoint Realty Company was signed and delivered on January 25, 1922. Salmon had not told Meinhard anything about it. Whatever his motive may have been, he had kept the negotiations to himself. Meinhard was not informed even of the bare existence of a project. The first that he knew of it was in February when the lease was an accomplished fact. He then made demand on the defendants that the lease be held in trust as an asset of the venture, making offer upon the trial to share the personal obligations incidental to the guaranty. The demand was followed by refusal, and later by this suit. A referee gave judgment for the plaintiff, limiting the plaintiff's interest in the lease, however, to 25 per cent. The limitation was on the theory that the plaintiff's equity was to be restricted to one-half of so much of the value of the lease as was contributed or represented by the occupation of the Bristol site. Upon cross-appeals to the Appellate Division, the judgment was modified so as to enlarge the equitable interest to one-half of the whole lease. With this enlargement of plaintiff's interest, there went, of course, a corresponding enlargement of his attendant obligations. The case is now here on an appeal by the defendants.

Joint adventurers, like copartners, owe to one another, while the enterprise continues, the duty of the finest loyalty. Many forms of conduct permissible in a workaday world for those acting at arm's length, are forbidden to those bound by fiduciary ties. A trustee is held to something stricter than the morals of the market place. Not honesty alone, but the punctilio of an honor the most sensitive, is then the standard of behavior. As to this there has developed a tradition that is unbending and inveterate. Uncompromising rigidity has been the attitude of courts of equity when petitioned to undermine the rule of undivided loyalty by the "disintegrating erosion" of particular exceptions

(*Wendt v. Fischer*, 243 N. Y. 439, 444). Only thus has the level of conduct for fiduciaries been kept at a level higher than that trodden by the crowd. It will not consciously be lowered by any judgment of this court.

The owner of the reversion, Mr. Gerry, had vainly striven to find a tenant who would favor his ambitious scheme of demolition and construction. Baffled in the search, he turned to the defendant Salmon in possession of the Bristol, the keystone of the project. He figured to himself beyond a doubt that the man in possession would prove a likely customer. To the eye of an observer, Salmon held the lease as owner in his own right, for himself and no one else. In fact he held it as a fiduciary, for himself and another, sharers in a common venture. If this fact had been proclaimed, if the lease by its terms had run in favor of a partnership, Mr. Gerry, we may fairly assume, would have laid before the partners, and not merely before one of them, his plan of reconstruction. The pre-emptive privilege, or, better, the pre-emptive opportunity, that was thus an incident of the enterprise, Salmon appropriated to himself in secrecy and silence. He might have warned Meinhard that the plan had been submitted, and that either would be free to compete for the award. If he had done this, we do not need to say whether he would have been under a duty, if successful in the competition, to hold the lease so acquired for the benefit of a venture then about to end, and thus prolong by indirection its responsibilities and duties. The trouble about his conduct is that he excluded his coadventurer from any chance to compete, from any chance to enjoy the opportunity for benefit that had come to him alone by virtue of his agency. This chance, if nothing more, he was under a duty to concede. The price of its denial is an extension of the trust at the option and for the benefit of the one whom he excluded.

No answer is it to say that the chance would have been of little value even if seasonably offered. Such a calculus of probabilities is beyond the science of the chancery. Salmon, the real estate operator, might have been preferred to Meinhard, the woolen merchant. On the other hand, Meinhard might have offered better terms, or reinforced his offer by alliance with the wealth of others. Perhaps he might even have persuaded the lessor to renew the Bristol lease alone, postponing for a time, in return for higher rentals, the improvement of adjoining lots. We know that even under the lease as made the time for the enlargement of the building was delayed for seven years. All these opportunities were cut away from him through another's intervention. He knew that Salmon was the manager. As the time drew near for the expiration of the lease, he would naturally assume from silence, if from nothing else, that the lessor was willing to extend it for a term of years, or at least to let it stand as a lease from year to year. Not impossibly the lessor would have done so, whatever his protestations of unwillingness, if Salmon had not given assent to a project more attractive. At all events, notice of termination, even if not necessary, might seem, not unreasonably, to be something to be looked for, if the business was over and another tenant was to enter. In the absence of such notice, the matter of an extension was one that would naturally be attended to by the manager of the enterprise, and not neglected altogether. At least, there was nothing in the situation to give warning to any one that while the lease was still in being, there had come to the manager an offer of extension which he had locked within his breast to be utilized by himself alone. The very fact that Salmon was in control with exclusive powers of direction charged him the more obviously with the duty of disclosure, since only through disclosure could opportunity be equalized. If he might cut off renewal by a purchase for his own benefit when four months were to pass before the lease would have an end, he might do so with equal right while there remained as many years (*cf. Mitchell v. Reed*, 61 N. Y. 123, 127). He might steal a march on his comrade under cover of the darkness, and then hold the captured ground. Loyalty and comradeship are not so easily abjured.

Salmon had put himself in a position in which thought of self was to be renounced, however hard the abnegation. He was much more than a coadventurer. He was a managing coadventurer (*Clegg v. Edmondson*, 8 D. M. & G. 787, 807). For him and for those like him, the rule of undivided loyalty is relentless and supreme (*Wendt v. Fischer, supra*; *Munson v. Syracuse*, etc., R. R. Co., 103 N. Y. 58, 74). A different question would be here if there were lacking any nexus of relation between the business conducted by the manager and the opportunity brought to him as an incident of management (*Dean v. MacDowell*, 8 Ch. D. 345, 354; *Aas v. Benham*, 1891, 2 Ch. 244, 258; *Latta v. Kilbourn*, 150 U. S. 524). For this problem, as for most, there are distinctions of degree. If Salmon had received from Gerry a proposition to lease a building at a location far removed, he might have held for himself the privilege thus acquired, or so we shall assume. Here the subject-matter of the new lease was an extension and enlargement of the subject-matter of the old one. A managing coadventurer appropriating the benefit of such a lease without warning to his partner might fairly expect to be reproached with conduct that was underhand, or lacking, to say the least, in reasonable candor, if the partner were to surprise him in the act of signing the new instrument. Conduct subject to that reproach does not receive from equity a healing benediction.

[The Court affirmed the Appellate Division's ruling in favor of Meinhard. The remainder of the opinion discusses the issue of assignment of a partnership interest, and what portion of the interest in the lease should be allotted to plaintiff.]

Enea v. The Superior Court of Monterey County
132 Cal.App.4th 1559 (2005)

RUSHING, P.J.

Defendants state that in 1980, they and other family members formed a general partnership known as 3-D. The partnership's sole asset was a building

Copyright in the Public Domain.

that had been converted from a residence into offices. Some portion of the property—apparently the greater part—has been rented since 1981 on a month-to-month basis by a law practice of which William Daniels is apparently the sole member. From time to time the property was rented on similar arrangements to others, including defendant Claudia Daniels. Plaintiff's counsel stipulated in the court below that "the partnership agreement has as its principal purpose the ownership, leasing and sale of the only partnership assets, which is the building. ..." He also stipulated that the partnership agreement contained no provision that the property "[would] be leased for fair market value." Defendants also assert, as the trial court ultimately found, that there was no evidence of any agreement to maximize rental profits.

In 1993, plaintiff, a client of William Daniels, purchased a one-third interest in the partnership from the latter's brother, John P. Daniels. Plaintiff testified in deposition that he sought to profit from this investment either by sale at some point to a third party, or by defendants' "just buying [him] out." In 2001, however, plaintiff questioned William Daniels about the rents being paid for the property. According to the trial court's order granting summary adjudication, their relationship "'began to unravel' and in 2003, Plaintiff was 'dissociated' from the partnership."

On August 6, 2003, plaintiff brought this action "to determine partner's buyout price and for damages." In his second cause of action, he alleged that defendants had occupied the partnership property without a written lease since the formation of the partnership; that they had told plaintiff they were paying fair market rent to the partnership; that they had "exclusive control of the books, records, accounts, and finances of the Partnership to the exclusion of plaintiff"; and that plaintiff was informed and believed they had in fact been paying significantly less than fair rental value, "in breach of their fiduciary duty to plaintiff." In their answer, defendants denied all of these allegations except to admit that defendant Claudia Daniels had occupied a portion of the premises at one time.

Defendants moved to summarily adjudicate the second cause of action on the ground, among others, that they owed no fiduciary duty to plaintiff to pay fair market rent. As an "undisputed" fact in support of the motion, defendants asserted that they "did not have a fiduciary duty to pay fair market value rent for occupancy of" the building. The "supporting evidence" cited for this assertion was "Corporations Code Section 16404(b) and (c)."

The trial court granted the motion. In its initial ruling it wrote that "whether or not Defendants were paying fair market rent, there was no breach of fiduciary duty to Plaintiff." The court noted that there was no evidence of any agreement to collect market or maximum rents. "Absent such an agreement ..., or some other evidence giving rise to a duty to pay fair market rent for the building, there can be no fiduciary duty to do so."

Despite the numerous diversions offered by defendants, the case presents a very simple set of facts and issues. For present purposes it must be assumed that defendants in fact leased the property to themselves, or associated enti- ties, at below-market rents. Therefore the sole question presented is whether defendants were categorically entitled to lease partnership property to themselves, or associated entities (or for that matter, to anyone) at less than it could yield in the open market. Remarkably, we have found no case squarely addressing this precise question. We are satisfied, however, that the answer is a resounding "No."

The defining characteristic of a partnership is the combination of two or more persons to jointly conduct business. (*Holmes v. Lerner* (1999) 74 Cal. App.4th 442, 454 ["association with the intent to carry on a business for profit"].) It is hornbook law that in forming such an arrangement the partners obligate themselves to share risks and benefits and to carry out the enterprise with the highest good faith toward one another—in short, with the loyalty and care of a fiduciary. "… [I]n all proceedings connected with the conduct of the partnership every partner is bound to act in the highest good faith to his copartner and may not obtain any advantage over him in the partnership affairs by the slightest misrepresentation, concealment, threat or adverse pressure of any kind." (*BT-I v. Equitable Life Assurance Society* (1999) 75 Cal. App.4th 1406, 1410–1411, quoting *Leff v. Gunter* (1983) 33 Cal.3d 508, 514.) Or to put the point more succinctly, "Partnership is a fiduciary relationship, and partners may not take advantages for themselves at the expense of the partnership." (*Jones v. Wells Fargo Bank* (2003) 112 Cal.App.4th 1527, 1540 .)

Here the facts as assumed by the parties and the trial court plainly depict defendants taking advantages for themselves from partnership property *at the expense of the partnership*. The advantage consisted of occupying partnership property at below-market rates, i.e., less than they would be required to pay to an independent landlord for equivalent premises. The cost to the partnership was the additional rent thereby rendered unavailable for collection from an independent tenant willing to pay the property's value.

Defendants' objections to this reasoning ring hollow. Defendants per- suaded the trial court that the conduct challenged by plaintiff was authorized by section 16404, subdivision (e), which states, "A partner does not violate a duty or obligation under this chapter or under the partnership agreement merely because the partner's conduct furthers the partner's own interest." The apparent purpose of this provision, which is drawn verbatim from RUPA section 404(e), is to excuse partners from accounting for incidental benefits obtained in the course of partnership activities *without detriment to the partner- ship*. It does not by its terms authorize the kind of conduct at issue here, which did not "merely" further defendants' own interests but did so by depriving the partnership of valuable assets, i.e., the space which would otherwise have been rented at market rates. Here, the statute entitled defendants to lease partnership property *at the same rent another tenant would have paid*. It did not empower them to occupy partnership property for their own exclusive benefit at partnership expense, in effect converting partnership assets to their own and appropriating the value it would otherwise have realized as distributable profits. Defendants' argument to the contrary seems conceptually indistinguishable from a claim that if a partnership's "primary purpose" is to purchase and hold investments, individual partners may freely pilfer its office supplies.

Defendants also persuaded the trial court that they had no duty to collect market rents in the absence of a contract expressly requiring them to do so. This argument turns partnership law on its head. Nowhere does the law declare that partners owe each other only those duties they explicitly assume by contract. On the contrary, the fiduciary duties at issue here are imposed by law, and their breach sounds in tort. (See *Everest Investors 8 v. Whitehall Real Estate Limited Partnership XI* (2002) 100 Cal.App.4th 1102, 1104 [one not having a fiduciary relationship with the plaintiff is "legally incapable of committing the tort" of breach of fiduciary duty].) We have no occasion here to consider the extent to which partners might effectively limit or modify those delictual duties by an explicit agreement or whether the partnership agreement in fact required market rents by its terms. There is no suggestion that it purported to affirmatively *excuse* defendants from the delictual duty not to engage in self-dealing. Instead, their argument is predicated on the wholly untenable notion that they were entitled to do so unless the agreement explicitly declared otherwise.

Defendants also assert, and the trial court found, that the "primary purpose" of the partnership was to hold the building for appreciation and eventual sale. This premise hardly justified summary adjudication. If the partners had explicitly agreed *not* to derive market rents from the property, but to let it be used for the exclusive advantage of some of them indefinitely, there would be some basis to contend that defendants were entitled to conduct themselves as they did—or at least that plaintiff was estopped to complain. But the mere anticipation of eventual capital gains as the main economic benefit to be derived from the venture has no tendency whatsoever to entitle individual partners to divert to their own advantage benefits that would otherwise flow to the partnership.

While this observation is sufficient to dispose of the point, we cannot help but note indications in the record that the falling-out between plaintiff and defendants apparently arose not only because William Daniels insisted on paying rents lower than plaintiff thought were proper, but also because he refused to sell the property until he was ready to retire from his law practice. Proof of such a dispute would highlight a direct conflict arising quite foreseeably from defendants' self-dealing. As emphasized by defendants, plaintiff testified in deposition that "he was 'looking to make a profit on the deal' either upon the sale of the Property at some point in time *or by [defendants] 'just buying [him] out.'*" (Italics added.) It is difficult to see why defendants would be in any hurry to buy plaintiff out so long as they could enjoy the property at a discounted rent. Presumably, they profited from the property every day this situation persisted, while plaintiff was deprived of any benefit whatsoever until it suited defendants to sell. By then, of course, they would have received months or years of direct financial advantage for which, according to them, they had no obligation to account to plaintiff or the partnership. This situation put them in direct conflict with both the partnership and plaintiff *even in terms of the "primary purpose"* they so emphatically claim for the partnership.

DISPOSITION

Let a peremptory writ of mandate issue directing respondent court to vacate its order granting defendants' motion for summary adjudication of plaintiff's second cause of action, and to enter a new order denying said motion.

B. WHAT ARE THE FINANCIAL ATTRIBUTES OF A PARTNERSHIP?

General partners jointly own a general partnership. Each partner shares in the success or failure of the business. If each partner is equally invested in the business, the partners will share equally in the profits or losses. This is the default rule in RUPA. Yet, if there is an unequal contribution of time, effort, or resources by partners, this rule may not be desirable. Partners can freely contract around this equal sharing system in their partnership agreement.

Section 401. Partner's Rights and Duties.

(a) Each partner is deemed to have an account that is:

   (1) credited with an amount equal to the money plus the value of any other property, net of the amount of any liabilities, the partner contributes to the partnership and the partner's share of the partnership profits; and

   (2) charged with an amount equal to the money plus the value of any other property, net of the amount of any liabilities, distributed by the partnership to the partner and the partner's share of the partnership losses.

(b) Each partner is entitled to an equal share of the partnership profits and is chargeable with a share of the partnership losses in proportion to the partner's share of the profits.

(c) A partnership shall reimburse a partner for payments made and indemnify a partner for liabilities incurred by the partner in the ordinary course of the business of the partnership or for the preservation of its business or property.

(d) A partnership shall reimburse a partner for an advance to the partnership beyond the amount of capital the partner agreed to contribute.

(e) A payment or advance made by a partner which gives rise to a partnership obligation under subsection (c) or (d) constitutes a loan to the partnership which accrues interest from the date of the payment or advance.

Source: Rev. Unif. Partnership Act § 401 (1994). Copyright © 1994 by National Conference of Commissioners on Uniform State Laws. Reprinted with permission.

(h) A partner is not entitled to remuneration for services performed for the partnership, except for reasonable compensation for services rendered in winding up the business of the partnership.

Comment

2. Subsection (a) provides that each partner is deemed to have an account that is credited with the partner's contributions and share of the partnership profits and charged with distributions to the partner and the partner's share of partnership losses. In the absence of another system of partnership accounts, these rules establish a rudimentary system of accounts for the partnership. The rules regarding the settlement of the partners' accounts upon the dissolution and winding up of the partnership business are found in Section 807.

3. Subsection (b) establishes the default rules for the sharing of partnership profits and losses. Partners share profits per capita and not in proportion to capital contribution as do corporate shareholders or partners in limited partnerships.

If partners agree to share profits other than equally, losses will be shared similarly to profits, absent agreement to do otherwise.

The default rules apply, as does UPA Section 18(a), where one or more of the partners contribute no capital, although there is case law to the contrary. *See, e.g., Kovacik v. Reed*, 49 Cal. 2d 166, 315 P.2d 314 (1957); *Becker v. Killarney*, 177 Ill. App. 3d 793, 523 N.E.2d 467 (1988). It may seem unfair that the contributor of services, who contributes little or no capital, should be obligated to contribute toward the capital loss of the large contributor who contributed no services. In entering a partnership with such a capital structure, the partners should foresee that application of the default rule may bring about unusual results and take advantage of their power to vary by agreement the allocation of capital losses.

4. Subsection (c) is derived from UPA Section 18(b) and provides that the partnership shall reimburse partners for payments made and indemnify them for liabilities incurred in the ordinary course of the partnership's business or for the preservation of its business or property. Reimbursement and indemnification is an obligation of the partnership. Indemnification may create a loss toward which the partners must contribute.

5. Subsection (d) is based on UPA Section 18(c). It makes explicit that the partnership must reimburse a partner for an advance of funds beyond the amount of the partner's agreed capital contribution, thereby treating the advance as a loan.

6. Subsection (e), which is also drawn from UPA Section 18(c), characterizes the partnership's obligation under subsection (c) or (d) as a loan to the partnership which accrues interest from the date of the payment or advance.

9. Subsection (h) continues the UPA Section 18(f) rule that a partner is not entitled to remuneration for services performed, except in winding up the partnership.

C. Who Owns Partnership Property?

Section 203. Partnership Property.

Property acquired by a partnership is property of the partnership and not of the partners individually.

Comment

All property acquired by a partnership, by transfer or otherwise, becomes partnership property and belongs to the partnership as an entity, rather than to the individual partners.

Section 501. Partner Not Co-Owner of Partnership Property.

A partner is not a co-owner of partnership property and has no interest in partnership property which can be transferred, either voluntarily or involuntarily.

Comment

Section 501 provides that a partner is not a co-owner of partnership property and has no interest in partnership property that can be transferred, either voluntarily or involuntarily. Thus, the section abolishes the UPA Section 25(1) concept of tenants in partnership and reflects the adoption of the entity theory. Partnership property is owned by the entity and not by the individual partners. See also Section 203, which provides that property transferred to or otherwise acquired by the partnership is property of the partnership and not of the partners individually.

Adoption of the entity theory also has the effect of protecting partnership property from execution or other process by a partner's personal creditors.

Section 101. Definitions.

In this [Act]:

(9) "Partnership interest" or "partner's interest in the partnership" means all of a partner's interests in the partnership, including the partner's transferable interest and all management and other rights.

Comment

"Partnership interest" or "partner's interest in the partnership" is defined to mean all of a partner's interests in the partnership, including the partner's transferable interest and all management and other rights. A partner's "transferable interest" is a more limited concept and means only his share of the profits and losses and right to receive distributions, that is, the partner's economic interests.

Source: Rev. Unif. Partnership Act §§ 101, 203, 501–503 (1994). Copyright © 1994 by National Conference of Commissioners on Uniform State Laws. Reprinted with permission.

Section 502. Partner's Transferable Interest in Partnership.

The only transferable interest of a partner in the partnership is the partner's share of the profits and losses of the partnership and the partner's right to receive distributions. The interest is personal property.

Comment

Section 502 continues the UPA Section 26 concept that a partner's only transferable interest in the partnership is the partner's share of profits and losses and right to receive distributions, that is, the partner's financial rights. The term "distribution" is defined in Section 101(3) [as "a transfer of money or other property from a partnership to a partner in the partner's capacity as a partner or to the partner's transferee."]

The partner's transferable interest is deemed to be personal property, regardless of the nature of the underlying partnership assets.

A partner has other interests in the partnership that may not be transferred, such as the right to participate in the management of the business. Those rights are included in the broader concept of a "partner's interest in the partnership."

Section 503. Transfer of Partner's Transferable Interest.

(a) A transfer, in whole or in part, of a partner's transferable interest in the partnership:

    (1) is permissible;

    (2) does not by itself cause the partner's dissociation or a dissolution and winding up of the partnership business; and

    (3) does not, as against the other partners or the partnership, entitle the transferee, during the continuance of the partnership, to participate in the management or conduct of the partnership business, to require access to information concerning partnership transactions, or to inspect or copy the partnership books or records.

(b) A transferee of a partner's transferable interest in the partnership has a right:

    (1) to receive, in accordance with the transfer, distributions to which the transferor would otherwise be entitled;

    (2) to receive upon the dissolution and winding up of the partnership business, in accordance with the transfer, the net amount otherwise distributable to the transferor; and

    (3) to seek under (6) a judicial determination that it is equitable to wind up the partnership business. ...

(d) Upon transfer, the transferor retains the rights and duties of a partner other than the interest in distributions transferred.

Comment

1. Section 503 is derived from UPA Section 27. Subsection (a)(1) states explicitly that a partner has the right to transfer his transferable interest in the partnership.

Subsection (a)(2) continues the UPA Section 27(1) rule that an assignment of a partner's interest in the partnership does not of itself cause a winding up of the partnership business. Under Section 601(4)(ii), however, a partner who has transferred substantially all of his partnership interest may be expelled by the other partners.

Subsection (a)(3), which is also derived from UPA Section 27(l), provides that a transferee is not, as against the other partners, entitled (i) to participate in the management or conduct of the partnership business; (ii) to inspect the partnership books or records; or (iii) to require any information concerning or an account of partnership transactions.

2. The rights of a transferee are set forth in subsection (b). Under subsection (b)(1), a transferee is entitled to receive, in accordance with the terms of the assignment, any distributions to which the transferor would otherwise have been entitled under the partnership agreement before dissolution. After dissolution, the transferee is also entitled to receive, under subsection (b)(2), the net amount that would otherwise have been distributed to the transferor upon the winding up of the business.

Subsection (b)(3) confers standing on a transferee to seek a judicial dissolution and winding up of the partnership business as provided in Section 801(6).

Section 504(b) accords the rights of a transferee to the purchaser at a sale foreclosing a charging order. The same rule should apply to creditors or other purchasers who acquire partnership interests by pursuing UCC remedies or statutory liens under federal or state law.

4. Subsection (d) is new. It makes clear that unless otherwise agreed the partner whose interest is transferred retains all of the rights and duties of a partner, other than the right to receive distributions. That means the transferor is entitled to participate in the management of the partnership and remains personally liable for all partnership obligations, unless and until he withdraws as a partner, is expelled under Section 601(4)(ii), or is otherwise dissociated under Section 601.

CHAPTER 10

EXITING GENERAL PARTNERSHIPS

At some point, partners may exit the general partnership. Typically, partners exit a partnership by quitting, being fired, retiring, or dying. Both UPA and RUPA provide a process for this. Under UPA, when a partner exits, it causes the partnership's dissolution. Under RUPA, a partner's exit does not necessarily cause dissolution. RUPA imposes a fairly complex procedure to determine whether a partner's exit will cause a partnership's dissolution or permit its continuation.

Recall that among RUPA's departures from UPA is its entity view of partnerships, as opposed to the aggregate view adopted under UPA. Given this understanding of the partnership, it makes sense that under RUPA, the rules governing a partner's exit were changed in a way that makes it much easier for the partnership to survive a partner's departure. RUPA affords the partnership many opportunities to continue its business after a partner exits the partnership.

Section 601. Events Causing Partner's Dissociation.

A partner is dissociated from a partnership upon the occurrence of any of the following events:

(1) the partnership's having notice of the partner's express will to withdraw as a partner or on a later date specified by the partner;

(2) an event agreed to in the partnership agreement as causing the partner's dissociation;

(3) the partner's expulsion pursuant to the partnership agreement;

(4) the partner's expulsion by the unanimous vote of the other partners if:

(i) it is unlawful to carry on the partnership business with that partner;

(ii) there has been a transfer of all or substantially all of that partner's transferable interest in the partnership, other than a transfer for

Source: Rev. Unif. Partnership Act §§ 601–603, 701, 801, 802, 807 (1994). Copyright © 1994 by National Conference of Commissioners on Uniform State Laws. Reprinted with permission.

security purposes, or a court order charging the partner's interest, which has not been foreclosed;

(iii) within 90 days after the partnership notifies a corporate partner that it will be expelled because it has filed a certificate of dissolution or the equivalent, its charter has been revoked, or its right to conduct business has been suspended by the jurisdiction of its incorporation, there is no revocation of the certificate of dissolution or no reinstatement of its charter or its right to conduct business; or

(iv) a partnership that is a partner has been dissolved and its business is being wound up;

(5) on application by the partnership or another partner, the partner's expulsion by judicial determination because:

(i) the partner engaged in wrongful conduct that adversely and materially affected the partnership business;

(ii) the partner willfully or persistently committed a material breach of the partnership agreement or of a duty owed to the partnership or the other partners under Section 404; or

(iii) the partner engaged in conduct relating to the partnership business which makes it not reasonably practicable to carry on the business in partnership with the partner;

(6) the partner's:

(i) becoming a debtor in bankruptcy;

(7) in the case of a partner who is an individual:

(i) the partner's death;

(ii) the appointment of a guardian or general conservator for the partner; or

(iii) a judicial determination that the partner has otherwise become incapable of performing the partner's duties under the partnership agreement; […]

(10) termination of a partner who is not an individual, partnership, corporation, trust, or estate.

Comment

RUPA dramatically changes the law governing partnership breakups and dissolution. An entirely new concept, "dissociation," is used in lieu of the UPA term "dissolution" to denote the change in the relationship caused by a partner's ceasing to be associated in the carrying on of the business. "Dissolution" is retained but with a different meaning. The entity theory of partnership provides a conceptual basis for continuing the firm itself despite a partner's withdrawal from the firm.

Under RUPA, unlike the UPA, the dissociation of a partner does not necessarily cause a dissolution and winding up of the business of the partnership. Section 801 identifies the situations in which the dissociation of a partner causes a winding up of the business. Section 701 provides that in all other situations there is a buyout of the partner's interest in the partnership, rather than a windup of the partnership business. In those other situations, the partnership entity continues, unaffected by the partner's dissociation.

A dissociated partner remains a partner for some purposes and still has some residual rights, duties, powers, and liabilities. Although Section 601 determines when a partner is dissociated from the partnership, the consequences of the partner's dissociation do not all occur at the same time. Thus, it is more useful to think of a dissociated partner as a partner for some purposes, but as a former partner for others. For example, see Section 403(b) (former partner's access to partnership books and records). The consequences of a partner's dissociation depend on whether the partnership continues or is wound up, as provided in Articles 6, 7, and 8.

Section 601 enumerates all of the events that cause a partner's dissociation.

Section 602. Partner's Power To Dissociate; Wrongful Dissociation.

(a) A partner has the power to dissociate at any time, rightfully or wrongfully, by express will pursuant to Section 601(1).

(b) A partner's dissociation is wrongful only if:

(1) it is in breach of an express provision of the partnership agreement; or

(2) in the case of a partnership for a definite term or particular undertaking, before the expiration of the term or the completion of the undertaking:

(i) the partner withdraws by express will, unless the withdrawal follows within 90 days after another partner's dissociation by death or otherwise under Section 601(6) through (10) or wrongful dissociation under this subsection;

(ii) the partner is expelled by judicial determination under Section 601(5);

(iii) the partner is dissociated by becoming a debtor in bankruptcy;

(c) A partner who wrongfully dissociates is liable to the partnership and to the other partners for damages caused by the dissociation. The liability is in addition to any other obligation of the partner to the partnership or to the other partners.

Comment

1. Subsection (a) states explicitly what is implicit in UPA Section 31(2) and RUPA Section 601(1)—that a partner has the power to dissociate at any time by expressing a will to withdraw, even in contravention of the

partnership agreement. The phrase "rightfully or wrongfully" reflects the distinction between a partner's *power* to withdraw in contravention of the partnership agreement and a partner's *right* to do so. In this context, although a partner cannot be enjoined from exercising the power to dissociate, the dissociation may be wrongful under subsection (b).

2. Subsection (b) provides that a partner's dissociation is wrongful only if it results from one of the enumerated events. The significance of a wrongful dissociation is that it may give rise to damages under subsection (c) and, if it results in the dissolution of the partnership, the wrongfully dissociating partner is not entitled to participate in winding up the business under Section 804.

3. Subsection (c) provides that a wrongfully dissociating partner is liable to the partnership and to the other partners for any damages caused by the wrongful nature of the dissociation. That liability is in addition to any other obligation of the partner to the partnership or to the other partners. For example, the partner would be liable for any damage caused by breach of the partnership agreement or other misconduct. The partnership might also incur substantial expenses resulting from a partner's premature withdrawal from a term partnership, such as replacing the partner's expertise or obtaining new financing. The wrongfully dissociating partner would be liable to the partnership for those and all other expenses and damages that are causally related to the wrongful dissociation.

Section 701(c) provides that any damages for wrongful dissociation may be offset against the amount of the buyout price due to the partner under Section 701(a), and Section 701(h) provides that a partner who wrongfully dissociates from a term partnership is not entitled to payment of the buyout price until the term expires.

Section 603. Effect of Partner's Dissociation.

(a) If a partner's dissociation results in a dissolution and winding up of the partnership business, [Article] 8 applies; otherwise, [Article] 7 applies.

(b) Upon a partner's dissociation:

   (1) the partner's right to participate in the management and conduct of the partnership business terminates, except as otherwise provided in Section 803;

   (2) the partner's duty of loyalty under Section 404(b)(3) terminates; and

   (3) the partner's duty of loyalty under Section 404(b)(1) and (2) and duty of care under Section 404(c) continue only with regard to matters arising and events occurring before the partner's dissociation, unless the partner participates in winding up the partnership's business pursuant to Section 803.

Comment

1. Section 603(a) is a "switching" provision. It provides that, after a partner's dissociation, the partner's interest in the partnership must be purchased pursuant to the buyout rules in Article 7 *unless* there is a dissolution and winding up of the partnership business under Article 8. Thus, a partner's dissociation will always result in either a buyout of the dissociated partner's interest or a dissolution and winding up of the business.

By contrast, under the UPA, every partner dissociation results in the dissolution of the partnership, most of which trigger a right to have the business wound up unless the partnership agreement provides otherwise.

2. Section 603(b) is new and deals with some of the internal effects of a partner's dissociation. Subsection (b)(1) makes it clear that one of the consequences of a partner's dissociation is the immediate loss of the right to participate in the management of the business, unless it results in a dissolution and winding up of the business. In that case, Section 804(a) provides that all of the partners who have not wrongfully dissociated may participate in winding up the business.

Section 701. Purchase of Dissociated Partner's Interest.

(a) If a partner is dissociated from a partnership without resulting in a dissolution and winding up of the partnership business under Section 801, the partnership shall cause the dissociated partner's interest in the partnership to be purchased for a buyout price determined pursuant to subsection (b).

(b) The buyout price of a dissociated partner's interest is the amount that would have been distributable to the dissociating partner under Section 807(b) if, on the date of dissociation, the assets of the partnership were sold at a price equal to the greater of the liquidation value or the value based on a sale of the entire business as a going concern without the dissociated partner and the partnership were wound up as of that date. Interest must be paid from the date of dissociation to the date of payment.

(c) Damages for wrongful dissociation under Section 602(b), and all other amounts owing, whether or not presently due, from the dissociated partner to the partnership, must be offset against the buyout price. Interest must be paid from the date the amount owed becomes due to the date of payment.

(h) A partner who wrongfully dissociates before the expiration of a definite term or the completion of a particular undertaking is not entitled to payment of any portion of the buyout price until the expiration of the term or completion of the undertaking, unless the partner establishes to the satisfaction of the court that earlier payment will not cause undue hardship to the business of the partnership. A deferred payment must be adequately secured and bear interest.

Comment

1. Article 7 is new and provides for the buyout of a dissociated partner's interest in the partnership when the partner's dissociation does not result in a dissolution and winding up of its business under Article 8. If there is no dissolution, the remaining partners have a right to continue the business and the dissociated partner has a right to be paid the value of his partnership interest. These rights can, of course, be varied in the partnership agreement. A dissociated partner has a continuing relationship with the partnership and third parties as provided in Sections 603(b), 702, and 703.

2. Subsection (a) provides that, if a partner's dissociation does not result in a windup of the business, the partnership shall cause the interest of the dissociating partner to be purchased for a buyout price determined pursuant to subsection (b). The buyout is mandatory. The "cause to be purchased" language is intended to accommodate a purchase by the partnership, one or more of the remaining partners, or a third party.

3. Subsection (b) provides how the "buyout price" is to be determined. The terms "fair market value" or "fair value" were not used because they are often considered terms of art having a special meaning depending on the context, such as in tax or corporate law. "Buyout price" is a new term. It is intended that the term be developed as an independent concept appropriate to the partnership buyout situation, while drawing on valuation principles developed elsewhere.

Under subsection (b), the buyout price is the amount that would have been distributable to the dissociating partner under Section 807(b) if, on the date of dissociation, the assets of the partnership were sold at a price equal to the greater of liquidation value or going concern value without the departing partner. Liquidation value is not intended to mean distress sale value. Under general principles of valuation, the hypothetical selling price in either case should be the price that a willing and informed buyer would pay a willing and informed seller, with neither being under any compulsion to deal. The notion of a minority discount in determining the buyout price is negated by valuing the business as a going concern. Other discounts, such as for a lack of marketability or the loss of a key partner, may be appropriate, however.

Since the buyout price is based on the value of the business at the time of dissociation, the partnership must pay interest on the amount due from the date of dissociation until payment to compensate the dissociating partner for the use of his interest in the firm. Section 104(b) provides that interest shall be at the legal rate unless otherwise provided in the partnership agreement.

The Section 701 rules are merely default rules. The partners may, in the partnership agreement, fix the method or formula for determining the buyout price and all of the other terms and conditions of the buyout right. Indeed, the very right to a buyout itself may be modified, although a provision providing for a complete forfeiture would probably not be enforceable.

4. Subsection (c) provides that the partnership may offset against the buyout price all amounts owing by the dissociated partner to the partnership, whether or not presently due, including any damages for wrongful dissociation under Section 602(c). This has the effect of accelerating payment of amounts not yet due from the departing partner to the partnership, including a long-term loan by the partnership to the dissociated partner. Where appropriate, the amounts not yet due should be discounted to present value. A dissociating partner, on the other hand, is not entitled to an add-on for amounts owing to him by the partnership. Thus, a departing partner who has made a long-term loan to the partnership must wait for repayment, unless the terms of the loan agreement provide for acceleration upon dissociation.

It is not intended that the partnership's right of setoff be construed to limit the amount of the damages for the partner's wrongful dissociation and any other amounts owing to the partnership to the value of the dissociated partner's interest. Those amounts may result in a net sum due to the partnership from the dissociated partner.

9. Under subsection (h), a wrongfully dissociating partner is not entitled to receive any portion of the buyout price before the expiration of the term or completion of the undertaking, unless the dissociated partner establishes to the satisfaction of the court that earlier payment will not cause undue hardship to the business of the partnership. In all other cases, there must be an immediate payment in cash.

Section 801. Events Causing Dissolution and Winding Up of Partnership Business.

A partnership is dissolved, and its business must be wound up, only upon the occurrence of any of the following events:

(1) in a partnership at will, the partnership's having notice from a partner, other than a partner who is dissociated under Section 601(2) through (10), of that partner's express will to withdraw as a partner, or on a later date specified by the partner;

(2) in a partnership for a definite term or particular undertaking:

    (i) within 90 days after a partner's dissociation by death or otherwise under Section 601(6) through (10) or wrongful dissociation under Section 602(b), the express will of at least half of the remaining partners to wind up the partnership business, for which purpose a partner's rightful dissociation pursuant to Section 602(b)(2)(i) constitutes the expression of that partner's will to wind up the partnership business;

    (i) the express will of all of the partners to wind up the partnership business; or

    (ii) the expiration of the term or the completion of the undertaking;

(3) an event agreed to in the partnership agreement resulting in the winding up of the partnership business;

(4) an event that makes it unlawful for all or substantially all of the business of the partnership to be continued, [...];

(5) on application by a partner, a judicial determination that:

(i) the economic purpose of the partnership is likely to be unreasonably frustrated;

(ii) another partner has engaged in conduct relating to the partnership business which makes it not reasonably practicable to carry on the business in partnership with that partner; or

(iii) it is not otherwise reasonably practicable to carry on the partnership business in conformity with the partnership agreement.

Comment

1. Under UPA Section 29, a partnership is dissolved every time a partner leaves. That reflects the aggregate nature of the partnership under the UPA. Even if the business of the partnership is continued by some of the partners, it is technically a new partnership. The dissolution of the old partnership and creation of a new partnership causes many unnecessary problems.

RUPA's move to the entity theory is driven in part by the need to prevent a technical dissolution or its consequences. Under RUPA, not every partner dissociation causes a dissolution of the partnership. Only certain departures trigger a dissolution. The basic rule is that a partnership is dissolved, and its business must be wound up, only upon the occurrence of one of the events listed in Section 801. All other dissociations result in a buyout of the partner's interest under Article 7 and a continuation of the partnership entity and business by the remaining partners.

2. Under RUPA, "dissolution" is merely the commencement of the winding up process. The partnership continues for the limited purpose of winding up the business. In effect, that means the scope of the partnership business contracts to completing work in process and taking such other actions as may be necessary to wind up the business. Winding up the partnership business entails selling its assets, paying its debts, and distributing the net balance, if any, to the partners in cash according to their interests. The partnership entity continues, and the partners are associated in the winding up of the business until winding up is completed. When the winding up is completed, the partnership entity terminates.

3. Section 801 continues two basic rules from the UPA. First, it continues the rule that any member of an *at-will* partnership has the right to force a liquidation. Second, by negative implication, it continues the rule that the partners who wish to continue the business of a *term* partnership cannot be forced to liquidate the business by a partner who withdraws prematurely in violation of the partnership agreement.

4. Section 801(1) provides that a partnership at will is dissolved and its business must be wound up upon the partnership's having notice of a partner's express will to withdraw as a partner, unless a later effective date is specified by the partner. A partner at will who has already been dissociated in some other manner, such as a partner who has been expelled, does not thereafter have a right to cause the partnership to be dissolved and its business wound up.

If, after dissolution, none of the partners wants the partnership wound up, Section 802(b) provides that, with the consent of all the partners, including the withdrawing partner, the remaining partners may continue the business. In that event, although there is a technical dissolution of the partnership and, at least in theory, a temporary contraction of the scope of the business, the partnership entity continues and the scope of its business is restored.

5. Section 801(2) provides three ways in which a term partnership may be dissolved before the expiration of the term:

> (i) Subsection (2)(i) provides for dissolution after a partner's dissociation by death or otherwise under Section 601(6) to (10) or wrongful dissociation under Section 602(b), if within 90 days after the dissociation at least half of the remaining partners express their will to dissolve the partnership. Thus, if a term partnership had six partners and one of the partners dies or wrongfully dissociates before the end of the term, the partnership will, as a result of the dissociation, be dissolved only if three of the remaining five partners affirmatively vote in favor of dissolution within 90 days after the dissociation. This reactive dissolution of a term partnership protects the remaining partners where the dissociating partner is crucial to the successful continuation of the business. Under UPA 1994, if the partnership is continued by the majority, any dissenting partner who wants to withdraw may do so rightfully under the exception to Section 602(b)(2)(i), in which case his interest in the partnership will be bought out under Article 7. By itself, however, a partner's vote not to continue the business is not necessarily an expression of the partner's will to withdraw, and a dissenting partner may still elect to remain a partner and continue in the business.
>
> The Section 601 dissociations giving rise to a reactive dissolution are: (6) a partner's bankruptcy or similar financial impairment; (7) a partner's death or incapacity; (8) the distribution by a trust-partner of its entire partnership interest; (9) the distribution by an estate-partner of its entire partnership interest; and (10) the termination of an entity-partner. Any dissociation during the term of the partnership that is wrongful under Section 602(b), including a partner's voluntary withdrawal, expulsion or bankruptcy, also gives rise to a reactive dissolution. Those statutory grounds may be varied by agreement or the reactive dissolution may be abolished entirely.

Under Section 601(6)(i), a partner is dissociated upon becoming a debtor in bankruptcy. The bankruptcy of a partner or of the partnership is not, however, an event of dissolution under Section 801. A partner's bankruptcy does, however, cause dissolution of a term partnership under Section 801(2)(i), unless a majority in interest of the remaining partners thereafter agree to continue the partnership. Affording the other partners the option of buying out the bankrupt partner's interest avoids the necessity of winding up a term partnership every time a partner becomes a debtor in bankruptcy.

Similarly, under Section 801(2)(i), the death of any partner will result in the dissolution of a term partnership, only if at least half of the remaining partners express their will to wind up the partnership's business. If dissolution does occur, the deceased partner's transferable interest in the partnership passes to his estate and must be bought out under Article 7.

(ii) Section 801(2)(ii) provides that a term partnership may be dissolved and wound up at any time by the express will of all the partners. That is merely an expression of the general rule that the partnership agreement may override the statutory default rules and that the partnership agreement, like any contract, can be amended at any time by unanimous consent.

(iii) Section 801(2)(iii) is based on UPA Section 31(1)(a) and provides for winding up a term partnership upon the expiration of the term or the completion of the undertaking.

6. Section 801(3) provides for dissolution upon the occurrence of an event specified in the partnership agreement as resulting in the winding up of the partnership business. The partners may, however, agree to continue the business and to ratify all acts taken since dissolution.

7. Section 801(4) continues the basic rule in UPA Section 31(3) and provides for dissolution if it is unlawful to continue the business of the partnership, unless cured. The "all or substantially all" proviso is intended to avoid dissolution for insubstantial or innocent regulatory violations.

8. Section 801(5) provides for judicial dissolution on application by a partner. A court may order a partnership dissolved upon a judicial determination that: (i) the economic purpose of the partnership is likely to be unreasonably frustrated; (ii) another partner has engaged in conduct relating to the partnership business which makes it not reasonably practicable to carry on the business in partnership with that partner; or (iii) it is not otherwise reasonably practicable to carry on the partnership business in conformity with the partnership agreement. The court's power to wind up the partnership under Section 801(5) cannot be varied in the partnership agreement.

Section 802. Partnership Continues After Dissolution.

(a) Subject to subsection (b), a partnership continues after dissolution only for the purpose of winding up its business. The partnership is terminated when the winding up of its business is completed.

(b) At any time after the dissolution of a partnership and before the winding up of its business is completed, all of the partners, including any dissociating partner other than a wrongfully dissociating partner, may waive the right to have the partnership's business wound up and the partnership terminated. In that event:

(1) the partnership resumes carrying on its business as if dissolution had never occurred, and any liability incurred by the partnership or a partner after the dissolution and before the waiver is determined as if dissolution had never occurred; and

(2) the rights of a third party accruing under Section 804(1) or arising out of conduct in reliance on the dissolution before the third party knew or received a notification of the waiver may not be adversely affected.

Comment

1. Section 802(a) provides that a partnership continues after dissolution only for the purpose of winding up its business, after which it is terminated. RUPA continues the concept of "termination" to mark the completion of the winding up process. Since no filing or other formality is required, the date will often be determined only by hindsight. No legal rights turn on the partnership's termination or the date thereof. Even after termination, if a previously unknown liability is asserted, all of the partners are still liable.

2. Section 802(b) makes explicit the right of the remaining partners to continue the business after an event of dissolution if all of the partners, including the dissociating partner or partners, waive the right to have the business wound up and the partnership terminated. Only those "dissociating" partners whose dissociation was the immediate cause of the dissolution must waive the right to have the business wound up. The consent of wrongfully dissociating partners is not required.

3. Upon waiver of the right to have the business wound up, Paragraph (1) of the subsection provides that the partnership entity may resume carrying on its business as if dissolution had never occurred, thereby restoring the scope of its business to normal. "Resumes" is intended to mean that acts appropriate to winding up, authorized when taken, are in effect ratified, and the partnership remains liable for those acts, as provided explicitly in paragraph (2).

Section 807. Settlement of Accounts and Contributions Among Partners.

(a) In winding up a partnership's business, the assets of the partnership, including the contributions of the partners required by this section, must be applied to discharge its obligations to creditors, including, to the extent permitted by law, partners who are creditors. Any surplus must be applied to pay in cash the net amount distributable to partners in accordance with their right to distributions under subsection (b).

(b) Each partner is entitled to a settlement of all partnership accounts upon winding up the partnership business. In settling accounts among the partners, profits and losses that result from the liquidation of the partnership assets must be credited and charged to the partners' accounts. The partnership shall make a distribution to a partner in an amount equal to any excess of the credits over the charges in the partner's account. A partner shall contribute to the partnership an amount equal to any excess of the charges over the credits in the partner's account but excluding from the calculation charges attributable to an obligation for which the partner is not personally liable under Section 306.

(c) If a partner fails to contribute the full amount required under subsection (b), all of the other partners shall contribute, in the proportions in which those partners share partnership losses, the additional amount necessary to satisfy the partnership obligations for which they are personally liable under Section 306. A partner or partner's legal representative may recover from the other partners any contributions the partner makes to the extent the amount contributed exceeds that partner's share of the partnership obligations for which the partner is personally liable under Section 306.

Comment

1. Section 807 provides the default rules for the settlement of accounts and contributions among the partners in winding up the business.

2. Subsection (a) continues the rule in UPA Section 38(l) that, in winding up the business, the partnership assets must first be applied to discharge partnership liabilities to creditors. For this purpose, any required contribution by the partners is treated as an asset of the partnership. After the payment of all partnership liabilities, any surplus must be applied to pay in cash the net amount due the partners under subsection (b) by way of a liquidating distribution.

3. Subsection (b) provides that each partner is entitled to a settlement of all partnership accounts upon winding up. It also establishes the default rules for closing out the partners' accounts. First, the profits and losses resulting from the liquidation of the partnership assets must be credited or charged to the partners' accounts, according to their respective shares of profits and losses. Then, the partnership must make a final liquidating distribution to those partners with a positive account balance. That distribution should be in the amount of the excess of credits over the charges in the account. Any

partner with a negative account balance must contribute to the partnership an amount equal to the excess of charges over the credits in the account provided the excess relates to an obligation for which the partner is personally liable under Section 306. The partners may, however, agree that a negative account does not reflect a debt to the partnership and need not be repaid in settling the partners' accounts.

4. Subsection (c) continues the UPA Section 40(d) rule that solvent partners share proportionately in the shortfall caused by insolvent partners who fail to contribute their proportionate share. The partnership may enforce a partner's obligation to contribute. A partner is entitled to recover from the other partners any contributions in excess of that partner's share of the partnership's liabilities.

PART 4

Corporations

CHAPTER 11

INTRODUCTION TO CORPORATIONS

A. WHAT IS A CORPORATION?

A corporation is an independent legal entity owned by shareholders. This means that the corporation itself, not the shareholders who own it, is legally liable for the debts and obligations the business incurs. A corporation provides limited liability protection to shareholders, so that shareholders generally can lose only their investment in the stock of the corporation. Limited liability provides a corporation with a significant advantage when it comes to raising capital for the business through the sale of stock. Investors are more willing to invest given that their liability is limited, unlike in a partnership, where there is potential unlimited personal liability.

B. THE MODEL BUSINESS CORPORATIONS ACT (MBCA 2016)

The Model Business Corporation Act (2016 Revision) is the first complete revision of the Model Act since 1984. The Model Act is a free-standing corporation statute that can be enacted in its entirety by a state legislation. It is the basis for the general corporation statute in 32 states and the District of Columbia, and is the source for many provisions in the general corporation statutes of other states. It is an important and often cited reference for courts, lawyers, and scholars, as well as a useful source of study and discussion in law schools in the U.S. and elsewhere. Through periodic amendments, the Model Act has evolved in significant ways since 1984. This evolution, however, has been incremental and has not been published in a comprehensive form that could be easily adopted by state legislatures as a means to capture all the changes since 1984. Nor had there been any systematic attempt to revise the Model Act to eliminate inconsistent terminology and adjust provisions that had become outdated since the 1984 revision.

Accordingly, beginning in 2010, the Business Law Section's Corporate Laws Committee has undertaken a thorough review and revision of the Model Act and its Official Comment. This effort has resulted in the adoption and publication of the Model Business Corporation

Excerpt from Model Business Coporations Act (2016 Revision): *Item Details*, Am. Bar Ass'n, https://shop.americanbar.org/eBus/Store/ProductDetails.aspx?productId=264484089 (last visited Sep. 26, 1977). Copyright © 2016 by American Bar Association. Reprinted with permission.

Act (2016 Revision). The 2016 Revision is based on the 1984 version and incorporates the amendments to the Model Act published in supplements regularly thereafter, with changes to both the Act and its Official Comment. Also included are notes on adoption and revised transitional provisions that are intended to facilitate legislative consideration in adopting the new version of the Model Act. The Committee intends and hopes that the publication of the 2016 Revision will encourage state legislatures—in states that have already adopted all or a substantial part of the Model Act and in other states as well—to consider adopting the Model Act in full and thereby bring their corporate statutes into line with recent developments in corporate law.

CHAPTER 12

FORMING CORPORATIONS

A. CHOOSING WHERE TO INCORPORATE

The first decision in forming a corporation is choosing a state in which to incorporate the business. Each state has its own laws and regulations for corporations. The laws of the state of incorporation apply to the "internal affairs" of a company. This rule, known as the internal affairs doctrine, requires that the laws of the state of incorporation govern the rights and duties of the shareholders, directors and officers. The doctrine applies even if the corporation conducts no business within the state of incorporation.

An extraordinarily high percentage of corporations are incorporated in Delaware. Around 300 of the Fortune 500 and half of the companies listed on the NYSE are incorporated in Delaware. The high percentage of corporations incorporated in Delaware is a result of the internal affairs doctrine. Delaware's corporate law is widely respected and considered one of the country's most advanced and flexible. Additionally, Delaware has developed a speedy and specialized court system (the Delaware Court of Chancery) to address business issues. Accordingly, corporate management seeks the benefit and protection of Delaware's corporate law and specialized courts.

B. PLANNING FOR INCORPORATION

The process of incorporation is very simple; in most states, it requires filling out a form and submitting that form to the Secretary of State. Once incorporated, a corporation must then be organized. That is, shares must be issued, directors elected and officers appointed.

§ 4.01. Corporate Name

(a) A corporate name:

    (1) must contain the word "corporation," "incorporated," "company," or "limited," or the abbreviation "corp.," "inc.," "co.," or "ltd.," or words or abbreviations of like import in another language; and

    (2) may not contain language stating or implying that the corporation is organized for a purpose other than that permitted by section 3.01 and its articles of incorporation.

§ 2.04. Liability for Preincorporation Transactions

All persons purporting to act as or on behalf of a corporation, knowing there was no incorporation under this Act, are jointly and severally liable for all liabilities created while so acting.

Official Comment

Ordinarily, only the filing of articles of incorporation should create the privilege of limited liability. Situations may arise, however, in which the protection of limited liability arguably should be recognized even though the simple incorporation process established by the Act has not been completed.

As a result, the Act imposes liability only on persons who act as or on behalf of corporations "knowing" that no corporation exists. In addition, section 2.04 does not foreclose the possibility that persons who urge defendants to execute contracts in the corporate name knowing that no steps to incorporate have been taken may be estopped to impose personal liability on individual defendants. This estoppel may be based on the inequity perceived when persons, unwilling or reluctant to enter into a commitment under their own name, are persuaded to use the name of a nonexistent corporation, and then are sought to be held personally liable under section 2.04 by the party advocating execution in the name of the corporation.

§ 3.01. Purposes

(a) Every corporation incorporated under this Act has the purpose of engaging in any lawful business unless a more limited purpose is set forth in the articles of incorporation.

Official Comment

The choice of an "any lawful business" clause has become nearly universal in states that permit the clause. Even if the articles of incorporation limit lines of business in which the corporation may engage, the limited scope of the ultra vires concept in litigation between the corporation and outsiders means that a third person entering into a transaction that violates the restrictions in the purpose clause may be able to enforce the transaction in accordance with its terms if the third person was unaware of the narrow purpose clause when entering into the transaction.

Source: Model Bus. Corp. Act §§ 2.02, 2.04, 3.01, 3.02, 3.04, 4.01, 5.01, 5.04 (2016). Copyright © 2016 by American Bar Association. Reprinted with permission.

Many corporations may also find it desirable to supplement a general purpose clause with an additional statement of business purposes. This may be necessary for licensing or for qualification or registration purposes in some states.

§ 3.02. General Powers

Unless its articles of incorporation provide otherwise, every corporation has perpetual duration and succession in its corporate name and has the same powers as an individual to do all things necessary or convenient to carry out its business and affairs, including power:

(a) to sue and be sued, complain and defend in its corporate name;

(b) to have a corporate seal, which may be altered at will, and to use it, or a facsimile of it, by impressing or affixing it or in any other manner reproducing it;

(c) to make and amend bylaws, not inconsistent with its articles of incorporation or with the laws of this state, for managing the business and regulating the affairs of the corporation;

(d) to purchase, receive, lease, or otherwise acquire, and own, hold, improve, use, and otherwise deal with, real or personal property, or any legal or equitable interest in property, wherever located;

(e) to sell, convey, mortgage, pledge, lease, exchange, and otherwise dispose of all or any part of its property;

(f) to purchase, receive, subscribe for, or otherwise acquire, own, hold, vote, use, sell, mortgage, lend, pledge, or otherwise dispose of, and deal in and with shares or other interests in, or obligations of, any other entity;

(g) to make contracts and guarantees, incur liabilities, borrow money, issue its notes, bonds, and other securities and obligations (which may be convertible into or include the option to purchase other securities of the corporation), and secure any of its obligations by mortgage or pledge of any of its property, franchises, or income;

(h) to lend money, invest and reinvest its funds, and receive and hold real and personal property as security for repayment;

(i) to be a promoter, partner, member, associate, or manager of any partnership, joint venture, trust, or other entity;

(j) to conduct its business, locate offices, and exercise the powers granted by this Act within or without this state;

(k) to elect directors and appoint officers, employees, and agents of the corporation, define their duties, fix their compensation, and lend them money and credit;

(l) to pay pensions and establish pension plans, pension trusts, profit sharing plans, share bonus plans, share option plans, and benefit or incentive plans for any or all of its current or former directors, officers, employees, and agents;

(m) to make donations for the public welfare or for charitable, scientific, or educational purposes;

(n) to transact any lawful business that will aid governmental policy; and

(o) to make payments or donations, or do any other act, not inconsistent with law, that furthers the business and affairs of the corporation.

Official Comment

The general philosophy of section 3.02 is that corporations formed under the Act should be automatically authorized to engage in all acts and have all powers that an individual may have. Because broad grants of power of this nature may not be desired in some corporations, section 3.02 generally authorizes articles of incorporation to deny or limit specific powers to a corporation.

The powers of a corporation under the Act exist independently of whether a corporation has a broad or narrow purpose clause. A corporation with a narrow purpose clause nevertheless has the same powers as an individual to do all things necessary or convenient to carry out its business. Many actions are therefore within the corporation's powers even if they do not directly affect the limited purpose for which the corporation is formed. For example, a corporation may generally make charitable contributions without regard to the purpose for which the charity will use the funds or may invest money in shares of other corporations without regard to whether the corporate purpose of the other corporation is broader or narrower than the limited purpose clause of the investing corporation. In some instances, however, a limited or narrow purpose clause may be considered to be a restriction on corporate powers as well as a restriction on purposes. Since the same ultra vires rule is applicable to corporations that exceed their purposes or powers, it is not necessary to determine whether a narrow purpose clause also limits the powers of the corporation but simply whether the purpose of the transaction in question is consistent with the purpose clause. These issues do not arise in corporations with an "any lawful business" purpose clause.

§ 3.04. Lack of Power to Act

(a) Except as provided in subsection (b), the validity of corporate action may not be challenged on the ground that the corporation lacks or lacked power to act.

(b) A corporation's power to act may be challenged:

    (1) in a proceeding by a shareholder against the corporation to enjoin the act;

(2) in a proceeding by the corporation, directly, derivatively, or through a receiver, trustee, or other legal representative, against an incumbent or former director, officer, employee, or agent of the corporation; or

(3) in a proceeding by the attorney general under section 14.30.

(c) In a shareholder's proceeding under subsection (b)(1) to enjoin an unauthorized corporate act, the court may enjoin or set aside the act, if equitable and if all affected persons are parties to the proceeding, and may award damages for loss (other than anticipated profits) suffered by the corporation or another party because of enjoining the unauthorized act.

Official Comment

Under section 3.04, it is unnecessary for persons dealing with a corporation to inquire into limitations on its purpose or powers that may appear in its articles of incorporation. A person who is unaware of these limitations when dealing with the corporation is not bound by them. The phrase in section 3.04(a) that the "validity of corporate action may not be challenged on the ground that the corporation lacks or lacked power to act" applies equally to the use of the doctrine as a sword or as a shield: a third person may no more avoid an undesired contract with a corporation on the ground the corporation was without authority to make the contract than a corporation may defend a suit on a contract on the ground that the contract is ultra vires.

The language of section 3.04 extends beyond contracts and conveyances of property; "corporate action" of any kind cannot be challenged on the ground of ultra vires. For this reason, it makes no difference whether a limitation in articles of incorporation is considered to be a limitation on a purpose or a limitation on a power; both are equally subject to section 3.04. Corporate action also includes inaction or refusal to act.

§ 5.01. Registered Office and Agent of Domestic and Registered Foreign Corporations

(a) Each corporation shall continuously maintain in this state:

(1) a registered office that may be the same as any of its places of business; and

(2) a registered agent, which may be:

(i) an individual who resides in this state and whose business office is identical with the registered office; or

(ii) a domestic or foreign corporation or eligible entity whose business office is identical with the registered office and, in the case of a foreign corporation or foreign eligible entity, is registered to do business in this state.

Official Comment

The requirements that a corporation organized under the Act or a registered foreign corporation continuously maintain a registered office and a registered agent at that office are based on the premises that at all times such a corporation should have an office where it may be found and a registered agent at that office to receive any notice or process required or permitted by law to be served.

Many corporations designate their registered office to be a business office of the corporation and a corporate officer at that office to be the registered agent. Because most of the communication to the registered agent at the registered office deals with legal matters, however, corporations sometimes designate their regular legal counsel or the counsel's nominee as their registered agent and the counsel's office as the registered office of the corporation.

The registered agent need not be an individual. Corporation service businesses often provide, as a commercial service, registered offices and registered agents at the office of the corporation service business.

§ 5.04. Service on Corporation

(a) A corporation's registered agent is the corporation's agent for service of process, notice, or demand required or permitted by law to be served on the corporation.

(b) If a corporation has no registered agent, or the agent cannot with reasonable diligence be served, the corporation may be served by registered or certified mail, return receipt requested, addressed to the secretary at the corporation's principal office.

§ 2.02. Articles of Incorporation

(a) The articles of incorporation must set forth:

(1) a corporate name for the corporation that satisfies the requirements of section 4.01;

(2) the number of shares the corporation is authorized to issue;

(3) the street and mailing addresses of the corporation's initial registered office and the name of its initial registered agent at that office; and

(4) the name and address of each incorporator.

(b) The articles of incorporation may set forth:

(1) the names and addresses of the individuals who are to serve as the initial directors;

(2) provisions not inconsistent with law regarding:

(i) the purpose or purposes for which the corporation is organized;

(ii) managing the business and regulating the affairs of the corporation;

   (iii) defining, limiting, and regulating the powers of the corporation, its board of directors, and shareholders;

   (iv) a par value for authorized shares or classes of shares; or

   (v) the imposition of interest holder liability on shareholders;

  (3) any provision that under this Act is required or permitted to be set forth in the bylaws;

  (4) a provision eliminating or limiting the liability of a director to the corporation or its shareholders for money damages for any action taken, or any failure to take any action, as a director, except liability for (i) the amount of a financial benefit received by a director to which the director is not entitled; (ii) an intentional infliction of harm on the corporation or the shareholders; (iii) a violation of section 8.32; or (iv) an intentional violation of criminal law;

  (5) a provision permitting or making obligatory indemnification of a director for liability as defined in section 8.50 to any person for any action taken, or any failure to take any action, as a director, except liability for (i) receipt of a financial benefit to which the director is not entitled, (ii) an intentional infliction of harm on the corporation or its shareholders, (iii) a violation of section 8.32, or (iv) an intentional violation of criminal law; and

  (6) a provision limiting or eliminating any duty of a director or any other person to offer the corporation the right to have or participate in any, or one or more classes or categories of, business opportunities, before the pursuit or taking of the opportunity by the director or other person; provided that any application of such a provision to an officer or a related person of that officer (i) also requires approval of that application by the board of directors, subsequent to the effective date of the provision, by action of qualified directors taken in compliance with the same procedures as are set forth in section 8.62, and (ii) may be limited by the authorizing action of the board.

(c) The articles of incorporation need not set forth any of the corporate powers enumerated in this Act.

Official Comment

Required Provisions

If a single class of shares is authorized, only the number of shares authorized need be stated; if more than one class of shares is authorized, however, both the number of authorized shares of each class and a description of the rights of each class must be included. It is unnecessary to specify par value, expected minimum capitalization, or contemplated issue price.

The corporation's initial registered office and agent must be included, and a mailing address alone, such as a post office box, is not sufficient since the registered office is the designated location for service of process.

Optional Provisions

Section 2.02(b) allows the articles of incorporation to contain optional provisions deemed sufficiently important to be of public record or subject to amendment only by the processes applicable to amendments of articles of incorporation.

C. INCORPORATION & ORGANIZATION

§ 2.01. Incorporators

One or more persons may act as the incorporator or incorporators of a corporation by delivering articles of incorporation to the secretary of state for filing.

Official Comment

The only functions of incorporators under the Act are (i) to sign the articles of incorporation, (ii) to deliver them to the secretary of state for filing, and (iii) to complete the formation of the corporation to the extent set forth in section 2.05. "Person" is defined in section 1.40 and includes both individuals and entities.

§ 2.03. Incorporation

(a) Unless a delayed effective date is specified, the corporate existence begins when the articles of incorporation are filed.

(b) The secretary of state's filing of the articles of incorporation is conclusive proof that the incorporators satisfied all conditions precedent to incorporation except in a proceeding by the state to cancel or revoke the incorporation or involuntarily dissolve the corporation.

§ 2.05. Organization Of Corporation

(a) After incorporation:

    (1) if initial directors are named in the articles of incorporation, the initial directors shall hold an organizational meeting, at the call of a majority of the directors, to complete the organization of the corporation by appointing officers, adopting bylaws, and carrying on any other business brought before the meeting; or

    (2) if initial directors are not named in the articles of incorporation, the incorporator or incorporators shall hold an organizational meeting at the call of a majority of the incorporators:

Source: Model Bus. Corp. Act §§ 2.01, 2.03, 2.05, 2.06, 2.08 (2016). Copyright © 2016 by American Bar Association. Reprinted with permission.

(i) to elect initial directors and complete the organization of the corporation; or

(ii) to elect a board of directors who shall complete the organization of the corporation.

(b) Action required or permitted by this Act to be taken by incorporators at an organizational meeting may be taken without a meeting if the action taken is evidenced by one or more written consents describing the action taken and signed by each incorporator.

Official Comment

Following incorporation, the organization of a new corporation must be completed so that it may engage in business. This usually requires adoption of bylaws, the appointment of officers and agents, the raising of equity capital by the issuance of shares to the participants in the venture, and the election of directors.

§ 2.06. Bylaws

(a) The incorporators or board of directors of a corporation shall adopt initial bylaws for the corporation.

(b) The bylaws of a corporation may contain any provision that is not inconsistent with law or the articles of incorporation.

(c) The bylaws may contain one or both of the following provisions:

(1) a requirement that if the corporation solicits proxies or consents with respect to an election of directors, the corporation include in its proxy statement and any form of its proxy or consent, to the extent and subject to such procedures or conditions as are provided in the bylaws, one or more individuals nominated by a shareholder in addition to individuals nominated by the board of directors; and

(2) a requirement that the corporation reimburse the expenses incurred by a shareholder in soliciting proxies or consents in connection with an election of directors, to the extent and subject to such procedures and conditions as are provided in the bylaws, provided that no bylaw so adopted shall apply to elections for which any record date precedes its adoption.

(d) Notwithstanding section 10.20(b)(2), the shareholders in amending, repealing, or adopting a bylaw described in subsection (c) may not limit the authority of the board of directors to amend or repeal any condition or procedure set forth in or to add any procedure or condition to such a bylaw to provide for a reasonable, practical, and orderly process.

Official Comment

The responsibility for adopting the original bylaws is placed on the person or persons completing the organization of the corporation. Section 2.06(b) permits any bylaw provision that is not inconsistent with law or the articles of incorporation. This limitation precludes bylaw provisions that limit the managerial authority of directors established by section 8.01(b).

The power to amend or repeal bylaws, or adopt new bylaws after the organization of the corporation is completed, is addressed in sections 10.20, 10.21 and 10.22.

Section 2.06(c) expressly authorizes bylaws that require the corporation to include individuals nominated by shareholders for election as directors in its proxy statement and proxy cards (or consents) and that require the reimbursement by the corporation of expenses incurred by a shareholder in soliciting proxies (or consents) in an election of directors, in each case subject to such procedures or conditions as may be provided in the bylaws.

Examples of the procedures and conditions that may be included in bylaws contemplated by section 2.06(c) include provisions that relate to the ownership of shares (including requirements as to the duration of ownership); informational requirements; restrictions on the number of directors to be nominated or on the use of the provisions by shareholders seeking to acquire control; provisions requiring the nominating shareholder to indemnify the corporation; limitations on reimbursement based on the amount spent by the corporation or the proportion of votes cast for the nominee; and limitations concerning the election of directors by cumulative voting.

Section 2.06(c) clarifies that proxy access and expense reimbursement provisions do not infringe upon the scope of authority granted to the board of directors of a corporation under section 8.01(b). Section 2.06(c) underscores the model of corporate governance embodied by the Act and reflected in section 8.01, but recognizes that different corporations may wish to grant shareholders varying rights in selecting directors through the election process.

Section 2.06(d) limits the rule set forth in section 10.20(b)(2) that shareholder adopted bylaws may limit the authority of directors to amend bylaws, by specifying that such a limit will not apply absolutely to conditions and procedures set forth in access or reimbursement bylaws authorized by section 2.06(c). Section 2.06(d) allows directors to ensure that such bylaws adequately provide for a reasonable, practical, and orderly process, but is not intended to allow the board of directors to frustrate the purpose of a shareholder-adopted proxy access or expense reimbursement provision.

§ 2.08. Forum Selection Provisions

(a) The articles of incorporation or the bylaws may require that any or all internal corporate claims shall be brought exclusively in any specified court or courts of this state and, if so specified, in any additional courts in this state or in any other jurisdictions with which the corporation has a reasonable relationship.

(b) A provision of the articles of incorporation or bylaws adopted under subsection (a) shall not have the effect of conferring jurisdiction on any court or over any person or claim, and shall not apply if none of the courts specified by such provision has the requisite personal and subject matter jurisdiction.

(c) No provision of the articles of incorporation or the bylaws may prohibit bringing an internal corporate claim in the courts of this state or require such claims to be determined by arbitration.

(d) "Internal corporate claim" means, for the purposes of this section, (i) any claim that is based upon a violation of a duty under the laws of this state by a current or former director, officer, or shareholder in such capacity, (ii) any derivative action or proceeding brought on behalf of the corporation, (iii) any action asserting a claim arising pursuant to any provision of this Act or the articles of incorporation or bylaws, or (iv) any action asserting a claim governed by the internal affairs doctrine that is not included in (i) through (iii) above.

Official Comment

Section 2.08(a) authorizes a provision in either the articles of incorporation or the bylaws creating an exclusive forum or forums for the adjudication of internal corporate claims. Under section 2.08(a), the provision must specify at least one court of this state (*i.e.*, a state court rather than a federal court). The provision may also include additional specified courts or all courts of this state or courts in this state (such as federal courts) or in one or more additional jurisdictions with a reasonable relationship to the corporation. In addition, the provision may prioritize among the specified courts. For example, the provision may specify that the claim shall be brought exclusively in a particular court of this state unless such court does not have the requisite personal and subject matter jurisdiction, in which case the claim shall be brought in other specified courts.

CHAPTER 13

PRESERVING LIMITED LIABILITY

Corporations can be an attractive choice for individuals when they are creating their business because, as previously discussed, the corporate form provides shareholders with limited liability protection. Under certain circumstances, however, limited liability will not apply, or will be judicially removed, and the owner will be subject to unlimited personal liability.

A. SHAREHOLDER LIABILITY

§ 6.22. Liability of Shareholders

(a) A purchaser from a corporation of the corporation's own shares is not liable to the corporation or its creditors with respect to the shares except to pay the consideration for which the shares were authorized to be issued or specified in the subscription agreement.

(b) A shareholder of a corporation is not personally liable for any liabilities of the corporation (including liabilities arising from acts of the corporation) except (i) to the extent provided in a provision of the articles of incorporation permitted by section 2.02(b)(2)(v), and (ii) that a shareholder may become personally liable by reason of the shareholder's own acts or conduct.

Official Comment

The sole obligation of a purchaser of shares from the corporation is to pay the consideration determined by the board of directors (or the consideration specified in the subscription agreement, in the case of preincorporation subscriptions). Upon the transfer to the corporation of the consideration so determined or specified, the shareholder has no further responsibility to the corporation or its creditors "with respect to the shares," although the

Source: Model Bus. Corp. Act § 6.22 (2016). Copyright © 2016 by American Bar Association. Reprinted with permission.

shareholder may have continuing obligations under a contract or promissory note entered into in connection with the acquisition of shares.

Section 6.22(b) sets forth the basic rule of nonliability of shareholders for corporate acts or debts that underlies corporation law. Unless such liability is provided for in the articles of incorporation, shareholders are not liable for corporate obligations, although the last clause of section 6.22(b) recognizes that such liability may be assumed voluntarily or by other conduct.

B. Exceptions to Limited Liability for Shareholders

1. Contract & Tort Exceptions

Generally, shareholders of a corporation are not personally liable for the acts or debts of the corporation. There are exceptions to this rule, though. A shareholder is liable for her own tortious conduct—even if committed while conducting the business of the corporation. Additionally, a shareholder will be held personally responsible for a contract if she gave a personal guarantee for the performance of the contract.

2. Judicial Exceptions

i. Piercing the Corporate Veil

Sea-land Services, Inc. v. Pepper Source

941 F.2d 519 (7th Cir. 1991)

BAUER, Chief Judge.

This spicy case finds its origin in several shipments of Jamaican sweet peppers. Appellee Sea-Land Services, Inc. ("Sea-Land"), an ocean carrier, shipped the peppers on behalf of The Pepper Source ("PS"), one of the appellants here. PS then stiffed Sea-Land on the freight bill, which was rather substantial. Sea-Land filed a federal diversity action for the money it was owed. On December 2, 1987, the district court entered a default judgment in favor of Sea-Land and against PS in the amount of $86,767.70. But PS was nowhere to be found; it had been "dissolved" in mid-1987 for failure to pay the annual state franchise tax. Worse yet for Sea-Land, even had it not been dissolved, PS apparently had no assets. With the well empty, Sea-Land could not recover its judgment against PS. Hence the instant lawsuit.

In June 1988, Sea-Land brought this action against Gerald J. Marchese and five business entities he owns: PS, Caribe Crown, Inc., Jamar Corp., Salescaster Distributors, Inc., and Marchese Fegan Associates. Marchese also was named individually. Sea-Land sought by this suit to pierce PS's corporate veil and render Marchese personally liable for the judgment owed to Sea-Land, and then "reverse pierce" Marchese's other corporations so that they, too, would be on the hook for the $87,000. Thus, Sea-Land alleged in its

Copyright in the public domain.

complaint that all of these corporations "are alter egos of each other and hide behind the veils of alleged separate corporate existence for the purpose of defrauding plaintiff and other creditors." Count I, ¶ 11. Not only are the corporations alter egos of each other, alleged Sea-Land, but also they are alter egos of Marchese, who should be held individually liable for the judgment because he created and manipulated these corporations and their assets for his own personal uses. Count III, ¶¶ 9–10. (Hot on the heels of the filing of Sea-Land's complaint, PS took the necessary steps to be reinstated as a corporation in Illinois.)

In early 1989, Sea-Land filed an amended complaint adding Tie-Net International, Inc., as a defendant. Unlike the other corporate defendants, Tie-Net is not owned solely by Marchese: he holds half of the stock, and an individual named George Andre owns the other half. Sea-Land alleged that, despite this shared ownership, Tie-Net is but another alter ego of Marchese and the other corporate defendants, and thus it also should be held liable for the judgment against PS.

In December 1989, Sea-Land moved for summary judgment. In that motion—which, with the brief in support and the appendices, was about three inches thick—Sea-Land argued that it was "entitled to judgment as a matter of law, since the evidence including deposition testimony and exhibits in the appendix will show that piercing the corporate veil and finding the status of an alter ego is merited in this case." Marchese and the other defendants filed brief responses.

In an order dated June 22, 1990, the court granted Sea-Land's motion. The court discussed and applied the test for corporate veil-piercing explicated in *Van Dorn Co. v. Future Chemical and Oil Corp.*, 753 F.2d 565 (7th Cir.1985). *Analyzing Illinois law, we held in Van Dorn* that a corporate entity will be disregarded and the veil of limited liability pierced when two requirements are met:

> [F]irst, there must be such unity of interest and ownership that the separate personalities of the corporation and the individual [or other corporation] no longer exist; and second, circumstances must be such that adherence to the fiction of separate corporate existence would sanction a fraud or promote injustice.

As for determining whether a corporation is so controlled by another to justify disregarding their separate identities, the Illinois cases, as we summarized them in *Van Dorn*, focus on four factors: "(1) the failure to maintain adequate corporate records or to comply with corporate formalities, (2) the commingling of funds or assets, (3) undercapitalization, and (4) one corporation treating the assets of another corporation as its own." 753 F.2d at 570 (citations omitted).

Following the lead of the parties, the district court in the instant case laid the template of *Van Dorn* over the facts of this case. The court concluded that both halves and all features of the test had been satisfied, and, therefore, entered judgment in favor of Sea-Land and against PS, Caribe Crown, Jamar,

Salescaster, Tie-Net, and Marchese individually. These defendants were held jointly liable for Sea-Land's $87,000 judgment, as well as for post-judgment interest under Illinois law. From that judgment Marchese and the other defendants brought a timely appeal.

Because this is an appeal from a grant of summary judgment, our review is *de novo*.

The first and most striking feature that emerges from our examination of the record is that these corporate defendants are, indeed, little but Marchese's playthings. Marchese is the sole shareholder of PS, Caribe Crown, Jamar, and Salescaster. He is one of the two shareholders of Tie-Net. Except for Tie-Net, none of the corporations ever held a single corporate meeting. (At the handful of Tie-Net meetings held by Marchese and Andre, no minutes were taken.) During his deposition, Marchese did not remember any of these corporations ever passing articles of incorporation, bylaws, or other agreements. As for physical facilities, Marchese runs all of these corporations (including Tie-Net) out of the same, single office, with the same phone line, the same expense accounts, and the like. And how he does "run" the expense accounts! When he fancies to, Marchese "borrows" substantial sums of money from these corporations-interest free, of course. The corporations also "borrow" money from each other when need be, which left at least PS completely out of capital when the Sea-Land bills came due. What's more, Marchese has used the bank accounts of these corporations to pay all kinds of personal expenses, including alimony and child support payments to his ex-wife, education expenses for his children, maintenance of his personal automobiles, health care for his pet—the list goes on and on. Marchese did not even have a personal bank account! (With "corporate" accounts like these, who needs one?)

And Tie-Net is just as much a part of this as the other corporations. On appeal, Marchese makes much of the fact that he shares ownership of Tie-Net, and that Sea-Land has not been able to find an example of funds flowing from PS to Tie-Net to the detriment of Sea-Land and PS's other creditors. So what? The record reveals that, in all material senses, Marchese treated Tie-Net like his other corporations: he "borrowed" over $30,000 from Tie-Net; money and "loans" flowed freely between Tie-Net and the other corporations; and Marchese charged up various personal expenses (including $460 for a picture of himself with President Bush) on Tie-Net's credit card. Marchese was not deterred by the fact that he did not hold all of the stock of Tie-Net; why should his creditors be?

In sum, we agree with the district court that there can be no doubt that the "shared control/unity of interest and ownership" part of the *Van Dorn* test is met in this case: corporate records and formalities have not been maintained; funds and assets have been commingled with abandon; PS, the offending corporation, and perhaps others have been undercapitalized; and corporate assets have been moved and tapped and "borrowed" without regard to their source. Indeed, Marchese basically punted this part of the inquiry before the district court by coming forward with little or no evidence in response to Sea-Land's extensively supported argument on these points. Thus, Sea-Land is entitled to judgment on these points.

The second part of the *Van Dorn* test is more problematic, however. "Unity of interest and ownership" is not enough; Sea-Land also must show that honoring the separate corporate existences of the defendants "would sanction a fraud or promote injustice." *Van Dorn*, 753 F.2d at 570. This last phrase truly is disjunctive:

> Although an intent to defraud creditors would surely play a part if established, the Illinois test does not require proof of such intent. Once the first element of the test is established, *either* the sanctioning of a fraud (intentional wrongdoing) or the promotion of injustice, will satisfy the second element.

Id. (emphasis in original). Seizing on this, Sea-Land has abandoned the language in its two complaints that make repeated references to "fraud" by Marchese, and has chosen not to attempt to *prove* that PS and Marchese intended to defraud it—which would be quite difficult on summary judgment. Instead, Sea-Land has argued that honoring the defendants' separate identities would "promote injustice."

But what, exactly, does "promote injustice" mean, and how does one establish it on summary judgment? These are the critical, troublesome questions in this case. To start with, as the above passage from *Van Dorn* makes clear, "promote injustice" means something less than an affirmative showing of fraud—but how much less? In its one-sentence treatment of this point, the district court held that it was enough that "Sea-Land would be denied a judicially-imposed recovery." Dist.Ct.Op. at 11–12. Sea-Land defends this reasoning on appeal, arguing that "permitting the appellants to hide behind the shield of limited liability would clearly serve as an injustice against appellee" because it would "impermissibly deny appellee satisfaction." Appellee's Brief at 14–15. But that cannot be what is meant by "promote injustice." The prospect of an unsatisfied judgment looms in every veil-piercing action; why else would a plaintiff bring such an action? Thus, if an unsatisfied judgment is enough for the "promote injustice" feature of the test, then *every* plaintiff will pass on that score, and *Van Dorn* collapses into a one-step "unity of interest and ownership" test.

Because we cannot abide such a result, we will undertake our own review of Illinois cases to determine how the "promote injustice" feature of the veil-piercing inquiry has been interpreted. In *Pederson*, a recent case from the Illinois court of appeals, the court offered the following summary: "Some element of unfairness, something akin to fraud or deception or the existence of a compelling public interest must be present in order to disregard the corporate fiction." 214 Ill.App.3d at 821.

The light shed on this point by other Illinois cases can be seen only if we examine the cases on their facts. [...].

Federal district courts sitting in Illinois also have on occasion discussed what kind of "injustice" suffices under the second half of the *Van Dorn* test. [...].

Generalizing from these cases, we see that the courts that properly have pierced corporate veils to avoid "promoting injustice" have found that, unless it did so, some "wrong" beyond a creditor's inability to collect would result: the common sense rules of adverse possession would be undermined; former partners would be permitted to skirt the legal rules concerning monetary obligations; a party would be unjustly enriched; a parent corporation that caused a sub's liabilities and its inability to pay for them would escape those liabilities; or an intentional scheme to squirrel assets into a liability-free corporation while heaping liabilities upon an asset-free corporation would be successful. Sea-Land, although it alleged in its complaint the kind of intentional asset- and liability-shifting found in *Van Dorn*, has yet to come forward with evidence akin to the "wrongs" found in these cases. Apparently, it believed, as did the district court, that its unsatisfied judgment was enough. That belief was in error, and the entry of summary judgment premature. We, therefore, reverse the judgment and remand the case to the district court.

On remand, the court should require that Sea-Land produce, if it desires summary judgment, evidence and argument that would establish the kind of additional "wrong" present in the above cases. For example, perhaps Sea-Land could establish that Marchese, like Roth in *Van Dorn*, used these corporate facades to avoid its responsibilities to creditors; or that PS, Marchese, or one of the other corporations will be "unjustly enriched" unless liability is shared by all. Of course, Sea-Land is not required fully to prove intent to defraud, which it probably could not do on summary judgment anyway. But it is required to show the kind of injustice to merit the evocation of the court's essentially equitable power to prevent "injustice." It may well be that, after more of such evidence is adduced, no genuine issue of fact exists to prevent Sea-Land from reaching Marchese's other pet corporations for PS's debt. Or it may be that only a finder of fact will be able to determine whether fraud or "injustice" is involved here. In any event, the record as it currently stands is insufficient to uphold the entry of summary judgment.

REVERSED and REMANDED with instructions.

Baatz v. Arrow Bar, Inc.

452 N.W.2d 138 (S.D. 1990)

SABERS, Justice.

Kenny and Peggy were seriously injured in 1982 when Roland McBride crossed the center line of a Sioux Falls street with his automobile and struck

Copyright in the public domain.

them while they were riding on a motorcycle. McBride was uninsured at the time of the accident and apparently is judgment proof.

Baatz alleges that Arrow Bar served alcoholic beverages to McBride prior to the accident while he was already intoxicated. Baatz commenced this action in 1984, claiming that Arrow Bar's negligence in serving alcoholic beverages to McBride contributed to the injuries they sustained in the accident. Baatz supports his claim against Arrow Bar with the affidavit of Jimmy Larson. Larson says he knew McBride and observed him being served alcoholic beverages in the Arrow Bar during the afternoon prior to the accident, while McBride was intoxicated.

Edmond and LaVella Neuroth formed the Arrow Bar, Inc. in May 1980. During the next two years they contributed $50,000 to the corporation pursuant to a stock subscription agreement. The corporation purchased the Arrow Bar business in June 1980 for $155,000 with a $5,000 down payment. Edmond and LaVella executed a promissory note personally guaranteeing payment of the $150,000 balance. In 1983 the corporation obtained bank financing in the amount of $145,000 to pay off the purchase agreement. Edmond and LaVella again personally guaranteed payment of the corporate debt. Edmond is the president of the corporation, and Jacquette Neuroth serves as the manager of the business.

In 1987 the trial court entered summary judgment in favor of Arrow Bar and the individual defendants. Baatz appealed that judgment and we reversed and remanded to the trial court for trial. Shortly before the trial date, Edmond, LaVella, and Jacquette moved for and obtained summary judgment dismissing them as individual defendants. Baatz appeals. We affirm.

Baatz claims that even if Arrow Bar, Inc. is the licensee, the corporate veil should be pierced, leaving the Neuroths, as the shareholders of the corporation, individually liable. A corporation shall be considered a separate legal entity until there is *sufficient reason* to the contrary. When continued recognition of a corporation as a separate legal entity would "produce injustices and inequitable consequences," then a court has sufficient reason to pierce the corporate veil. Factors that indicate injustices and inequitable consequences and allow a court to pierce the corporate veil are:

1. fraudulent representation by corporation directors;

2. undercapitalization;

3. failure to observe corporate formalities;

4. absence of corporate records;

5. payment by the corporation of individual obligations; or

6. use of the corporation to promote fraud, injustice, or illegalities.

When the court deems it appropriate to pierce the corporate veil, the corporation and its stockholders will be treated identically.

Baatz advances several arguments to support his claim that the corporate veil of Arrow Bar, Inc. should be pierced, but fails to support them with facts, or misconstrues the facts.

First, Baatz claims that since Edmond and LaVella personally guaranteed corporate obligations, they should also be personally liable to Baatz. However, the personal guarantee of a loan is a contractual agreement and cannot be enlarged to impose tort liability. Moreover, the personal guarantee creates individual liability for a corporate obligation, the opposite of factor 5), above. As such, it supports, rather than detracts from, recognition of the corporate entity.

Baatz also argues that the corporation is simply the alter ego of the Neuroths, and the corporate veil should be pierced. Baatz' discussion of the law is adequate, but he fails to present evidence that would support a decision in his favor in accordance with that law. When an individual treats a corporation "as an instrumentality through which he [is] conducting his personal business," a court may disregard the corporate entity. Baatz fails to demonstrate how the Neuroths were transacting personal business through the corporation. In fact, the evidence indicates the Neuroths treated the corporation separately from their individual affairs.

Baatz next argues that the corporation is undercapitalized. Shareholders must equip a corporation with a reasonable amount of capital for the nature of the business involved. Baatz claims the corporation was started with only $5,000 in borrowed capital, but does not explain how that amount failed to equip the corporation with a reasonable amount of capital. In addition, Baatz fails to consider the personal guarantees to pay off the purchase contract in the amount of $150,000, and the $50,000 stock subscription agreement. There simply is no evidence that the corporation's capital in whatever amount was inadequate for the operation of the business. Normally questions relating to individual shareholder liability resulting from corporate undercapitalization should not be reached until the primary question of corporate liability is determined. Questions depending in part upon other determinations are not normally ready for summary judgment. However, simply asserting that the corporation is undercapitalized does not make it so. Without some evidence of the inadequacy of the capital, Baatz fails to present specific facts demonstrating a genuine issue of material fact.

Finally, Baatz argues that Arrow Bar, Inc. failed to observe corporate formalities because none of the business' signs or advertising indicated that the business was a corporation. Baatz cites SDCL 47–2–36 as requiring the name of any corporation to contain the word corporation, company, incorporated, or limited, or an abbreviation for such a word. In spite of Baatz' contentions, the corporation is in compliance with the statute because its corporate name—Arrow Bar, Inc.—includes the abbreviation of the word incorporated. Furthermore, the "mere failure upon occasion to follow all the forms prescribed by law for the conduct of corporate activities will not justify" disregarding the corporate entity. Even if the corporation is improperly using its name, that alone is not a sufficient reason to pierce the corporate veil. This is especially so where, as here, there is no relationship between the claimed defect and the resulting harm.

In addition, the record is void of any evidence which would support imposition of individual liability by piercing the corporate veil under any of the other factors listed above in 1), 4) or 6).

In summary, Baatz fails to present specific facts that would allow the trial court to find the existence of a genuine issue of material fact. There is no indication that any of the Neuroths personally served an alcoholic beverage to McBride on the day of the accident. Nor is there any evidence indicating that the Neuroths treated the corporation in any way that would produce the injustices and inequitable consequences necessary to justify piercing the corporate veil. In fact, the only evidence offered is otherwise. Therefore, we affirm summary judgment dismissing the Neuroths as individual defendants.

ii. Enterprise Liability

v. Carlton

18 N.Y.2d 414 (NY Ct. App. 1966)

FULD, Judge.

This case involves what appears to be a rather common practice in the taxicab industry of vesting the ownership of a taxi fleet in many corporations, each owning only one or two cabs.

The complaint alleges that the plaintiff was severely injured four years ago in New York City when he was run down by a taxicab owned by the defendant Seon Cab Corporation and negligently operated at the time by the defendant Marchese. The individual defendant, Carlton, is claimed to be a stockholder of 10 corporations, including Seon, each of which has but two cabs registered in its name, and it is implied that only the minimum automobile liability insurance required by law (in the amount of $10,000) is carried on any one cab. Although seemingly independent of one another, these corporations are alleged to be 'operated as a single entity, unit and enterprise' with regard to financing, supplies, repairs, employees and garaging, and all are named as defendants. The plaintiff asserts that he is also entitled to hold their stockholders personally liable for the damages sought because the multiple corporate structure constitutes an unlawful attempt 'to defraud members of the general public' who might be injured by the cabs.

The defendant Carlton has moved, pursuant to CPLR 3211(a)7, to dismiss the complaint on the ground that as to him it 'fails to state a cause of action'. The court at Special Term granted the motion but the Appellate Division, by a divided vote, reversed, holding that a valid cause of action was sufficiently

Copyright in the public domain.

stated. The defendant Carlton appeals to us, from the nonfinal order, by leave of the Appellate Division on a certified question.

The law permits the incorporation of a business for the very purpose of enabling its proprietors to escape personal liability but, manifestly, the privilege is not without its limits. Broadly speaking, the courts will disregard the corporate form, or, to use accepted terminology, 'pierce the corporate veil', whenever necessary 'to prevent fraud or to achieve equity' In determining whether liability should be extended to reach assets beyond those belonging to the corporation, we are guided, as Judge Cardozo noted, by 'general rules of agency'. In other words, whenever anyone uses control of the corporation to further his own rather than the corporation's business, he will be liable for the corporation's acts 'upon the principle of Respondeat superior applicable even where the agent is a natural person'. Such liability, moreover, extends not only to the corporation's commercial dealings but to its negligent acts as well.

In the case before us, the plaintiff has explicitly alleged that none of the corporations 'had a separate existence of their own' and, as indicated above, all are named as defendants. However, it is one thing to assert that a corporation is a fragment of a larger corporate combine which actually conducts the business. It is quite another to claim that the corporation is a 'dummy' for its individual stockholders who are in reality carrying on the business in their personal capacities for purely personal rather than corporate ends. Either circumstance would justify treating the corporation as an agent and piercing the corporate veil to reach the principal but a different result would follow in each case. In the first, only a larger Corporate entity would be held financially responsible (while, in the other, the stockholder would be personally liable. Either the stockholder is conducting the business in his individual capacity or he is not. If he is, he will be liable; if he is not, then it does not matter—insofar as his personal liability is concerned—that the enterprise is actually being carried on by a larger 'enterprise entity'.

Reading the complaint in this case most favorably and liberally, we do not believe that there can be gathered from its averments the allegations required to spell out a valid cause of action against the defendant Carlton.

The individual defendant is charged with having 'organized, managed, dominated and controlled' a fragmented corporate entity but there are no allegations that he was conducting business in his individual capacity. Had the taxicab fleet been owned by a single corporation, it would be readily apparent that the plaintiff would face formidable barriers in attempting to establish personal liability on the part of the corporation's stockholders. The fact that the fleet ownership has been deliberately split up among many corporations does not ease the plaintiff's burden in that respect. The corporate form may not be disregarded merely because the assets of the corporation, together with the mandatory insurance coverage of the vehicle which struck the plaintiff, are insufficient to assure him the recovery sought. If Carlton were to be held individually liable on those facts alone, the decision would apply equally to the thousands of cabs which are owned by their individual drivers who conduct their businesses through corporations organized pursuant to section 401 of the Business Corporation Law, Consol.Laws, c. 4 and carry the minimum insurance required by subdivision 1 (par. (a)) of section 370 of the Vehicle and Traffic Law, Consol.Laws, c. 71. These taxi owner-operators are entitled to form such corporations and we agree with the court at Special Term that, if the insurance coverage required by statute 'is inadequate for the protection of the public, the remedy lies not with the courts but with the Legislature.' It may very well be sound policy to require that certain corporations must take out liability insurance which will afford adequate compensation to their potential tort victims. However, the responsibility for imposing conditions on the privilege of incorporation has been committed by the Constitution to the Legislature and it may not be fairly implied, from any statute, that the Legislature intended, without the slightest discussion or debate, to require of taxi corporations that they carry automobile liability insurance over and above that mandated by the Vehicle and Traffic Law.

This is not to say that it is impossible for the plaintiff to state a valid cause of action against the defendant Carlton. However, the simple fact is that the plaintiff has just not done so here. While the complaint alleges that the separate corporations were undercapitalized and that their assets have been intermingled, it is barren of any 'sufficiently particular(ized) statements' that the defendant Carlton and his associates are actually doing business in their individual capacities, shuttling their personal funds in and out of the corporations 'without regard to formality and to suit their immediate convenience.' Such a 'perversion of the privilege to do business in a corporate form' would justify imposing personal liability on the individual stockholders. Nothing of the sort has in fact been charged, and it cannot reasonably or logically be inferred from the happenstance that the business of Seon Cab Corporation may actually be carried on by a larger corporate entity composed of many corporations which, under general principles of agency, would be liable to each other's creditors in contract and in tort.

In point of fact, the principle relied upon in the complaint to sustain the imposition of personal liability is not agency but fraud. Such a cause of action cannot withstand analysis. If it is not fraudulent for the owner-operator of a single cab corporation to take out only the minimum required liability insurance, the enterprise does not become either illicit or fraudulent merely because it consists of many such corporations. The plaintiff's injuries are the same regardless of whether the cab which strikes him is owned by a single corporation or part of a fleet with ownership fragmented among many corporations. Whatever rights he may be able to assert against parties other than the registered owner of the vehicle come into being not because he has been defrauded but because, under the principle of Respondeat superior, he is entitled to hold the whole enterprise responsible for the acts of its agents.

In sum, then, the complaint falls short of adequately stating a cause of action against the defendant Carlton in his individual capacity.

The order of the Appellate Division should be reversed, with costs in this court and in the Appellate Division, the certified question answered in the negative and the order of the Supreme Court, Richmond County, reinstated, with leave to serve an amended complaint.

KEATING, Judge (dissenting).

The defendant Carlton, the shareholder here sought to be held for the negligence of the driver of a taxicab, was a principal shareholder and organizer of the defendant corporation which owned the taxicab. The corporation was one of 10 organized by the defendant, each containing two cabs and each cab having the 'minimum liability' insurance coverage mandated by section 370 of the Vehicle and Traffic Law. The sole assets of these operating corporations are the vehicles themselves and they are apparently subject to mortgages.*

From their inception these corporations were intentionally undercapitalized for the purpose of avoiding responsibility for acts which were bound to arise as a result of the operation of a large taxi fleet having cars out on the street 24 hours a day and engaged in public transportation. And during the course of the corporations' existence all income was continually drained out of the corporations for the same purpose.

The issue presented by this action is whether the policy of this State, which affords those desiring to engage in a business enterprise the privilege of limited liability through the use of the corporate device, is so strong that it will permit that privilege to continue no matter how much it is abused, no matter how irresponsibly the corporation is operated, no matter what the cost to the public. I do not believe that it is.

Under the circumstances of this case the shareholders should all be held individually liable to this plaintiff for the injuries he suffered. At least, the matter should not be disposed of on the pleadings by a dismissal of the complaint. 'If a corporation is organized and carries on business without substantial capital in such a way that the corporation is likely to have no sufficient assets available to meet its debts, it is inequitable that shareholders should set up such a flimsy organization to escape personal liability. The attempt to do corporate business without providing any sufficient basis of financial responsibility to creditors is an abuse of the separate entity and will be ineffectual to exempt the shareholders from corporate debts. It is coming to be recognized as the policy of law that shareholders should in good faith put at the risk of the business unincumbered capital reasonably adequate for its prospective liabilities. If capital is illusory or trifling compared with the business to be done and the risks of loss, this is a ground for denying the separate entity privilege.' (Ballantine, Corporations (rev.ed., 1946), s 129, pp. 302–303.)

CHAPTER 14

Capitalizing & Financing Corporations

A. Overview of Corporate Finance

Corporations generate capital and founders may self-fund a start-up, but they also may turn to external sources for funding in the form of debt or equity financing.

Equity Financing

Through equity financing, a company seeks to raise capital by granting an ownership interest in the business. The company gives up a degree of control but reduces risks associated with the timing of and the liability for repayment. The scope and scale of equity financing can range from a few thousand dollars for shares purchased privately by friends and family to billion-dollar initial public offerings with shares sold on public exchanges. A company may go through several rounds of equity financing as it issues stock throughout its lifetime.

Stock is typically issued as either common stock or preferred stock. Common stock usually retains a right to vote, to receive dividends, to obtain certain information, and to receive any remaining funds after liquidation. Preferred stock is often senior to common stock in terms of its right to a share of dividends or assets upon liquidation and may have other rights not possessed by common stock. Investor interest and bargaining power shape the terms on which stocks are offered.

Debt Financing

Corporations may borrow funds in the form of bank loans, payable notes, bonds, or other debt instruments. While the lender does not gain an ownership interest, debt financing usually comes with the added cost of interest.

Lenders seek to limit their risk by securing debt against a company's assets or obtaining a personal guarantee from borrowers. Additionally, if a company defaults, lenders will be paid back before stockholders. For many companies, the added cost associated with debt offers better rates than equity financing.

The balance between debt and equity financing affects the valuation of a firm and its ability to obtain further financing.

B Shares of Stock

§ 1.40. Act Definitions

In this Act, unless otherwise specified:

"Shares" means the units into which the proprietary interests in a domestic or foreign corporation are divided.

§ 6.01. Authorized Shares

(a) The articles of incorporation must set forth any classes of shares and series of shares within a class, and the number of shares of each class and series, that the corporation is authorized to issue. If more than one class or series of shares is authorized, the articles of incorporation must prescribe a distinguishing designation for each class or series and, before the issuance of shares of a class or series, describe the terms, including the preferences, rights, and limitations, of that class or series. Except to the extent varied as permitted by this section, all shares of a class or series must have terms, including preferences, rights, and limitations, that are identical with those of other shares of the same class or series.

(b) The articles of incorporation must authorize:

    (1) one or more classes or series of shares that together have full voting rights, and

    (2) one or more classes or series of shares (which may be the same class, classes or series as those with voting rights) that together are entitled to receive the net assets of the corporation upon dissolution.

(c) The articles of incorporation may authorize one or more classes or series of shares that:

    (1) have special, conditional, or limited voting rights, or no right to vote, except to the extent otherwise provided by this Act;

    (2) are redeemable or convertible as specified in the articles of incorporation:

Source: Model Bus. Corp. Act §§ 1.40, 6.01, 6.03, 6.21, 6.30, 6.31 (2016). Copyright © 2016 by American Bar Association. Reprinted with permission.

(i) at the option of the corporation, the shareholder, or another person or upon the occurrence of a specified event;

(ii) for cash, indebtedness, securities, or other property; and

(iii) at prices and in amounts specified or determined in accordance with a formula;

(3) entitle the holders to distributions calculated in any manner, including dividends that may be cumulative, noncumulative, or partially cumulative; or

(4) have preference over any other class or series of shares with respect to distributions, including distributions upon the dissolution of the corporation.

(d) Terms of shares may be made dependent upon facts objectively ascertainable outside the articles of incorporation in accordance with section 1.20(k).

(e) Any of the terms of shares may vary among holders of the same class or series so long as such variations are expressly set forth in the articles of incorporation.

(f) The description of the preferences, rights, and limitations of classes or series of shares in subsection (c) is not exhaustive.

Official Comment

Section 6.01(a)

Section 6.01(a) requires that the articles of incorporation prescribe the classes and series of shares and the number of shares of each class and series that the corporation is authorized to issue. If the articles of incorporation authorize the issue of only one class of shares, no designation or description of the shares is required, it being understood that these shares have both the power to vote and the power to receive the net assets of the corporation upon dissolution. Shares with both of these characteristics are usually referred to as "common shares" but no specific designation is required by the Act. The articles of incorporation may set forth the number of shares authorized and permit the board of directors under section 6.02 to allocate the authorized shares among designated classes or series of shares.

The preferences, rights and limitations of each class or series of shares constitute the "contract" of the holders of those classes and series of shares with respect to the holders' interest in the corporation and must be set forth in sufficient detail reasonably to define their interest. The terms, including the preferences, rights and limitations, of shares with one or more special or preferential rights which may be authorized are further described in section 6.01(c).

If more than one class or series is authorized (or if only one class or series is originally authorized but at some future time one or more other classes or series of shares are added by amendment), the terms, including the preferences, rights and limitations of each class, classes or series of shares, including the class, classes or series that possess the fundamental characteristics of voting and residual equity financial interests, must be described before shares of those classes or series are issued. If both fundamental characteristics are placed exclusively in a single class of shares, that class may be described simply as "common shares" or by statements such as the "shares have the general distribution and voting rights," the "shares have all the rights of common shares," or the "shares have all rights not granted to the class A shares."

If the articles of incorporation create classes or series of shares that divide these fundamental rights among two or more classes or series of shares, it is necessary that the rights be clearly allocated among the classes and series. Specificity is required only to the extent necessary to differentiate the relative rights of the respective classes and series. For example, where one class or series has a liquidation preference over another, it is necessary to specify only the preferential liquidation right of that class or series; in the absence of a contrary provision in the articles of incorporation, the remaining class or series would be entitled to receive the net assets remaining after the liquidation preference has been satisfied. More than one class or series of shares may be designated as "common shares;" however, each must have a "distinguishing designation" under section 6.01(a), *e.g.*, "nonvoting common shares" or "class A common shares," and the rights of the classes and series must be described. For example, if a corporation authorizes two classes of shares with equal rights to share in all distributions and with identical voting rights except that one class is entitled exclusively to elect one director and the second class is entitled exclusively to elect a second director, the two classes may be designated, *e.g.*, as "Class A common" and "Class B common." What is required is language that makes the allocation of these rights clear.

Rather than describing the terms of each class or series of shares in the articles of incorporation, the corporation may delegate to the board of directors under section 6.02 the power to establish the terms of a class of shares or a series within a class if no shares of that class or series have previously been issued. Those terms, however, must be set forth in an amendment to the articles of incorporation that is effective before the shares are issued.

Section 6.01(b)

Section 6.01(b) requires that every corporation authorize one or more classes or series of shares that in the aggregate have the two fundamental characteristics of full voting rights and the right to receive the net assets of the corporation upon its dissolution. The phrase "full voting rights" refers to the right to vote on all matters for which voting is required by either the Act or the articles of incorporation.

The two fundamental characteristics need not be placed in a single class or series of shares but may be divided as desired. It is nevertheless essential that the corporation always have authorized shares having in the aggregate these two characteristics, and section 6.03 requires that shares having in the aggregate these characteristics always be outstanding.

Section 6.01(c)

Section 6.01(c) provides a non-exhaustive list of the principal features that are customarily incorporated into classes or series of shares.

A. In General

Section 6.01(c) authorizes creation of classes or series of shares with a range of preferences, rights and limitations as further described below. The Act permits the creation of shares convertible into, or redeemable in exchange for, cash, other property, or shares or debt securities of the corporation ranking senior to the shares, at the option of either the holder or the corporation. Such a conversion or redemption is subject to the restrictions on distributions under section 6.40.

B. Voting of Shares

Any class or series of shares may be granted multiple or fractional votes per share without limitation. Shares of any class or series may also be made nonvoting "except to the extent otherwise provided by this Act." This "except" clause refers to the provisions in the Act that permit shares which are designated to be nonvoting to vote as separate voting groups on amendments to articles of incorporation and other organic changes in the corporation that directly affect that class or series. In addition, shares may be given voting rights that are limited or conditional (*e.g.*, voting rights triggered by the failure to pay specified dividends).

C. Redemption and Conversion of Shares

Section 6.01(c)(2) permits redemption for any class or series of shares and thereby permits the creation of redeemable or callable shares without limitation (subject only to the provisions that the class, classes or series of shares described in section 6.01(b) must always be authorized and that at least one or more shares which together have those rights must be outstanding under section 6.03).

The prices to be paid upon the redemption of shares under section 6.01(c)(2) and the amounts to be redeemed may be fixed in the articles of incorporation or "determined in accordance with a formula." The formula could be self contained or, pursuant to the provisions of section 6.01(d), could be determined by reference to extrinsic data or events. This permits the redemption price and the amounts to be redeemed to be established on the basis of matters external to the corporation, such as the purchase price of other shares, the level of market reference rates, the effective interest rate at which the corporation may obtain short or long-term financing, the consumer price index or a designated currency ratio.

All redemptions of shares are subject to the restrictions on distributions set forth in section 6.40.

D. Extrinsic Facts

Section 6.01(d) permits the creation of classes or series of shares with terms that are dependent upon facts objectively ascertainable outside the articles of incorporation. Terms that depend upon reference to extrinsic facts may include dividend rates that vary according to some external index or event. Because such a "variable rate" class or series of shares would be intended to respond to current market conditions, it would most often be used with "blank check" provisions in the articles of incorporation with the terms of shares set by the board of directors immediately before issuance.

E. Variation Among Holders

Section 6.01(e) permits the creation of classes or series of shares with terms that may vary among holders of the same class or series of shares. An example of such variation would be a provision that shares held by a bank or bank holding company in excess of a certain percentage would not have voting rights. In addition, section 6.24(b) expressly permits the issuance of rights, options or warrants for the purchase of shares or other securities of the corporation that contain terms and conditions which vary the rights of the holders of such rights, warrants or options based on a holder's ownership of, or offer to acquire, a specified number or percentage of the outstanding shares or other securities of the corporation.

Examples of Classes or Series of Shares Permitted by Section 6.01

Section 6.01 is enabling rather than restrictive given that corporations often find it necessary to create new classes or series of shares for a variety of reasons, for instance in connection with raising debt or equity capital. Classes or series of shares may also be used in connection with desired control relationships among the participants in a venture. Under section 7.21, only securities classified as "shares" in the articles of incorporation can have the power to vote.

Examples of such classes and series of shares include:

- Shares of one class or series may be authorized to elect a specified number of directors while shares of a second class or series may be authorized to elect the same or a different number of directors.

- Shares of one class or series may be entitled to vote as a separate voting group on certain transactions, but shares of two or more classes or series may be only entitled to vote together as a single voting group on the election of directors and other matters.

- Shares of one class or series may be nonvoting or may be given multiple or fractional votes per share.

- Shares of one class or series may be entitled to different dividend rights or rights on dissolution than shares of another class or series.

- Shares of one class or series may be created to include some characteristics of debt securities.

A corporation has power to issue debt securities under section 3.02. Although 6.01 authorizes the creation of interests that usually will be classed as "equity" rather than "debt," it is permissible to create classes or series of securities under section 6.01 that have some of the characteristics of debt securities. These securities are often referred to as "hybrid securities." Section 6.01 does not limit the development of hybrid securities, and equity securities may be created under the Act that embody any characteristics of debt. As noted above, however, the Act restricts the power to vote to securities classified as "shares" in the articles of incorporation.

§ 6.03. Issued and Outstanding Shares

(a) A corporation may issue the number of shares of each class or series authorized by the articles of incorporation. Shares that are issued are outstanding shares until they are reacquired, redeemed, converted, or cancelled.

(b) The reacquisition, redemption, or conversion of outstanding shares is subject to the limitations of subsection (c) and to section 6.40.

(c) At all times that shares of the corporation are outstanding, one or more shares that together have full voting rights and one or more shares that together are entitled to receive the net assets of the corporation upon dissolution must be outstanding.

Official Comment

The determination of the number of shares to be issued under section 6.03 is usually made by the board of directors but may be reserved by the articles of incorporation to the shareholders. The only requirements are that no class or series of shares be overissued and that one or more shares of a class, classes or series that together have full voting rights and one or more shares of a class, classes or series that together are entitled to the net assets of the corporation upon dissolution at all times must be outstanding.

The corporation may acquire outstanding shares pursuant to a voluntary transaction between a shareholder and the corporation. Also, shares may be made subject to transfer restrictions that may result in contractual obligations by the corporation to reacquire shares. Further, the corporation may reacquire shares pursuant to a right of redemption (or an obligation to redeem) established in the articles of incorporation. All voluntary or contractual reacquisitions are subject to the limitations set forth in section 6.03(c) and to section 6.40.

§ 6.21. Issuance of Shares

(a) The powers granted in this section to the board of directors may be reserved to the shareholders by the articles of incorporation.

(b) The board of directors may authorize shares to be issued for consideration consisting of any tangible or intangible property or benefit to the corporation, including cash, promissory notes, services performed, contracts for services to be performed, or other securities of the corporation.

(c) Before the corporation issues shares, the board of directors shall determine that the consideration received or to be received for shares to be issued is adequate. That determination by the board of directors is conclusive insofar as the adequacy of consideration for the issuance of shares relates to whether the shares are validly issued, fully paid, and nonassessable.

(d) When the corporation receives the consideration for which the board of directors authorized the issuance of shares, the shares issued therefor are fully paid and nonassessable.

Official Comment

Because a statutory structure embodying "par value" and "stated capital" concepts does not protect creditors and senior security holders from payments to junior security holders, section 6.21 does not use these concepts.

Consideration

Because shares need not have a par value under section 6.21, there is no minimum price at which shares must be issued. Section 6.21(b) specifically validates "any tangible or intangible property or benefit to the corporation," as consideration for the present issue of shares, specifically including contracts for future services (including promoters' services) and promissory notes. The term "benefit" should be broadly construed also to include, for example, a reduction of a liability, a release of a claim, or intangible gain obtained by a corporation. Business judgment should determine what kind of property or benefit should be obtained for shares, and a determination by the directors meeting the requirements of section 8.30 to accept a specific kind of property or benefit for shares should be accepted and not circumscribed by artificial or arbitrary rules.

Board Determination of Adequacy

Protection of shareholders against abuse of the power granted to the board of directors to determine that shares should be issued for intangible property or benefit is provided by the requirements of section 8.30 applicable to a determination that the consideration received for shares is adequate.

In many instances, property or benefit received by the corporation will be of uncertain value; if the board of directors determines that the issuance of shares for the property or benefit is an appropriate transaction, that is sufficient under section 6.21. The board of directors does not have to make an explicit "adequacy" determination by formal resolution; that determination may be inferred from a determination to authorize the issuance of shares for a specified consideration.

The second sentence of section 6.21(c) describes the effect of the determination by the board of directors that consideration is adequate for the issuance of shares. That determination, without more, is conclusive to the extent that adequacy is relevant to the question whether the shares are validly issued, fully paid, and nonassessable. Whether shares are validly issued may depend on compliance with corporate procedural requirements, such as issuance within the amount authorized in the articles of incorporation or holding a directors' meeting upon proper notice and with a quorum present.

§ 1.40. Act Definitions

In this Act, unless otherwise specified:

> "Record shareholder" means (i) the person in whose name shares are registered in the records of the corporation or (ii) the person identified as the beneficial owner of shares in a beneficial ownership certificate pursuant to section 7.23 on file with the corporation to the extent of the rights granted by such certificate.

Official Comment

Shareholder and Record Shareholder

The term "shareholder" is usually used in the Act to mean a "record shareholder" as defined in section 1.40, but section 1.40 contemplates that definitions may be expanded or limited by the Act for purposes of specific provisions. The definition of "record shareholder" in section 1.40 includes a beneficial owner of shares named in a beneficial ownership certificate under section 7.23, but only to the extent of the rights granted the beneficial owner in the certificate—for example, the right to receive notice of, and vote at, shareholders' meetings. Various substantive sections of the Act also permit holders of voting trust certificates or beneficial owners of shares (not subject to a beneficial ownership certificate under section 7.23) to exercise some of the rights of a "shareholder."

§ 6.30. Shareholders' Preemptive Rights

(a) The shareholders of a corporation do not have a preemptive right to acquire the corporation's unissued shares except to the extent the articles of incorporation so provide.

(b) A statement included in the articles of incorporation that "the corporation elects to have preemptive rights" (or words of similar effect) means that the following principles apply except to the extent the articles of incorporation expressly provide otherwise:

(1) The shareholders of the corporation have a preemptive right, granted on uniform terms and conditions prescribed by the board of directors to provide a fair and reasonable opportunity to exercise the right, to acquire proportional amounts of the corporation's unisssued shares upon the decision of the board of directors to issue them.

(2) A preemptive right may be waived by a shareholder. A waiver evidenced by a writing is irrevocable even though it is not supported by consideration.

(3) There is no preemptive right with respect to:

    (i) shares issued as compensation to directors, officers, employees or agents of the corporation, its subsidiaries or affiliates;

    (ii) shares issued to satisfy conversion or option rights created to provide compensation to directors, officers, employees or agents of the corporation, its subsidiaries or affiliates;

    (iii) shares authorized in the articles of incorporation that are issued within six months from the effective date of incorporation; or

    (iv) shares sold otherwise than for cash.

(c) For purposes of this section, "shares" includes a security convertible into or carrying a right to subscribe for or acquire shares.

Official Comment

Section 6.30(a) adopts an "opt in" provision for preemptive rights: unless an affirmative reference to these rights appears in the articles of incorporation, no preemptive rights exist.

Section 6.30(b) provides a standard model for preemptive rights if the corporation desires to exercise the "opt in" alternative of section 6.30(a). A corporation may qualify or limit any of the rules set forth in this section by express provisions in the articles of incorporation. The purposes of this standard model for preemptive rights are (i) to simplify drafting articles of incorporation and (ii) to provide a simple checklist of business considerations for the benefit of attorneys who are considering the inclusion of preemptive rights in articles of incorporation.

Preemptive rights can protect the voting power and equity participation of shareholders. This combination of functions creates no problem in a corporation that has authorized only a single class of shares but may occasionally create problems in corporations with more complex capital structures. In many capital structures, the issuance of additional shares of one class or series typically does not adversely affect other classes or series. For example, the issuance of additional shares with voting power but without preferential rights normally does not affect either the limited voting power or equity participation of holders of shares with preferential rights; holders of shares with preferential equity participation rights but without voting power should therefore have no preemptive rights with respect to shares with voting power but without preferential rights. Classes or series of shares that may give rise to possible conflict between the protection of voting interests and equity participation when the board of directors desires to issue additional shares include classes or series of nonvoting shares without preferential rights and classes or series of shares with both voting power and preferential rights to distributions. These conflicts can be dealt with by specific provisions in the articles of incorporation.

§ 6.31. Corporation's Acquisition of Its Own Shares

(a) A corporation may acquire its own shares, and shares so acquired constitute authorized but unissued shares.

(b) If the articles of incorporation prohibit the reissue of the acquired shares, the number of authorized shares is reduced by the number of shares acquired.

Official Comment

Shares that are acquired by the corporation become authorized but unissued shares under section 6.31 unless the articles of incorporation prohibit reissue, in which event the shares are cancelled and the number of authorized shares is automatically reduced.

If the number of authorized shares of a class is reduced as a result of the operation of section 6.31(b), the board of directors should amend the articles of incorporation under section 10.05(f) to reflect that reduction. If there are no remaining authorized shares in a class as a result of the operation of section 6.31, the board should amend the articles of incorporation under section 10.05(g) to delete the class from the classes of shares authorized by the articles of incorporation.

C. DISTRIBUTIONS & DIVIDENDS

§ 1.40. Act Definitions

In this Act, unless otherwise specified:

> "Distribution" means a direct or indirect transfer of cash or other property (except a corporation's own shares) or incurrence of indebtedness by a corporation to or for the benefit of its shareholders in respect of any of its shares. A distribution may be in the form of a payment of a dividend; a purchase, redemption, or other acquisition of shares; a distribution of indebtedness; a distribution in liquidation; or otherwise.

Source: Model Bus. Corp. Act §§ 1.40, 6.40 (2016). Copyright © 2016 by American Bar Association. Reprinted with permission.

Official Comment

Section 1.40 defines "distribution" to include all transfers of cash or other property made by a corporation to any shareholder in respect of the corporation's shares, except mere changes in the unit of interest such as share dividends and share splits. Thus, a "distribution" includes the payment of a dividend, a purchase by a corporation of its own shares, a distribution of evidences of indebtedness or promissory notes of the corporation, and a distribution in voluntary or involuntary liquidation. If a corporation incurs indebtedness to shareholders in connection with a distribution (as in the case of a distribution of a debt instrument or an installment purchase of shares), the creation, incurrence, or distribution of the indebtedness is the event which constitutes the distribution rather than the subsequent payment of the debt by the corporation, except in the situation addressed in section 6.40(g).

The term "indirect" in the definition of "distribution" is intended to address transactions like the repurchase of parent company shares by a subsidiary whose actions are controlled by the parent. It also is intended to address any other transaction in which the substance is clearly the same as a typical dividend or share repurchase, no matter how structured or labeled.

The test for validity of distributions other than distributions in liquidation is set forth in section 6.40, and for distributions in liquidation in chapter 14.

§ 6.40. Distributions to Shareholders

(a) A board of directors may authorize and the corporation may make distributions to its shareholders subject to restriction by the articles of incorporation and the limitation in subsection (c).

(b) The board of directors may fix the record date for determining shareholders entitled to a distribution, which date may not be retroactive. If the board of directors does not fix a record date for determining shareholders entitled to a distribution (other than one involving a purchase, redemption, or other acquisition of the corporation's shares), the record date is the date the board of directors authorizes the distribution.

(c) No distribution may be made if, after giving it effect:

  (1) the corporation would not be able to pay its debts as they become due in the usual course of business; or

  (2) the corporation's total assets would be less than the sum of its total liabilities plus (unless the articles of incorporation permit otherwise) the amount that would be needed, if the corporation were to be dissolved at the time of the distribution, to satisfy the preferential

rights upon dissolution of shareholders whose preferential rights are superior to those receiving the distribution.

(d) The board of directors may base a determination that a distribution is not prohibited under subsection (c) either on financial statements prepared on the basis of accounting practices and principles that are reasonable in the circumstances or on a fair valuation or other method that is reasonable in the circumstances.

Official Comment

The Scope of Section 6.40

Section 6.40 imposes a single, uniform test on all distributions other than distributions in liquidation under chapter 14. Section 1.40 defines "distribution" broadly to include transfers of cash and other property (excluding a corporation's own shares) to a shareholder in respect of the corporation's shares. Examples of such transfers are cash or property dividends, payments by a corporation to purchase its own shares, and distributions of promissory notes or indebtedness. The financial provisions of the Act do not use the concept of surplus but do have restrictions on distributions built around both equity insolvency and balance sheet tests.

Equity Insolvency Test

In most cases involving a corporation operating as a going concern in the normal course, it will be apparent from information generally available that no particular inquiry concerning the equity insolvency test in section 6.40(c)(1) is needed. Although neither a balance sheet nor an income statement can be conclusive as to this test, the existence of significant shareholders' equity and normal operating conditions are of themselves a strong indication that no issue should arise under that test. In the case of a corporation having regularly audited financial statements, the absence of any qualification in the most recent auditor's opinion as to the corporation's status as a "going concern," coupled with a lack of subsequent adverse events, would normally be decisive.

It is only when circumstances indicate that the corporation is encountering difficulties or is in an uncertain position concerning its liquidity and operations that the board of directors or, more commonly, the officers or others upon whom they may place reliance under section 8.30(d), may need to address the issue. Because of the overall judgment required in evaluating the equity insolvency test, no "bright line" test is provided. However, in determining whether the equity insolvency test has been met, certain judgments or assumptions as to the future course of the corporation's business are customarily justified, absent clear evidence to the contrary. These include the likelihood that (i) based on existing and contemplated demand for the corporation's products or services, it will be able to generate funds over a period of time sufficient to satisfy its existing and reasonably anticipated obligations as they mature, and (ii) indebtedness which matures in the near-term will be refinanced where, on the basis of the corporation's financial condition and future prospects and the general availability of credit to businesses similarly situated, it is reasonable to assume that such refinancing may be accomplished. To the extent that the corporation may be subject to asserted or unasserted contingent liabilities, reasonable judgments as to the likelihood, amount, and time of any recovery against the corporation, after giving consideration to the extent to which the corporation is insured or otherwise protected against loss, may be utilized. There may be occasions when it would be useful to consider a cash flow analysis, based on a business forecast and budget, covering a sufficient period of time to permit a conclusion that known obligations of the corporation can reasonably be expected to be satisfied over the period of time that they will mature.

In exercising their judgment, the directors are entitled to rely, as provided in section 8.30(e), on information, opinions, reports, and statements prepared by others. Ordinarily, they should not be expected to become involved in the details of the various analyses or market or economic projections that may be relevant.

Balance Sheet Test

The determination of a corporation's assets and liabilities for purposes of the balance sheet test of section 6.40(c)(2) and the choice of the permissible basis on which to do so are left to the judgment of its board of directors. In making a judgment under section 6.40(d), the board may rely as provided in section 8.30(e) upon information, opinions, reports, and statements, including financial statements and other financial data, prepared or presented by public accountants or others.

Section 6.40 does not utilize particular accounting terminology of a technical nature or specify particular accounting concepts. In making determinations under this section, the board of directors may make judgments about accounting matters.

In a corporation with subsidiaries, the board of directors may rely on unconsolidated statements prepared on the basis of the equity method of accounting as to the corporation's investee corporations, including corporate joint ventures and subsidiaries, although other evidence would be relevant in the total determination. The board of directors is entitled to rely as provided by section 8.30(e) upon reasonably current financial statements in determining whether the balance sheet test of section 6.40(c)(2) has been met, unless the board has knowledge that makes such reliance unwarranted. Section 6.40 does not mandate the use of generally accepted accounting principles; it only requires the use of accounting practices and principles that are reasonable in the circumstances. Although corporations subject to registration under the Securities Exchange Act of 1934 must, and many other corporations in fact do, use financial statements prepared on the basis of generally accepted accounting principles, a great number of smaller or closely held corporations do not. Some of these corporations maintain records solely on a tax accounting basis and their financial statements are of necessity prepared on that basis. Others prepare financial statements that substantially reflect generally accepted accounting principles but may depart from them in some respects (*e.g.*, footnote disclosure). A statutory standard of reasonableness, rather than stipulating generally accepted accounting principles as the normative standard, is appropriate to achieve a reasonable degree of flexibility and to accommodate the needs of the many different types of business corporations which might be subject to these provisions, including in particular closely held corporations.

Preferential Dissolution Rights and the Balance Sheet Test

Section 6.40(c)(2) treats preferential dissolution rights of shares for distribution purposes as if they were liabilities for the sole purpose of determining the amount available for distributions. In making the calculation of the amount that must be added to the liabilities of the corporation to reflect the preferential dissolution rights, the assumption should be made that the preferential dissolution rights are to be established pursuant to the articles of incorporation as of the date of the distribution or proposed distribution. The amount so determined must include arrearages in preferential dividends if the articles of incorporation require that they be paid upon the dissolution of the corporation. In the case of shares having both preferential rights upon dissolution and other nonpreferential rights, only the preferential rights should be taken into account. The treatment of preferential dissolution rights of classes or series of shares set forth in section 6.40(c)(2) is applicable only to the balance sheet test and is not applicable to the equity insolvency test of section 6.40(c)(1). The treatment of preferential rights mandated by section 6.40(c)(2) may always be eliminated by an appropriate provision in the articles of incorporation.

CHAPTER 15

GOVERNING CORPORATIONS: THE ROLE OF SHAREHOLDERS

Shareholders are the owners of a corporation. Unless they desire otherwise, by default, shareholders do not manage the corporation; directors do. Shareholders, though, are entitled to voting rights. Shareholders may elect and remove directors, amend the corporation's articles and bylaws, and approve fundamental transactions. Additionally, shareholders can exercise some level of control through other rights, such as the right to inspect the corporation's books, and the right to sue the board of directors or officers on behalf of the corporation for breaching their fiduciary duties to the corporation.

A. SHAREHOLDER MEETINGS

§ 7.01. Annual Meeting

(a) Unless directors are elected by written consent in lieu of an annual meeting as permitted by section 7.04, a corporation shall hold a meeting of shareholders annually at a time stated in or fixed in accordance with the bylaws at which directors shall be elected.

(b) Annual meetings may be held in or out of this state at the place stated in or fixed in accordance with the bylaws. If no place is so stated or fixed, annual meetings shall be held at the corporation's principal office.

(c) The failure to hold an annual meeting at the time stated in or fixed in accordance with a corporation's bylaws does not affect the validity of any corporate action.

Official Comment

The principal action to be taken at the annual meeting is the election of directors pursuant to section 8.03, but the purposes of the annual meeting are not limited by the Act. The requirement of section 7.01(a) that an annual

Source: Model Bus. Corp. Act §§ 1.40, 7.01, 7.02, 7.04–07 (2016). Copyright © 2016 by American Bar Association. Reprinted with permission.

meeting be held is phrased in mandatory terms to ensure that every share-holder entitled to participate in an annual meeting has the unqualified rights to (i) demand that an annual meeting be held and (ii) compel the holding of the meeting under section 7.03 if the corporation does not promptly hold the meeting and if the shareholders have not elected directors by written consent.

Many corporations, such as nonpublic subsidiaries and closely held corporations, do not regularly hold annual meetings and, if no shareholder objects or action has been taken by written consent, that practice creates no problem under section 7.01, because section 7.01(c) provides that failure to hold an annual meeting does not affect the validity of any corporate action.

§ 7.02. Special Meeting

(a) A corporation shall hold a special meeting of shareholders:

  (1) on call of its board of directors or the person or persons authorized to do so by the articles of incorporation or bylaws; or

  (2) if shareholders holding at least 10% of all the votes entitled to be cast on an issue proposed to be considered at the proposed special meeting sign, date, and deliver to the corporation one or more written demands for the meeting describing the purpose or purposes for which it is to be held, provided that the articles of incorporation may fix a lower percentage or a higher percentage not exceeding 25% of all the votes entitled to be cast on any issue proposed to be considered.

(b) If not otherwise fixed under section 7.03 or 7.07, the record date for determining shareholders entitled to demand a special meeting shall be the first date on which a signed shareholder demand is delivered to the corporation.

(c) Special meetings of shareholders may be held in or out of this state at the place stated in or fixed in accordance with the bylaws. If no place is so stated or fixed, special meetings shall be held at the corporation's principal office.

(d) Only business within the purpose or purposes described in the meeting notice required by section 7.05(c) may be conducted at a special meeting of shareholders.

Official Comment

Any meeting other than an annual meeting is a special meeting under section 7.02. The principal differences between an annual meeting and a special meeting are that at an annual meeting directors are elected and, subject to any applicable special notice requirement prescribed by the Act or by the articles of incorporation, any relevant issue pertaining to the corporation may be considered, while at a special meeting only matters within the specific purposes for which the meeting is called may be considered.

Who May Call a Special Meeting

A special meeting may be called by the board of directors, a person or persons authorized to do so by the articles of incorporation or bylaws, or upon written demand by shareholders as described below. Typically, the person or persons holding certain designated offices within the corporation, *e.g.*, the president, chairman of the board of directors, or chief executive officer, are given authority to call special meetings of the shareholders. In addition, the shareholders holding at least 10% of all the votes entitled to be cast on a proposed issue at the special meeting may require the corporation to hold a special meeting by signing, dating, and delivering one or more writings that demand a special meeting and set forth the purpose or purposes of the desired meeting. That percentage may be decreased or increased (but to not more than 25%) by a provision in the articles of incorporation fixing a different percentage. Shareholders demanding a special meeting do not have to sign a single document, but the writings signed must all describe essentially the same purpose or purposes. Upon receipt of demands from holders with the requisite number of votes, the corporation (through an appropriate officer) must call the special meeting at a reasonable time and place. The shareholders' demand may suggest a time and place but the final decision on such matters belongs to the corporation. If no meeting is held within the time periods specified in section 7.03, a shareholder, as defined in section 7.03(c), who signed the demand may seek judicial relief under that section requiring that the meeting be held.

The Business That May Be Conducted at a Special Meeting

Section 7.05(c) provides that a notice of a special meeting must include a "description of the purpose or purposes for which the meeting is called." Section 7.02(d) states that only business that is "within" that purpose or those purposes may be conducted at the special meeting. The word "within" was chosen, rather than a broader phrase like "reasonably related to," to describe the relationship between the notice and the authorized business to assure a shareholder who does not attend a special meeting that new or unexpected matters will not be considered in the shareholder's absence.

§ 7.04. Action Without Meeting

(a) Action required or permitted by this Act to be taken at a shareholders' meeting may be taken without a meeting if the action is taken by all the shareholders entitled to vote on the action. The action must be evidenced by one or more written consents bearing the date of signature and describing the action taken, signed by all the shareholders entitled to vote on the action and delivered to the corporation for filing by the corporation with the minutes or corporate records.

(b) The articles of incorporation may provide that any action required or permitted by this Act to be taken at a shareholders' meeting may be taken without a meeting, and without prior notice, if consents in writing setting forth the action so taken are signed by the holders of outstanding shares having not less than the minimum number of votes that would be required to authorize or take the action at a meeting at which all shares entitled to vote on the action were present and voted; provided, however, that if a corporation's articles of incorporation authorize shareholders to cumulate their votes when electing directors pursuant to section 7.28, directors may not be elected by less than unanimous written consent.

Official Comment

Section 7.04(a) permits shareholders to act by unanimous written consent without holding a meeting. This applies to any shareholder action, including election of directors, approval of mergers, domestications, conversions, sales of the corporation's assets requiring shareholder approval, amendments of articles of incorporation, and dissolution. Unanimous written consent is generally obtainable only for matters on which there are relatively few shareholders entitled to vote and is thus generally not used by public corporations. Under section 7.04(b), however, a corporation may include in its articles of incorporation a provision that permits shareholder action by less than unanimous written consent except with respect to the election of directors by written consent where cumulative voting applies. If the articles of incorporation permit action by less than unanimous written consent, they may also limit or otherwise specify the shareholder actions that may be approved by less than unanimous consent.

§ 7.05. Notice of Meeting

(a) A corporation shall notify shareholders of the date, time, and place of each annual and special shareholders' meeting no fewer than 10 nor more than 60 days before the meeting date. The notice must include the record date for determining the shareholders entitled to vote at the meeting, if such date is different from the record date for determining shareholders entitled to notice of the meeting. Unless this Act or the articles of incorporation require otherwise, the corporation is required to give notice only to shareholders entitled to vote at the meeting as of the record date for determining the shareholders entitled to notice of the meeting.

(b) Unless this Act or the articles of incorporation require otherwise, the notice of an annual meeting of shareholders need not include a description of the purpose or purposes for which the meeting is called.

(c) Notice of a special meeting of shareholders must include a description of the purpose or purposes for which the meeting is called.

(d) If not otherwise fixed under section 7.03 or 7.07, the record date for determining shareholders entitled to notice of and to vote at an annual or special shareholders' meeting is the day before the first notice is delivered to shareholders.

(e) Unless the bylaws require otherwise, if an annual or special shareholders' meeting is adjourned to a different date, time, or place, notice need not be given of the new date, time, or place if the new date, time, or place is announced at the meeting before adjournment. If a new record date for the adjourned meeting is or must be fixed under section 7.07, however, notice of the adjourned meeting shall be given under this section to shareholders entitled to vote at such adjourned meeting as of the record date fixed for notice of such adjourned meeting.

Official Comment

The Act does not require that the notice of an annual meeting refer to any specific purpose or purposes, and any matter appropriate for shareholder action may be considered. Section 7.05(b) recognizes, however, that other provisions of the Act or the corporation's articles of incorporation may require that specific reference to a proposed action appear in the notice of meeting. In addition, as a condition to relying upon shareholder action to establish the safe harbor protection of section 8.61(b), section 8.63 requires notice to shareholders providing information regarding any director's conflict of interest in a transaction. If the board of directors chooses, a notice of an annual meeting may contain references to purposes or proposals not required by statute. If a notice of an annual meeting refers specifically to one or more purposes, the meeting is not limited to those purposes. Although the corporation is not required to give notice of the purpose or purposes of an annual meeting unless the Act or the articles of incorporation so provide, a shareholder, in order to raise a matter at an annual meeting (for example, to nominate an individual for election as a director or to propose a resolution for adoption), may have to comply with any advance notice provisions in the corporation's articles of incorporation or bylaws. Such provisions might include requirements that shareholder nominations for election to the board of directors or resolutions intended to be voted on at the annual meeting be submitted in writing and received by the corporation a prescribed number of days in advance of the meeting.

The selection of the day before the notice is delivered as the catch-all record date under section 7.05(d) is intended to permit the corporation to deliver notices to shareholders on a given day without regard to any requests for transfer that may have been received during that day. For this reason, this section is consistent with the general principle set forth in section 7.07(b) that the board of directors may not fix a retroactive record date.

Section 7.05(e) provides rules for adjourned meetings and determines whether new notice must be given to shareholders. If a new record date is or must be fixed under section 7.07, the 10- to 60-day notice requirement and all other requirements of section 7.05 must be complied with because notice must be given to the persons who are shareholders as of the new record date. In such circumstances, a new quorum for the adjourned meeting must also be established.

§ 7.06. Waiver of Notice

(a) A shareholder may waive any notice required by this Act or the articles of incorporation or bylaws, before or after the date and time stated in the notice. The waiver must be in writing, be signed by the shareholder entitled to the notice, and be delivered to the corporation for filing by the corporation with the minutes or corporate records.

(b) A shareholder's attendance at a meeting:

(1) waives objection to lack of notice or defective notice of the meeting, unless the shareholder at the beginning of the meeting objects to holding the meeting or transacting business at the meeting; and

(2) waives objection to consideration of a particular matter at the meeting that is not within the purpose or purposes described in the meeting notice, unless the shareholder objects to considering the matter when it is presented.

Official Comment

A notice of shareholders' meeting serves two principal purposes: (i) it advises shareholders of the date, time, and place of the annual or special meeting, and (ii) in the case of a special shareholders' meeting (or an annual meeting at which fundamental changes may be made), it advises shareholders of the purposes of the meeting. Section 7.06(b)(1) provides that attendance at a meeting constitutes waiver of any failure to receive the notice or defects in the statement of the date, time, and place of any meeting. Defects waived by attendance for this purpose include a failure to send the notice altogether, delivery to the wrong address, a misstatement of the date, time, or place of the meeting, and a failure to notice the meeting within the time periods specified in section 7.05(a). If a shareholder believes that the defect in or failure of notice was in some way prejudicial, the shareholder must state at the beginning of the meeting an objection to holding the meeting or transacting any business or the objection is waived. If this objection is made, the corporation may correct the defect by sending proper notice to the shareholders for a subsequent meeting or by obtaining written waivers of notice from all shareholders who did not receive the notice required by section 7.05.

For purposes of this section, "attendance" at a meeting involves the presence of the shareholder in person or by proxy or, if authorized in accordance with section 7.09(b), the shareholder or proxy may attend by means of remote communication. A shareholder who attends a meeting solely for the purpose of objecting to the notice is counted as present for purposes of determining whether a quorum is present.

In the case of special shareholders' meetings, or annual meetings at which certain fundamental corporate changes are considered, a second purpose of the notice is to inform shareholders of the matters to be considered at the meeting. An objection that a particular matter is not within the stated purposes of the meeting cannot be raised until the matter is presented. Thus section 7.06(b)(2) provides that a shareholder waives this kind of objection by failing to object when the matter is presented. If this objection is made, the corporation may correct the defect by sending proper notice to the shareholders for a subsequent meeting or obtaining written waivers of notice from all shareholders. Whether a specific matter is within a stated purpose of a meeting is ultimately a matter for judicial determination, typically in a suit to invalidate action taken at the meeting brought by a shareholder who was not present at the meeting or who was present at the meeting and preserved an objection under section 7.06(b).

The purpose of both waiver rules in section 7.06(b) is to require shareholders with technical objections to holding the meeting or considering a specific matter to raise them at the outset and not reserve them to be raised only if they are unhappy with the outcome of the meeting. The rules set forth in this section differ in some respects from the waiver rules for directors set forth in section 8.23 where a waiver is inferred if the director acquiesces in the action taken at a meeting even if the director raised a technical objection to the notice of a meeting at the outset.

§ 1.40. Act Definitions

In this Act, unless otherwise specified:

> "Record date" means the date fixed for determining the identity of the corporation's shareholders and their shareholdings for purposes of this Act.

§ 7.07. Record Date for Meeting

(a) The bylaws may fix or provide the manner of fixing the record date or dates for one or more voting groups to determine the shareholders entitled to notice of a shareholders' meeting, to demand a special meeting, to vote, or to take any other action. If the bylaws do not fix or provide for fixing a record date, the board of directors may fix the record date.

(b) A record date fixed under this section may not be more than 70 days before the meeting or action requiring a determination of shareholders and may not be retroactive.

(c) A determination of shareholders entitled to notice of or to vote at a shareholders' meeting is effective for any adjournment of the meeting unless the board of directors fixes a new record date or dates, which it shall do if the meeting is adjourned to a date more than 120 days after the date fixed for the original meeting.

Official Comment

Section 7.07 authorizes the board of directors to fix record dates for determining shareholders entitled to take any action unless the bylaws themselves fix or otherwise provide for the fixing of a record date. A separate record date may be established for each voting group entitled to vote separately on a matter at a meeting, or a single record date may be established for all voting groups entitled to participate in the meeting. If neither the bylaws nor the board of directors fixes a record date for a specific action, the section of the Act that deals with that action itself fixes the record date. For example, section 7.05(d), relating to giving notice of a meeting, provides that the record date for determining who is entitled to notice of and to vote at a meeting (if not fixed by the directors or the bylaws) is the close of business on the day before the date the corporation first gives notice to shareholders of the meeting.

After a record date is fixed, if a new record date subsequently is or must be fixed under section 7.07, section 7.05 requires that new notice be given to the persons who are shareholders as of the new record date, and section 7.25 requires that a quorum be reestablished for that meeting.

B. SHAREHOLDER VOTING

§ 1.40. Act Definitions

In this Act, unless otherwise specified:

> "Voting power" means the current power to vote in the election of directors.

Official Comment

Application of the definition of "voting power" turns on whether the relevant shares carry the power to vote in the election of directors as of the time for voting on the relevant transaction. If shares carry the power to vote in the election of directors only under a certain contingency, as is often the case with preferred stock, the shares would not carry voting power within the meaning of section 1.40 unless the contingency has occurred, and then only during the period when the voting rights are in effect. Shares that carry the power to vote for any directors as of the time to vote on the relevant transaction have the current power to vote in the election of directors within the meaning of the definition, even if the shares do not carry the power to vote for all directors.

§ 7.21. Voting Entitlement of Shares

(a) Except as provided in subsections (b) and (d) or unless the articles of incorporation provide otherwise, each outstanding share, regardless of class or series, is entitled to one vote on each matter voted on at a shareholders' meeting. Only shares are entitled to vote.

(b) Shares of a corporation are not entitled to vote if they are owned by or otherwise belong to the corporation directly, or indirectly through an entity of which a majority of the voting power is held directly or indirectly by the corporation or which is otherwise controlled by the corporation.

Source: Model Bus. Corp. Act §§ 1.40, 7.21, 7.22, 7.25–28, 7.31 (2016). Copyright © 2016 by American Bar Association. Reprinted with permission.

Official Comment

Voting Power of Shares

Section 7.21(a) provides that each outstanding share, regardless of class or series, is entitled to one vote per share unless otherwise provided in the articles of incorporation. The articles of incorporation may provide for multiple or fractional votes per share and may provide that some classes or series of shares are nonvoting on some or all matters, or that some classes or series have a single vote per share or different multiple or fractional votes per share, or that some classes or series constitute one or more separate voting groups and are entitled to vote separately on the matter. To reflect the possibility that shares may have multiple or fractional votes per share, the provisions relating to quorums, voting, and similar matters in the Act are phrased in terms of votes represented by shares.

Voting Power of Nonshareholders

Under the last sentence of section 7.21(a), the power to vote may only be vested in shares. For example, bondholders may not be given the direct power to vote under the Act. They may, however, be given the power to vote by issuing them special classes or series of shares.

Circular Holdings

The purpose of the prohibition in section 7.21(b) is to prevent a board of directors or management from using a corporate investment to perpetuate itself in power. While shares acquired by a corporation cease to be outstanding under section 6.31, except as provided in that section, and therefore are not entitled to vote, other arrangements may be devised seeking to obtain the benefits of ownership without actually acquiring the shares at all or not acquiring the shares at the time the right to vote is determined. The concept of shares that "otherwise belong to" is included in addition to "owned by" to ensure that courts will have the flexibility to apply public policy considerations to arrangements under which shares are not technically "owned," or under which shares may or will be owned at a later time, but which have a similar effect. For example, if the corporation or a controlled entity has entered into a forward purchase contract for shares with the right to vote or direct the vote of the shares, a court could find that the shares belong to the corporation and are not entitled to be voted under section 7.21. Similarly, if the voting power is exercised by someone acting on behalf of the corporation or by a member of management of the corporation, a court could find that the shares otherwise belong to the corporation, and are not entitled to vote under section 7.21.

§ 7.22. Proxies

(a) A shareholder may vote the shareholder's shares in person or by proxy.

(b) A shareholder, or the shareholder's agent or attorney-in-fact, may appoint a proxy to vote or otherwise act for the shareholder by signing an appointment form, or by an electronic transmission. An electronic transmission must contain or be accompanied by information from which the recipient can determine the date of the transmission and that the transmission was authorized by the sender or the sender's agent or attorney-in-fact.

(c) An appointment of a proxy is effective when a signed appointment form or an electronic transmission of the appointment is received by the inspector of election or the officer or agent of the corporation authorized to count votes. An appointment is valid for the term provided in the appointment form, and, if no term is provided, is valid for 11 months unless the appointment is irrevocable under subsection (d).

(d) An appointment of a proxy is revocable unless the appointment form or electronic transmission states that it is irrevocable and the appointment is coupled with an interest. Appointments coupled with an interest include the appointment of:

    (1) a pledgee;

    (2) a person who purchased or agreed to purchase the shares;

    (3) a creditor of the corporation who extended it credit under terms requiring the appointment;

    (4) an employee of the corporation whose employment contract requires the appointment; or

    (5) a party to a voting agreement created under section 7.31.

(e) [...]

(f) An appointment made irrevocable under subsection (d) is revoked when the interest with which it is coupled is extinguished.

Official Comment

Nomenclature

The word "proxy" is often used ambiguously, sometimes referring to the grant of authority to vote, sometimes to the document granting the authority, and sometimes to the person to whom the authority is granted. In the Act, the word "proxy" is used only in the last sense; the terms "proxy appointment," "appointment form" and "electronic transmission" are used to describe the document or communication appointing the proxy; and the word "appointment" is used to describe the grant of authority to vote.

Duration of Appointment

An appointment form that contains no expiration date is valid for 11 months unless it is irrevocable. This ensures that in the normal course a new appointment will be solicited at least once every 12 months. An appointment form may validly specify its term if the parties agree, which may be longer or shorter than 11 months. An irrevocable appointment is valid for so long as it is irrevocable unless it terminates earlier in accordance with its terms.

The appointment of a proxy is essentially the appointment of an agent and is revocable in accordance with the principles of agency law unless it is "coupled with an interest." An appointment may be revoked either expressly or by implication, as when a shareholder later signs a second appointment form inconsistent with an earlier one, or attends the meeting in person and seeks to vote on the shareholder's own behalf.

Irrevocable Appointment of Proxies

Section 7.22(d) deals with the irrevocable appointment of a proxy. The general test adopted is the common law test that all appointments are revocable unless "coupled with an interest." Section 7.22(d) provides considerable certainty as it describes several accepted forms of relationship as examples of "proxies coupled with an interest." These examples are not exhaustive and other arrangements may also be "coupled with an interest."

Section 7.22(f) provides that an irrevocable appointment is revoked when the interest with which it was coupled is extinguished—for example, by repayment of the loan or release of the pledge.

§ 1.40. Act Definitions

In this Act, unless otherwise specified:

> "Voting group" means all shares of one or more classes or series that under the articles of incorporation or this Act are entitled to vote and be counted together collectively on a matter at a meeting of shareholders. All shares entitled by the articles of incorporation or this Act to vote generally on the matter are for that purpose a single voting group.

Official Comment

Section 1.40 defines "voting group" for purposes of the Act as a matter of convenient reference. When the definition refers to shares entitled to vote "generally" on a matter, it signifies all shares entitled to vote together on the matter by the articles of incorporation or the Act, regardless of whether they also have the right to be counted or tabulated separately. "Voting groups" are thus the basic units of collective voting by shareholders, and voting by voting groups may provide essential protection to one or more classes or series of shares against actions that are detrimental to the rights or interests of that class or series.

The determination of which shares form part of a single voting group must be made from the provisions of the articles of incorporation and of the Act. In a few instances under the Act, the board of directors may establish the right to vote by voting groups. On most matters to be voted on by shareholders, only a single voting group, consisting of a class of voting or common shares, will be involved, and action on such a matter is effective when approved by that voting group pursuant to section 7.25. In other circumstances, the vote of multiple groups may be required.

§ 7.25. Quorum and Voting Requirements for Voting Groups

(a) Shares entitled to vote as a separate voting group may take action on a matter at a meeting only if a quorum of those shares exists with respect to that matter. Unless the articles of incorporation provide otherwise, shares representing a majority of the votes entitled to be cast on the matter by the voting group constitutes a quorum of that voting group for action on that matter. Whenever this Act requires a particular quorum for a specified action, the articles of incorporation may not provide for a lower quorum.

(b) Once a share is represented for any purpose at a meeting, it is deemed present for quorum purposes for the remainder of the meeting and for any adjournment of that meeting unless a new record date is or must be fixed for that adjourned meeting.

(c) If a quorum exists, action on a matter (other than the election of directors) by a voting group is approved if the votes cast within the voting group favoring the action exceed the votes cast opposing the action, unless the articles of incorporation require a greater number of affirmative votes.

(d) An amendment of the articles of incorporation adding, changing, or deleting a quorum or voting requirement for a voting group greater than specified in subsection (a) or (c) is governed by section 7.27.

(e) The election of directors is governed by section 7.28.

(f) Whenever a provision of this Act provides for voting of classes or series as separate voting groups, the rules provided in section 10.04(c) for amendments of the articles of incorporation apply to that provision.

Official Comment

Section 7.25 establishes general quorum and voting requirements for voting groups for purposes of the Act. As defined in section 1.40, a "voting group" consists of all shares of one or more classes or series that under the articles of incorporation or the Act are entitled to vote and be counted together collectively on a matter. Shares entitled to vote "generally" on a matter (that is, all shares entitled to vote on the matter by the articles of incorporation or the Act that do not expressly have the right to be counted separately) are a single voting group. On most matters coming before shareholders' meetings, only a single voting group, consisting of a class of voting shares, will be involved, and action on such a matter is effective when approved by that voting group pursuant to section 7.25.

Section 7.25 covers quorum and voting requirements for all actions by the shareholders of a corporation with a single class of voting shares. It also covers quorum and voting requirements for a matter on which only a class or series of shares is entitled to vote under the articles of incorporation, for example, when a class with preferential rights may vote to elect directors because of a default in the payment of dividends (a vote which is often described as a "class vote"). Finally, section 7.25 also covers quorum and voting requirements for a matter on which both common and preferred shares or separate classes or series of common or preferred shares are entitled to vote, either together as a single voting group under the articles of incorporation or separately as two or more voting groups under either the articles of incorporation or the Act.

Determination of Voting Groups under the Act

Under the Act, classes or series of shares are generally not entitled to vote separately by voting group except to the extent specifically authorized by the articles of incorporation. But sections 9.21, 9.32, 10.04, and 11.04 of the Act grant classes or series of shares the right to vote separately when fundamental changes are proposed that may adversely affect that class or series.

Section 10.04(c) further provides that when two or more classes or series are affected by an amendment covered by section 10.04 in essentially the same way, the classes or series are grouped together and must vote as a single voting group rather than as multiple voting groups on the matter, unless otherwise provided in the articles of incorporation or required by the board of directors. Section 7.25(f) provides that the group voting rule of section 10.04(c), including the ability to vary that rule in the articles of incorporation or by action of the board of directors, also applies to the group voting provisions in sections 9.21, 9.32, and 11.04. Under the Act even a class or series of shares that is expressly described as nonvoting under the articles of incorporation may be entitled to vote separately on an amendment to the articles of incorporation that affects the class or series in a designated way.

In addition to the provisions of the Act, separate voting by voting group may be authorized by the articles of incorporation (except that the statutory privilege of voting by separate voting groups cannot be diluted or reduced). On some matters, the board of directors may condition its submission of matters to shareholders on their approval by specific voting groups designated by the board of directors. Sections 7.25 and 7.26 establish the mechanics by which all voting by single or multiple voting groups is carried out.

Quorum and Voting Requirements in General

A corporation's determination of the voting groups entitled to vote, and the quorum and voting requirements applicable to that determination, should be determined separately for each matter coming before a meeting. As a result, different quorum and voting requirements may be applicable to different portions of a meeting, depending on the matter being considered. In the normal case where only a single voting group is entitled to vote on all matters coming before a meeting of shareholders, a single quorum and voting requirement will usually be applicable to the entire meeting. To reflect the possibility that shares may have multiple or fractional votes per share, the provisions relating to quorums are phrased in terms of votes represented by shares.

Quorum Requirements for Action by Voting Group

Under Section 7.25(b), once a share is present at a meeting, it is deemed present for quorum purposes throughout the meeting. Thus, a voting group may continue to act despite the withdrawal of persons having the power to vote one or more shares.

The shares owned by a shareholder who comes to the meeting to object on grounds of lack of notice are considered present for purposes of determining the presence of a quorum. Similarly, shares owned by a shareholder who attends a meeting solely for purposes of raising the objection that a quorum is not present are considered present for purposes of determining the presence of a quorum. Attendance at a meeting, however, does not constitute a waiver of other objections to the meeting such as the lack of notice.

Voting Requirements for Approval by Voting Group

Section 7.25(c) provides that an action (other than the election of directors, which is governed by section 7.28) is approved by a voting group at a meeting at which a quorum is present if the votes cast in favor of the action exceed the votes cast opposing the action, unless the articles of incorporation require a greater number of votes. This default rule differs from a formulation appearing in some state statutes that an action is approved at a meeting at which a quorum is present if it receives the affirmative vote of a majority of the shares represented at that meeting. That formulation in effect treats abstentions as negative votes; the Act treats them truly as abstentions. For example, if a corporation (that has not, through the articles of incorporation, modified quorum and voting requirements) has 1,000 shares of a single class outstanding, each share entitled to cast one vote, a quorum consists of 501 shares; if 600 shares are represented at the meeting and the vote on a proposed action is 280 in favor, 225 opposed, and 95 abstaining, the action would not be approved in a state following the formulation that treats abstentions as negative votes because fewer than a majority of the 600 shares attending voted in favor of the action. Under section 7.25(c) the action would be approved and not be defeated by the 95 abstaining votes.

Modification of Standard Requirements

The articles of incorporation may modify the quorum and voting requirements of section 7.25 for a single voting group or for all voting groups entitled to vote on any matter. The articles of incorporation may increase the quorum and voting requirements to any extent desired up to and including unanimity, subject to section 7.27. They may also require that shares of different classes or series are entitled to vote separately or together on specific issues or provide that actions are approved only if they receive the favorable vote of a majority of the shares of a voting group present at a meeting at which a quorum is present. The articles may also decrease the quorum requirement as desired, subject to section 7.25(a) and section 7.27.

§ 7.26. Action by Single and Multiple Voting Groups

(a) If the articles of incorporation or this Act provide for voting by a single voting group on a matter, action on that matter is taken when voted upon by that voting group as provided in section 7.25.

(b) If the articles of incorporation or this Act provide for voting by two or more voting groups on a matter, action on that matter is taken only when voted upon by each of those voting groups counted separately as provided in section 7.25. Action may be taken by different voting groups on a matter at different times.

Official Comment

Section 7.26(a) provides that when a matter is to be voted upon by a single voting group, action is taken when the voting group votes upon the action as provided in section 7.25. In most instances, a single voting group will consist of all the shares of the class or classes or series entitled to vote by the articles of incorporation. Voting by two or more voting groups as contemplated by section 7.26(b) is the exceptional case.

Implicit in section 7.26(b) are the concepts that (i) different quorum and voting requirements may be applicable to different matters considered at a single meeting and (ii) different quorum and voting requirements may be applicable to different voting groups voting on the same matter. Each group entitled to vote must independently meet the quorum and voting requirements established by section 7.25. If a quorum is present for one or more voting groups but not for all voting groups, section 7.26(b) provides that the voting groups for which a quorum is present may vote upon the matter, even though their vote alone will not be sufficient for the matter to be approved.

A single meeting, furthermore, may consider matters on which action by several voting groups is required and also matters on which only a single voting group may act. Action may be taken on the matters on which the single voting group may act even though no quorum is present to take action on other matters. For example, in a corporation with one class of nonvoting shares with preferential rights ("preferred shares") and one class of general voting shares without preferential rights ("common shares"), a matter to be considered at the annual meeting might be a proposed amendment to the articles of incorporation that reduces the cumulative dividend right of the preferred shares (a matter on which the preferred shares have a statutory right to vote as a separate voting group). Other matters to be considered might include the election of directors and the ratification of the appointment of an auditor, both matters on which the preferred shares may have no vote. If a quorum of the voting group consisting of the common shares but no quorum of the voting group consisting of the preferred shares is present, the common shares may proceed to elect directors and ratify the appointment of the auditor. The common shares voting group may also vote to approve the proposed amendment to the articles of incorporation, but that amendment will not be approved until the preferred shares voting group also votes to approve the amendment, which could occur at a different time.

Normally, each class or series of shares will participate in only a single voting group. But because holders of shares entitled by the articles of incorporation to vote generally on a matter are always entitled to vote in the voting group consisting of the general voting shares, in some instances classes or series of shares may be entitled to be counted in two voting groups. This will occur whenever a class or series of shares entitled to vote generally on a matter under the articles of incorporation is affected by the matter in a way that gives rise to the right to have its vote counted separately as an independent voting group under the Act. For example, assume that corporation Y has outstanding one class of common shares, 500 shares issued and outstanding, and one class of preferred shares, 100 shares issued and outstanding, that also have full voting rights under the articles of incorporation, *i.e.*, the preferred may vote for election of directors and on all other matters on which common may vote. The preferred and the common therefore are part of the general voting group. The directors propose to amend the articles of incorporation to change the preferential dividend rights of the preferred from cumulative to noncumulative. All shares are present at the meeting and they divide as follows on the proposal to adopt the amendment.

Yes	Common	230
	Preferred	80
No	Common	270
	Preferred	20

Both the preferred and the common are entitled to vote on the amendment to the articles of incorporation because they are part of a general voting group pursuant to the articles. But the vote of the preferred is also entitled to be counted separately on the proposal by section 10.04(a)(3). The result is that the proposal passes by a vote of 310 to 290 in the voting group consisting of the shares entitled to vote generally and 80 to 20 in the voting group consisting solely of the preferred shares.

In this situation, in the absence of a special quorum requirement, a meeting could approve the proposal to amend the articles of incorporation if—and only if—a quorum of each voting group is present, *i.e.*, at least 51 shares of preferred and 301 shares of common and preferred were represented at the meeting.

§ 7.27. Modifying Quorum or Voting Requirements

An amendment to the articles of incorporation that adds, changes, or deletes a quorum or voting requirement shall meet the same quorum requirement and be adopted by the same vote and voting groups required to take action under the quorum and voting requirements then in effect or proposed to be adopted, whichever is greater.

Official Comment

Section 7.27 permits the articles of incorporation to change the quorum or voting requirements for approval of an action by shareholders up to any desired amount so long as the change is adopted in accordance with the requirements of section 7.27. For example, a supermajority provision that requires an 80% affirmative vote of all eligible votes of a voting group present at the meeting may not be removed from the articles of incorporation or reduced in any way except by an 80% affirmative vote. If the 80% requirement is coupled with a quorum requirement for a voting group that shares representing two-thirds of the total votes must be present in person or by proxy, both the 80% voting requirement and the two-thirds quorum requirement are immune from reduction except at a meeting of the voting group at which the two- thirds quorum requirement is met and the reduction is approved by an 80% affirmative vote. If the proposal is to increase the 80% voting require-ment to 90%, that proposal must be approved by a 90% affirmative vote at a meeting of the voting group at which the two-thirds quorum requirement is met; if the proposal is to increase the two-thirds quorum requirement to three-quarters without changing the 80% voting requirement, that proposal must be approved by an 80% affirmative vote at a meeting of the voting group at which a three-quarters quorum requirement is met.

§ 7.28. Voting for Directors; Cumulative Voting

(a) Unless otherwise provided in the articles of incorporation, directors are elected by a plurality of the votes cast by the shares entitled to vote in the election at a meeting at which a quorum is present.

(b) Shareholders do not have a right to cumulate their votes for directors unless the articles of incorporation so provide.

(c) A statement included in the articles of incorporation that "[all] [a desig-nated voting group of] shareholders are entitled to cumulate their votes for directors" (or words of similar import) means that the shareholders designated are entitled to multiply the number of votes they are entitled to cast by the number of directors for whom they are entitled to vote and cast the product for a single candidate or distribute the product among two or more candidates.

Official Comment

As used in section 7.28(a), election by a "plurality" means that the individuals with the largest number of votes are elected as directors up to the maximum number of directors to be chosen at the election. In elections in which several factions are competing within a voting group, an individual may be elected with votes of fewer than a majority of the votes cast. The articles of incorporation of the corporation may, however, provide a different vote requirement for the election of directors and the bylaws may also do so to the extent provided in section 10.22.

The entire board of directors may be elected by a single voting group or the articles of incorporation may provide that different voting groups are entitled to elect a designated number or fraction of the board of directors. Elections are contested only within specific voting groups.

Under section 7.28(b), each corporation may determine whether to elect its directors by cumulative voting. If directors are elected by different voting groups, the articles of incorporation may provide that specified voting groups are entitled to vote cumulatively while others are not.

Cumulative voting affects the manner in which votes may be cast by shares participating in the election but does not affect the plurality principle set forth in section 7.28(a).

If a corporation has determined to elect directors by cumulative voting, such directors may not be elected by written consent unless that consent is unanimous.

Section 7.28(c) describes the mechanics of cumulative voting. By casting all of the shareholder's votes for a single candidate or a limited number of candidates, a minority shareholder's voting power with respect to a given candidate can be increased, and such shareholder may be able to elect one or more directors.

§ 7.31. Voting Agreements

(a) Two or more shareholders may provide for the manner in which they will vote their shares by signing an agreement for that purpose. A voting agreement created under this section is not subject to the provisions of section 7.30.

(b) A voting agreement created under this section is specifically enforceable.

Official Comment

Section 7.31(a) explicitly recognizes agreements among two or more shareholders as to the voting of shares and makes clear that these agreements are not subject to the rules relating to a voting trust. The only formal requirements are that they be in writing and signed by all the participating shareholders. In other respects, their validity is to be judged like any other contract.

A voting agreement may provide its own enforcement mechanism, as by the appointment of a proxy to vote all shares subject to the agreement; the appointment may be made irrevocable under section 7.22. If no enforcement mechanism is provided, a court may order specific enforcement of the agreement and order the votes cast as the agreement contemplates. Section 7.31(b) recognizes that damages are not likely to be an appropriate remedy for breach of a voting agreement.

C. BOOKS, RECORDS & REPORTS

§ 16.01. Corporate Records

(a) A corporation shall maintain the following records:

   (1) its articles of incorporation as currently in effect;

   (2) any notices to shareholders referred to in section 1.20(k)(5) specifying facts on which a filed document is dependent if those facts are not included in the articles of incorporation or otherwise available as specified in section 1.20(k)(5);

   (3) its bylaws as currently in effect;

   (4) all written communications within the past three years to shareholders generally;

   (5) minutes of all meetings of, and records of all actions taken without a meeting by, its shareholders, its board of directors, and board committees established under section 8.25;

   (6) a list of the names and business addresses of its current directors and officers; and

   (7) its most recent annual report delivered to the secretary of state under section 16.21.

(b) A corporation shall maintain all annual financial statements prepared for the corporation for its last three fiscal years (or such shorter period of existence) and any audit or other reports with respect to such financial statements.

(c) A corporation shall maintain accounting records in a form that permits preparation of its financial statements.

(d) A corporation shall maintain a record of its current shareholders in alphabetical order by class or series of shares showing the address of, and the number and class or series of shares held by, each shareholder.

Source: Model Bus. Corp. Act §§ 16.01, 16.02, 16.05, 16.20 (2016). Copyright © 2016 by American Bar Association. Reprinted with permission.

Official Comment

Records to be Maintained

Section 16.01(a) requires certain basic records to be maintained by the corporation. The Act does not generally specify how records must be maintained (other than in a manner so that they may be made available for inspection within a reasonable time), where they must be located or, with the exception of section 16.02(a), where they must be available. They may be maintained in one or more offices within or without the state and in some cases, such as shareholder records, may be maintained by agents of the corporation; indeed, in the case of records in intangible form, it may be impossible to determine where they are located.

Minutes and Related Documents

Section 16.01(a) does not address the amount of detail that should appear in minutes or written actions. Minutes of meetings customarily include the formalities of notice, the time and place of the meeting, those in attendance, and the results of any votes. Minutes of meetings and written actions without a meeting show formal action taken. The extent to which further detail is included is a matter of judgment which may depend upon the circumstances.

Financial Statements and Accounting Records

The Act does not provide normative standards for the financial statements and accounting records to be prepared or maintained. The financial statements to be maintained under section 16.01(b) are those that the corporation prepares in the operation of its business, including in response to third party requirements. The form of the financial statements prepared by a corporation depends to some extent on the nature and complexity of the corporation's business and third party requirements such as those governing the preparation and filing of tax returns with applicable tax authorities. To accommodate the needs of the many different types of business corporations that may be subject to these provisions, including closely held corporations, the Act does not require that the corporation prepare and maintain financial statements on the basis of generally accepted accounting principles ("GAAP") if it is not otherwise required to prepare GAAP financial statements. The Act does not define what accounting records must be maintained or mandate how long they must be maintained. The accounting records to be maintained under section 16.01(c) depend upon the form of the corporation's financial statements. For example, annual tax returns filed with the relevant taxing authorities may be the only annual financial statements prepared by small businesses operating on a cash basis and, in those instances, the requisite accounting records to be maintained might consist of only a check register, vouchers and receipts.

Shareholders' Lists

Section 16.01(d) requires the corporation to maintain such records of its shareholders as will permit it to compile a list of current shareholders when required. These records may vary from stubs from which certificates have been detached in the case of corporations with a few shareholders to elaborate electronic data in the case of large corporations whose shares are publicly traded.

§ 16.02. Inspection Rights Of Shareholders

(a) A shareholder of a corporation is entitled to inspect and copy, during regular business hours at the corporation's principal office, any of the records of the corporation described in section 16.01(a), excluding minutes of meetings of, and records of actions taken without a meeting by, the corporation's board of directors and board committees established under section 8.25, if the shareholder gives the corporation a signed written notice of the shareholder's demand at least five business days before the date on which the shareholder wishes to inspect and copy.

(b) A shareholder of a corporation is entitled to inspect and copy, during regular business hours at a reasonable location specified by the corporation, any of the following records of the corporation if the shareholder meets the requirements of subsection (c) and gives the corporation a signed written notice of the shareholder's demand at least five business days before the date on which the shareholder wishes to inspect and copy:

   (1) the financial statements of the corporation maintained in accordance with section 16.01(b);

   (2) accounting records of the corporation;

   (3) excerpts from minutes of any meeting of, or records of any actions taken without a meeting by, the corporation's board of directors and board committees maintained in accordance with section 16.01(a); and

   (4) the record of shareholders maintained in accordance with section 16.01(d).

(c) A shareholder may inspect and copy the records described in subsection (b) only if:

   (1) the shareholder's demand is made in good faith and for a proper purpose;

   (2) the shareholder's demand describes with reasonable particularity the shareholder's purpose and the records the shareholder desires to inspect; and

(3) the records are directly connected with the shareholder's purpose.

(d) The corporation may impose reasonable restrictions on the confidentiality, use or distribution of records described in subsection (b).

(e) [...]

(f) The right of inspection granted by this section may not be abolished or limited by a corporation's articles of incorporation or bylaws.

Official Comment

Section 16.02(a)

Under section 16.02(a), each shareholder is entitled to inspect all documents that deal with the shareholder's interest in the corporation. The right to inspection includes the right to make copies, as further described in section 16.03. Although some of these documents may also be a matter of public record in the office of the secretary of state, a shareholder should not be compelled to go to a public office that may be physically distant to examine the basic documents relating to the corporation. The "principal office" of the corporation is defined in section 1.40 to be the location of the executive offices of the corporation at its address as set forth by the corporation in its annual report required by section 16.21.

Section 16.02(b)

In contrast to the right to inspect minutes of meetings of, and written actions taken without a meeting by, shareholders, a shareholder is entitled to inspect only excerpts of meetings of, and records of written actions taken by, the board of directors and board committees related to the purpose of the inspection. A shareholder is entitled to inspect the record of shareholders under section 16.02(b) without regard to the size or value of the shareholder's holding. This right is independent of the right to inspect a shareholders' list under section 7.20.

Section 16.02(c)

Section 16.02(c) permits inspection of the financial statements and records described in section 16.02(b) by a shareholder only if the demand is made in good faith and for a "proper purpose." Although not defined in the Act, "proper purpose" under section 16.02(c) has been defined in case law to involve a purpose that is reasonably relevant to the demanding shareholder's interest as a shareholder.

Section 16.02(c) requires that a shareholder designate "with reasonable particularity" the purpose for the demand and the records he or she desires to inspect. Also, the records demanded must be "directly connected" with that purpose. If disputed by the corporation, the "connection" of the records to the shareholder's purpose may be determined by a court's examination of the records.

Section 16.02(d)

The reasonable restrictions on the confidentiality, use or distribution of financial statements and records permitted by section 16.02(d) allow for the protection of confidential or proprietary information in the corporation's records or sensitive matters that might be disclosed in a shareholder inspection. Such restrictions might include, for example, requiring the demanding shareholder to sign a confidentiality and use agreement.

Sections 16.02(f)

The prohibition in section 16.02(f) does not apply to a shareholder agreement permissible under section 7.32. No inference should be drawn from the prohibition in section 16.02(f) as to whether other, unrelated sections of the Act may be modified by provisions in the articles of incorporation or bylaws.

§ 16.05. Inspection Rights Of Directors

(a) A director of a corporation is entitled to inspect and copy the books, records and documents of the corporation at any reasonable time to the extent reasonably related to the performance of the director's duties as a director, including duties as a member of a board committee, but not for any other purpose or in any manner that would violate any duty to the corporation.

(b) The [name or describe court] may order inspection and copying of the books, records and documents at the corporation's expense, upon application of a director who has been refused such inspection rights, unless the corporation establishes that the director is not entitled to such inspection rights. The court shall dispose of an application under this subsection on an expedited basis.

Official Comment

The purpose of section 16.05(a) is to confirm the principle that a director always is entitled to inspect books, records and documents to the extent reasonably related to the performance of the director's duties, provided that the requested inspection is not for an improper purpose and the director's use of the information obtained would not violate any duty to the corporation. In addition, section 16.05 sets forth a remedy for the director in circumstances where the corporation improperly denies the right of inspection.

Section 16.05(b) provides for a court order on an expedited basis because there is a presumption that significant latitude and discretion should be granted to the director, and the corporation has the burden of establishing that the director is not entitled to inspection of the documents requested. There may be circumstances where the director's inspection right might be denied, for example, when it would be contrary to the interest of the corporation because of adversity with the director, and the courts have broad discretion to address these circumstances.

§ 16.20. Financial Statements for Shareholders

(a) Upon the written request of a shareholder, a corporation shall deliver or make available to such requesting shareholder by posting on its website or by other generally recognized means annual financial statements for the most recent fiscal year of the corporation for which annual financial statements have been prepared for the corporation. If financial statements have been prepared for the corporation on the basis of generally accepted accounting principles for such specified period, the corporation shall deliver or make available such financial statements to the requesting shareholder. If the annual financial statements to be delivered or made available to the requesting shareholder are audited or otherwise reported upon by a public accountant, the report shall also be delivered or made available to the requesting shareholder.

Official Comment

Although section 16.20 requires a corporation, upon the written request of a shareholder, to deliver or make available annual financial statements that have been prepared, it does not require a corporation to prepare financial statements. This recognizes that many small, closely held corporations do not regularly prepare formal financial statements unless required by banks, suppliers or other third parties.

Section 16.20 does not limit the financial statements to be delivered or made available to shareholders to financial statements prepared on the basis of generally accepted accounting principles. Many small corporations have never prepared financial statements on the basis of GAAP. "Cash basis" financial statements (often used in preparing the tax returns of small corporations) do not comply with GAAP. Smaller corporations that keep accrual basis records, and file their federal income tax returns on that basis, frequently do not make the adjustments that may be required to present their financial statements on a GAAP basis.

Failure to comply with the requirements of section 16.20 does not adversely affect the existence or good standing of the corporation. Rather, failure to comply gives an aggrieved shareholder rights to compel compliance or to obtain damages, if they can be established, under general principles of law.

A shareholder may also seek access to the financial statements of the corporation through the inspection rights established in section 16.02.

CHAPTER 16

GOVERNING CORPORATIONS: THE ROLE OF DIRECTORS & OFFICERS

While shareholders are the owners of corporations, the power to manage a corporation resides with the directors and officers.

A. BOARD OF DIRECTORS & ELECTIONS

§ 8.01. Requirement For And Functions Of Board Of Directors

(a) Except as may be provided in an agreement authorized under section 7.32, each corporation shall have a board of directors.

(b) Except as may be provided in an agreement authorized under section 7.32, and subject to any limitation in the articles of incorporation permitted by section 2.02(b), all corporate powers shall be exercised by or under the authority of the board of directors, and the business and affairs of the corporation shall be managed by or under the direction, and subject to the oversight, of the board of directors.

Official Comment

As provided in Section 8.01(a), the board of directors is the traditional form of governance, but the shareholders of a corporation may, in an agreement that satisfies the requirements of section 7.32, dispense with a board of directors and structure the corporation's management and governance to address specific needs of the enterprise.

In section 8.01(b), the phrase "by or under the direction, and subject to the oversight, of" encompasses the varying functions of boards of directors of different corporations. In some corporations, particularly closely held

Source: Model Bus. Corp. Act §§ 8.01–06, 8.08, 8.11 (2016). Copyright © 2016 by American Bar Association. Reprinted with permission.

corporations, the board of directors may be involved in the day-to-day business and affairs and it may be reasonable to describe management as being "by" the board of directors. In many other corporations, including most public corporations, the business and affairs are managed "under the direction, and subject to the oversight, of" the board of directors, and operational management is delegated to executive officers and other professional managers.

Section 8.01(b) often is considered to constitute the heart of the governance provisions of the Act. Giving the board of directors the power, and the responsibility, to oversee and direct the business of the corporation permits separation of ownership of the corporation from control of its oversight and direction. The Act's broad grant of authority and responsibility to the board of directors constitutes the rejection of the concept that the directors, having been elected by the shareholders, merely serve as agents to implement the will of the shareholders.

Section 8.01(b), in providing for corporate powers to be exercised under the direction of the board of directors, allows the board of directors to delegate to appropriate officers, employees or agents of the corporation authority to exercise powers and perform functions not required by law to be exercised or performed by the board of directors itself. Although such delegation does not relieve the board of directors from its responsibility to oversee the business and affairs of the corporation, directors are not personally responsible for actions or omissions of officers, employees, or agents of the corporation so long as the directors have relied reasonably and in good faith upon these officers, employees, or agents.

The scope of the board's oversight responsibility will vary depending on the nature of the corporation and its business. At least for public corporations, the board's responsibilities generally include oversight of the following:

- business performance, plans and strategy;
- management's assessment of major risks to which the corporation is or may be exposed;
- the performance and compensation of executive officers;
- policies and practices to foster the corporation's compliance with law and ethical conduct;
- management's preparation of the corporation's financial statements;
- management's design and assessment of effectiveness of the corporation's internal controls;
- plans for the succession of the chief executive officer and other executive officers;
- the composition of the board and of board committees; and
- whether the corporation has information and reporting systems in place to provide directors with appropriate information in a timely manner.

In giving attention to the composition of the board, directors of public corporations should consider the corporation's processes for obtaining and evaluating the views of shareholders, including processes for considering individuals proposed by shareholders as nominees for election as directors. Directors of public corporations also should take into account the important role of independent directors. When ownership is separated from responsibility for oversight and direction, as is the case with public corporations, having nonmanagement independent directors who participate actively in the board's oversight functions increases the likelihood that actions taken by the board, if challenged, will be given deference by the courts. The listing standards of most public securities markets have requirements for independent directors to serve on boards; in many cases, they must constitute a majority of the board, and certain board committees must be composed entirely of independent directors. The listing standards have differing rules as to what constitutes an independent director. The Act does not attempt to define "independent director." Ordinarily, an independent director may not be a present or recent member of senior management and must be free of significant professional, financial or similar relationships with the corporation, and the director and members of the director's immediate family must be free of similar relationships with the corporation's senior management. Judgment is required to determine independence in light of the particular circumstances, subject to any specific requirements of a listing standard. The qualifications for disinterestedness required of directors for specific purposes under the Act are similar, but not necessarily identical, to those that are prerequisites to independence. For the requirements for a director to be considered disinterested and qualified to act in those specified situations. An individual who is an independent director may not be eligible to act in a particular case under those other provisions of the Act. Conversely, a director who is not independent (for example, a member of management) may be disinterested and qualified to act in a particular case.

Section 8.01(b) recognizes that the powers of the board of directors may be limited by express provisions in the articles of incorporation and in an agreement among all shareholders under section 7.32. In an agreement under section 7.32, board powers also may be assigned to others. Because all of the shareholders must approve a section 7.32 agreement, the only restriction on limiting or assigning board powers is that any limitation or assignment must be provided for in sections 7.32(a)(1) through (a)(7) or must not be contrary to public policy under section 7.32(a)(8). In contrast, as is provided in section 2.02(b)(2), any limitation on board powers in the articles of incorporation cannot be "inconsistent with law." As a result of this difference in standards, any such limitation under section 2.02 should not, for example, be inconsistent with requirements of section 8.30 regarding standards of conduct for directors or otherwise preclude the directors from fulfilling their duties to the corporation.

§ 8.02. Qualifications Of Directors

(a) The articles of incorporation or bylaws may prescribe qualifications for directors or for nominees for directors. Qualifications must be reasonable as applied to the corporation and be lawful.

(b) A requirement that is based on a past, prospective, or current action, or expression of opinion, by a nominee or director that could limit the ability of a nominee or director to discharge his or her duties as a director is not a permissible qualification under this section. Notwithstanding the foregoing, qualifications may include not being or having been subject to specified criminal, civil, or regulatory sanctions or not having been removed as a director by judicial action or for cause.

(c) A director need not be a resident of this state or a shareholder unless the articles of incorporation or bylaws so prescribe.

Official Comment

Some corporations have adopted qualifications for individuals to be directors or to be nominated as directors. One use of qualifications may be by closely held corporations, to ensure representation and voting power on the board of directors. Other provisions of the Act also are designed to accomplish these purposes.

Qualifications may apply to all board members or to a specified percentage or number of directors. An example of a qualification applying to fewer than all directors would be a requirement that at least two directors must have specified business or professional experience or a particular educational degree or background.

The purpose of section 8.02(a) is to permit qualifications that may benefit the corporation by enhancing the board's ability to perform its role effectively. However, this needs to be balanced against the risk that qualifications could be misused for entrenchment purposes by incumbents or for other improper purposes. To address these concerns, section 8.02(a) requires that qualifications must be reasonable as applied to the corporation and must be lawful. For example, a qualification that seeks to favor incumbent directors or distinguish between a director elected from the slate nominated by a corporation's board and a director elected as the result of being nominated by one or more shareholders, including under a bylaw adopted pursuant to section 2.06(c), would not ordinarily be reasonable and thus not ordinarily authorized by section 8.02(a). An example of a qualification that would not be lawful would be a requirement that is impermissibly discriminatory under the Civil Rights Act of 1964.

Scope of Permitted Qualifications

Examples of qualifications that may be permissible under section 8.02 are eligibility requirements based on residence, shareholdings, age, length of service, experience, expertise, and professional licenses or certifications.

Under section 8.02(b) a qualification that is based on a past, current, or prospective action, or expression of opinion, by a nominee or director that could limit the ability of a nominee or director to discharge his or her duties as a director is not a permissible qualification. The discharge of duties of a director is referenced in section 8.30. A requirement based on a director's having voted for or against, or expressed an intent to vote for or against, a particular type of resolution, such as a resolution in favor of or against a bylaw pursuant to section 2.06(c) or a resolution in favor of or against a shareholder rights plan, would be impermissible.

A shareholder agreement that meets the requirements of section 7.32 could override the terms of section 8.02, including with respect to the requirement of reasonableness in section 8.02(a) and the limitation on permitted qualifications in section 8.02(b).

§ 8.03. Number And Election Of Directors

(a) A board of directors shall consist of one or more individuals, with the number specified in or fixed in accordance with the articles of incorporation or bylaws.

(b) The number of directors may be increased or decreased from time to time by amendment to, or in the manner provided in, the articles of incorporation or bylaws.

(c) Directors are elected at the first annual shareholders' meeting and at each annual shareholders' meeting thereafter unless elected by written consent in lieu of an annual meeting as permitted by section 7.04 or unless their terms are staggered under section 8.06.

Official Comment

Number of Directors

Under section 8.03(a), the size of the board of directors may be fixed initially in one or more of the fundamental corporate documents, or the decision as to the size of the initial board of directors may be made thereafter in the manner authorized in those documents.

Changes in the Size of the Board of Directors

Section 8.03(b) provides a corporation with the freedom to design its articles of incorporation and bylaw provisions relating to the size of its board with a view to achieving the combination of flexibility for the board of directors and protection for shareholders that it deems appropriate. The articles of incorporation could provide for a specified number of directors or a board size within a range from a minimum to a maximum, or an unlimited size not fewer than one as determined by the board or the shareholders. If the shareholders or the board of directors want to change the specified size of the board, to change the range established for the size of the board or to change from a board size within a range or of unlimited size to a specified board size or vice versa, board of directors and shareholder action would be required to make those changes by amending the articles of incorporation. Alternatively, the bylaws could provide for a specified number of directors or a size within a stated range or unlimited size, with the number to be fixed by the board of directors. Any change would be made in the manner provided by the bylaws. The bylaws could permit amendment by the board of directors or the bylaws could require that any amendment, in whole or in part, be made only by the shareholders in accordance with section 10.20(a). Typically, the board of directors would be permitted to change the board size within the established range. If a corporation wishes to ensure that any change in the number of directors be approved by shareholders, then an appropriate restriction would have to be included in the articles of incorporation or bylaws.

The board's power to change the number of directors, like all other board powers, is subject to compliance with applicable standards governing director conduct. In particular, it may be inappropriate to change the size of the board for the primary purpose of maintaining control or defeating particular candidates for the board.

In many closely held corporations, shareholder approval for a change in the size of the board of directors may be readily accomplished if that is desired. In many closely held corporations a board of directors of a fixed size may be an essential part of a control arrangement. In these situations, an increase or decrease in the size of the board of directors by even a single member may significantly affect control. To maintain control arrangements dependent on a board of directors of a fixed size, the power of the board of directors to change its own size must be negated. This may be accomplished by fixing the size of the board of directors in the articles of incorporation or by expressly negating the power of the board of directors to change the size of the board, whether by amendment of the bylaws or otherwise.

§ 8.04. Election Of Directors By Certain Classes Or Series Of Shares

If the articles of incorporation or action by the board of directors pursuant to section 6.02 authorize dividing the shares into classes or series, the articles of incorporation may also authorize the election of all or a specified number of directors by the holders of one or more authorized classes or series of shares. A class or series (or multiple classes or series) of shares entitled to elect one or more directors is a separate voting group for purposes of the election of directors.

Official Comment

Provisions allowing separate classes or series of shares each to elect a specified number of directors are often used in corporations to effect an agreed upon allocation of control, for example, to ensure representation on the board of directors by particular shareholders by issuing to those shareholders a class or series of shares entitled to elect one or more directors. Each class or series (or multiple classes or series) entitled to elect separately one or more directors constitutes a separate voting group for this purpose, and the quorum and voting requirements must be separately met by each voting group as provided in sections 7.25, 7.26 and 7.28.

§ 8.05. Terms Of Directors Generally

(a) The terms of the initial directors of a corporation expire at the first shareholders' meeting at which directors are elected.

(b) The terms of all other directors expire at the next, or if their terms are staggered in accordance with section 8.06, at the applicable second or third, annual shareholders' meeting following their election, except to the extent (i) provided in section 10.22 if a bylaw electing to be governed by that section is in effect, or (ii) a shorter term is specified in the articles of incorporation in the event of a director nominee failing to receive a specified vote for election.

(c) A decrease in the number of directors does not shorten an incumbent director's term.

(d) The term of a director elected to fill a vacancy expires at the next shareholders' meeting at which directors are elected.

(e) Except to the extent otherwise provided in the articles of incorporation or under section 10.22 if a bylaw electing to be governed by that section is in effect, despite the expiration of a director's term, the director continues to serve until the director's successor is elected and qualifies or there is a decrease in the number of directors.

Official Comment

Section 8.05 provides for the annual election of directors at the annual shareholders' meeting with the single exception that terms may be staggered as permitted in section 8.06.

Under section 8.05(d), if terms are staggered, the term of a director elected to fill a vacant term with more than a year to run is shorter than the term of the director's predecessor. The board of directors may take appropriate steps, by designation of short terms or otherwise, to return the rotation of election of directors to the original staggered terms established or fixed by the articles of incorporation or bylaws.

Section 8.05(e), with two exceptions, provides for "holdover" directors so that directorships do not automatically become vacant at the expiration of their terms. This means that the power of the board of directors to act continues uninterrupted even if an annual shareholders' meeting is not held or the shareholders are deadlocked or otherwise do not elect directors at the meeting. The articles of incorporation may modify or eliminate this holdover concept. Also, if a bylaw is adopted invoking section 10.22, the effect will be that directors who are elected by a plurality vote but receive more votes against than for their election will not hold over past the abbreviated 90-day term of office specified in section 10.22.

§ 8.06. Staggered Terms For Directors

The articles of incorporation may provide for staggering the terms of directors by dividing the total number of directors into two or three groups, with each group containing half or one-third of the total, as near as may be practicable. In that event, the terms of directors in the first group expire at the first annual shareholders' meeting after their election, the terms of the second group expire at the second annual shareholders' meeting after their election, and the terms of the third group, if any, expire at the third annual shareholders' meeting after their election. At each annual shareholders' meeting held thereafter, directors shall be elected for a term of two years or three years, as the case may be, to succeed those whose terms expire.

Official Comment

Section 8.06 permits the practice of "classifying" the board or "staggering" the terms of directors. The requirement that these provisions be in the articles of incorporation ensures that, unless included in the corporation's original articles, a staggered board may only be implemented with shareholder approval.

§ 8.08. Removal Of Directors By Shareholders

(a) The shareholders may remove one or more directors with or without cause unless the articles of incorporation provide that directors may be removed only for cause.

(b) If a director is elected by a voting group of shareholders, only the shareholders of that voting group may participate in the vote to remove that director.

(c) A director may be removed if the number of votes cast to remove exceeds the number of votes cast not to remove the director, except to the extent the articles of incorporation or bylaws require a greater number; provided that if cumulative voting is authorized, a director may not be removed if, in the case of a meeting, the number of votes sufficient to elect the director under cumulative voting is voted against removal and, if action is taken by less than unanimous written consent, voting shareholders entitled to the number of votes sufficient to elect the director under cumulative voting do not consent to the removal.

(d) A director may be removed by the shareholders only at a meeting called for the purpose of removing the director and the meeting notice must state that removal of the director is a purpose of the meeting.

Official Comment

Section 8.08(a) provides a default rule that shareholders have the power to change the directors at will. However, that section permits the power to remove directors without cause to be eliminated by a provision in the articles of incorporation. Section 8.08(c) assures that a minority faction with sufficient votes to guarantee the election of a director under cumulative voting will be able to protect that director from removal by the remaining shareholders. In computing whether a director elected by cumulative voting is protected from removal under that section, the votes should be counted as though (i) the vote to remove the director occurred in an election to elect the number of directors normally elected by the relevant voting group along with the director whose removal is sought, (ii) the number of votes cast cumulatively against removal had been cast for election of the director, and (iii) all votes cast for removal of the director had been cast cumulatively in an efficient pattern for the election of a sufficient number of candidates so as to deprive the director whose removal is being sought of the director's office.

Although sections 8.08(b) and (c) have specific requirements with respect to removal of directors elected by particular voting groups or by cumulative voting, such directors nevertheless may be removed by court proceeding under section 8.09. Section 8.08(d) acknowledges the seriousness of director removal by requiring the meeting notice to state that removal of specific directors will be proposed. Section 8.08(d) governs removal of directors at a meeting of shareholders, but does not preclude removal by means of shareholder action by written consent under section 7.04. Unless cumulative voting is authorized, and in the absence of a greater vote requirement in the articles of incorporation or bylaws, removal of a director by less than unanimous written consent would require that a majority of the outstanding shares of the relevant voting group consent to the removal.

§ 8.11. Compensation Of Directors

Unless the articles of incorporation or bylaws provide otherwise, the board of directors may fix the compensation of directors.

Official Comment

Section 8.11 reflects the view that director compensation is an appropriate function of the board of directors. Board action on directors' compensation and benefits is a director's conflicting interest transaction subject to chapter 8F.

B. MEETINGS & ACTION OF THE BOARD

§ 8.20. Meetings

(a) The board of directors may hold regular or special meetings in or out of this state.

(b) Unless restricted by the articles of incorporation or bylaws, any or all directors may participate in any meeting of the board of directors through the use of any means of communication by which all directors participating may simultaneously hear each other during the meeting. A director participating in a meeting by this means is deemed to be present in person at the meeting.

Official Comment

Section 8.20 provides flexibility with respect to holding meetings of directors. Under section 8.20, a meeting in which any or all of the directors participate through any means of communication that complies with section 8.20(b) will meet the statutory requirements. Depending on the nature of the matters to be considered at the meeting, however, a board of directors may wish to consider whether holding an in-person meeting at which some or all directors are physically present provides greater opportunity for interchange.

§ 8.21. Action Without Meeting

(a) Except to the extent that the articles of incorporation or bylaws require that action by the board of directors be taken at a meeting, action required or permitted by this Act to be taken by the board of directors may be taken without a meeting if each director signs a consent describing the action to be taken and delivers it to the corporation.

(b) Action taken under this section is the act of the board of directors when one or more consents signed by all the directors are delivered to the corporation. The consent may specify a later time as the time at which the action taken is to be effective. A director's consent may be withdrawn by a revocation signed by the director and delivered to the corporation before delivery to the corporation of unrevoked written consents signed by all the directors.

(c) A consent signed under this section has the effect of action taken at a meeting of the board of directors and may be described as such in any document.

Source: Model Bus. Corp. Act §§ 8.20–25 (2016). Copyright © 2016 by American Bar Association. Reprinted with permission.

Official Comment

Directors may take action by written consent without a meeting only when approval of an action is unanimous. Accordingly, if a director abstains, is recused or withholds consent on an action, the action could not be authorized by consent, and a meeting would need to be held for the action to be approved.

§ 8.22. Notice Of Meeting

(a) Unless the articles of incorporation or bylaws provide otherwise, regular meetings of the board of directors may be held without notice of the date, time, place, or purpose of the meeting.

(b) Unless the articles of incorporation or bylaws provide for a longer or shorter period, special meetings of the board of directors shall be preceded by at least two days' notice of the date, time, and place of the meeting. The notice need not describe the purpose of the special meeting unless required by the articles of incorporation or bylaws.

Official Comment

Unlike regular meetings of the board of directors, special meetings always require notice, the timing of which may be varied by the articles of incorporation or bylaws. The notice may be written, or oral if oral notice is reasonable in the circumstances. No statement of the purpose of any meeting of the board of directors is necessary in the notice unless required by the articles of incorporation or bylaws. These requirements differ from the requirements applicable to meetings of shareholders because of the fundamental differences in the roles and involvement of directors and shareholders.

§ 8.23. Waiver Of Notice

(a) A director may waive any notice required by this Act, the articles of incorporation or the bylaws before or after the date and time stated in the notice. Except as provided by subsection (b), the waiver must be in writing, signed by the director entitled to the notice and delivered to the corporation for filing by the corporation with the minutes or corporate records.

(b) A director's attendance at or participation in a meeting waives any required notice to the director of the meeting unless the director at the beginning of the meeting (or promptly upon arrival) objects to holding the meeting or transacting business at the meeting and does not after objecting vote for or assent to action taken at the meeting.

Official Comment

If a director actually attends the meeting, section 8.23(b) generally provides the director may not subsequently raise an objection based on lack of notice. If a director does wish to object, he or she must call attention to the lack of notice at the outset of the meeting or promptly upon arriving and not vote for any action taken at the meeting. That director may then attack the validity of any action taken at the meeting on the grounds of lack of notice, as may any other director who was not given notice and was not present at the meeting.

§ 8.24. Quorum And Voting

(a) Unless the articles of incorporation or bylaws provide for a greater or lesser number or unless otherwise expressly provided in this Act, a quorum of a board of directors consists of a majority of the number of directors specified in or fixed in accordance with the articles of incorporation or bylaws.

(b) The quorum of the board of directors specified in or fixed in accordance with the articles of incorporation or bylaws may not consist of less than one-third of the specified or fixed number of directors.

(c) If a quorum is present when a vote is taken, the affirmative vote of a majority of directors present is the act of the board of directors unless the articles of incorporation or bylaws require the vote of a greater number of directors or unless otherwise expressly provided in this Act.

(d) A director who is present at a meeting of the board of directors or a committee when corporate action is taken is deemed to have assented to the action taken unless: (i) the director objects at the beginning of the meeting (or promptly upon arrival) to holding it or transacting business at the meeting; (ii) the dissent or abstention from the action taken is entered in the minutes of the meeting; or (iii) the director delivers written notice of the director's dissent or abstention to the presiding officer of the meeting before its adjournment or to the corporation immediately after adjournment of the meeting. The right of dissent or abstention is not available to a director who votes in favor of the action taken.

Official Comment

In the absence of a provision in the articles of incorporation or bylaws, a quorum is a majority of the total number of directors specified (*e.g.*, "the number of directors shall be X") in or fixed (*e.g.*, "the number of directors shall be not less than Y or more than Z as determined by the board of directors") in accordance with the articles of incorporation or the bylaws.

Section 8.24(a) recognizes that the Act itself may provide for a different quorum in certain specified situations.

Section 8.24 allows the articles of incorporation or bylaws to decrease the required quorum (but not below one-third) or to increase the quorum or the vote necessary to take action up to and including unanimity. The articles of incorporation or bylaws may also establish quorum or voting requirements with respect to directors elected by voting groups of shareholders pursuant to section 8.04. The options to increase the quorum and vote requirements might be used, for example, in closely held corporations where a greater degree of participation is thought appropriate or where a minority participant in the venture seeks to obtain a veto power over corporate action.

The phrase "when the vote is taken" in section 8.24(c) is designed to make clear that the board of directors may act only when a quorum is present. If directors leave during the course of a meeting, the board of directors may not act after the number of directors present is reduced to less than a quorum.

If a director who is present at a meeting wishes to object or abstain with respect to action taken by the board of directors or a committee, that director must make his or her position clear in one of the ways described in section 8.24(d). If objection is made in the form of a written dissent under clause (iii) of section 8.24(d), it may be transmitted by any form of delivery authorized by the definition of that term in section 1.40, including electronic transmission, if authorized by section 1.41. Section 8.24(d) serves the important purpose of bringing the position of the dissenting director clearly to the attention of the other directors. The provision that a director who is present is deemed to have assented unless an objection is noted also prevents a director from later seeking to avoid responsibility because of unexpressed doubts about the wisdom of the action taken.

Section 8.24(d) applies only to directors who are present at the meeting. Directors who are not present are not deemed to have assented to any action taken at the meeting in their absence.

§ 8.25. Committees Of The Board

(a) Unless this Act, the articles of incorporation or the bylaws provide otherwise, a board of directors may establish one or more board committees composed exclusively of one or more directors to perform functions of the board of directors.

(b) The establishment of a board committee and appointment of members to it shall be approved by the greater of (i) a majority of all the directors in office when the action is taken or (ii) the number of directors required by the articles of incorporation or bylaws to take action under section 8.24, unless, in either case, this Act or the articles of incorporation provide otherwise.

(c) Sections 8.20 through 8.24 apply to board committees and their members.

(d) A board committee may exercise the powers of the board of directors under section 8.01, to the extent specified by the board of directors or in the articles of incorporation or bylaws, except that a board committee may not:

(1) authorize or approve distributions, except according to a formula or method, or within limits, prescribed by the board of directors;

(2) approve or propose to shareholders action that this Act requires be approved by shareholders;

(3) fill vacancies on the board of directors or, subject to subsection (e), on any board committees; or

(4) adopt, amend, or repeal bylaws.

Official Comment

Section 8.25 deals only with board committees authorized to perform functions of the board of directors. The board of directors or management, independently of section 8.25, may establish non-board committees composed in whole or in part of directors, employees, or others to address matters in ways that do not constitute performing functions required to be performed by the board of directors under section 8.01, including acting in an advisory capacity.

Under section 8.25(a), except as otherwise provided by the Act, the articles of incorporation or the bylaws, a board committee may consist of a single director. This accommodates situations in which only one director may be present or available to make a decision on short notice, as well as situations in which it is unnecessary or inconvenient to have more than one member on a board committee or where only one board member is disinterested or independent with respect to a matter. Various other sections of the Act require the participation or approval of at least two qualified directors in order for the decision of the board or committee to have effect. These include a determination that maintenance of a derivative suit is not in the corporation's best interests (section 7.44(b)(2)), a determination that indemnification is permissible (section 8.55(b)(1)), an approval of a director's conflicting interest transaction (section 8.62(a)), and disclaimer of the corporation's interest in a business opportunity (section 8.70(a)).

The requirement of section 8.25(b) that, unless the Act or the articles of incorporation otherwise provide, a board committee may be created only by the affirmative vote of a majority of the board of directors then in office, or, if greater, by the number of directors required to take action by the articles of incorporation or bylaws, reflects the importance of the decision to invest board committees with power to act under section 8.25. Sections 7.44(b), 8.55(b), 8.62(a) and 8.70 contain exceptions to this rule.

The limitations in section 8.25(d)(1) through (4) are based on the principle that the listed actions so substantially affect the rights of shareholders or are so fundamental to the governance of the corporation that they should be determined by the full board and not delegated to a committee. On the other hand, section 8.25(d) allows board committees to take many actions that may be material, such as the authorization of long-term debt and capital investment or the issuance of shares.

Although section 8.25(d)(1) generally makes nondelegable the decision whether to authorize or approve distributions, including dividends, it does permit the delegation to a board committee of power to approve a distribution pursuant to a formula or method or within limits prescribed by the board of directors. Therefore, the board of directors could set a dollar range and timeframe for a prospective dividend and delegate to a board committee the authority to determine the exact amount and record and payment dates of the dividend. The board of directors also could establish certain conditions to the payment of a distribution and delegate to a board committee the power to determine whether the conditions have been satisfied.

C. CORPORATE OFFICERS

§ 8.40. Officers

(a) A corporation has the officers described in its bylaws or appointed by the board of directors in accordance with the bylaws.

(b) The board of directors may elect individuals to fill one or more offices of the corporation. An officer may appoint one or more officers if authorized by the bylaws or the board of directors.

(c) The bylaws or the board of directors shall assign to an officer responsibility for maintaining and authenticating the records of the corporation required to be kept under section 16.01(a).

(d) The same individual may simultaneously hold more than one office in a corporation.

Official Comment

Section 8.40 permits every corporation to designate the officers it will have. No particular officers are required.

The board of directors, as well as duly authorized officers, employees or agents, may also appoint other agents for the corporation. In addition, a board of directors has the intrinsic power to organize its own internal affairs, including designating officers of the board.

The officer who has the responsibility to maintain the minutes and authenticate the corporate records referred to in section 16.01(a) is referred to as the "secretary" of the corporation throughout the Act. The person so designated has authority to bind the corporation by that officer's authentication under this section. This assignment of authority, traditionally vested in the corporate "secretary," allows third persons to rely on authenticated records without inquiry as to their truth or accuracy.

Source: Model Bus. Corp. Act §§ 8.40, 8.41, 8.43, 8.44 (2016). Copyright © 2016 by American Bar Association. Reprinted with permission.

§ 8.41. Functions of Officers

Each officer has the authority and shall perform the functions set forth in the bylaws or, to the extent consistent with the bylaws, the functions prescribed by the board of directors or by direction of an officer authorized by the board of directors to prescribe the functions of other officers.

Official Comment

The methods of investing officers with formal authority in section 8.41 do not exhaust the sources of an officer's actual or apparent authority. Specific officers, particularly the chief executive officer, may have implied authority to take certain actions on behalf of a corporation merely by virtue of their positions. Officers may also be vested with apparent authority by reason of corporate conduct on which third persons reasonably rely.

In addition to express, implied, or apparent authority, a corporation is bound by unauthorized acts of officers if they are ratified by the board of directors. Generally, ratification may extend only to acts that could have been authorized as an original matter. Ratification may itself be express or implied and may in some cases serve as the basis of apparent authority.

§ 8.43. Resignation and Removal of Officers

(a) An officer may resign at any time by delivering a written notice to the board of directors, or its chair, or to the appointing officer or the secretary. A resignation is effective as provided in section 1.41(i) unless the notice provides for a delayed effectiveness, including effectiveness determined upon a future event or events. If effectiveness of a resignation is stated to be delayed and the board of directors or the appointing officer accepts the delay, the board of directors or the appointing officer may fill the pending vacancy before the delayed effectiveness but the new officer may not take office until the vacancy occurs.

(b) An officer may be removed at any time with or without cause by (i) the board of directors; (ii) the appointing officer, unless the bylaws or the board of directors provide otherwise; or (iii) any other officer if authorized by the bylaws or the board of directors.

(c) In this section, "appointing officer" means the officer (including any successor to that officer) who appointed the officer resigning or being removed.

Official Comment

In part because of the unlimited power of removal under section 8.43(b), a corporation may enter into an employment agreement with the holder of an office that gives the officer rights in the event of removal or failure to be reelected or reappointed to office. This type of contract is binding on the corporation even if the articles of incorporation or bylaws provide that officers are elected for a term shorter than the period of the employment contract. Such an employment agreement does not override the removal power set forth in section 8.43(b) and may give the officer the right to damages, but not specific performance, if employment is terminated before the end of the contract term.

Section 8.43(b) provides the corporation with the flexibility to determine when, if ever, an officer will be permitted to remove another officer. To the extent that the corporation wishes to permit an officer, other than the appointing officer, to remove another officer, the bylaws or a board resolution should set forth clearly the persons having removal authority.

A person may be removed from office irrespective of contract rights or the presence or absence of "cause" in a legal sense.

§ 8.44. Contract Rights Of Officers

(a) The election or appointment of an officer does not itself create contract rights.

(b) An officer's removal does not affect the officer's contract rights, if any, with the corporation. An officer's resignation does not affect the corporation's contract rights, if any, with the officer.

Official Comment

The removal of an officer with contract rights is without prejudice to the officer's rights in a proceeding seeking damages for breach of contract. Similarly, an officer with an employment contract who prematurely resigns may be in breach of his or her employment contract. The mere election or appointment of an officer for a term does not create a contractual obligation on the officer's part to complete the term.

CHAPTER 17

CONSTRAINING DIRECTORS & OFFICERS

A. INTRODUCTION

Similar to partners' duties to one another in a partnership, a corporation's board of directors has fiduciary duties to the corporation and its shareholders. The policy behind these duties is the same as it is in partnership law. These duties are imposed upon the directors of a corporation to ensure that they undertake actions carefully, with the best interests of the shareholders in mind, and do not abuse their position of power.

In Re Walt Disney Co. Derivative Litigation
907 A. 2d 693, 745–756 (Del. Ch. 2005).

The fiduciary duties owed by directors of a Delaware corporation are the duties of due care and loyalty. …[I]ssues of good faith are (to a certain degree) inseparably and necessarily intertwined with the duties of care and loyalty, as well as a principal reason the distinctness of these duties make a difference—namely § 102(b)(7) of the Delaware General Corporation Law.

A. The Business Judgment Rule

Delaware law is clear that the business and affairs of a corporation are managed by or under the direction of its board of directors. The business judgment rule serves to protect and promote the role of the board as the ultimate manager of the corporation. Because courts are ill equipped to engage in *post hoc* substantive review of business decisions, the business judgment rule "operates to preclude a court from imposing itself unreasonably on the business and affairs of a corporation."

The business judgment rule is not actually a substantive rule of law, but instead it is a presumption that "in making a business decision the directors

Copyright in the Public Domain.

of a corporation acted on an informed basis, ... and in the honest belief that the action taken was in the best interests of the company [and its shareholders]." This presumption applies when there is no evidence of "fraud, bad faith, or self-dealing in the usual sense of personal profit or betterment" on the part of the directors. In the absence of this evidence, the board's decision will be upheld unless it cannot be "attributed to any rational business purpose." When a plaintiff fails to rebut the presumption of the business judgment rule, she is not entitled to any remedy, be it legal or equitable, unless the transaction constitutes waste.

This presumption can be rebutted by a showing that the board violated one of its fiduciary duties in connection with the challenged transaction. In that event, the burden shifts to the director defendants to demonstrate that the challenged transaction was "entirely fair" to the corporation and its shareholders.

In *Van Gorkom*, the Delaware Supreme Court analyzed the Trans Union board of directors *as a whole* in determining whether the protections of the business judgment rule applied. More recent cases understand that liability determinations must be on a director-by-director basis. In *Emerging Communications*, Justice Jacobs wrote (while sitting as a Vice Chancellor) that the "liability of the directors must be determined on an individual basis because the nature of their breach of duty (if any), and whether they are exculpated from liability for that breach, can vary for each director."

Even if the directors have exercised their business judgment, the protections of the business judgment rule will not apply if the directors have made an "unintelligent or unadvised judgment." Furthermore, in instances where directors have not exercised business judgment, that is, in the event of director inaction, the protections of the business judgment rule do not apply. Under those circumstances, the appropriate standard for determining liability is widely believed to be gross negligence, but a single Delaware case has held that ordinary negligence would be the appropriate standard.

C. The Fiduciary Duty of Due Care

The fiduciary duty of due care requires that directors of a Delaware corporation "use that amount of care which ordinarily careful and prudent men would use in similar circumstances," and "consider all material information reasonably available" in making business decisions, and that deficiencies in the directors' process are actionable only if the directors' actions are grossly negligent. Chancellor Allen described the two contexts in which liability for a breach of the duty of care can arise:

First, such liability may be said to follow *from a board decision* that results in a loss because that decision was ill advised or "negligent". Second, liability to the corporation for a loss may be said to arise from an *unconsidered failure of the board to act* in circumstances in which due attention would, arguably, have prevented the loss.

Chancellor Allen then explained with respect to board decisions:

... [These] cases will typically be subject to review under the director-protective business judgment rule, assuming the decision made was the product of *a process* that was *either* deliberately considered in good faith or was otherwise rational. What should be understood, but may not widely be understood by courts or commentators who are not often required to face such questions, is that compliance with a director's duty of care can never appropriately be judicially determined by reference to *the content of the board decision* that leads to a corporate loss, apart from consideration of the good faith or rationality of the process employed. That is, whether a judge or jury considering the matter after the fact, believes a decision substantively wrong, or degrees of wrong extending through "stupid" to "egregious" or "irrational", provides no ground for director liability, so long as the court determines that the process employed was either rational or employed in *a good faith* effort to advance corporate interests. To employ a different rule—one that permitted an "objective" evaluation of the decision—would expose directors to substantive second guessing by ill-equipped judges or juries, which would, in the long-run, be injurious to investor interests. Thus, the business judgment rule is process oriented and informed by a deep respect for all *good faith* board decisions.

Indeed, one wonders on what moral basis might shareholders attack a *good faith* business decision of a director as "unreasonable" or "irrational". Where a director *in fact exercises a good faith effort to be informed and to exercise appropriate judgment*, he or she should be deemed to satisfy fully the duty of attention.

With respect to liability for director inaction, Chancellor Allen wrote that in order for the inaction to be so great as to constitute a breach of the director's duty of care, a plaintiff must show a "lack of good faith as evidenced by sustained or systematic failure of a director to exercise reasonable oversight." The Chancellor rationalized this extremely high standard of liability for violations of the duty of care through inaction by concluding that:

[A] demanding test of liability in the oversight context is probably beneficial to corporate shareholders as a class, as it is in the board decision context, since it makes board service by qualified persons more likely, while continuing to act as a stimulus to *good faith performance of duty* by such directors.

In the duty of care context with respect to corporate fiduciaries, gross negligence has been defined as a "'reckless indifference to or a deliberate disregard of the whole body of stockholders' or actions which are 'without the bounds of reason.'" Because duty of care violations are actionable only if the directors acted with gross negligence, and because in most instances money damages are unavailable to a plaintiff who could theoretically prove a duty of care violation, duty of care violations are rarely found.

D. The Fiduciary Duty of Loyalty

The fiduciary duty of loyalty was described in the seminal case of *Guth v. Loft, Inc.*, in these strict and unyielding terms:

Corporate officers and directors are not permitted to use their position of trust and confidence to further their private interests.... A public policy, existing through the years, and derived from a profound knowledge of human characteristics and motives, has established a rule that demands of a corporate officer or director, peremptorily and inexorably, the most scrupulous observance of his duty, not only affirmatively to protect the interests of the corporation committed to his charge, but also to refrain from doing anything that would work injury to the corporation, or to deprive it of profit or advantage which his skill and ability might properly bring to it, or to enable it to make in the reasonable and lawful exercise of its powers. The rule that requires an undivided and unselfish loyalty to the corporation demands that there be no conflict between duty and self-interest.

More recently, the Delaware Supreme Court stated that there is no safe-harbor for divided loyalties in Delaware, and that the duty of loyalty, in essence, "mandates that the best interest of the corporation and its shareholders take precedence over any interest possessed by a director, officer or controlling shareholder and not shared by the stockholders generally." The classic example that implicates the duty of loyalty is when a fiduciary either appears on both sides of a transaction or receives a personal benefit not shared by all shareholders.

E. Section 102(b)(7)

Following the Delaware Supreme Court's landmark decision in *Van Gorkom*, the Delaware General Assembly acted swiftly to enact 8 *Del. C.* § 102(b)(7). Section 102(b)(7) states that a corporation may include in its certificate of incorporation:

(7) A provision eliminating or limiting the personal liability of a director to the corporation or its stockholders for monetary damages for breach of fiduciary duty as a director, provided that such provision shall not eliminate or limit the liability of a director: (i) For any breach of the director's duty of loyalty to the corporation or its stockholders; (ii) for acts or omissions not in good faith or which involve intentional misconduct or a knowing violation of law; (iii) under § 174 of this title; or (iv) for any transaction from which the director derived an improper personal benefit. No such provision shall eliminate or limit the liability of a director for any act or omission occurring prior to the date when such provision becomes effective. All references in this paragraph to a director shall also be deemed to refer (x) to a member of the governing body of a corporation which is not authorized to issue capital stock, and (y) to such other person or persons, if any, who, pursuant to a provision of the certificate of incorporation in accordance with § 141(a) of this

title, exercise or perform any of the powers or duties otherwise conferred or imposed upon the board of directors by this title.

The purpose of Section 102(b)(7) was explained by the Delaware Supreme Court in this manner:

The purpose of Section 102(b)(7) was to *permit shareholders*—who are entitled to rely upon directors to discharge their fiduciary duties at all times—to adopt a provision in the certificate of incorporation to exculpate directors from any personal liability for the payment of monetary damages for breaches of their duty of care, but not for duty of loyalty violations, good faith violations and certain other conduct.

Recently, Vice Chancellor Strine wrote that, "[o]ne of the primary purposes of § 102(b)(7) is to encourage directors to undertake risky, but potentially value-maximizing, business strategies, so long as they do so in good faith." Or in other words, § 102(b)(7) is most useful "when, despite the directors' good intentions, [the challenged transaction] did not generate financial success and … the possibility of hindsight bias about the directors' prior ability to foresee that their business plans would not pan out" could improperly influence a *post hoc* judicial evaluation of the directors' actions.

The vast majority of Delaware corporations have a provision in their certificate of incorporation that permits exculpation to the extent provided for by § 102(b)(7). This provision prohibits recovery of monetary damages from directors for a successful shareholder claim, either direct or derivative, that is exclusively based upon establishing a violation of the duty of due care. The existence of an exculpation provision authorized by § 102(b)(7) does not, however, eliminate a director's fiduciary duty of care, because a court may still grant injunctive relief for violations of that duty.

An exculpation provision such as that authorized by § 102(b)(7) is in the nature of an affirmative defense. As a result, it is the burden of the director defendants to demonstrate that they are entitled to the protections of the relevant charter provision

F. Acting in Good Faith

Decisions from the Delaware Supreme Court and the Court of Chancery are far from clear with respect to whether there is a separate fiduciary duty of good faith. Good faith has been said to require an "honesty of purpose," and a genuine care for the fiduciary's constituents, but, at least in the corporate fiduciary context, it is probably easier to define bad faith rather than good faith. This may be so because Delaware law presumes that directors act in good faith when making business judgments. Bad faith has been defined as authorizing a transaction "for some purpose *other than* a genuine attempt to advance corporate welfare or [when the transaction] is *known to constitute* a violation of applicable positive law." In other words, an action taken with the intent to harm the corporation is a disloyal act in bad faith. A similar definition was used seven years earlier, when Chancellor Allen wrote that bad faith (or lack of good faith) is when a director acts in a manner "unrelated to a pursuit of the corporation's best interests." It makes no difference the reason why the director intentionally fails to pursue the best interests of the corporation.

Bad faith can be the result of "any emotion [that] may cause a director to [intentionally] place his own interests, preferences or appetites before the welfare of the corporation," including greed, "hatred, lust, envy, revenge, … shame or pride." Sloth could certainly be an appropriate addition to that incomplete list if it constitutes a systematic or sustained shirking of duty. Ignorance, in and of itself, probably does not belong on the list, but ignorance attributable to any of the moral failings previously listed could constitute bad faith. It is unclear, based upon existing jurisprudence, whether motive is a necessary element for a successful claim that a director has acted in bad faith, and, if so, whether that motive must be shown explicitly or whether it can be inferred from the directors' conduct.

[T]he concept of *intentional dereliction of duty*, a *conscious disregard for one's responsibilities*, is an appropriate (although not the only) standard for determining whether fiduciaries have acted in good faith. Deliberate indifference and inaction *in the face of a duty to act* is, in my mind, conduct that is clearly disloyal to the corporation. It is the epitome of faithless conduct.

To act in good faith, a director must act at all times with an honesty of purpose and in the best interests and welfare of the corporation. The presumption of the business judgment rule creates a presumption that a director acted in good faith. In order to overcome that presumption, a plaintiff must prove an act of bad faith by a preponderance of the evidence. To create a definitive and categorical definition of the universe of acts that would constitute bad faith would be difficult, if not impossible. And it would misconceive how, in my judgment, the concept of good faith operates in our common law of corporations. Fundamentally, the duties traditionally analyzed as belonging to corporate fiduciaries, loyalty and care, are but constituent elements of the overarching concepts of allegiance, devotion and faithfulness that must guide the conduct of every fiduciary. The good faith required of a corporate fiduciary includes not simply the duties of care and loyalty, in the narrow sense that I have discussed them above, but all actions required by a true faithfulness and devotion to the interests of the corporation and its shareholders. A failure to act in good faith may be shown, for instance, where the fiduciary intentionally acts with a purpose other than that of advancing the best interests of the corporation, where the fiduciary acts with the intent to violate applicable positive law, or where the fiduciary intentionally fails to act in the face of a known duty to act, demonstrating a conscious disregard for his duties. There may be other examples of bad faith yet to be proven or alleged, but these three are the most salient.

B. FIDUCIARY DUTY OF CARE

§ 8.30. Standards Of Conduct For Directors

(a) Each member of the board of directors, when discharging the duties of a director, shall act:

    (i) in good faith, and (ii) in a manner the director reasonably believes to be in the best interests of the corporation.

(b) The members of the board of directors or a board committee, when becoming informed in connection with their decision-making function or devoting attention to their oversight function, shall discharge their duties with the care that a person in a like position would reasonably believe appropriate under similar circumstances.

(c) In discharging board or board committee duties, a director shall disclose, or cause to be disclosed, to the other board or committee members information not already known by them but known by the director to be material to the discharge of their decision-making or oversight functions, except that disclosure is not required to the extent that the director reasonably believes that doing so would violate a duty imposed under law, a legally enforceable obligation of confidentiality, or a professional ethics rule.

(d) In discharging board or board committee duties, a director who does not have knowledge that makes reliance unwarranted is entitled to rely on the performance by any of the persons specified in subsection (f)(1) or subsection (f)(3) to whom the board may have delegated, formally or informally by course of conduct, the authority or duty to perform one or more of the board's functions that are delegable under applicable law.

(e) In discharging board or board committee duties, a director who does not have knowledge that makes reliance unwarranted is entitled to rely on information, opinions, reports, or statements, including financial statements and other financial data, prepared or presented by any of the persons specified in subsection (f).

(f) A director is entitled to rely, in accordance with subsection (d) or (e), on:

    (1) one or more officers or employees of the corporation whom the director reasonably believes to be reliable and competent in the functions performed or the information, opinions, reports or statements provided;

    (2) legal counsel, public accountants, or other persons retained by the corporation as to matters involving skills or expertise the director reasonably believes are matters (i) within the particular person's

Source: Source: Model Bus. Corp. Act §§ 8.30, 8.31, 8.42 (2016). Copyright © 2016 by American Bar Association. Reprinted with permission.

professional or expert competence, or (ii) as to which the particular person merits confidence; or

(3) a board committee of which the director is not a member if the director reasonably believes the committee merits confidence.

Official Comment

Section 8.30 sets standards of conduct for directors that focus on the manner in which directors make their decisions, not the correctness of the decisions made. Section 8.30 should be read in light of the basic role of directors set forth in section 8.01(b), which provides that the "business and affairs of a corporation shall be managed by or under the direction and subject to the oversight of the board of directors," as supplemented by various provisions of the Act assigning specific powers or responsibilities to the board. The standards of conduct for directors established by section 8.30 are analogous to those generally articulated by courts in evaluating director conduct, often referred to as the duties of care and loyalty.

Section 8.30 addresses standards of conduct—the level of performance expected of directors undertaking the role and responsibilities of the office of director. The section does not address the liability of a director, although exposure to liability may result from a failure to honor the standards of conduct required to be observed. The issue of director liability is addressed in sections 8.31 and 8.32. Section 8.30 does, however, play an important role in evaluating a director's conduct and the effectiveness of board action. It has relevance in assessing, under section 8.31, the reasonableness of a director's belief. Similarly, it has relevance in assessing a director's timely attention to appropriate inquiry when particular facts and circumstances of significant concern materialize. It also serves as a frame of reference for determining, under section 8.32(a), liability for an unlawful distribution. Finally, section 8.30 compliance may influence a court's analysis where injunctive relief against a transaction is being sought. Directors act both individually and collectively as a board in performing their functions and discharging their duties. Section 8.30 addresses actions in both capacities.

Under the standards of section 8.30, the board may delegate or assign to appropriate officers or employees of the corporation the authority or duty to exercise powers that the law does not require the board to retain. Because the directors are entitled to rely on these persons absent knowledge making reliance unwarranted, the directors will not be in breach of the standards under section 8.30 as a result of their delegatees' actions or omissions so long as the board acted in good faith and complied with the other standards of conduct set forth in section 8.30 in delegating responsibility and, where appropriate, monitoring performance of the duties delegated. In addition, subsections (d), (e) and (f) permit a director to rely on enumerated third parties for specified purposes, although reliance is prohibited when a director has knowledge that makes reliance unwarranted. Section 8.30(a)'s standards of good faith and reasonable belief in the best interests of the corporation also apply to a director's reliance under subsections (d), (e) and (f).

Section 8.30(a)

Section 8.30(a) establishes the basic standards of conduct for all directors and its mandate governs all aspects of directors' conduct, including the requirements in other subsections. It includes concepts courts have used in defining the duty of loyalty. Two of the phrases used in section 8.30(a) deserve further comment:

- The phrase "reasonably believes" is both subjective and objective in character. Its first level of analysis is geared to what the particular director, acting in good faith, actually believes—not what objective analysis would lead another director (in a like position and acting in similar circumstances) to conclude. The second level of analysis is focused specifically on "reasonably." Although a director has wide discretion in gathering information and reaching conclusions, whether a director's belief is reasonable (*i.e.*, could—not would—a reasonable person in a like position and acting in similar circumstances, taking into account that director's knowledge and experience, have arrived at that belief) ultimately involves an overview that is objective in character.

- The phrase "best interests of the corporation" is key to an understanding of a director's duties. The term "corporation" is a surrogate for the business enterprise as well as a frame of reference encompassing the shareholder body. In determining the corporation's "best interests," the director has wide discretion in deciding how to weigh near-term opportunities versus long-term benefits as well as in making judgments where the interests of various groups of shareholders or other corporate constituencies may differ.

Section 8.30 operates as a "baseline" principle governing director conduct in circumstances uncomplicated by self-interest. The Act recognizes, however, that directors' personal interests may not always align with the corporation's best interests and provides procedures by which situations and transactions involving conflicts of interest can be processed. See subchapter D (derivative proceedings) of chapter 7 and subchapters E (indemnification and advance for expenses), F (directors' conflicting interest transactions), and G (business opportunities) of this chapter 8. Those procedures generally contemplate that the interested director will provide appropriate disclosure and will not be involved in taking action on the matter giving rise to the conflict of interest.

Section 8.30(b)

Section 8.30(b) establishes a general standard of care for directors in the context of their dealing with the board's decision-making and oversight functions. Although certain aspects will involve individual conduct (*e.g.*, preparation for meetings), these functions are generally performed by the board of directors through collective action, as recognized by the reference in subsection (b) to board and committee "members" and "their duties." In contrast with section 8.30(a)'s individual conduct mandate, section 8.30(b) has a two-fold thrust: it provides a standard of conduct for individual action and, more broadly, it states a conduct obligation— "shall discharge their duties"—concerning the degree of care to be used collectively by the directors when performing those functions. The standard is not what care a particular director might believe appropriate in the circumstances but what a person—in a like position and acting under similar circumstances—would reasonably believe to be appropriate. Thus, the degree of care that directors should employ under section 8.30(b) involves an objective standard.

The process by which a director becomes informed, in carrying out the decision-making and oversight functions, will vary. The directors' decision-making function is reflected in various sections of the Act, including: the issuance of shares (section 6.21); distributions (section 6.40); dismissal of derivative proceedings (section 7.44); indemnification (section 8.55); conflict of interest transaction authorization (section 8.62); articles of incorporation amendments (sections 10.2 and 10.03); bylaw amendments (section 10.20); mergers and share exchanges (section 11.04); asset dispositions (section 12.02); and dissolution (section 14.02). The directors' oversight function is established under section 8.01. In discharging the section 8.01 duties associated with the board's oversight function, the standard of care entails primarily a requirement of attention. In contrast with the board's decision-making function, which generally involves informed action at a point in time, the oversight function is concerned with a continuum and the attention of the directors accordingly involves participatory performance over a period of time.

Several of the phrases chosen to define the standard of conduct in section 8.30(b) deserve specific mention:

- The phrase "becoming informed," in the context of the decision--making function, refers to the process of gaining sufficient familiarity with the background facts and circumstances to make an informed judgment. Unless the circumstances would permit a reasonable director to conclude that he or she is already sufficiently informed, the standard of care requires every director to take steps to become informed about the background facts and circumstances before taking action on the matter at hand. The process typically involves review of written materials provided before or at the meeting and attention to or participation in the deliberations leading up to a vote. In addition to considering information and data on which a director is expressly entitled to rely under section 8.30(e), "becoming informed" can also involve consideration of information and data generated by other persons, for example, review of industry studies or research articles prepared by third parties. It can also involve direct communications, outside of the boardroom, with members of management or other directors. There is no one way for "becoming informed," and both the method and measure—"how to" and "how much"— are matters of reasonable judgment for the director to exercise.

- The phrase "devoting attention," in the context of the oversight function, refers to considering such matters as the corporation's information and reporting systems generally and not to an independent investigation into particular system inadequacies or noncompliance. Although directors typically give attention to future plans and trends as well as current activities, they should not be expected to anticipate any particular problems which the corporation may face except in those circumstances where something has occurred to make it obvious to the board that the corporation should be addressing a particular problem. The standard of care associated with the oversight function involves gaining assurances from management and advisers that appropriate systems have been established, such as those concerned with legal compliance, risk assessment or internal controls. Such assurances also should cover establishment of ongoing monitoring of the systems in place, with appropriate follow-up responses when alerted to the issues requiring attention.

- The reference to "person," without embellishment, is intended to avoid implying any qualifications, such as specialized expertise or experience requirements, beyond the basic attributes of common sense, practical wisdom, and informed judgment (however, see the last bullet below).

- The phrase "reasonably believe appropriate" refers to the array of possible options that a person possessing the basic attributes of common sense, practical wisdom and informed judgment would recognize to be available, in terms of the degree of care that might be appropriate, and from which a choice by such person would be made. The measure of care that such person might determine to be appropriate, in a given instance, would normally involve a selection from the range of options and any choice within the realm of reason would be an appropriate decision under the standard of care called for under section 8.30(b). However, a decision that is so removed from the realm of reason, or is so unreasonable, that it falls outside the permissible bounds of sound discretion, and thus is an abuse of discretion, will not satisfy the standard.

- The phrase "in a like position" recognizes that the "care" under consideration is that which would be used by the "person" if he or she were a director of the particular corporation.

- The combined phrase "in a like position ... under similar circumstances" is intended to recognize that (i) the nature and extent of responsibilities will vary, depending upon such factors as the size, complexity, urgency, and location of activities carried on by the particular corporation, (ii) decisions must be made on the basis of the information known to the directors without the benefit of hindsight, and (iii) the special background, qualifications, and oversight responsibilities of a particular director may be relevant in evaluating that director's compliance with the standard of care.

Section 8.30(c)

A requirement to disclose to other directors information that a director knows to be material to the decision-making or oversight functions of the board of directors or a board committee is implicit in the standards of conduct set forth in sections 8.30(a) and (b), but section 8.30(c) makes this explicit. Thus, for example, when a member of the board of directors knows information that the director recognizes is material to a decision by the board but is not known to the other directors, the director is obligated to disclose that information to the other members of the board. Such disclosure can occur through direct statements in meetings of the board, or by any other timely means, including, for example, communicating the information to the chairman of the board or the chairman of a committee, or to the corporation's general counsel, and requesting that the recipient inform the other board or committee members of the information.

Section 8.30(c) recognizes that a duty of confidentiality to a third party can override a director's obligation to share with other directors information pertaining to a current corporate matter. In some circumstances, a duty of confidentiality to a third party may even prohibit disclosure of the nature or the existence of the duty itself. Ordinarily, however, a director who withholds material information based on a reasonable belief that a duty of confidentiality to a third party prohibits disclosure should advise the other directors of the existence and nature of that duty.

The requirement that a director disclose information to other directors as set forth in section 8.30(c) is different from any common law duty the board may have to cause the corporation to make disclosures to shareholders under certain circumstances. The Act does not seek to codify such a duty of disclosure, but leaves its existence and scope, the circumstances for its application, and the consequences of any failure to satisfy it, to be developed by courts on a case-by-case basis.

Section 8.30(d)

The delegation of authority and responsibility described in section 8.30(d) may take a variety of forms, including (i) formal action through a board resolution, (ii) implicit action through the election of corporate officers (*e.g.*, chief financial officer or controller) or the appointment of corporate managers (*e.g.*, credit manager), or (iii) informal action through a course of conduct (*e.g.*, involvement through corporate officers and managers in the management of a significant 50%-owned joint venture). Under section 8.30(d), a director may properly rely on those to whom authority has been delegated pursuant to section 8.30(d) respecting particular matters calling for specific action or attention in connection with the directors' decision-making function as well as matters on the board's continuing agenda, such as legal compliance and internal controls, in connection with the directors' oversight function. Delegation should be carried out in accordance with the standard of care set forth in section 8.30(b).

By identifying those persons upon whom a director may rely in connection with the discharge of duties, section 8.30(d) does not limit the ability of directors to delegate their powers under section 8.01(b) except where delegation is expressly prohibited by the Act or otherwise by applicable law. By employing the concept of delegation, the Act does not limit the ability of directors to establish baseline principles as to management responsibilities. Specifically, section 8.01(b) provides that "all corporate powers shall be exercised by or under the authority of" the board, and a basic board function involves the allocation of management responsibilities and the related assignment (or delegation) of corporate powers. For example, a board can properly decide to retain a third party to assume responsibility for the administration of designated aspects of risk management for the corporation (*e.g.*, health insurance or disability claims).

Although the board of directors may delegate the authority or duty to perform one or more of its functions, delegation and reliance under section 8.30(d) may not alone constitute compliance with sections 8.30(a) and (b) and the action taken by the delegatee may not alone satisfy the directors or a noncommittee board member's section 8.01 responsibilities. On the other hand, failure of the board committee or the corporate officer or employee performing the function delegated to meet section 8.30(b)'s standard of care will not automatically result in violation by the board of section 8.01. Factors to be considered in determining whether a violation of section 8.01 has occurred will include the care used in the delegation to and supervision over the delegatee, and the amount of knowledge regarding the particular matter which is reasonably available to the particular director. Care in delegation and supervision includes appraisal of the capabilities and diligence of the delegatee in light of the subject and its relative importance and may be satisfied, in the usual case, by receipt of reports concerning the delegatee's activities. The enumeration of these factors is intended to emphasize that directors may not abdicate their responsibilities and avoid accountability simply by delegating authority to others. Rather, a director who is accountable for the acts of delegatees will fulfill the director's duties if the standards contained in section 8.30 are met.

Section 8.30(e)

Reliance under section 8.30(e) on a report, statement, opinion, or other information is permitted only if the director has read or heard orally presented the information, opinion, report or statement in question, or took other steps to become generally familiar with it. A director must comply with the general standard of care of section 8.30(b) in making a judgment as to the reliability and competence of the source of information upon which the director proposes to rely or, as appropriate, that it otherwise merits confidence.

Section 8.30(f)

In determining whether a corporate officer or employee is "reliable," for purposes of section 8.30(f)(1), the director would typically consider (i) the individual's background experience and scope of responsibility within the corporation in gauging the individual's familiarity and knowledge respecting the subject matter and (ii) the individual's record and reputation for honesty, care and ability in discharging responsibilities which he or she undertakes. In determining whether a person is "competent," the director would normally take into account the same considerations and, if expertise should be relevant, the director would consider the individual's technical skills as well. Recognition of the right of one director to rely on the expertise and experience of another director, in the context of board or committee deliberations, is unnecessary, for reliance on shared experience and wisdom of other board members is an implicit underpinning of collective board conduct. In relying on another member of the board, a director would quite properly take advantage of the colleague's knowledge and experience in becoming informed about the matter at hand before taking action; however, the director would be expected to exercise independent judgment when it comes time to vote.

Advisers on whom a director may rely under section 8.30(f)(2) include not only licensed professionals, such as lawyers, accountants, and engineers, but also those in other fields involving special experience and skills, such as investment bankers, geologists, management consultants, actuaries, and appraisers. The adviser could be an individual or an organization, such as a law or investment banking firm. Reliance on a nonmanagement director, who is specifically engaged (and, normally, additionally compensated) to undertake a special assignment or a particular consulting role, would fall within this outside adviser frame of reference. The concept of "expert competence" embraces a wide variety of qualifications and is not limited to the more precise and narrower recognition of experts under the Securities Act of 1933. In addition, a director may also rely on outside advisers where skills or expertise of a technical nature is not a prerequisite, or where the person's professional or expert competence has not been established, so long as the director reasonably believes the person merits confidence. For example, a board might choose to engage a private investigator to inquire into a particular matter (*e.g.*, follow up on rumors about a senior executive's alleged misconduct) and properly rely on the private investigator's report.

Section 8.30(f)(3) permits reliance on a board committee when it is submitting recommendations for action by the full board of directors as well as when it is performing supervisory or other functions in instances where neither the full board of directors nor the committee takes dispositive action. For example, the compensation committee typically reviews proposals and makes recommendations for action by the full board of directors. There also might be reliance upon an investigation undertaken by a board committee and reported to the full board, which forms the basis for a decision by the board of directors not to take dispositive action. Another example is reliance on a board committee, such as an audit committee with respect to the board's ongoing role of oversight of the accounting and auditing functions of the corporation. In addition, where reliance on information or materials prepared or presented by a board committee is not involved in connection with board action, a director may properly rely on oversight monitoring or dispositive action by a board committee (of which the director is not a member) empowered to act pursuant to authority delegated under section 8.25 or acting with the acquiescence of the board of directors. In parallel with section 8.30(f)(2)(ii), the concept of "confidence" is used instead of "competence" to avoid any inference that technical skills are a prerequisite. In the usual case, the appointment of committee members or the reconstitution of the membership of a standing committee (*e.g.*, the audit committee), following an annual shareholders' meeting, would alone manifest the noncommittee members' belief that the committee "merits confidence." Depending on the circumstances, the reliance contemplated by section 8.30(f)(3) is geared to the point in time when the board takes action or the period of time over which a committee is engaged in an oversight function; consequently, the judgment to be made (*i.e.*, whether a committee "merits confidence") will arise at varying points in time. Ordinarily, after making an initial judgment that a committee (of which a director is not a member) merits confidence, a director may continue to rely on that committee so long as the director has no reason to believe that confidence is no longer warranted.

Application to Officers

Section 8.30 generally deals only with directors. Section 8.42 and its Official Comment explain the extent to which the principles set forth in section 8.30 apply to officers.

§ 8.31. Standards of Liability for Directors

(a) A director shall not be liable to the corporation or its shareholders for any decision to take or not to take action, or any failure to take any action, as a director, unless the party asserting liability in a proceeding establishes that:

    (1) no defense interposed by the director based on (i) any provision in the articles of incorporation authorized by section 2.02(b)(4) or by section 2.02(b)(6), (ii) the protection afforded by section 8.61 (for action taken in compliance with section 8.62 or section 8.63), or (iii) the protection afforded by section 8.70, precludes liability; and

    (2) the challenged conduct consisted or was the result of:

        (i) action not in good faith; or

        (ii) a decision

            (A) which the director did not reasonably believe to be in the best interests of the corporation, or

(B) as to which the director was not informed to an extent the director reasonably believed appropriate in the circumstances; or

(iii) a lack of objectivity due to the director's familial, financial or business relationship with, or a lack of independence due to the director's domination or control by, another person having a material interest in the challenged conduct,

(A) which relationship or which domination or control could reasonably be expected to have affected the director's judgment respecting the challenged conduct in a manner adverse to the corporation, and

(B) after a reasonable expectation to such effect has been established, the director shall not have established that the challenged conduct was reasonably believed by the director to be in the best interests of the corporation; or

(iv) a sustained failure of the director to devote attention to ongoing oversight of the business and affairs of the corporation, or a failure to devote timely attention, by making (or causing to be made) appropriate inquiry, when particular facts and circumstances of significant concern materialize that would alert a reasonably attentive director to the need for such inquiry; or

(v) receipt of a financial benefit to which the director was not entitled or any other breach of the director's duties to deal fairly with the corporation and its shareholders that is actionable under applicable law.

(b) The party seeking to hold the director liable:

(1) for money damages, shall also have the burden of establishing that:

(i) harm to the corporation or its shareholders has been suffered, and

(ii) the harm suffered was proximately caused by the director's challenged conduct; or

(2) for other money payment under a legal remedy, such as compensation for the unauthorized use of corporate assets, shall also have whatever persuasion burden may be called for to establish that the payment sought is appropriate in the circumstances; or

(3) for other money payment under an equitable remedy, such as profit recovery by or disgorgement to the corporation, shall also have whatever persuasion burden may be called for to establish that the equitable remedy sought is appropriate in the circumstances.

Official Comment

Boards of directors and corporate managers make numerous decisions that involve the balancing of risks and benefits for the enterprise. Although some decisions turn out to have been unwise or the result of a mistake of judgment, it is not reasonable to impose liability for an informed decision made in good faith which with the benefit of hindsight turns out to be wrong or unwise. Therefore, as a general rule, a director is not exposed to personal liability for injury or damage caused by an unwise decision and conduct conforming with the standards of section 8.30 will almost always be protected regardless of the end result. Moreover, the fact that a director's performance fails to meet the standards of section 8.30 does not in itself establish personal liability for damages that the corporation or its shareholders may have suffered as a consequence. Nevertheless, a director can be held liable for misfeasance or nonfeasance in performing his or her duties. Section 8.31 sets forth the standards of liability of directors as distinct from the standards of conduct set forth in section 8.30.

Courts have developed the broad common law concept of the business judgment rule. Although formulations vary, in basic principle, a board of directors generally enjoys a presumption of sound business judgment and its decisions will not be disturbed by a court substituting its own notions of what is or is not sound business judgment if the board's decisions can be attributed to any rational business purpose. It is also presumed that, in making a business decision, directors act in good faith, on an informed basis, and in the honest belief that the action taken is in the best interests of the corporation. The elements of the business judgment rule and the circumstances for its application continue to be developed and refined by courts. Accordingly, it would not be desirable to freeze the concept in a statute. Thus, section 8.31 does not codify the business judgment rule as a whole, although certain of its principal elements, relating to personal liability issues, are reflected in section 8.31(a)(2).

Section 8.31(a)

A. Section 8.31(A)(1)—Affirmative Defenses

Under section 8.31(a)(1), if a provision in the articles of incorporation (i) (adopted pursuant to section 2.02(b)(4)) shelters the director from liability for money damages, or (ii) (adopted pursuant to section 2.02(b)(6)) limits or eliminates any duty to offer the particular business opportunity to the corporation, or if a safe harbor procedure under sections 8.61(b)(1) or (b)(2) or section 8.70(a)(1) shelters the director's conduct in connection with a conflicting interest transaction or the pursuit or taking of a business opportunity, and such defense applies to all claims in plaintiff's complaint, there is no need to consider further the application of section 8.31's standards of liability. In that event, the court would presumably grant the defendant director's motion for dismissal or summary judgment (or the equivalent) and the proceeding would be ended.

If a claim of liability arising out of a challenged act or omission of a director is not resolved and disposed of under section 8.31(a)(1), section 8.31(a)(2) provides the basis for evaluating whether the conduct in question can be challenged. One of the elements in section 8.31(a)(2) must be established for a director to have liability under section 8.31.

B. Section 8.31(A)(2)(I)—Good Faith

It is a basic standard under section 8.31(a)(2)(i) that a director's conduct in performing his or her duties be in good faith. If a director's conduct can be successfully challenged pursuant to other clauses of section 8.31(a)(2), there is a substantial likelihood that the conduct in question will also present an issue of good faith implicating section 8.31(a)(2)(i). Similarly, if section 8.31(a)(2) included only subsection (i), much of the conduct with which the other clauses are concerned could still be considered under that subsection, on the basis that such conduct evidenced the director's lack of good faith. Where conduct has not been found deficient on other grounds, decision-making outside the bounds of reasonable judgment can give rise to an inference of bad faith. That form of conduct, sometimes characterized as "reckless indifference" or "deliberate disregard," giving rise to an inference of bad faith can also raise a question whether the director could have reasonably believed that the best interests of the corporation would be served. These issues could arise, for example, in approval of conflicting interest transactions.

C. Section 8.31(A)(2)(Ii)—Reasonable Belief

Liability under section 8.31(a)(2)(ii) turns on a director's reasonable belief with respect to the nature of his or her decision and the degree to which he or she has become informed. In each case, the director must have an actual subjective belief and, so long as it is his or her honest and good faith belief, a director has wide discretion. There is also an objective element to be met, in that the director's belief must also be reasonable. The inquiry is similar to that in section 8.30(a)—could a reasonable person in a like position and acting in similar circumstances have arrived at that belief? In the rare case where a decision respecting the corporation's best interests is so removed from the realm of reason (*e.g.*, corporate waste), or a belief as to the sufficiency of the director's preparation to make an informed judgment is so unreasonable as to fall outside the permissible bounds of sound discretion (*e.g.*, if the director has undertaken no preparation and is completely uninformed), the director's judgment will not be sustained.

D. Section 8.31(A)(2)(Iii)—Lack of Objectivity or Independence

If the matter at issue involves a director's transactional interest, such as a "director's conflicting interest transaction" in which a "related person" is involved, it will be governed by section 8.61; otherwise, a lack of objectivity due to a relationship's influence on the director's judgment will be evaluated, in the context of the pending challenge of director conduct, under section 8.31. If the matter at issue involves lack of independence, the proof of domination or control and its influence on the director's judgment will typically entail different (and perhaps more convincing) evidence than what may be involved in a lack of objectivity case. The variables are manifold, and the facts must be sorted out and weighed on a case-by-case basis. For example, the closeness or nature of the relationship with the person allegedly exerting influence on the director could be a factor. If the director is required under section 8.31(a)(2)(iii)(B) to establish that the action taken by him or her was reasonably believed to be in the best interests of the corporation, the inquiry will involve the elements of actual subjective belief and objective reasonableness similar to those found in section 8.31(a)(2)(ii) and section 8.30(a).

To call into question the director's objectivity or independence on the basis of a person's relationship with, or exertion of dominance over, the director, the person must have a material interest in the challenged conduct. In the typical case, analysis of another's interest would first consider the materiality of the transaction or conduct at issue—in most cases, any transaction or other action involving the attention of the board of directors or a board committee will cross the materiality threshold, but not always—and would then consider the materiality of that person's interest in the matter. The possibility that a director's judgment would be adversely affected by another's interest in a transaction or conduct that is not material, or another's immaterial interest in a transaction or conduct, is sufficiently remote that it should not be made subject to judicial review.

In situations where there may be a lack of objectivity, domination, a conflict of interest or divided loyalty, or even where there may be grounds for the issue to be raised, the better course to follow where board or committee action is required is usually for the director to disclose the facts and circumstances posing the possible issue, and then to withdraw from the meeting (or, in the alternative, to abstain from the deliberations and voting). The board members free of any possible taint may then take appropriate action as contemplated by section 8.30 (or section 8.61 if applicable). If this course is followed, the director's conduct respecting the matter in question should be beyond challenge.

E. Section 8.31(A)(2)(Iv)—Failure to Devote Attention

The director's role involves two fundamental components: the decision-making function and the oversight function. In contrast with the decision-making function, which generally involves action taken at a point in time, the oversight function under section 8.01(b) involves ongoing monitoring of the corporation's business and affairs over a period of time. Although the facts will be outcome-determinative, deficient conduct involving a sustained failure to exercise oversight—where found actionable—has typically been characterized by the courts in terms of abdication and continued neglect by a director to devote attention, not a brief distraction or temporary interruption. Also embedded in the oversight function is the need to inquire when suspicions are aroused. This need to inquire is not a component of ongoing oversight, and does not entail proactive vigilance, but arises under section 8.31(a)(2)(iv) when, and only when, particular facts and circumstances of material concern (*e.g.*, evidence of embezzlement at a high level or the discovery of significant inventory shortages) surface.

F. Section 8.31(A)(2)(V)—Improper Financial Benefit and Other Breaches of Duties

Subchapter 8F deals in detail with directors' transactional interests. Its coverage of those interests is exclusive and its safe harbor procedures for director's conflicting interest transactions (as defined)—providing shelter from legal challenges based on interest conflicts, when properly observed—will establish a director's entitlement to any financial benefit gained from the transactional event. A director's conflicting interest transaction that is not protected by the fairness standard set forth in section 8.61(b)(3), pursuant to which the conflicted director may establish the transaction to have been fair to the corporation, would often involve receipt of a financial benefit to which the director was not entitled (*i.e.*, the transaction was not "fair" to the corporation). Unauthorized use of corporate assets, such as aircraft or hotel suites, would also provide a basis for the proper challenge of a director's conduct. There can be other forms of improper financial benefit not involving a transaction with the corporation or use of its facilities, such as where a director profits from unauthorized use of proprietary information.

There is no materiality threshold that applies to a financial benefit to which a director is not properly entitled. The Act observes this principle in several places, for example, the exception to liability elimination prescribed in section 2.02(b)(4)(i) and the indemnification restriction in section 8.51(d)(2), as well as the liability standard in section 8.31(a)(2)(v).

The second clause of section 8.31(a)(2)(v) is, in part, a catchall provision that implements the intention to make section 8.31 a generally inclusive provision but, at the same time, to recognize the existence of other breaches of common-law principles that can give rise to liability for directors. As developed in the case law, these actionable breaches may include unauthorized use of corporate property or information (which as noted above, might also be characterized as receipt of an improper financial benefit), unfair competition with the corporation or the taking of a corporate opportunity.

Section 8.31(b)

Whether a corporation or its shareholders have suffered harm and whether a particular director's conduct was the proximate cause of that harm may be affected by the collective nature of board action. Proper performance of the relevant duty through the action taken by the director's colleagues can overcome the consequences of his or her deficient conduct. For example, where a director's conduct can be challenged under section 8.31(a)(2)(ii)(B) by reason of having been uninformed about the decision or not reading the materials distributed before the meeting, or arriving late at the board meeting just in time for the vote but, nonetheless, voting in favor solely because the others were in favor—the favorable action by a quorum of properly informed directors would ordinarily protect the director against liability, either because there was no harm or the offending director's actions were not the proximate cause of the harm. Although the concept of "proximate cause" is a term of art that is basic to tort law, for purposes of section 8.31(b)(1), a useful approach for the concept's application would be that the challenged conduct must have been a "substantial factor in producing the harm."

§ 8.42. Standards of Conduct For Officers

(a) An officer, when performing in such capacity, has the duty to act:

> (1) in good faith;
>
> (2) with the care that a person in a like position would reasonably exercise under similar circumstances; and
>
> (3) in a manner the officer reasonably believes to be in the best interests of the corporation.

(b) The duty of an officer includes the obligation

> (1) to inform the superior officer to whom, or the board of directors or the board committee to which, the officer reports of information about the affairs of the corporation known to the officer, within the scope of the officer's functions, and known to the officer to be material to such superior officer, board or committee; and
>
> (2) to inform his or her superior officer, or another appropriate person within the corporation, or the board of directors, or a board committee, of any actual or probable material violation of law involving the corporation or material breach of duty to the corporation by an officer, employee, or agent of the corporation, that the officer believes has occurred or is likely to occur.

(c) In discharging his or her duties, an officer who does not have knowledge that makes reliance unwarranted is entitled to rely on:

> (1) the performance of properly delegated responsibilities by one or more employees of the corporation whom the officer reasonably believes to be reliable and competent in performing the responsibilities delegated; or
>
> (2) (information, opinions, reports or statements, including financial statements and other financial data, prepared or presented by one or more employees of the corporation whom the officer reasonably

believes to be reliable and competent in the matters presented or by legal counsel, public accountants, or other persons retained by the corporation as to matters involving skills or expertise the officer reasonably believes are matters (i) within the particular person's professional or expert competence or (ii) as to which the particular person merits confidence.

(d) An officer shall not be liable to the corporation or its shareholders for any decision to take or not to take action, or any failure to take any action, as an officer, if the duties of the office are performed in compliance with this section. Whether an officer who does not comply with this section shall have liability will depend in such instance on applicable law, including those principles of section 8.31 that have relevance.

Official Comment

Under section 8.42(a), an officer, when performing in such officer's official capacity, has to meet standards of conduct generally specified for directors under section 8.30. This section is not intended to modify, diminish or qualify the duties or standards of conduct that may be imposed upon specific officers by other law or regulation.

Common law has generally recognized a duty on the part of officers and key employees to disclose to their superiors material information relevant to the affairs of the corporation. This duty is implicit in, and embraced under, the broader standard of section 8.42(a), but section 8.42(b) sets forth this disclosure obligation explicitly. Section 8.42(b)(1) specifies that business information shall be transmitted through the officer's regular reporting channels. Section 8.42(b)(2) specifies the reporting responsibility differently with respect to actual or probable material violations of law or material breaches of duty. The use of the term "appropriate" in subsection (b)(2) accommodates any normative standard that the corporation may have prescribed for reporting potential violations of law or duty to a specified person, such as an ombudsperson, ethics officer, internal auditor, general counsel or the like, as well as situations where there is no designated person but the officer's immediate superior is not appropriate (for example, because the officer believes that individual is complicit in the unlawful activity or breach of duty).

Section 8.42(b)(1) should not be interpreted so broadly as to discourage efficient delegation of functions. It addresses the flow of information to the board of directors and to superior officers necessary to enable them to perform their decision-making and oversight functions. The officer's duties under subsection (b) may not be negated by agreement; however, their scope under section 8.42(b)(1) may be shaped by prescribing the scope of an officer's functional responsibilities.

With respect to the duties under section 8.42(b)(2), codes of conduct or codes of ethics may prescribe the circumstances in which and mechanisms by which officers and employees may discharge their duty to report material information to superior officers or the board of directors, or to other designated persons.

The term "material" modifying violations of law or breaches of duty in section 8.42(b)(2) denotes a qualitative as well as quantitative standard. It relates not only to the potential direct financial impact on the corporation, but also to the nature of the violation or breach. For example, an embezzlement of $10,000, or even less, would be material because of the seriousness of the offense, even though the amount involved would ordinarily not be material to the financial position or results of operations of the corporation.

The duty under section 8.42(b)(2) is triggered by an officer's subjective belief that a material violation of law or breach of duty actually or probably has occurred or is likely to occur. This duty is not triggered by objective knowledge concepts, such as whether the officer should have concluded that such misconduct was occurring. The subjectivity of the trigger under subsection (b)(2), however, does not excuse officers from their obligations under subsection (a) to act in good faith and with due care in the performance of the functions assigned to them, including oversight duties within their respective areas of responsibility. There may be occasions when the principles applicable under section 8.30(c) limiting the duty of disclosure by directors where a duty of confidentiality is overriding may also apply to officers.

An officer's ability to rely on others in meeting the standards prescribed in section 8.42 may be more limited, depending upon the circumstances of the particular case, than the measure and scope of reliance permitted a director under section 8.30, in view of the greater obligation the officer may have to be familiar with the affairs of the corporation. The proper delegation of responsibilities by an officer, separate and apart from the exercise of judgment as to the delegatee's reliability and competence, is concerned with the procedure employed. This will involve, in the usual case, sufficient communication such that the delegatee understands the scope of the assignment and, in turn, manifests to the officer a willingness and commitment to undertake its performance. The entitlement to rely upon employees assumes that a delegating officer will maintain a sufficient level of communication with the officer's subordinates to fulfill his or her supervisory responsibilities. The definition of "employee" in section 1.40 includes an officer; accordingly, section 8.42 contemplates the delegation of responsibilities to other officers as well as to non-officer employees.

Although under section 8.42(d), performance meeting that section's standards of conduct will eliminate an officer's exposure to any liability to the corporation or its shareholders, failure by an officer to meet that section's standards will not automatically result in liability. Deficient performance of duties by an officer, depending upon the facts and circumstances, will normally be dealt with through intracorporate disciplinary procedures, such as reprimand, compensation adjustment, delayed promotion, demotion or discharge. These procedures may be subject to (and limited by) the terms of an officer's employment agreement.

In some cases, failure to observe relevant standards of conduct can give rise to an officer's liability to the corporation or its shareholders. A court review of challenged conduct will involve an evaluation of the particular facts and circumstances in light of applicable law. In this connection, section 8.42(d) recognizes that relevant principles of section 8.31, such as duties to deal fairly with the corporation and its shareholders and the challenger's burden of establishing proximately caused harm, should be taken into account. In addition, the business judgment rule will normally apply to decisions within an officer's discretionary authority. Liability to others can also arise from an officer's own acts or omissions (*e.g.*, violations of law or tort claims) and, in some cases, an officer with supervisory responsibilities can have risk exposure in connection with the acts or omissions of others.

The Official Comment to section 8.30 supplements this Official Comment to the extent that it can be appropriately viewed as generally applicable to officers as well as directors.

C. DUTY OF LOYALTY

§ 8.60. Subchapter Definitions

In this subchapter:

"Control" (including the term "controlled by") means (i) having the power, directly or indirectly, to elect or remove a majority of the members of the board of directors or other governing body of an entity, whether through the ownership of voting shares or interests, by contract, or otherwise, or (ii) being subject to a majority of the risk of loss from the entity's activities or entitled to receive a majority of the entity's residual returns.

"Director's conflicting interest transaction" means a transaction effected or proposed to be effected by the corporation (or by an entity controlled by the corporation)

> (i)   to which, at the relevant time, the director is a party;
>
> (ii) respecting which, at the relevant time, the director had knowledge and a material financial interest known to the director; or
>
> (iii) respecting which, at the relevant time, the director knew that a related person was a party or had a material financial interest.

"Fair to the corporation" means, for purposes of section 8.61(b)(3), that the transaction as a whole was beneficial to the corporation, taking into appropriate account whether it was (i) fair in terms of the director's dealings with the corporation, and (ii) comparable to what might have been obtainable in an arm's length transaction, given the consideration paid or received by the corporation.

Source: Model Bus. Corp. Act §§ 1.43, 8.60–8.63 (2016). Copyright © 2016 by American Bar Association. Reprinted with permission.

"Material financial interest" means a financial interest in a transaction that would reasonably be expected to impair the objectivity of the director's judgment when participating in action on the authorization of the transaction.

"Related person" means:

(i)   the individual's spouse;

(ii) a child, stepchild, grandchild, parent, step parent, grandparent, sibling, step sibling, half sibling, aunt, uncle, niece or nephew (or spouse of any such person) of the individual or of the individual's spouse;

(iii) a natural person living in the same home as the individual;

(iv) an entity (other than the corporation or an entity controlled by the corporation) controlled by the individual or any person specified above in this definition;

(v)   a domestic or foreign (A) business or nonprofit corporation (other than the corporation or an entity controlled by the corporation) of which the individual is a director, (B) unincorporated entity of which the individual is a general partner or a member of the governing body, or (C) individual, trust or estate for whom or of which the individual is a trustee, guardian, personal representative or like fiduciary; or

(vi) a person that is, or an entity that is controlled by, an employer of the individual.

"Relevant time" means (i) the time at which directors' action respecting the transaction is taken in compliance with section 8.62, or (ii) if the transaction is not brought before the board of directors (or a committee) for action under section 8.62, at the time the corporation (or an entity controlled by the corporation) becomes legally obligated to consummate the transaction.

"Required disclosure" means disclosure of (i) the existence and nature of the director's conflicting interest, and (ii) all facts known to the director respecting the subject matter of the transaction that a director free of such conflicting interest would reasonably believe to be material in deciding whether to proceed with the transaction.

Official Comment

Director's Conflicting Interest Transaction

The definition of "director's conflicting interest transaction" in section 8.60 is the core concept underlying subchapter F. The definition operates preclusively in that, as used in section 8.61, it denies the power of a court to invalidate transactions or otherwise to remedy conduct on the ground that the director has a conflict of interest if it falls outside the statutory definition of "director's conflicting interest transaction."

A. Transaction

For purposes of subchapter F, "transaction" requires a bilateral (or multilateral) arrangement to which the corporation or an entity controlled by the corporation is a party. Subchapter F does not apply to transactions to which no such entity is a party. For example, a purchase or sale by the director of the corporation's shares on the open market or from or to a third party is not a "director's conflicting interest transaction" within the meaning of subchapter F.

B. Party to the Transaction—The Corporation or a Controlled Entity

In the usual case, the transaction would be effected by X Co. Assume, however, that X Co. controls the vote for directors of S Co. D wishes to sell a building D owns to X Co. and X Co. is willing to buy it. As a business matter, it makes no difference to X Co. whether it takes the title directly or indirectly through its subsidiary S Co. or some other entity that X Co. controls. The applicability of subchapter F does not depend upon that formal distinction, because the subchapter includes within its operative framework transactions by entities controlled by X Co. Thus, subchapter F would apply to a sale of the building by D to S Co.

C. Party to the Transaction—The Director or a Related Person

D can have a conflicting interest in only two ways.

First, a conflicting interest can arise under either clause (i) or (ii) of the definition of "director's conflicting interest transaction." This will be the case if, under clause (i), the transaction is between D and X Co. A conflicting interest also will arise under clause (ii) if D is not a party to the transaction, but knows about it and knows that he or she has a material financial interest in it. The personal economic stake of the director must be in the transaction itself—that is, the director's gain must flow directly from the transaction. A remote gain (for example, a future reduction in tax rates in the local community) is not enough to give rise to a conflicting interest under clause (ii) of the definition.

Second, a conflicting interest for D can arise under clause (iii) of the definition from the involvement in the transaction of a "related person" of D that is either a party to the transaction or has a "material financial interest" in it. "Related person" is defined in section 8.60.

Circumstances may arise where a director could have a conflicting interest under more than one clause of the definition. For example, if Y Co. is a party to or interested in the transaction with X Co. and Y Co. is a related person of D, the matter would fall under clause (iii), but D also may have a conflicting interest under clause (ii) if D's economic interest in Y Co. is sufficiently material and if the importance of the transaction to Y Co. is sufficiently material.

A director may have relationships and connections to persons and institutions that are not specified in clause (iii) of the definition. Such relationships and connections fall outside subchapter F because the categories of persons described in clause (iii) constitute the exclusive universe for purposes of subchapter F. For example, in a challenged transaction between X Co. and Y Co., suppose the court confronts the argument that D also is a major creditor of Y Co. and that creditor status in Y Co. gives D a conflicting interest. The court should rule that D's creditor status in Y Co. does not fit any category of the definition; and therefore, the conflict of interest claim must be rejected by reason of section 8.61(a). The result would be different if Y Co.'s debt to D were of such economic significance to D that it would either fall under clause (ii) of the definition or, if it placed D in control of Y Co., it would fall under clause (iii) (because Y Co. is a related person of D under clause (iv) of the definition). To explore the example further, if D is also a shareholder of Y Co., but D does not have a material financial interest in the transaction and does not control Y Co., no director's conflicting interest transaction arises and the transaction cannot be challenged on conflict of interest grounds. To avoid any appearance of impropriety, D, nonetheless, could consider recusal from the other directors' deliberations and voting on the transaction between X Co. and Y Co.

Any director's interest in a transaction that meets the criteria of the definition renders the transaction a "director's conflicting interest transaction." If the director's interest satisfies those criteria, subchapter F draws no distinction between a director's interest that clashes with the interests of the corporation and a director's interest that coincides with, or is parallel to, or even furthers the interests of the corporation.

Routine business transactions frequently occur between companies with overlapping directors. If X Co. and Y Co. have routine, frequent business dealings with terms dictated by competitive market forces, then even if a director of X Co. has a relevant relationship with Y Co., the transactions would almost always be defensible, regardless of approval by disinterested directors or shareholders, on the ground that they are "fair." For example, a common transaction involves a purchase of the corporation's products or services by Y Co., or perhaps by D or a related person, at prices normally charged by the corporation. In such circumstances, it usually will not be difficult for D to show that the transaction was on arms-length terms and was fair. Even a purchase by D of a product of X Co. at a usual "employee's discount," although technically assailable as a conflicting interest transaction, would customarily be viewed as a routine incident of the office of director and, thus, "fair" to the corporation.

Control

The definition of "control" in section 8.60 contains two independent clauses. The first clause addresses the ability to elect or remove a majority of the members of an entity's governing body. That power can arise, for example, from articles of incorporation or a shareholders' agreement. The second clause addresses economic interest in the entity and may include, among other circumstances, financial structures that do not have voting interests or a governing body in the traditional sense, such as special purpose entities.

Relevant Time

The definition of director's conflicting interest transaction requires that, except where he or she is a party, the director know of the transaction at the "relevant time" as defined in section 8.60. Where the director lacks such knowledge, the risk to the corporation that the director's judgment might be improperly influenced, or the risk of unfair dealing by the director, is not present. In a corporation of significant size, routine transactions in the ordinary course of business, which typically involve decision making at lower management levels, normally will not be known to the director and, if that is the case, will not meet the "knowledge" requirement of clauses (ii) or (iii) of the definition of director's conflicting interest transaction.

Material Financial Interest

The "interest" of a director or a related person in a transaction can be direct or indirect (*e.g.*, as an owner of an entity or a beneficiary of a trust or estate), but it must be financial for there to exist a "director's conflicting interest transaction." Thus, for example, an interest in a transaction between X Co. and a director's alma mater, or any other transaction involving X Co. and a party with which D might have emotional involvement but no financial interest, would not give rise to a director's conflicting interest transaction. Moreover, whether a financial interest is material does not turn on any asser- tion by the possibly conflicted director that the interest in question would not impair his or her objectivity if called upon to vote on the authorization of the transaction. Instead, assuming a court challenge asserting the materiality of the financial interest, the standard calls upon the trier of fact to determine whether the objectivity of the director would reasonably be expected to have been impaired by the financial interest when voting on the matter. Thus, the standard is objective, not subjective.

Under clause (ii) of the definition of "director's conflicting interest transaction," at the relevant time a director must have knowledge of his or her financial interest in the transaction in addition to knowing about the transaction itself. As a practical matter, a director could not be influenced by a financial interest about which that director had no knowledge. For example, the possibly conflicted director might know about X Co.'s transaction with Y Co., but might not know that his or her money manager recently established a significant position in Y Co. stock for the director's portfolio. In such circumstances, the transaction with Y Co. would not fall within clause (ii), notwithstanding the portfolio investment's significance. If the director did not know about the Y Co. portfolio investment, it could not reasonably be expected to impair the objectivity of that director's judgment.

Similarly, under clause (iii) of that definition, a director must know about his or her related person's financial interest in the transaction for the matter to give rise to a "material financial interest" as defined in section 8.60. If there is such knowledge and "interest" (*i.e.*, the financial interest could reasonably be expected to influence the director's judgment), then the matter involves a director's conflicting interest transaction.

Related Person

Six categories of "related person" of the director are set out in the definition of that term.

These categories are specific, exclusive and preemptive.

The first three categories involve closely related family, or near-family, individuals as specified in clauses (i) through (iii). These clauses are exclusive insofar as family relationships are concerned and include adoptive relationships. The references to a "spouse" include a common law spouse. Clause (iii) covers personal, as opposed to business, relationships; for example, clause (iii) does not cover a lessee.

Regarding the subcategories of persons described in clause (v) from the perspective of X Co., certain of D's relationships with other entities and D's fiduciary relationships are always a sensitive concern, separate and apart from whether D has a financial interest in the transaction. Clause (v) reflects the policy judgment that D cannot escape D's legal obligation to act in the best interests of another person for whom D has such a relationship and, accordingly, that such a relationship (without regard to any financial interest on D's part) should cause the relevant entity to have "related person" status.

The term "employer" as used in clause (vi) is not separately defined but should be interpreted in light of the purpose of subchapter F. The relevant inquiry is whether D, because of an employment relationship with an employer who has a significant stake in the outcome of the transaction, is likely to be influenced to act in the interest of that employer rather than in the interest of X Co.

References in the foregoing to "director" or "D" include the term "officer" where relevant in section 2.02(b)(6) and section 8.70.

Fair to the Corporation

The term "fair" to the corporation in subchapter F has a special meaning. The transaction, viewed as a whole, must have been beneficial to the corporation.

In considering the "fairness" of the transaction, the court will be required to consider not only the market fairness of the terms of the deal—whether it is comparable to what might have been obtainable in an arm's length transaction—but also (as the board of directors would have been required to do) whether the transaction was one that was reasonably likely to yield favorable results (or reduce detrimental results). Thus, if a manufacturing company that lacks sufficient working capital allocates some of its scarce funds to purchase at a market price a sailing yacht owned by one of its directors, it will not be easy to persuade the court that the transaction was "fair" in the sense that it was reasonably made to further the business interests of the corporation. The fact that the price paid for the yacht was a "fair" market price, and that the full measure of disclosures made by the director is beyond challenge, may still not be enough to defend and uphold the transaction.

A. Consideration and Other Terms of the Transaction

The fairness of the consideration and other transaction terms are to be judged at the relevant time. See section 8.61(b)(3). The relevant inquiry is whether the consideration paid or received by the corporation or the benefit expected to be realized by the corporation was adequate in relation to the obligations assumed or received or other consideration provided by or to the corporation. If the issue in a transaction is the "fairness" of a price, "fair" is not to be taken to imply that there is one single "fair" price, all others being "unfair." Generally, a "fair" price is any price within a range that an unrelated party might have been willing to pay or willing to accept, as the case may be, for the relevant property, asset, service or commitment, following a normal arm's-length business negotiation. The same approach applies not only to gauging the fairness of price, but also to the fairness evaluation of any other key term of the deal. Although the "fair" criterion used to assess the consideration under section 8.61(b)(3) is also a range rather than a point, the width of that range may be narrower than would be the case in an arm's-length transaction. For example, the quality and completeness of disclosures, if any, made by the conflicted director that bear upon the consideration in question are relevant in determining whether the consideration paid or received by the corporation, although otherwise commercially reasonable, was "fair" for purposes of section 8.61(b)(3).

B. Process of Decision and the Director's Conduct

In some circumstances, the behavior of the director having the conflicting interest may affect the finding and content of "fairness." Fair dealing requires that the director make "required disclosure" at the "relevant time" (both as defined) even if the director plays no role in arranging or negotiating the terms of the transaction. One illustration of unfair dealing is the director's failure to disclose fully the director's interest or hidden defects known to the director regarding the transaction. Another illustration would be the exertion by the director of improper pressure upon the other directors or other parties that might be involved with the transaction. Whether a transaction can be successfully challenged by reason of deficient or improper conduct, notwithstanding the fairness of the economic terms, will turn on the court's evaluation of the conduct and its impact on the transaction.

Required Disclosure

An important element of subchapter F's safe harbor procedures is that those acting for the corporation be able to make an informed judgment. As an example of "required disclosure" (as defined), if D knows that the land the corporation is proposing to buy from D is sinking into an abandoned coal mine, D must disclose not only D's interest in the transaction but also that the land is subsiding. As a director of X Co., D may not invoke the "buyer beware" doctrine. On the other hand, D does not have any obligation to reveal the price that D paid for the property 10 years ago, or the fact that D inherited the property, because that information is not material to the board's evaluation of the property and its business decision whether to proceed with the transaction. Further, although material facts respecting the subject of the transaction must be disclosed, D is not required to reveal personal or subjective information that bears upon D's negotiating position (such as, for example, D's urgent need for cash, or the lowest price D would be willing to accept). This is true even though such information would be highly relevant to the corporation's decision-making in that, if the information were known to the corporation, it could enable the corporation to hold out for more favorable terms.

§ 8.61. Judicial Action

(a) A transaction effected or proposed to be effected by the corporation (or by an entity controlled by the corporation) may not be the subject of equitable relief, or give rise to an award of damages or other sanctions against a director of the corporation, in a proceeding by a shareholder or by or in the right of the corporation, on the ground that the director has an interest respecting the transaction, if it is not a director's conflicting interest transaction.

(b) A director's conflicting interest transaction may not be the subject of equitable relief, or give rise to an award of damages or other sanctions against a director of the corporation, in a proceeding by a shareholder or by or in the right of the corporation, on the ground that the director has an interest respecting the transaction, if:

    (1) directors' action respecting the transaction was taken in compliance with section 8.62 at any time; or

(2) shareholders' action respecting the transaction was taken in compliance with section 8.63 at any time; or

(3) the transaction, judged according to the circumstances at the relevant time, is established to have been fair to the corporation.

Official Comment

Section 8.61 is the operational section of subchapter F, as it prescribes the judicial consequences of the other sections. In general terms:

- If the section 8.62 or 8.63 procedures are complied with, or if it is established that at the relevant time a director's conflicting interest transaction was fair to the corporation, then a director's conflicting interest transaction is immune from attack by a shareholder or the corporation on the ground of an interest of the director. However, if the transaction is vulnerable to attack on some other ground, observance of subchapter F's procedures does not make it less so.

- If a transaction is *not* a director's conflicting interest transaction as defined in section 8.60, then the transaction may *not* be enjoined, rescinded, or made the basis of other sanction on the ground of a conflict of interest of a director, regardless of whether it went through the procedures of subchapter F. In that sense, subchapter F is specifically intended to be both comprehensive and exclusive.

- If a director's conflicting interest transaction that was not at any time the subject of action taken in compliance with section 8.62 or 8.63 is challenged on grounds of the director's conflicting interest, and is not shown to be fair to the corporation, then the court may take such remedial action as it considers appropriate under the applicable law of the jurisdiction.

Section 8.61(a)

Section 8.61(a) makes clear that the bright-line definition of "director's conflicting interest transaction" is exclusive with respect to a court's review of a director's interest in a transaction. So, for example, a transaction will not constitute a director's conflicting interest transaction and, therefore, will not be subject to judicial review on the ground that a director had an interest in the transaction, where the transaction is made with a relative of a director who is not one of the relatives specified in the definition of "related person," or on the ground of an alleged interest other than a material financial interest, such as a financial interest of the director that is not material, as defined in section 8.60, or a nonfinancial interest. If, however, there is reason to believe that the fairness of a transaction involving D could be questioned, D should subject the transaction to the safe harbor procedures of subchapter F. The procedures of section 8.62 (and, to a lesser extent, section 8.63) may be used for many transactions that lie outside the definitions of section 8.60.

Section 8.61(b)

Section 8.61(b)(1) provides a defense in a proceeding challenging a director's conflicting interest transaction if the procedures of section 8.62 have been properly followed.

The plaintiff may challenge the availability of that defense based on a failure to meet the specific requirements of section 8.62 or to conform with general standards of director conduct. For example, a challenge addressed to section 8.62 compliance might question whether the acting directors were "qualified directors" or might dispute the quality and completeness of the disclosures made by D to the qualified directors. If such a challenge is successful, the board action is ineffective for purposes of section 8.61(b)(1) and both D and the transaction may be subject to the full range of remedies that might apply, absent the safe harbor, unless the fairness of the transaction can be established under section 8.61(b)(3). The fact that a transaction has been nominally passed through safe harbor procedures does not preclude a subsequent challenge based on any failure to meet the requirements of section 8.62. A challenge to the effectiveness of board action for purposes of section 8.61(b)(1) might also assert that, although the conflicted director's conduct in connection with the process of approval by qualified directors may have been consistent with the statute's expectations, the qualified directors dealing with the matter did not act in good faith or on reasonable inquiry. The kind of relief that may be appropriate when qualified directors have approved a transaction but have not acted in good faith or have failed to become reasonably informed—and, again, where the fairness of the transaction has not been established under section 8.61(b)(3)—will depend heavily on the facts of the individual case.

Section 8.61(b)(2) regarding shareholders' approval of the transaction is the matching piece to section 8.61(b)(1) regarding directors' approval.

The language "at any time" in these provisions permits the directors or the shareholders to ratify a director's conflicting interest transaction after the fact for purposes of subchapter F.

Section 8.61(b)(3) permits a showing that a director's conflicting interest transaction was fair to the corporation even if there was no compliance with section 8.62 or 8.63. Under section 8.61(b)(3) the interested director has the burden of establishing that the transaction was fair.

Note on Directors' Compensation

Although directors' fees and other forms of director compensation are typically set by the board of directors and are specifically authorized by section 8.11 of the Act, they do involve a director's conflicting interest transaction in which most if not all of the directors may not be qualified directors. Therefore, board action on directors' compensation and benefits would be subject to judicial sanction if they are not favorably acted upon by shareholders pursuant to section 8.63 or if they are not in the circumstances fair to the corporation pursuant to section 8.61(b)(3).

§ 8.62. Directors' Action

(a) Directors' action respecting a director's conflicting interest transaction is effective for purposes of section 8.61(b)(1) if the transaction has been authorized by the affirmative vote of a majority (but no fewer than two) of the qualified directors who voted on the transaction, after required disclosure by the conflicted director of information not already known by such qualified directors, or after modified disclosure in compliance with subsection (b), provided that:

  (1) the qualified directors have deliberated and voted outside the presence of and without the participation by any other director; and

  (2) where the action has been taken by a board committee, all members of the committee were qualified directors, and either (i) the committee was composed of all the qualified directors on the board of directors or (ii) the members of the committee were appointed by the affirmative vote of a majority of the qualified directors on the board of directors.

(b) [...].

(c) A majority (but no fewer than two) of all the qualified directors on the board of directors, or on the board committee, constitutes a quorum for purposes of action that complies with this section.

Official Comment

Section 8.62 provides the procedure for action by the board of directors or by a board committee under subchapter F. In the normal course this section, together with section 8.61(b), will be the key method for addressing directors' conflicting interest transactions. Any discussion of section 8.62 must have in mind the requirements that directors act in good faith and on reasonable inquiry. Director action that does not comply with those requirements, even if otherwise in compliance with section 8.62, will be subject to challenge and not be given effect under section 8.62.

The definition of "qualified director" in section 1.43(a)(4) excludes not only a director who is conflicted directly or because of a person specified in the categories of the "related person" definition in section 8.60, but also any director with a familial, financial, employment, professional or other relationship with *another director for whom the transaction is a director's conflicting interest transaction* that would be likely to impair the objectivity of the first director's judgment when participating in a vote on the transaction.

Action under section 8.62 may take the form of committee action meeting the requirements of subsection (a)(2). The requirements for effective committee action are intended to preclude the appointment as committee members of a favorably inclined minority from among all the qualified directors. With respect to required disclosure under subsection (a), if there is more than one conflicted director interested in the transaction, the need for required disclosure would apply to each.

§ 1.43. Qualified Director

(a) A "qualified director" is a director who, at the time action is to be taken under:

   [...]

   (4) section 8.62, is not a director (i) as to whom the transaction is a director's conflicting interest transaction, or (ii) who has a material relationship with another director as to whom the transaction is a director's conflicting interest transaction; or

(b) For purposes of this section:

   (1) "material relationship" means a familial, financial, professional, employment or other relationship that would reasonably be expected to impair the objectivity of the director's judgment when participating in the action to be taken; and

   (2) "material interest" means an actual or potential benefit or detriment (other than one which would devolve on the corporation or the shareholders generally) that would reasonably be expected to impair the objectivity of the director's judgment when participating in the action to be taken.

Official Comment

Although the term "qualified director" embraces the concept of independence, it does so only in relation to the director's interest or involvement in the specific situations to which the definition applies. The judicial decisions that have examined the qualifications of directors for such purposes have generally required that directors be both *disinterested*, in the sense of no having exposure to an actual or potential benefit or detriment arising out of the action being taken (as opposed to an actual or potential benefit or detriment to the corporation or all shareholders generally), and *independent*, in the sense of having no personal or other relationship with an interested director (*e.g.*, a director who is a party to a transaction with the corporation) that presents a reasonable likelihood that the director's objectivity will be impaired. The "qualified director" concept embraces both of those requirements, and its application is situation-specific; that is, "qualified director" determinations will depend upon the directly relevant facts and circumstances, and the disqualification of a director to act arises from factors that would reasonably be expected to impair the objectivity of the director's judgment. On the other hand, the concept does not suggest that a "qualified director" has or should have special expertise to act on the matter in question.

In each context in which the "qualified director" definition applies, it also excludes any director who has a "material relationship" with another director (or, with respect to a provision applying to an officer under section 2.02(b)(6) or section 8.70, a "material relationship" with that officer) who is not disinterested for one or more of the reasons outlined in the preceding paragraph. Any relationship with such a person, whether the relationship is familial, financial, professional, employment or otherwise, is a "material relationship," as that term is defined in section 1.43(b)(1), if it would reasonably be expected to impair the objectivity of the director's judgment when voting or otherwise participating in action to be taken on a matter referred to in section 1.43(a). The determination of whether there is a "material relationship" should be based on the practicalities of the situation rather than on formalistic considerations. For example, a director employed by a corporation controlled by another director should be regarded as having an employment relationship with that director. On the other hand, a casual social acquaintance with another director should not be regarded as a disqualifying relationship.

The term "qualified director" is distinct from the generic term "independent director," which is not used in the Act. As a result, a director who might typically be viewed as an "independent director" may in some circumstances not be a "qualified director," and vice versa.

§ 8.63. Shareholders' Action

(a) Shareholders' action respecting a director's conflicting interest transaction is effective for purposes of section 8.61(b)(2) if a majority of the votes cast by the holders of all qualified shares are in favor of the transaction after (i) notice to shareholders describing the action to be taken respecting the transaction, (ii) provision to the corporation of the information referred to in subsection (b), and (iii) communication to the shareholders entitled to vote on the transaction of the information that is the subject of required disclosure, to the extent the information is not known by them.

(b) A director who has a conflicting interest respecting the transaction shall, before the shareholders' vote, inform the secretary or other officer or agent of the corporation authorized to tabulate votes, in writing, of the number of shares that the director knows are not qualified shares under subsection (c), and the identity of the holders of those shares.

(c) For purposes of this section: (i) "holder" means and "held by" refers to shares held by a record shareholder, a beneficial shareholder, and an unrestricted voting trust beneficial owner; and (ii) "qualified shares" means all shares entitled to be voted with respect to the transaction except for shares that the secretary or other officer or agent of the corporation authorized to tabulate votes either knows, or under subsection (b) is notified, are held by (A) a director who has a conflicting interest respecting the transaction or (B) a related person of the director (excluding a person described in clause (vi) of the definition of "related person" in section 8.60).

(d) A majority of the votes entitled to be cast by the holders of all qualified shares constitutes a quorum for purposes of compliance with this section. Subject to the provisions of subsection (e), shareholders' action that otherwise complies with this section is not affected by the presence of holders, or by the voting, of shares that are not qualified shares.

Official Comment

Section 8.63 provides the machinery for shareholders' action that confers safe harbor protection for a director's conflicting interest transaction, just as section 8.62 provides the machinery for directors' action that confers subchapter F safe harbor protection for such a transaction.

Section 8.63(a)

Section 8.63(a) specifies the procedure required to confer effective safe harbor protection for a director's conflicting interest transaction through a vote of shareholders. In advance of the vote, three steps must be taken: (i) shareholders must be given timely and adequate notice describing the transaction; (ii) D must disclose the information called for in subsection (b); and (iii) required disclosure (as defined in section 8.60) must be made to the shareholders entitled to vote.

Shareholder action that complies with subsection (a) may be taken at any time, before or after the corporation becomes legally obligated to complete the transaction.

Section 8.63(b)

In many circumstances, the secretary or other person charged with counting votes on behalf of X Co. will have no way to know which of X Co.'s outstanding shares should be excluded from the vote. Section 8.63(b) (together with subsection (c)) therefore obligates a director who has a conflicting interest respecting the transaction, as a prerequisite to safe harbor protection by shareholder action, to provide information known to the director with respect to the shares that are not qualified.

Section 8.63(c)

The definition of "qualified shares" in section 8.63(c) does not exclude shares held by entities or persons described in clause (vi) of the definition of "related person" in section 8.60, *i.e.*, a person that is, or is an entity that is controlled by, an employer of D. If D is an employee of Y Co., that fact does not prevent Y Co. from exercising its usual rights to vote any shares it may hold in X Co. D may be unaware of, and would not necessarily monitor, whether his or her employer holds X Co. shares. Moreover, D will typically have no control over his or her employer and how it may vote its X Co. shares.

D. BUSINESS OPPORTUNITIES

§ 8.70. Business Opportunities

(a) If a director or officer pursues or takes advantage of a business opportunity directly, or indirectly through or on behalf of another person, that action may not be the subject of equitable relief, or give rise to an award of damages or other sanctions against the director, officer or other person, in a proceeding by or in the right of the corporation on the ground that the opportunity should have first been offered to the corporation, if

   (1) before the director, officer or other person becomes legally obligated respecting the opportunity the director or officer brings it to the attention of the corporation and either:

      (i) action by qualified directors disclaiming the corporation's interest in the opportunity is taken in compliance with the same procedures as are set forth in section 8.62, or

      (ii) shareholders' action disclaiming the corporation's interest in the opportunity is taken in compliance with the procedures set forth in section 8.63, in either case as if the decision being made concerned a director's conflicting interest transaction, except that, rather than making "required disclosure" as defined in section 8.60, the director or officer shall have made prior disclosure to those acting on behalf of the corporation of all material facts concerning the business opportunity known to the director or officer; or

   (2) the duty to offer the corporation the business opportunity has been limited or eliminated pursuant to a provision of the articles of incorporation adopted (and where required, made effective by action of qualified directors) in accordance with section 2.02(b)(6).

(b) In any proceeding seeking equitable relief or other remedies based upon an alleged improper pursuit or taking advantage of a business opportunity by a director or officer, directly, or indirectly through or on behalf of another person, the fact that the director or officer did not employ the procedure described in subsection (a)(1)(i) or (ii) before pursuing or taking advantage of the opportunity shall not create an implication that the opportunity should have been first presented to the corporation or alter the burden of proof otherwise applicable to establish that the director or officer breached a duty to the corporation in the circumstances.

Source: Model Bus. Corp. Act §§ 1.43, 8.70 (2016). Copyright © 2016 by American Bar Association. Reprinted with permission.

Official Comment

Section 8.70(a)(1) provides a safe harbor for a director or officer weighing possible involvement with a prospective business opportunity that might constitute a "corporate opportunity." The phrase "directly, or indirectly through or on behalf of another person" recognizes the need to cover transactions pursued or effected either directly by the director or officer or indirectly through or on behalf of another person, which might be a related person as defined in section 8.60 or a person which is not a related person. By action of the board of directors or shareholders of the corporation under section 8.70(a) (1), the director or officer can obtain a disclaimer of the corporation's interest in the matter before proceeding with such involvement. In the alternative, the corporation may, among other things, (i) decline to disclaim its interest, (ii) delay a decision respecting granting a disclaimer pending receipt from the director or officer of additional information (or for any other reason), or (iii) attach conditions to the disclaimer it grants under section 8.70(a)(1).

The safe harbor provided under section 8.70(a)(1) may be utilized only for a specific business opportunity. A broader advance safe harbor for any, or one or more classes or categories of, business opportunities must meet the requirements of section 2.02(b)(6). Section 8.70(a)(2) confirms that if the duty of an officer or director to present an opportunity has been limited or eliminated by a provision in the articles of incorporation under section 2.02(b)(6) (and, in the case of officers, appropriate action by qualified directors as required by that section), a safe harbor exists in connection with the pursuit or taking of the opportunity. The common law doctrine of "corporate opportunity" has long been recognized as a part of the director's duty of loyalty and, under court decisions, extends to officers. The doctrine recognizes that the corporation has a right prior to that of its directors or officers to act on certain business opportunities that come to the attention of the directors or officers. In such situations, a director or officer who acts on the opportunity for the benefit of the director or officer or another person without having first presented it to the corporation can be held to have "usurped" or "intercepted" a right of the corporation. A defendant director or officer who is found by a court to have violated the duty of loyalty in this regard, as well as related or other persons involved in the transaction, may be subject to damages or possible equitable remedies, including injunction, disgorgement or the imposition of a constructive trust in favor of the corporation. Although the doctrine's concept is easily described, whether it will be found to apply in a given case depends on the facts and circumstances of the particular situation and is thus frequently unpredictable.

In recognition that the corporation need not pursue every business opportunity of which it becomes aware, an opportunity coming within the doctrine's criteria that has been properly presented to and declined by the corporation may then be pursued or taken by the presenting director or officer without breach of the duty of loyalty.

The fact-intensive nature of the corporate opportunity doctrine resists statutory definition. Instead, subchapter G employs the broader notion of "business opportunity" that encompasses any opportunity, without regard to whether it would come within the judicial definition of a "corporate opportunity," as it may have been developed by courts in a jurisdiction. When properly employed, subchapter G provides a safe-harbor mechanism enabling a director or officer to pursue an opportunity directly, or indirectly through or on behalf of another person, free of possible challenge claiming conflict with the director's or officer's duty on the ground that the opportunity should first have been offered to the corporation. Section 8.70 is modeled on the safe-harbor and approval procedures of subchapter F pertaining to directors' conflicting interest transactions with, however, some modifications necessary to accommodate differences in the two matters addressed.

Section 8.70(a)(1)

Section 8.70(a)(1) describes the safe harbor available to a director or officer who elects to subject a business opportunity, regardless of whether the opportunity would be classified as a "corporate opportunity," to the disclosure and approval procedures set forth in that section. The safe harbor provided is as broad as that provided for a director's conflicting interest transaction in section 8.61. If the director or officer makes the prescribed disclosure of the facts specified and the corporation's interest in the opportunity is disclaimed by director action under subsection (a)(1)(i) or shareholder action under subsection (a)(1)(ii), the director or officer has foreclosed any claimed breach of the duty of loyalty and may not be subject to equitable relief, damages or other sanctions if the director or officer thereafter pursues or takes the opportunity for his or her own account or through or for the benefit of another person. As a general proposition, disclaimer by director action under subsection (a)(1)(i) must meet all of the requirements provided in section 8.62 with respect to a director's conflicting interest transaction and disclaimer by shareholder action under subsection (a)(1)(ii) must likewise meet all of the requirements for shareholder action under section 8.63. Note, however, several important differences.

First, in contrast to director or shareholder action under sections 8.62 and 8.63, which may be taken at any time, section 8.70(a)(1) requires that the director or officer present the opportunity and secure director or shareholder action disclaiming it *before* the director of officer or other person involved through or on behalf of the director or officer becomes legally obligated respecting the opportunity. The safe harbor concept contemplates that the corporation's decision maker will have full freedom of action in deciding whether the corporation should take over a proffered opportunity or disclaim the corporation's interest in it. If the director or officer could seek ratification after the legal obligation respecting the opportunity arises, the option of taking over the opportunity would, in most cases, be foreclosed to the corporation. The safe harbor's benefit is available only when the corporation can entertain the opportunity in a fully objective way.

The second difference relates to the necessary disclosure. Instead of employing section 8.60's definition of "required disclosure" which is incorporated in sections 8.62 and 8.63 and includes "the existence and nature of the director's conflicting interest," the disclosure obligation of section 8.70(a)(1) requires only that the director or officer reveal all material facts concerning the business opportunity known to the director or officer. The safe harbor procedure shields the director or officer even if a material fact regarding the business opportunity is not disclosed, so long as the proffering director or officer had no knowledge of that fact.

Section 8.70(b)

Section 8.70(b) reflects a fundamental difference between the coverage of subchapters F and

Because subchapter F provides an exclusive definition of "director's conflicting interest transaction," any transaction meeting the definition that is not approved in accordance with the provisions of subchapter F is not entitled to its safe harbor. Unless the interested director can, upon challenge, establish the transaction's fairness, the director's conduct is presumptively actionable and subject to the full range of remedies that might otherwise be awarded by a court. In contrast, the concept of "business opportunity" under section 8.70 is not defined but is intended to be broader than what might be regarded as an actionable "corporate opportunity." This approach reflects the fact-intensive nature of the corporate opportunity doctrine, with the result that a director or officer may be inclined to seek safe harbor protection under section 8.70 before pursuing an opportunity that may or may not be a "corporate opportunity." Likewise, a director or officer may conclude that a business opportunity is not a "corporate opportunity" under applicable law and choose to pursue it without seeking a disclaimer by the corporation under subsection (a)(1). Accordingly, subsection (b) provides that a decision not to seek the safe harbor offered by subsection (a)(1) neither creates a negative implication nor alters the burden of proof in any subsequent proceeding seeking damages or equitable relief based upon an alleged improper taking of a "corporate opportunity."

§ 1.43. Qualified Director

(a) A "qualified director" is a director who, at the time action is to be taken under:
[…]

   (5) section 8.70, is not a director who (i) pursues or takes advantage of the business opportunity, directly, or indirectly through or on behalf of another person, or (ii) has a material relationship with a director or officer who pursues or takes advantage of the business opportunity, directly, or indirectly through or on behalf of another person.

(b) For purposes of this section:

    (1) "material relationship" means a familial, financial, professional, employment or other relationship that would reasonably be expected to impair the objectivity of the director's judgment when participating in the action to be taken.

CHAPTER 18

PROTECTING DIRECTORS AND OFFICERS

We have previously discussed how directors may find themselves in lawsuits for breaching their fiduciary duties to the corporation. Given the possibility of being sued for breaching these fiduciary duties, a corporation's directors' actually bear a great deal of potential personal liability. To mitigate this liability, corporations may have certain directors' protections, such as exculpatory clauses, indemnification, or insurance.

A. EXCULPATION OF DIRECTOR LIABILITY

§ 2.02. Articles of Incorporation

(b) The articles of incorporation may set forth:

(4) a provision eliminating or limiting the liability of a director to the corporation or its shareholders for money damages for any action taken, or any failure to take any action, as a director, except liability for (i) the amount of a financial benefit received by a director to which the director is not entitled; (ii) an intentional infliction of harm on the corporation or the shareholders; (iii) a violation of section 8.32; or (iv) an intentional violation of criminal law;

(6) a provision limiting or eliminating any duty of a director or any other person to offer the corporation the right to have or participate in any, or one or more classes or categories of, business opportunities, before the pursuit or taking of the opportunity by the director or other person; provided that any application of such a provision to an officer or a related person of that officer (i) also requires approval of that application by the board of directors, subsequent to the effective

Source: Model Bus. Corp. Act § 2.02 (2016). Copyright © 2016 by American Bar Association. Reprinted with permission.

date of the provision, by action of qualified directors taken in compliance with the same procedures as are set forth in section 8.62, and (ii) may be limited by the authorizing action of the board.

Official Comment

Optional Provisions

Section 2.02(b) allows the articles of incorporation to contain optional provisions deemed sufficiently important to be of public record or subject to amendment only by the processes applicable to amendments of articles of incorporation.

A. Limitations of Director Liability

Section 2.02(b)(4) authorizes the inclusion of a provision in the articles of incorporation eliminating or limiting, with certain exceptions, the liability of the directors to the corporation or its shareholders for money damages. This section is optional rather than self-executing and does not apply to equitable relief. Likewise, nothing in section 2.02(b)(4) in any way affects the right of the shareholders to remove directors, under section 8.08(a), with or without cause. The phrase "as a director" emphasizes that section 2.02(b)(4) applies to a director's actions or failures to take action in the director's capacity as a director and not in any other capacity, such as officer, employee or controlling shareholder. However, it is not intended to exclude coverage of conduct by individuals, even though they are also officers, employees or controlling shareholders, to the extent they are acting in their capacity as directors.

Shareholders are given considerable latitude in limiting directors' liability for money damages. The statutory exceptions to permitted limitations of director liability are few and narrow and are discussed below.

Financial Benefit

Corporate law subjects transactions from which a director could benefit personally to special scrutiny. The financial benefits exception is limited to the amount of the benefit actually received. Thus, liability for punitive damages could be eliminated, except in cases of intentional infliction of harm or for violation of criminal law (as described below) where, in a particular case (for example, theft), punitive damages may be available. The benefit must be financial rather than in less easily measured and more conjectural forms, such as business goodwill, personal reputation, or social ingratiation. The phrase "received by a director" is not intended to be a "bright line." As a director's conduct moves toward the edge of what may be exculpated, the director should bear the risk of miscalculation. Depending upon the circumstances, a director may be deemed to have received a benefit that the director caused to be directed to another person, for example, a relative, friend, or affiliate.

What constitutes a financial benefit "to which the director is not entitled" is left to judicial development. For example, a director is entitled to reasonable compensation for the performance of services or to an increase in the value of stock or stock options held by the director; on the other hand, a director is not entitled to a bribe, a kick-back, or the profits from a corporate opportunity improperly taken by the director.

Intentional Infliction of Harm

There may be situations in which a director intentionally causes harm to the corporation even though the director does not receive any improper benefit. The use of the word "intentional," rather than a less precise term such as "knowing," is meant to refer to the specific intent to perform, or fail to perform, the acts with actual knowledge that the director's action, or failure to act, will cause harm, rather than a general intent to perform the acts which cause the harm.

Unlawful Distributions

Section 8.32(a) indicates a strong policy in favor of liability for unlawful distributions approved by directors who have not complied with the standards of conduct of section 8.30. Accordingly, the exception in section 2.02(b)(4) (iii) prohibits the shareholders from eliminating or limiting the liability of directors for a violation of section 8.32.

Intentional Violation of Criminal Law

Even though a director committing a crime may intend to benefit the corporation, the shareholders should not be permitted to exculpate the director for any harm caused by an intentional violation of criminal law, including, for example, fines and legal expenses of the corporation in defending a criminal prosecution. The use of the word "intentional," rather than a less precise term such as "knowing," is meant to refer to the specific intent to perform, or fail to perform, the acts with actual knowledge that the director's action, or failure to act, constitutes a violation of criminal law.

B. Business Opportunities

Section 2.02(b)(6) authorizes the inclusion of a provision in the articles of incorporation to limit or eliminate, in advance, the duty of a director or other person to bring a business opportunity to the corporation. The limitation or elimination may be blanket in nature and apply to any business opportunities, or it may extend only to one or more specified classes or categories of business opportunities. The adoption of such a provision constitutes a curtailment of the duty of loyalty which includes the doctrine of corporate opportunity. If such a provision is included in the articles, taking advantage of a business opportunity covered by the provision of the articles without offering it to the corporation will not expose the director or other person to whom it is made applicable either to monetary damages or to equitable or any other relief in favor of the corporation upon compliance with the requirements of section 2.02(b)(6).

This provision may be useful, for example, in the context of a private equity investor that wishes to have a nominee on the board but conditions its investment on an advance limitation or elimination of the corporate opportunity doctrine because of the uncertainty over the application of the corporate opportunity doctrine inherent when investments are made in multiple enterprises in specific industries. Another example is a joint venture in corporate form where the participants in the joint venture want to be sure that the corporate opportunity doctrine would not apply to their activities outside the joint venture.

The focus of the advance limitation or elimination is on the duty of the director which extends indirectly to the investor through the application of the related party definition in section 8.60. This provision also permits extension of the limitation or elimination of the duty to any other persons who might be deemed to have a duty to offer business opportunities to the corporation. For example, courts have held that the corporate opportunity doctrine extends to officers of the corporation.

Whether a provision for advance limitation or elimination of duty in the articles of incorporation should be a broad "blanket" provision or one more tailored to specific categories or classes of transactions deserves careful consideration given the particular circumstances of the corporation.

Limitation or elimination of the duty of a director or officer to present a business opportunity to the corporation does not limit or eliminate the director's or officer's duty not to make unauthorized use of corporate property or information or to compete unfairly with the corporation.

B. INDEMNIFICATION

§ 8.51. Permissible Indemnification

(a) Except as otherwise provided in this section, a corporation may indemnify an individual who is a party to a proceeding because the individual is a director against liability incurred in the proceeding if:

(1) (i) the director conducted himself or herself in good faith; and

(ii) the director reasonably believed:

(A) in the case of conduct in an official capacity, that his or her conduct was in the best interests of the corporation; and

(B) in all other cases, that his or her conduct was at least not opposed to the best interests of the corporation; and

(iii) in the case of any criminal proceeding, the director had no reasonable cause to believe his or her conduct was unlawful; or

Source: Model Bus. Corp. Act §§ 8.51, 8.52, 8.56 (2016). Copyright © 2016 by American Bar Association. Reprinted with permission.

(2) the director engaged in conduct for which broader indemnification has been made permissible or obligatory under a provision of the articles of incorporation (as authorized by section 2.02(b)(5)).

Official Comment

The standards for indemnification of directors contained in section 8.51(a) define the limits of the conduct for which discretionary indemnification is permitted under the Act, except to the extent that court-ordered indemnification is available under section 8.54(a)(3). Conduct that falls within these limits does not automatically entitle directors to indemnification, although a corporation may obligate itself to indemnify directors to the maximum extent permitted by applicable law. Absent such an obligatory provision, section 8.52 defines much narrower circumstances in which directors are entitled as a matter of right to indemnification.

§ 8.52. Mandatory Indemnification

A corporation shall indemnify a director who was wholly successful, on the merits or otherwise, in the defense of any proceeding to which the director was a party because he or she was a director of the corporation against expenses incurred by the director in connection with the proceeding.

Official Comment

Section 8.52 creates a right of indemnification in favor of the director who meets its requirements.

The basic standard for mandatory indemnification is that the director has been "wholly successful, on the merits or otherwise," in the defense of the proceeding. A defendant is "wholly successful" only if the entire proceeding is disposed of on a basis which does not involve a finding of liability. A director who is precluded from mandatory indemnification by this requirement may still be entitled to permissible indemnification under section 8.51(a) or court-ordered indemnification under section 8.54(a)(3).

Although the standard "on the merits or otherwise" may result in an occasional defendant becoming entitled to indemnification because of procedural defenses not related to the merits, e.g., the statute of limitations or disqualification of the plaintiff, it is unreasonable to require a defendant with a valid procedural defense to undergo a possibly prolonged and expensive trial on the merits to establish eligibility for mandatory indemnification.

§ 8.56. Indemnification Of Officers

(a) A corporation may indemnify and advance expenses under this subchapter to an officer who is a party to a proceeding because he or she is an officer

    (1) to the same extent as a director; and

    (2) if he or she is an officer but not a director, to such further extent as may be provided by the articles of incorporation or the bylaws, or by a resolution adopted or a contract approved by the board of directors or shareholders, except for

        (i) liability in connection with a proceeding by or in the right of the corporation other than for expenses incurred in connection with the proceeding, or

        (ii) liability arising out of conduct that constitutes

            (A) receipt by the officer of a financial benefit to which he or she is not entitled,

            (B) an intentional infliction of harm on the corporation or the shareholders, or

            (C) an intentional violation of criminal law.

Official Comment

Section 8.56 does not deal with indemnification of employees and agents because the concerns of self-dealing that arise when directors provide for their own indemnification and expense advance (and sometimes for senior executive officers) are not present when directors (or officers) provide for indemnification and expense advance for employees and agents who are not directors or officers.

Although subchapter E is silent with respect to such employees and agents, they may be indemnified using broad grants of powers to corporations under section 3.02, including powers to make contracts, appoint and fix the compensation of employees and agents and to make payments furthering the business and affairs of the corporation. Many corporations use these powers to provide for employees and agents in the same provisions in the articles, bylaws or otherwise in which they provide for expense advance and indemnification for directors and officers. Indemnification may also be provided to protect employees or agents from liabilities incurred while serving at a corporation's request as a director, officer, partner, trustee, or agent of another commercial, charitable, or nonprofit venture.

C. INSURANCE

§ 8.57. Insurance

A corporation may purchase and maintain insurance on behalf of an individual who is a director or officer of the corporation, or who, while a director or officer of the corporation, serves at the corporation's request as a director, officer, partner, trustee, employee, or agent of another domestic or foreign corporation or a joint venture, trust, employee benefit plan, or other entity, against liability asserted against or incurred by the individual in that capacity or arising from the individual's status as a director or officer, regardless of whether the corporation would have power to indemnify or advance expenses to the individual against the same liability under this subchapter.

Official Comment

In authorizing a corporation to purchase and maintain insurance on behalf of directors and officers, section 8.57 sets no limits on the type of insurance which a corporation may maintain or the type of persons who are covered. Insurance is not limited to claims against which a corporation is entitled to indemnify under this subchapter. Such insurance can provide protection to directors and officers in addition to the rights of indemnification created by or pursuant to subchapter E (as well as typically protecting the individual insureds against the corporation's failure to pay indemnification required or permitted by this subchapter) and can also provide a source of reimbursement for a corporation that indemnifies its directors and others for conduct covered by the insurance. On the other hand, policies typically do not cover uninsurable matters, such as actions involving dishonesty, self-dealing, bad faith, knowing violations of the securities laws, or other willful misconduct.

Source: Model Bus. Corp. Act § 8.57 (2016). Copyright © 2016 by American Bar Association. Reprinted with permission.

CHAPTER 19

Planning Issues for Closely Held Corporations

A corporation with a small number of shareholders, no ready market for its shares, and having a substantial participation in management by its majority shareholders is generally known as a closely held corporation. Closely held corporations have unique operating challenges. Given that controlling power is concentrated in a small number of shareholders, such a concentration of power could leave minority shareholders without any voice in the business and without any way to prevent the controlling shareholders from imposing their will on the company. There are both statutory and judicially-created protections for minority shareholders in closely held corporations. Many of these protections are also afforded to shareholders in publicly held corporations.

A. Shareholder Agreements

§ 7.32. Shareholder Agreements

(a) An agreement among the shareholders of a corporation that complies with this section is effective among the shareholders and the corporation even though it is inconsistent with one or more other provisions of this Act in that it:

   (1) eliminates the board of directors or restricts the discretion or powers of the board of directors;

   (2) governs the authorization or making of distributions, regardless of whether they are in proportion to ownership of shares, subject to the limitations in section 6.40;

   (3) establishes who shall be directors or officers of the corporation, or their terms of office or manner of selection or removal;

Source: Model Bus. Corp. Act § 7.32 (2016). Copyright © 2016 by American Bar Association. Reprinted with permission.

(4) governs, in general or in regard to specific matters, the exercise or division of voting power by or between the shareholders and directors or by or among any of them, including use of weighted voting rights or director proxies;

(5) establishes the terms and conditions of any agreement for the transfer or use of property or the provision of services between the corporation and any shareholder, director, officer or employee of the corporation or among any of them;

(6) transfers to one or more shareholders or other persons all or part of the authority to exercise the corporate powers or to manage the business and affairs of the corporation, including the resolution of any issue about which there exists a deadlock among directors or shareholders;

(7) requires dissolution of the corporation at the request of one or more of the shareholders or upon the occurrence of a specified event or contingency; or

(8) otherwise governs the exercise of the corporate powers or the management of the business and affairs of the corporation or the relationship among the shareholders, the directors and the corporation, or among any of them, and is not contrary to public policy.

(b) An agreement authorized by this section shall be:

(1) as set forth (i) in the articles of incorporation or bylaws and approved by all persons who are shareholders at the time of the agreement, or (ii) in a written agreement that is signed by all persons who are shareholders at the time of the agreement and is made known to the corporation; and

(2) subject to amendment only by all persons who are shareholders at the time of the amendment, unless the agreement provides otherwise.

(c) The existence of an agreement authorized by this section shall be noted conspicuously on the front or back of each certificate for outstanding shares or on the information statement required by section 6.26(b).

(d) If the agreement ceases to be effective for any reason, the board of directors may, if the agreement is contained or referred to in the corporation's articles of incorporation or bylaws, adopt an amendment to the articles of incorporation or bylaws, without shareholder action, to delete the agreement and any references to it.

(e) An agreement authorized by this section that limits the discretion or powers of the board of directors shall relieve the directors of, and impose upon the person or persons in whom such discretion or powers are vested, liability for acts or omissions imposed by law on directors to the extent that the discretion or powers of the directors are limited by the agreement.

(f)   The existence or performance of an agreement authorized by this section shall not be a ground for imposing personal liability on any shareholder for the acts or debts of the corporation even if the agreement or its performance treats the corporation as if it were a partnership or results in failure to observe the corporate formalities otherwise applicable to the matters governed by the agreement.

Official Comment

Shareholders of some corporations, especially those that are closely held, frequently enter into agreements that govern the operation of the enterprise.

Section 7.32 provides, within the context of the traditional corporate structure, legal certainty to such agreements that embody various aspects of the business arrangement established by the shareholders to meet their business and personal needs. The subject matter of these arrangements includes governance of the entity, allocation of the economic return from the business, and other aspects of the relationships among shareholders, directors, and the corporation which are part of the business arrangement. Section 7.32 also recognizes that many of the corporate norms contained in the Act were designed with an eye towards corporations whose management and share ownership are distinct. These functions are often conjoined in some corporations, such as the close corporation. Thus, section 7.32 validates agreements among shareholders even when the agreements are inconsistent with the statutory norms contained in the Act.

Importantly, section 7.32 only addresses the parties to the shareholder agreement, their transferees, and the corporation, and does not have any binding legal effect on the state, creditors, or other third persons.

Section 7.32 supplements the other provisions of the Act. If an agreement is not in conflict with another section of the Act, no resort need be made to section 7.32 with its requirement of unanimity. For example, special provisions may be included in the articles of incorporation or bylaws with less than unanimous shareholder agreement so long as such provisions are not in conflict with other provisions of the Act. Similarly, section 7.32 would not have to be relied upon to validate typical buy-sell agreements among two or more shareholders or the covenants and other terms of a stock purchase agreement entered into in connection with the issuance of shares by a corporation.

Section 7.32(a)

An agreement authorized by section 7.32 is "not inconsistent with law" within the meaning of sections 2.02(b)(2) and 2.06(b) of the Act.

The range of agreements validated by section 7.32(a) is expansive though not unlimited. Section 7.32 defines the types of agreements that can be validated largely by illustration. The seven specific categories that are listed are designed to cover some of the most frequently used arrangements. There are numerous other arrangements that may be made, and section 7.32(a)(8) provides an additional category for any provisions that, in a manner inconsistent with any other provision of the Act, otherwise govern the exercise of the corporate powers or the management of the business and affairs of the corporation or the relationship between and among the shareholders, the directors, and the corporation or any of them, and are not contrary to public policy.

The provisions of a shareholder agreement authorized by section 7.32(a) will often, in operation, conflict with the language of more than one section of the Act, and courts should in such cases construe all related sections of the Act flexibly and in a manner consistent with the underlying intent of the shareholder agreement. Thus, for example, in the case of an agreement that provides for weighted voting by directors, every reference in the Act to a majority or other proportion of directors should be construed to refer to a majority or other proportion of the votes of the directors.

Although the limits of section 7.32(a)(8) are left uncertain, there are provisions of the Act that may not be overridden if they reflect core principles of public policy with respect to corporate affairs. For example, a provision of a shareholder agreement that purports to eliminate all of the standards of conduct established under section 8.30 might be viewed as contrary to public policy and thus not validated under section 7.32(a)(8). Similarly, a provision that exculpates directors from liability more broadly than permitted by section 2.02(b)(4), or indemnifies them more broadly than permitted by section 2.02(b)(5), might not be validated under section 7.32 because of strong public policy reasons for the statutory limitations on the right to exculpate directors from liability and to indemnify them. The validity of some provisions may depend upon the circumstances. For example, a provision of a shareholder agreement that limited inspection rights under section 16.02 or the right to financial statements under section 16.20 might, as a general matter, be valid, but that provision might not be given effect if it prevented shareholders from obtaining information necessary to determine whether directors of the corporation have satisfied the standards of conduct under section 8.30. The foregoing are examples and are not intended to be exclusive.

As noted above, shareholder agreements otherwise validated by section 7.32 are not legally binding on the state, on creditors, or on other third parties. For example, an agreement that dispenses with the need to make corporate filings required by the Act would be ineffective. Similarly, an agreement among shareholders that provides that only the president has authority to enter into contracts for the corporation would not, without more, be binding against third parties, and ordinary principles of agency, including the concept of apparent authority, would continue to apply.

Section 7.32(b)

Section 7.32 minimizes the formal requirements for a shareholder agreement so as not to restrict unduly the shareholders' ability to take advantage of the flexibility the section provides. Thus, it is not necessary to "opt in" to a special class of close corporations to obtain the benefits of section 7.32. An agreement can be validated under section 7.32 whether it is set forth in the articles of incorporation, the bylaws or in a separate agreement, and regardless of whether section 7.32 is specifically referenced in the agreement. Where the corporation has a single shareholder, the requirement of an "agreement among the shareholders" is satisfied by the unilateral action of the shareholder in establishing the terms of the agreement, evidenced by provisions in the articles of incorporation or bylaws, or in a writing signed by the sole shareholder. Although a writing signed by all the shareholders is not required where the agreement is contained in articles of incorporation or bylaws unanimously approved, it may be desirable to have all the shareholders actually sign the instrument to establish unequivocally their agreement. Similarly, although transferees are bound by a valid shareholder agreement, subject to section 7.32(c), it may be desirable to obtain the affirmative written assent of the transferee at the time of the transfer.

Section 7.32(b) requires unanimous shareholder approval of the shareholder agreement regardless of entitlement to vote. Unanimity is required because an agreement authorized by section 7.32 can effect material organic changes in the corporation's operation and structure, and in the rights and obligations of shareholders.

The requirement that the shareholder agreement be made known to the corporation is the predicate for the requirement in section 7.32(c) that share certificates or information statements be legended to note the existence of the agreement. In the case of shareholder agreements in the articles of incorporation or bylaws, the corporation will necessarily have notice. In the case of a shareholder agreement outside the articles of incorporation or bylaws, the requirement of signatures by all of the shareholders should in virtually all cases be sufficient to make the corporation aware of the agreement, as one or more signatories will normally also be a director or an officer.

Section 7.32(c)

Section 7.32(c) addresses the effect of a shareholder agreement on subsequent purchasers or transferees of shares. Typically, corporations with shareholder agreements also have restrictions on the transferability of the shares as authorized by section 6.27, thus lessening the practical effects of the problem in the context of voluntary transferees. Transferees of shares without knowledge of the agreement or those acquiring shares upon the death of an original participant in a close corporation may, however, be heavily affected. Weighing the burdens on transferees against the burdens on the remaining shareholders in the enterprise, section 7.32(c) affirms the continued validity of the shareholder

272 BUSINESS ORGANIZATIONS

agreement on all transferees, whether by purchase, gift, operation of law, or otherwise. Unlike restrictions on transfer, it may be impossible to enforce a shareholder agreement against less than all of the shareholders. Thus, under section 7.32, one who inherits shares subject to a shareholder agreement must continue to abide by the agreement. If that is not the desired result, care must be exercised at the initiation of the shareholder agreement to ensure a different outcome, such as providing for a buy-back upon death.

Where shares are transferred to a purchaser without knowledge of a shareholder agreement, the validity of the agreement is similarly unaffected, but the purchaser is afforded a rescission remedy against the seller.

With respect to the related subject of restrictions on transferability of shares, note that section 7.32 does not directly address or validate such restrictions, which are governed instead by section 6.27 of the Act. However, if such restrictions are adopted as a part of a shareholder agreement that complies with the requirements of section 7.32, a court should apply the concept of reasonableness under section 6.27 in determining the validity of such restrictions.

Section 7.32(c) contains an affirmative requirement that the share certificate or information statement for the shares be legended to note the existence of a shareholder agreement. No specified form of legend is required, and a simple statement that "[t]he shares represented by this certificate are subject to a shareholder agreement" is sufficient. At that point, a purchaser must obtain a copy of the shareholder agreement from the transferor or proceed at the purchaser's peril. In the event a corporation fails to legend share certificates or information statements, a court may, in an appropriate case, imply a cause of action against the corporation in favor of an injured purchaser without knowledge of a shareholder agreement.

Section 7.32(d)

Section 7.32(d) recognizes that the terms of a shareholder agreement may provide for its termination upon the happening of a specified event or condition. An example may be when the corporation undergoes an initial public offering. This approach is consistent with the broad freedom of contract provided to participants in such enterprises.

Sections 7.32(e)

Section 7.32(e) provides a shift of liability from the directors to any person or persons in whom the discretion or powers otherwise exercised by the board of directors are vested under the shareholder agreement. A shareholder agreement which provides for such a shift of responsibility, with the concomitant shift of liability provided by subsection (e), could also provide for exculpation from that liability to the extent otherwise authorized by the Act. The transfer of liability provided by subsection (e) covers liabilities imposed on directors "by law," which is intended to include liabilities arising under the Act, the common law, and statutory law outside the Act.

B. TRANSFER RESTRICTIONS

§ 6.27. Restriction on Transfer of Shares

(a) The articles of incorporation, the bylaws, an agreement among share-holders, or an agreement between shareholders and the corporation may impose restrictions on the transfer or registration of transfer of shares of the corporation. A restriction does not affect shares issued before the restriction was adopted unless the holders of the shares are parties to the restriction agreement or voted in favor of the restriction.

(b) A restriction on the transfer or registration of transfer of shares is valid and enforceable against the holder or a transferee of the holder if the restriction is authorized by this section and its existence is noted conspicuously on the front or back of the certificate or is contained in the information statement required by section 6.26(b). Unless so noted or contained, a restriction is not enforceable against a person without knowledge of the restriction.

(c) A restriction on the transfer or registration of transfer of shares is authorized:

  (1) to maintain the corporation's status when it is dependent on the number or identity of its shareholders;

  (2) to preserve exemptions under federal or state securities law; or

  (3) for any other reasonable purpose.

(d) A restriction on the transfer or registration of transfer of shares may:

  (1) obligate the shareholder first to offer the corporation or other persons (separately, consecutively, or simultaneously) an opportunity to acquire the restricted shares;

  (2) obligate the corporation or other persons (separately, consecutively, or simultaneously) to acquire the restricted shares;

  (3) require the corporation, the holders of any class or series of its shares, or other persons to approve the transfer of the restricted shares, if the requirement is not manifestly unreasonable; or

  (4) prohibit the transfer of the restricted shares to designated persons or classes of persons, if the prohibition is not manifestly unreasonable.

(e) For purposes of this section, "shares" includes a security convertible into or carrying a right to subscribe for or acquire shares.

Source: Model Bus. Corp. Act § 6.27 (2016). Copyright © 2016 by American Bar Association. Reprinted with permission.

Official Comment

Share transfer restrictions are used by corporations for a variety of purposes. Section 6.27(c) enumerates certain purposes for which share transfer restrictions may be imposed, but does not limit the purposes given that section 6.27(c)(3) permits restrictions "for any other reasonable purpose." Examples of the "status" referred to in section 6.27(c)(1) include the subchapter S election under the Internal Revenue Code, and entitlement to a program or eligibility for a privilege administered by governmental agencies or national securities exchanges.

Examples of the uses of share transfer restrictions include:

- a corporation with few shareholders may impose share transfer restrictions to ensure that shareholders do not transfer their shares to a person not acceptable to the corporation or other shareholders;

- a corporation with few shareholders may impose share transfer restrictions to establish the value of the shares of deceased shareholders;

- a professional corporation may impose share transfer restrictions to ensure that its treatment of departing, retiring or deceased shareholders is consistent with rules applicable to the profession in question;

- a corporation may impose share transfer restrictions to ensure that its election of subchapter S treatment under the Internal Revenue Code will not be unexpectedly terminated; and

- a corporation issuing securities pursuant to an exemption from federal or state securities registration may impose share transfer restrictions to ensure that subsequent transfers of shares will not result in the loss of the exemption being relied upon.

Section 6.27(d) describes the types of restrictions that may be imposed. The types of restrictions referred to in sections 6.27(d)(1) (rights of first offer) and (d)(2) (buy-sell agreements) are imposed as a matter of contractual negotiation and do not prohibit the outright transfer of shares. Rather, they designate to whom shares or other securities must be offered at a price established in the agreement or by a formula or method agreed to in advance. By contrast, the restrictions described in clauses sections 6.27(d)(3) and (d)(4) may permanently limit the market for shares by disqualifying all or some potential purchasers. The restrictions imposed by these two provisions must not be "manifestly unreasonable."

C. PROTECTION AGAINST MINORITY OPPRESSION

1. Heightened Fiduciary Duties

Donahue v. Rodd Electrotype Co.

367 Mass. 578 (1974)

TAURO, Chief Justice.

The plaintiff, Euphemia Donahue, a minority stockholder in the Rodd Electrotype Company of New England, Inc. (Rodd Electrotype), a Massachusetts corporation, brings this suit against the directors of Rodd Electrotype, Charles H. Rodd, Frederick I. Rodd and Mr. Harold E. Magnuson, against Harry C. Rodd, a former director, officer, and controlling stockholder of Rodd Electrotype and against Rodd Electrotype (hereinafter called defendants). The plaintiff seeks to rescind Rodd Electrotype's purchase of Harry Rodd's shares in Rodd Electrotype and to compel Harry Rodd 'to repay to the corporation the purchase price of said shares, $36,000, together with interest from the date of purchase.' The plaintiff alleges that the defendants caused the corporation to purchase the shares in violation of their fiduciary duty to her, a minority stockholder of Rodd Electrotype.

The trial judge, after hearing oral testimony, dismissed the plaintiff's bill on the merits. He found that the purchase was without prejudice to the plaintiff and implicitly found that the transaction had been carried out in good faith and with inherent fairness. The Appeals Court affirmed with costs. The case is before us on the plaintiff's application for further appellate review.

[Statement of Facts]

In 1935, the defendant, Harry C. Rodd, began his employment with Rodd Electrotype, then styled the Royal Electrotype Company of New England, Inc. (Royal of New England). At that time, the company was a wholly-owned subsidiary of a Pennsylvania corporation, the Royal Electrotype Company (Royal Electrotype). Mr. Rodd's advancement within the company was rapid. The following year he was elected a director, and, in 1946, he succeeded to the position of general manager and treasurer.

In 1936, the plaintiff's husband, Joseph Donahue (now deceased), was hired by Royal of New England as a 'finisher' of electrotype plates. His duties were confined to operational matters within the plant. Although he ultimately achieved the positions of plant superintendent (1946) and corporate vice president (1955), Donahue never participated in the 'management' aspect of the business.

Copyright in the public domain.

In the years preceding 1955, the parent company, Royal Electrotype, made available to Harry Rodd and Joseph Donahue shares of the common stock in its subsidiary, Royal of New England. Harry Rodd took advantage of the opportunities offered to him and acquired 200 shares for $20 a share. Joseph Donahue, at the suggestion of Harry Rodd, who hoped to interest Donahue in the business, eventually obtained fifty shares in two twenty-five share lots priced at $20 a share. The parent company at all times retained 725 of the 1,000 outstanding shares. One Lawrence W. Kelley owned the remaining twenty-five shares.

In June of 1955, Royal of New England purchased all 725 of its shares owned by its parent company. The total price amounted to $135,000. Royal of New England remitted $75,000 of this total in cash and executed five promissory notes of $12,000 each, due in each of the succeeding five years. Lawrence W. Kelley's twenty-five shares were also purchased at this time for $1,000.

The stock purchases left Harry Rodd in control of Royal of New England. Early in 1955, before the purchases, he had assumed the presidency of the company. His 200 shares gave him a dominant eighty per cent interest. Joseph Donahue, at this time, was the only minority stockholder.

Subsequent events reflected Harry Rodd's dominant influence. From 1959 to 1967, Harry Rodd pursued what may fairly be termed a gift program by which he distributed the majority of his shares equally among his two sons and his daughter, Phyllis E. Mason. Each child received thirty-nine shares.

We come now to the events of 1970 which form the grounds for the plaintiff's complaint. In May of 1970, Harry Rodd was seventy-seven years old. The record indicates that for some time he had not enjoyed the best of health and that he had undergone a number of operations. His sons wished him to retire. Mr. Rodd was not averse to this suggestion. However, he insisted that some financial arrangements be made with respect to his remaining eighty-one shares of stock. Harry Rodd and Charles Rodd (representing the company) negotiated terms of purchase for forty-five shares which, Charles Rodd testified, would reflect the book value and liquidating value of the shares.

A special board meeting convened on July 13, 1970. As the first order of business, Harry Rodd resigned his directorship of Rodd Electrotype. The remaining incumbent directors, Charles Rodd and Mr. Harold E. Magnuson (clerk of the company and a defendant), elected Frederick Rodd to replace his father. The three directors then authorized Rodd Electrotype's president (Charles Rodd) to execute an agreement between Harry Rodd and the company in which the company would purchase forty-five shares for $800 a share ($36,000).

The stock purchase agreement was formalized between the parties on July 13, 1970.

A special meeting of the stockholders of the company was held on March 30, 1971. At the meeting, Charles Rodd, company president and general manager, reported the tentative results of an audit conducted by the company auditors and reported generally on the company events of the year. For the first time, the Donahues learned that the corporation had purchased Harry Rodd's shares. According to the minutes of the meeting, following Charles Rodd's report, the Donahues raised questions about the purchase. They then voted against a resolution, ultimately adopted by the remaining stockholders, to approve Charles Rodd's report. Although the minutes of the meeting show that the stockholders unanimously voted to accept a second resolution ratifying all acts of the company president (he executed the stock purchase agreement) in the preceding year, the trial judge found, and there was evidence to support his finding, that the Donahues did not ratify the purchase of Harry Rodd's shares.

A few weeks after the meeting, the Donahues, acting through their attorney, offered their shares to the corporation on the same terms given to Harry Rodd. Mr. Harold E. Magnuson replied by letter that the corporation would not purchase the shares and was not in a financial position to do so. This suit followed.

In her argument before this court, the plaintiff has characterized the corporate purchase of Harry Rodd's shares as an unlawful distribution of corporate assets to controlling stockholders. She urges that the distribution constitutes a breach of the fiduciary duty owed by the Rodds, as controlling stockholders, to her, a minority stockholder in the enterprise, because the Rodds failed to accord her an equal opportunity to sell her shares to the corporation. The defendants reply that the stock purchase was within the powers of the corporation and met the requirements of good faith and inherent fairness imposed on a fiduciary in his dealings with the corporation. They assert that there is no right to equal opportunity in corporate stock purchases for the corporate treasury. For the reasons hereinafter noted, we agree with the plaintiff and reverse the decree of the Superior Court. However, we limit the applicability of our holding to 'close corporations,' as hereinafter defined. Whether the holding should apply to other corporations is left for decision in another case, on a proper record.

A. Close Corporations.

In previous opinions, we have alluded to the distinctive nature of the close corporation but have never defined precisely what is meant by a close corporation. There is no single, generally accepted definition. Some commentators emphasize an 'integration of ownership and management' in which the stockholders occupy most management positions. Others focus on the number of stockholders and the nature of the market for the stock. In this view, close corporations have few stockholders; there is little market for corporate stock. The Supreme Court of Illinois adopted this latter view in Galler v. Galler, 32 Ill.2d 16, 203 N.E.2d 577 (1965): 'For our purposes, a close corporation is one in which the stock is held in a few hands, or in a few families, and wherein it is not at all, or only rarely, dealt in by buying or selling.' We accept aspects of both definitions. We deem a close corporation to the typified by: (1) a small number of stockholders; (2) no ready market for the corporate stock; and (3) substantial majority stockholder participation in the management, direction and operations of the corporation.

As thus defined, the close corporation bears striking resemblance to a partnership. The stockholders 'clothe' their partnership 'with the benefits peculiar to a corporation, limited liability, perpetuity and the like. In essence, though, the enterprise remains one in which ownership is limited to the original parties or transferees of their stock to whom the other stockholders have agreed, in which ownership and management are in the same hands, and in which the owners are quite dependent on one another for the success of the enterprise. Many close corporations are 'really partnerships, between two or three people who contribute their capital, skills, experience and labor. Just as in a partnership, the relationship among the stockholders must be one of trust, confidence and absolute loyalty if the enterprise is to succeed. Close corporations with substantial assets and with more numerous stockholders are no different from smaller close corporations in this regard. All participants rely on the fidelity and abilities of those stockholders who hold office. Disloyalty and self-seeking conduct on the part of any stockholder will engender bickering, corporate stalemates, and, perhaps, efforts to achieve dissolution.

Although the corporate form provides the above-mentioned advantages for the stockholders (limited liability, perpetuity, and so forth), it also supplies an opportunity for the majority stockholders to oppress or disadvantage minority stockholders. The minority is vulnerable to a variety of oppressive devices, termed 'freezeouts,' which the majority may employ. An authoritative study of such 'freeze-outs' enumerates some of the possibilities: 'The squeezers (those who employ the freeze-out techniques) may refuse to declare dividends; they may drain off the corporation's earnings in the form of exorbitant salaries and bonuses to the majority shareholder-officers and perhaps to their relatives, or in the form of high rent by the corporation for property leased from majority shareholders ... ; they may deprive minority shareholders of corporate offices and of employment by the company; they may cause the corporation to sell its assets at an inadequate price to the majority shareholders . ...' F. H. O'Neal and J. Derwin, Expulsion or Oppression of Business Associates, 42 (1961). In particular, the power of the board of directors, controlled by the majority, to declare or withhold dividends and to deny the minority employment is easily converted to a device to disadvantage minority stockholders.

The minority can, of course, initiate suit against the majority and their directors. Self-serving conduct by directors is proscribed by the director's fiduciary obligation to the corporation. However, in practice, the plaintiff will find difficulty in challenging dividend or employment policies. Such policies are considered to be within the judgment of the directors. This court has said: 'The courts prefer not to interfere ... with the sound financial management of the corporation by its directors, but declare as general rule that the declaration of dividends rests within the sound discretion of the directors, refusing to interfere with their determination unless a plain abuse of discretion is made to appear.' Judicial reluctance to interfere combines with the difficulty of proof when the standard is 'plain abuse of discretion' or bad faith, see Perry v. Perry, supra, to limit the possibilities for relief.

Thus, when these types of 'freeze-outs' are attempted by the majority stockholders, the minority stockholders, cut off from all corporation-related revenues, must either suffer their losses or seek a buyer for their shares. Many minority stockholders will be unwilling or unable to wait for an alteration in majority policy. Typically, the minority stockholder in a close corporation has a substantial percentage of his personal assets invested in the corporation. The stockholder may have anticipated that his salary from his position with the corporation would be his livelihood. Thus, he cannot afford to wait passively. He must liquidate his investment in the close corporation in order to reinvest the funds in income-producing enterprises.

At this point, the true plight of the minority stockholder in a close corporation becomes manifest. He cannot easily reclaim his capital. In a large public corporation, the oppressed or dissident minority stockholder could sell his stock in order to extricate some of his invested capital. By definition, this market is not available for shares in the close corporation. In a partnership, a partner who feels abused by his fellow partners may cause dissolution by his 'express will ... at any time' (G.L. c. 108A, s 31(1)(b) and (2)) and recover his share of partnership assets and accumulated profits. If dissolution results in a breach of the partnership articles, the culpable partner will be liable in damages. G.L. c. 108A, s 38(2)(a) II. By contrast, the stockholder in the close corporation or 'incorporated partnership' may achieve dissolution and recovery of his share of the enterprise assets only by compliance with the rigorous terms of the applicable chapter of the General Laws. 'The dissolution of a corporation which is a creature of the Legislature is primarily a legislative function, and the only authority courts have to deal with this subject is the power conferred upon them by the Legislature.' To secure dissolution of the ordinary close corporation subject to G.L. c. 156B, the stockholder, in the absence of corporate deadlock, must own at least fifty per cent of the shares (G.L. c. 156B, s 99(a)) or have the advantage of a favorable provision in the articles of organization (G.L. c. 156B, s 100(a)(2)). The minority stockholder, by definition lacking fifty per cent of the corporate shares, can never 'authorize' the corporation to file a petition for dissolution under G.L. c. 156B, s 99(a), by his own vote. He will seldom have at his disposal the requisite favorable provision in the articles of organization.

Thus, in a close corporation, the minority stockholders may be trapped in a disadvantageous situation. No outsider would knowingly assume the position of the disadvantaged minority. The outsider would have the same difficulties. To cut losses, the minority stockholder may be compelled to deal with the majority. This is the capstone of the majority plan. Majority 'freeze-out' schemes which withhold dividends are designed to compel the minority to relinquish stock at inadequate prices. When the minority stockholder agrees to sell out at less than fair value, the majority has won.

Because of the fundamental resemblance of the close corporation to the partnership, the trust and confidence which are essential to this scale and manner of enterprise, and the inherent danger to minority interests in the close corporation, we hold that stockholders in the close corporation owe one another substantially the same fiduciary duty in the operation of the enterprise that partners owe to one another. In our previous decisions, we have defined the standard of duty owed by partners to one another as the 'utmost good faith and loyalty.' Cardullo v. Landau, 329 Mass. 5, 8, 105 N.E.2d 843 (1952). Stockholders in close corporations must discharge their management and stockholder responsibilities in conformity with this strict good faith standard. They may not act out of avarice, expediency or self-interest in derogation of their duty of loyalty to the other stockholders and to the corporation.

We contrast this strict good faith standard with the somewhat less stringent standard of fiduciary duty to which directors and stockholders of all corporations must adhere in the discharge of their corporate responsibilities. Corporate directors are held to a good faith and inherent fairness standard of conduct (Winchell v. Plywood Corp., 324 Mass. 171, 177, 85 N.E.2d 313 (1949)) and are not 'permitted to serve two masters whose interests are antagonistic.' Spiegel v. Beacon Participations, Inc., 297 Mass. 398, 411, 8 N.E.2d 859, 904 (1937). 'Their paramount duty is to the corporation, and their personal pecuniary interests are subordinate to that duty.' Durfee v. Durfee & Canning, Inc., 323 Mass. 187, 196, 80 N.E.2d 522, 527 (1948).

The more rigorous duty of partners and participants in a joint adventure, here extended to stockholders in a close corporation, was described by then Chief Judge Cardozo of the New York Court of Appeals in Meinhard v. Salmon, 249 N.Y. 458, 164 N.E. 545 (1928): 'Joint adventurers, like copartners, owe to one another, while the enterprise continues, the duty of the finest loyalty. Many forms of conduct permissible in a workaday world for those acting at arm's length, are forbidden to those bound by fiduciary ties. ... Not honesty alone, but the punctilio of an honor the most sensitive, is then the standard of behavior.' Id. at 463—464, 164 N.E. at 546.

B. Equal Opportunity in a Close Corporation.

Under settled Massachusetts law, a domestic corporation, unless forbidden by statute, has the power to purchase its own shares. An agreement to reacquire stock '(is) enforceable, subject, at least, to the limitations that the purchase must be made in good faith and without prejudice to creditors and stockholders.' When the corporation reacquiring its own stock is a close corporation, the purchase is subject to the additional requirement, in the light of our holding in this opinion, that the stockholders, who, as directors or controlling stockholders, caused the corporation to enter into the stock purchase agreement, must have acted with the utmost good faith and loyalty to the other stockholders.

To meet this test, if the stockholder whose shares were purchased was a member of the controlling group, the controlling stockholders must cause the corporation to offer each stockholder an equal opportunity to sell a ratable number of his shares to the corporation at an identical price. Purchase by the corporation confers substantial benefits on the members of the controlling group whose shares were purchased. These benefits are not available to the minority stockholders if the corporation does not also offer them an opportunity to sell their shares. The controlling group may not, consistent with its strict duty to the minority, utilize its control of the corporation to obtain special advantages and disproportionate benefit from its share ownership.

The benefits conferred by the purchase are twofold: (1) provision of a market for shares; (2) access to corporate assets for personal use. By definition, there is no ready market for shares of a close corporation. The purchase creates a market for shares which previously had been unmarketable. It transforms a previously illiquid investment into a liquid one. If the close corporation purchases shares only from a member of the controlling group, the controlling stockholder can convert his shares into cash at a time when none of the other stockholders can. Consistent with its strict fiduciary duty, the controlling group may not utilize its control of the corporation to establish an exclusive market in previously unmarketable shares from which the minority stockholders are excluded.

The purchase also distributes corporate assets to the stockholder whose shares were purchased. Unless an equal opportunity is given to all stockholders, the purchase of shares from a member of the controlling group operates as a preferential distribution of assets. In exchange for his shares, he receives a percentage of the contributed capital and accumulated profits of the enterprise. The funds he so receives are available for his personal use. The other stockholders benefit from no such access to corporate property and cannot withdraw their shares of the corporate profits and capital in this manner unless the controlling group acquiesces. Although the purchase price for the controlling stockholder's shares may seem fair to the corporation and other stockholders under the tests established in the prior case law, the controlling stockholder whose stock has been purchased has still received a relative advantage over his fellow stockholders, inconsistent with his strict fiduciary duty—an opportunity to turn corporate funds to personal use.

The rule of equal opportunity in stock purchases by close corporations provides equal access to these benefits for all stockholders. We hold that, in any case in which the controlling stockholders have exercised their power over the corporation to deny the minority such equal opportunity, the minority shall be entitled to appropriate relief. To the extent that language in Spiegel v. Beacon Participations, Inc., 297 Mass. 398, 431, 8 N.E.2d 895 (1937), and other cases suggests that there is no requirement of equal opportunity for minority stockholders when a close corporation purchases shares from a controlling stockholder, it is not to be followed.

C. Application of the Law to this Case.

We turn now to the application of the learning set forth above to the facts of the instant case. The strict standard of duty is plainly applicable to the stockholders in Rodd Electrotype. Rodd Electrotype is a close corporation. Members of the Rodd and Donahue families are the sole owners of the corporation's stock. In actual numbers, the corporation, immediately prior to the corporate purchase of Harry Rodd's shares, had six stockholders. The shares have not been traded, and no market for them seems to exist. Harry Rodd, Charles Rodd, Frederick Rodd, William G. Mason (Phyllis Mason's husband), and the plaintiff's husband all worked for the corporation. The Rodds have retained the paramount management positions.

Through their control of these management positions and of the majority of the Rodd Electrotype stock, the Rodds effectively controlled the corporation. In testing the stock purchase from Harry Rodd against the applicable strict fiduciary standard, we treat the Rodd family as a single controlling group. We reject the defendants' contention that the Rodd family cannot be treated as a unit for this purpose. From the evidence, it is clear that the Rodd family was a close-knit one with strong community of interest. Harry Rodd had hired his sons to work in the family business, Rodd Electrotype. As he aged, he transferred portions of his stock holdings to his children. Charles Rodd and Frederick Rodd were given positions of responsibility in the business as he withdrew from active management. In these circumstances, it is realistic to assume that appreciation, gratitude, and filial devotion would prevent the younger Rodds from opposing a plan which would provide funds for their father's retirement.

On its face, then, the purchase of Harry Rodd's shares by the corporation is a breach of the duty which the controlling stockholders, the Rodds, owed to the minority stockholders, the plaintiff and her son. The purchase distributed a portion of the corporate assets to Harry Rodd, a member of the controlling group, in exchange for his shares. The plaintiff and her son were not offered an equal opportunity to sell their shares to the corporation. In fact, their efforts to obtain an equal opportunity were rebuffed by the corporate representative.

Because of the foregoing, we hold that the plaintiff is entitled to relief. Two forms of suitable relief are set out hereinafter. The judgment may require Harry Rodd to remit $36,000 with interest at the legal rate from July 15, 1970, to Rodd Electrotype in exchange for forty-five shares of Rodd Electrotype treasury stock. In the alternative, the judgment may require Rodd Electrotype to purchase all of the plaintiff's shares for $36,000 without interest. In the circumstances of this case, we view this as the equal opportunity which the plaintiff should have received. Harry Rodd's retention of thirty-six shares, which were to be sold and given to his children within a year of the Rodd Electrotype purchase, cannot disguise the fact that the corporation acquired one hundred per cent of that portion of his holdings (forty-five shares) which he did not intend his children to own. The plaintiff is entitled to have one hundred per cent of her forty-five shares similarly purchased.

Wilkes v. Springside Nursing Home, Inc.

370 Mass. 842 (1976)

HENNESSEY, Chief Justice.

On August 5, 1971, the plaintiff (Wilkes) filed for declaratory judgment in the Probate Court, naming as defendants T. Edward Quinn (Quinn), Leon L. Riche (Riche), the First Agricultural National Bank of Berkshire County and Frank Sutherland MacShane as executors under the will of Lawrence R. Connor (Connor), and the Springside Nursing Home, Inc. (Springside or the corporation). Wilkes alleged that he, Quinn, Riche and Dr. Hubert A. Pipkin (Pipkin) entered into a partnership agreement in 1951, prior to the incorporation of Springside, which agreement was breached in 1967 when Wilkes's salary was terminated and he was voted out as an officer and director of the corporation. Wilkes sought, among other forms of relief, damages in the amount of the salary he would have received had he continued as a director and officer of Springside subsequent to March, 1967.

A judge of the Probate Court referred the suit to a master, who issued his final report in late 1973. A judgment was entered dismissing Wilkes's action on the merits. We granted direct appellate review. On appeal, Wilkes argued in the alternative that (1) he should recover damages for breach of the alleged partnership agreement; and (2) he should recover damages because the defendants, as majority stockholders in Springside, breached their fiduciary duty to him as a minority stockholder by their action in February and March, 1967.

We conclude that the master's findings were warranted by the evidence and that his report was properly confirmed. However, we reverse so much of the judgment as dismisses Wilkes's complaint and order the entry of a judgment substantially granting the relief sought by Wilkes under the second alternative set forth above.

[Statement of Facts]

In 1951 Wilkes acquired an option to purchase a building and lot located in Pittsfield, Massachusetts, the building having previously housed the Hillcrest Hospital. Though Wilkes was principally engaged in the roofing and siding business, he had gained a reputation locally for profitable dealings in real estate. Riche, an acquaintance of Wilkes, learned of the option, and interested Quinn (who was known to Wilkes through membership on the draft board in

Copyright in the public domain.

Pittsfield) and Pipkin (an acquaintance of both Wilkes and Riche) in joining Wilkes in his investment. The four men met and decided to participate jointly in the purchase of the building and lot as a real estate investment which, they believed, had good profit potential on resale or rental.

The parties later determined that the property would have its greatest potential for profit if it were operated by them as a nursing home. Wilkes consulted his attorney, who advised him that if the four men were to operate the contemplated nursing home as planned, they would be partners and would be liable for any debts incurred by the partnership and by each other. On the attorney's suggestion, and after consultation among themselves, ownership of the property was vested in Springside, a corporation organized under Massachusetts law.

Each of the four men invested $1,000 and subscribed to ten shares of $100 par value stock in Springside. At the time of incorporation it was understood by all of the parties that each would be a director of Springside and each would participate actively in the management and decision making involved in operating the corporation. It was, further, the understanding and intention of all the parties that, corporate resources permitting, each would receive money from the corporation in equal amounts as long as each assumed an active and ongoing responsibility for carrying a portion of the burdens necessary to operate the business.

The work involved in establishing and operating a nursing home was roughly apportioned, and each of the four men undertook his respective tasks. Initially, Riche was elected president of Springside, Wilkes was elected treasurer, and Quinn was elected clerk. Each of the four was listed in the articles of organization as a director of the corporation.

At some time in 1952, it became apparent that the operational income and cash flow from the business were sufficient to permit the four stockholders to draw money from the corporation on a regular basis. Each of the four original parties initially received $35 a week from the corporation. As time went on the weekly return to each was increased until, in 1955, it totaled $100.

In 1959, after a long illness, Pipkin sold his shares in the corporation to Connor, who was known to Wilkes, Riche and Quinn through past transactions with Springside in his capacity as president of the First Agricultural National Bank. Connor received a weekly stipend from the corporation equal to that received by Wilkes, Riche and Quinn. He was elected a director of the corporation but never held any other office. He was assigned no specific area of responsibility in the operation of the nursing home but did participate in business discussions and decisions as a director and served additionally as financial adviser to the corporation.

In 1965 the stockholders decided to sell a portion of the corporate property to Quinn who, in addition to being a stockholder in Springside, possessed an interest in another corporation which desired to operate a rest home on the property. Wilkes was successful in prevailing on the other stockholders of

Springside to procure a higher sale price for the property than Quinn apparently anticipated paying or desired to pay. After the sale was consummated, the relationship between Quinn and Wilkes began to deteriorate.

The bad blood between Quinn and Wilkes affected the attitudes of both Riche and Connor. As a consequence of the strained relations among the parties, Wilkes, in January of 1967, gave notice of his intention to sell his shares for an amount based on an appraisal of their value. In February of 1967 a directors' meeting was held and the board exercised its right to establish the salaries of its officers and employees. A schedule of payments was established whereby Quinn was to receive a substantial weekly increase and Riche and Connor were to continue receiving $100 a week. Wilkes, however, was left off the list of those to whom a salary was to be paid. The directors also set the annual meeting of the stockholders for March, 1967.

At the annual meeting in March, Wilkes was not reelected as a director, nor was he reelected as an officer of the corporation. He was further informed that neither his services nor his presence at the nursing home was wanted by his associates.

The meetings of the directors and stockholders in early 1967 were used as a vehicle to force Wilkes out of active participation in the management and operation of the corporation and to cut off all corporate payments to him. Though the board of directors had the power to dismiss any officers or employees for misconduct or neglect of duties, there was no indication in the minutes of the board of directors' meeting of February, 1967, that the failure to establish a salary for Wilkes was based on either ground. The severance of Wilkes from the payroll resulted not from misconduct or neglect of duties, but because of the personal desire of Quinn, Riche and Connor to prevent him from continuing to receive money from the corporation. Despite a continuing deterioration in his personal relationship with his associates, Wilkes had consistently endeavored to carry on his responsibilities to the corporation in the same satisfactory manner and with the same degree of competence he had previously shown. Wilkes was at all times willing to carry on his responsibilities and participation if permitted so to do and provided that he receive his weekly stipend.

[Legal Analysis]

We turn to Wilkes's claim for damages based on a breach of the fiduciary duty owed to him by the other participants in this venture. In light of the theory underlying this claim, we do not consider it vital to our approach to this case whether the claim is governed by partnership law or the law applicable to business corporations. This is so because, as all the parties agree, Springside was at all times relevant to this action, a close corporation as we have recently defined such an entity in Donahue v. Rodd Electrotype Co. of New England, Inc., — Mass. —, ———, 328 N.E.2d 505 (1975).

In Donahue, we held that 'stockholders in the close corporation owe one another substantially the same fiduciary duty in the operation of the enterprise that partners owe to one another.' As determined in previous decisions of this court, the standard of duty owed by partners to one another is one of 'utmost good faith and loyalty.' Thus, we concluded in Donahue, with regard to 'their actions relative to the operations of the enterprise and the effects of that operation on the rights and investments of other stockholders,' '(s)tockholders in close corporations must discharge their management and stockholder responsibilities in conformity with this strict good faith standard. They may not act out of avarice, expediency or self-interest in derogation of their duty of loyalty to the other stockholders and to the corporation.'

In the Donahue case we recognized that one peculiar aspect of close corporations was the opportunity afforded to majority stockholders to oppress, disadvantage or 'freeze out' minority stockholders. In Donahue itself, for example, the majority refused the minority an equal opportunity to sell a ratable number of shares to the corporation at the same price available to the majority. The net result of this refusal, we said, was that the minority could be forced to 'sell out at less than fair value,' since there is by definition no ready market for minority stock in a close corporation.

'Freeze outs,' however, may be accomplished by the use of other devices. One such device which has proved to be particularly effective in accomplishing the purpose of the majority is to deprive minority stockholders of corporate offices and of employment with the corporation. F. H. O'Neal, 'Squeeze-Outs' of Minority Shareholders 59, 78—79 (1975). This 'freeze-out' technique has been successful because courts fairly consistently have been disinclined to interfere in those facets of internal corporate operations, such as the selection and retention or dismissal of officers, directors and employees, which essentially involve management decisions subject to the principle of majority control. As one authoritative source has said, '(M)any courts apparently feel that there is a legitimate sphere in which the controlling (directors or) shareholders can act in their own interest even if the minority suffers.' F. H. O'Neal, supra at 59 (footnote omitted).

The denial of employment to the minority at the hands of the majority is especially pernicious in some instances. A guaranty of employment with the corporation may have been one of the 'basic reason(s) why a minority owner has invested capital in the firm.' The minority stockholder typically depends on his salary as the principal return on his investment, since the 'earnings of a close corporation ... are distributed in major part in salaries, bonuses and retirement benefits.' Other noneconomic interests of the minority stockholder are likewise injuriously affected by barring him from corporate office. Such action severely restricts his participation in the management of the enterprise, and he is relegated to enjoying those benefits incident to his status as a stockholder. In sum, by terminating a minority stockholder's employment or by severing him from a position as an officer or director, the majority effectively frustrate the minority stockholder's purposes in entering on the corporate venture and also deny him an equal return on his investment.

The Donahue decision acknowledged, as a 'natural outgrowth' of the case law of this Commonwealth, a strict obligation on the part of majority stockholders in a close corporation to deal with the minority with the utmost good faith and loyalty. On its face, this strict standard is applicable in the instant case. The distinction between the majority action in Donahue and the majority action in this case is more one of form than of substance. Nevertheless, we are concerned that untempered application of the strict good faith standard enunciated in Donahue to cases such as the one before us will result in the imposition of limitations on legitimate action by the controlling group in a close corporation which will unduly hamper its effectiveness in managing the corporation in the best interests of all concerned. The majority, concededly, have certain rights to what has been termed 'selfish ownership' in the corporation which should be balanced against the concept of their fiduciary obligation to the minority.

Therefore, when minority stockholders in a close corporation bring suit against the majority alleging a breach of the strict good faith duty owed to them by the majority, we must carefully analyze the action taken by the controlling stockholders in the individual case. It must be asked whether the controlling group can demonstrate a legitimate business purpose for its action. In asking this question, we acknowledge the fact that the controlling group in a close corporation must have some room to maneuver in establishing the business policy of the corporation. It must have a large measure of discretion, for example, in declaring or withholding dividends, deciding whether to merge or consolidate, establishing the salaries of corporate officers, dismissing directors with or without cause, and hiring and firing corporate employees.

When an asserted business purpose for their action is advanced by the majority, however, we think it is open to minority stockholders to demonstrate that the same legitimate objective could have been achieved through an alternative course of action less harmful to the minority's interest. If called on to settle a dispute, our courts must weigh the legitimate business purpose, if any, against the practicability of a less harmful alternative.

Applying this approach to the instant case it is apparent that the majority stockholders in Springside have not shown a legitimate business purpose for severing Wilkes from the payroll of the corporation or for refusing to reelect him as a salaried officer and director. The master's subsidiary findings relating to the purpose of the meetings of the directors and stockholders in February and March, 1967, are supported by the evidence. There was no showing of misconduct on Wilkes's part as a director, officer or employee of the corporation which would lead us to approve the majority action as a legitimate response to the disruptive nature of an undesirable individual bent on injuring or destroying the corporation. On the contrary, it appears that Wilkes had always accomplished his assigned share of the duties competently, and that he had never indicated an unwillingness to continue to do so.

It is an inescapable conclusion from all the evidence that the action of the majority stockholders here was a designed 'freeze out' for which no legitimate business purpose has been suggested. Furthermore, we may infer that a design to pressure Wilkes into selling his shares to the corporation at a price below their value well may have been at the heart of the majority's plan.

In the context of this case, several factors bear directly on the duty owed to Wilkes by his associates. At a minimum, the duty of utmost good faith and loyalty would demand that the majority consider that their action was in disregard of a long-standing policy of the stockholders that each would be a director of the corporation and that employment with the corporation would go hand in hand with stock ownership; that Wilkes was one of the four originators of the nursing home venture; and that Wilkes, like the others, had invested his capital and time for more than fifteen years with the expectation that he would continue to participate in corporate decisions. Most important is the plain fact that the cutting off of Wilkes's salary, together with the fact that the corporation never declared a dividend (see note 13 supra), assured that Wilkes would receive no return at all from the corporation.

Therefore our order is as follows: So much of the judgment as dismisses Wilkes's complaint and awards costs to the defendants is reversed. The case is remanded to the Probate Court for further proceedings concerning the issue of damages. Thereafter a judgment shall be entered declaring that Quinn, Riche and Connor breached their fiduciary duty to Wilkes as a minority stockholder in Springside, and awarding money damages therefor. Wilkes shall be allowed to recover the salary he would have received had he remained an officer and director of Springside.

2. CLAIM FOR OPPRESSION

§ 14.30. Grounds For Judicial Dissolution

(a) The [name or describe court or courts] may dissolve a corporation:

  (2) in a proceeding by a shareholder if it is established that:

    (i) the directors are deadlocked in the management of the corporate affairs, the shareholders are unable to break the deadlock, and irreparable injury to the corporation is threatened or being suffered, or the business and affairs of the corporation can no longer be conducted to the advantage of the shareholders generally, because of the deadlock;

Source: Model Bus. Corp. Act §§ 14.30, 14.34 (2016). Copyright © 2016 by American Bar Association. Reprinted with permission.

    (ii) the directors or those in control of the corporation have acted, are acting, or will act in a manner that is illegal, oppressive, or fraudulent;

    (iii) the shareholders are deadlocked in voting power and have failed, for a period that includes at least two consecutive annual meeting dates, to elect successors to directors whose terms have expired; or

    (iv) the corporate assets are being misapplied or wasted;

(b) Subsection (a)(2) shall not apply in the case of a corporation that, on the date of the filing of the proceeding, has a class or series of shares which is:

    (1) a covered security under section 18(b)(1)(A) or (B) of the Securities Act of 1933; or

    (2) not a covered security, but is held by at least 300 shareholders and the shares outstanding have a market value of at least $20 million (exclusive of the value of such shares held by the corporation's subsidiaries, senior executives, directors and beneficial shareholders and voting trust beneficial owners owning more than 10% of such shares).

Official Comment

Involuntary Dissolution by Shareholders

Section 14.30(a)(2) provides for involuntary dissolution at the request of a shareholder under circumstances involving deadlock or significant abuse of power by controlling shareholders or directors. The remedy of judicial dissolution is available only for shareholders of corporations that do not meet the tests in section 14.30(b). Even for those corporations to which section 14.30(a)(2) applies, however, the court can take into account the number of shareholders and the nature of the trading market for the shares in deciding whether to exercise its discretion to order dissolution. Shareholders of corporations that meet the tests of section 14.30(b) may often have the ability to sell their shares if they are dissatisfied with current management or may seek other remedies under the Act.

§ 14.34. Election To Purchase In Lieu Of Dissolution

(a) In a proceeding under section 14.30(a)(2) to dissolve a corporation, the corporation may elect or, if it fails to elect, one or more shareholders may elect to purchase all shares owned by the petitioning shareholder at the fair value of the shares. An election pursuant to this section shall be irrevocable unless the court determines that it is equitable to set aside or modify the election.

Official Comment

It is not always necessary to dissolve a corporation and liquidate its assets to provide relief for the situations covered in section 14.30(a)(2). Section 14.34 provides an alternative by means of which a dissolution proceeding under section 14.30(a)(2) can be terminated upon payment of the fair value of the petitioner's shares, allowing the corporation to continue in existence for the benefit of the remaining shareholders.

CHAPTER 20

REGULATING SECURITIES

The laws and rules that govern the securities industry in the United States derive from a simple and straightforward concept: all investors, whether large institutions or private individuals, should have access to certain basic information about an investment prior to buying it, and so long as they hold it. Only through access to timely, comprehensive, and accurate information can people make sound investment decisions.

A. THE FEDERAL SECURITIES LAWS

In the 1920s, companies often sold stocks and bonds on the basis of glittering promises of fantastic profits and without disclosing any meaningful information to investors. Following the stock market crash of 1929, the U.S. Congress enacted the federal securities laws and created the [Securities Exchange Commission ("SEC")] to administer them.

There are two primary sets of federal securities laws that come into play when a company wants to offer and sell its securities:

- Securities Act of 1933 ("Securities Act").

- Securities Exchange Act of 1934 ("Exchange Act").

1. SECURITIES ACT OF 1933

Often referred to as the "truth in securities" law, the Securities Act of 1933 has two basic objectives:

- require that investors receive financial and other significant information concerning securities being offered for public sale; and

- prohibit deceit, misrepresentations, and other fraud in the sale of securities.

Excerpts from *What We Do*, U.S. Security and Exchange Commission (June 10, 2013), https://www.sec.gov/Article/whatwedo.html#.U0MvglfLKa4; and *Small Business and the SEC*, U.S. Security and Exchange Commission (Feb. 1, 2016), https://www.sec.gov/info/smallbus/qasbsec.htm.

Purpose of Registration

A primary means of accomplishing these goals is the disclosure of important financial information through the registration of securities. This information enables investors, not the government, to make informed judgments about whether to purchase a company's securities. While the SEC requires that the information provided be accurate, it does not guarantee it. Investors who purchase securities and suffer losses have important recovery rights if they can prove that there was incomplete or inaccurate disclosure of important information.

The Registration Process

In general, securities sold in the U.S. must be registered. The Securities Act requires your company to file a registration statement with the SEC before it may offer its securities for sale. This process is often referred to as an initial public offering, or "IPO." Your company may not actually sell the securities covered by the registration statement until the SEC staff declares the registration statement "effective."

Registration statements have two principal parts:

* Part I is the prospectus, the legal offering or "selling" document. Your company—the "issuer" of the securities—must describe in the prospectus important facts about its business operations, financial condition, results of operations, risk factors, and management. It must also include audited financial statements. The prospectus must be delivered to everyone who buys the securities, as well as anyone who is made an offer to purchase the securities.

* Part II contains additional information that the company does not have to deliver to investors but must file with the SEC, such as copies of material contracts.

The Basic Form for Registration Statements—Form S-1

All companies may use SEC Form S-1 to prepare a registration statement for a securities offering. The prospectus you include in the registration statement should provide clear, readable information written in plain English.

If your company decides to prepare and file a registration statement using Form S-1, it must include specified disclosures about the company in the prospectus, including:

* a description of your company's business, properties, and competition;

* a description of the risks of investing in your company;

* a discussion and analysis of the company's financial results and financial condition as seen through the eyes of management;

* the identity of the company's officers and directors and their compensation;

- a description of material transactions between the company and its officers, directors, and significant shareholders;
- a description of material legal proceedings involving the company and its officers and directors; and
- a description of the company's material contracts.

The company must also provide information about the offering, including:

- a description of the securities being offered;
- the plan for distributing the securities; and
- the intended use of the proceeds of the offering.

Information about how to prepare these and other non-financial disclosures in the registration statement is set out in Regulation S-K, which contains form and content rules for non-financial portions of registration statements. In addition, the SEC staff has issued guidance to aid small businesses in preparing these disclosures for initial public offerings of securities.

Registration statements also must include financial statements that comply with the form and content requirements of Regulation S-X. For most companies, financial statements must be prepared in accordance with generally accepted accounting principles in the United States ("U.S. GAAP").

Annual financial statements must be audited by an independent certified public accountant registered with the Public Company Accounting Oversight Board or "PCAOB." The PCAOB registers and regulates public accounting firms that audit financial statements filed with the SEC.

In addition to the information expressly required by Form S-1, your company also must provide any other information that is necessary to make your disclosures not misleading.

The Filing Process

Registration statements must be filed with the SEC using the SEC's Electronic Data Gathering, Analysis and Retrieval (EDGAR) system. In general, anyone can see the information and documents your company files as part of Part I and Part II of the registration statement, by looking it up on the SEC website.

SEC Staff Review of Registration Statements

The SEC staff examines registration statements for compliance with disclosure requirements, but does not evaluate the merits of the securities offering or determine whether the securities offered are "good" investments or appropriate for a particular type of investor.

If a filing or confidential submission appears incomplete or if the staff has questions regarding the registration statement or the offering, they usually inform the company with an initial "comment letter," typically within 30 days after filing or confidential submission. The company may file correcting or clarifying amendments to respond to the comments. The initial comment letter may be followed by additional comment letters. The review process is not subject to time limits.

Once the company has satisfied the disclosure requirements, the staff declares the registration statement "effective." The company may then complete sales of its securities.

Reporting Obligations because of Securities Act Registration

Once the SEC staff declares your company's Securities Act registration statement effective, the company becomes subject to [1934 Securities] Exchange Act reporting requirements. These rules require your company to file annual reports on Form 10-K, quarterly reports on Form 10-Q and current reports on Form 8-K with the SEC on an ongoing basis. If your company qualifies as a "smaller reporting company" or an "emerging growth company," it will be eligible to follow scaled disclosure requirements for these reports.

Once your company begins reporting, it will be required to continue reporting unless it satisfies one of the following "thresholds," in which case its filing obligations are suspended:

- your company has fewer than 300 shareholders of record of the class of securities offered (1,200 shareholders of record if your company is a bank or bank holding company); or

- your company has fewer than 500 shareholders of record of the class of securities offered and less than $10 million in total assets for each of its last three fiscal years.

If your company is subject to Exchange Act reporting requirements, it must file with the SEC much of the same information about the company as is required in the registration statement for a public offering, described above.

All of this information must be filed electronically with the SEC through its EDGAR system, and will immediately become publicly available upon filing. Your company's CEO and CFO must certify the financial and certain other information contained in annual reports on Form 10-K and quarterly reports on Form 10-Q.

Can My Company Legally Offer and Sell Securities without Registering with the SEC?

Your company's securities offering may qualify for one of several exemptions from the registration requirements of the Securities Act. We explain the most common ones below. You must remember, however, that all securities transactions, even exempt transactions, are subject to the antifraud provisions of the federal securities laws. This means that you and your company will be responsible for false or misleading statements that you or others on your behalf make regarding your company, the securities offered, or the offering. You and your company are responsible for any such statements, whether made by your company or on behalf of the company, and regardless of whether they are made orally or in writing.

In addition, offerings that are exempt from provisions of the federal securities laws may still be subject to the notice and registration requirements of various state laws. You should make sure to check with the appropriate state securities regulators before proceeding with your company's offering.

Non-public Offering (Private Placement) Exemption

Section 4(a)(2) of the Securities Act exempts from registration "transactions by an issuer not involving any public offering." To qualify for this exemption, which is sometimes referred to as the "private placement" exemption, the purchasers of the securities must:

- either have enough knowledge and experience in finance and business matters to be "sophisticated investors" (able to evaluate the risks and merits of the investment), or be able to bear the investment's economic risk;

- have access to the type of information normally provided in a prospectus for a registered securities offering; and

- agree not to resell or distribute the securities to the public.

In general, public advertising of the offering, and general solicitation of investors, is incompatible with the non-public offering exemption.

The precise limits of the non-public offering exemption are not defined by rule. As the number of purchasers increases and their relationship to the company and its management becomes more remote, it is more difficult to show that the offering qualifies for this exemption. If your company offers securities to even one person who does not meet the necessary conditions, the entire offering may be in violation of the Securities Act.

Rule 506(b) provides objective standards that your company can rely on to meet the requirements of the Section 4(a)(2) non-public offering exemption. Rule 506(b) is part of Regulation D, which is described more fully below.

Regulation D—Rules 504, 505 and 506

Regulation D contains Rules 504, 505 and 506, which establish exemptions from Securities Act registration. The only filing requirement under each of these exemptions is the requirement to file a notice on Form D with the SEC. The notice must be filed within 15 days after the first sale of securities in the offering. Many states also require the filing of a Form D notice in a Regulation D offering. The main purpose of the Form D filing is to notify federal (and state) authorities of the amount and nature of the offering being undertaken in reliance upon Regulation D.

Some rules under Regulation D specify particular disclosures that must be made to investors, while others do not. Even if your company sells securities in a manner that is not subject to specific disclosure requirements, you should take care that sufficient information is available to investors. All sales of securities are subject to the antifraud provisions of the securities laws. This means that you should consider whether the necessary information was available to investors, and that any information provided to investors must be free from false or misleading statements. Similarly, information should not be omitted if, as a result of the omission, the information that is provided to investors is false or misleading.

We address each of the Regulation D exemptions separately below.

Rule 504. Rule 504, sometimes referred to as the "seed capital" exemption, provides an exemption for the offer and sale of up to $1,000,000 of securities in a 12-month period. Your company may use this exemption so long as it is not a blank check company and is not subject to Exchange Act reporting requirements. In general, you may not use general solicitation or advertising to market the securities, and purchasers generally receive "restricted securities." Purchasers of restricted securities may not sell them without SEC registration or using another exemption, which is further explained below under the heading "Resales of restricted securities." Investors should be informed that they may not be able to sell securities of a non-reporting company for at least a year without the issuer registering the transaction with the SEC.

Your company may, however, use the Rule 504 exemption for a public offering of its securities with general solicitation and advertising, and investors will receive non-restricted securities, under one of the following circumstances:

- It sells in accordance with a state law that requires the public filing and delivery to investors of a substantive disclosure document; or

- It sells in accordance with a state law that requires registration and disclosure document delivery and also sells in a state without those requirements, so long as your company delivers to all purchasers the disclosure documents mandated by a state in which it registered; or

- It sells exclusively according to state law exemptions that permit general solicitation and advertising, so long as sales are made only to "accredited investors" (we describe the term "accredited investor" in more detail below in connection with our description of Rule 506 offerings).

Rule 505. Rule 505 provides an exemption for offers and sales of securities totaling up to $5 million in any 12-month period. Under this exemption, your company may sell to an unlimited number of "accredited investors" and up to 35 persons that are not accredited investors. Purchasers must buy for investment purposes only, and not for the purpose of reselling the securities. The issued securities are "restricted securities," meaning purchasers may not resell them without registration or an applicable exemption, as explained below under the heading "Resales of restricted securities." If your company is not an

SEC reporting company, investors should be informed that they may not be able to sell securities for at least a year without the company registering the transaction with the SEC. Your company may not use general solicitation or advertising to sell the securities.

Under Rule 505, if your offering involves any purchasers that are not accredited investors, you must give these purchasers disclosure documents that generally contain the same information as those included in a registration statement for a registered offering. There are also financial statement requirements that apply to Rule 505 offerings involving purchasers that are not accredited investors. For instance, if financial statements are required, they must be audited by a certified public accountant. You must also be available to answer questions from prospective purchasers who are not accredited investors.

You may decide what information to give to accredited investors, so long as it does not violate the antifraud prohibitions of the federal securities laws. If your company provides information to accredited investors, it must make this information available to the non-accredited investors as well.

Rule 506. Rule 506 provides two different ways of conducting a securities offering that is exempt from registration: Rule 506(b) and Rule 506(c). Rule 506(b) is a long-standing rule. Rule 506(c) was added in 2013 to implement a statutory mandate under the JOBS Act.

Rule 506(b). As discussed earlier, Rule 506(b) is a "safe harbor" for the non-public offering exemption in Section 4(a)(2) of the Securities Act, which means it provides specific requirements that, if followed, establish that your transaction falls within the Section 4(a)(2) exemption. Rule 506 does not limit the amount of money your company can raise or the number of accredited investors it can sell securities to, but to qualify for the safe harbor, your company must:

- not use general solicitation or advertising to market the securities;

- not sell securities to more than 35 non-accredited investors (unlike Rule 505, all non-accredited investors, either alone or with a purchaser representative, must meet the legal standard of having sufficient knowledge and experience in financial and business matters to be capable of evaluating the merits and risks of the prospective investment);

- give non-accredited investors specified disclosure documents that generally contain the same information as provided in registered offerings (the company is not required to provide specified disclosure documents to accredited investors, but, if it does provide information to accredited investors, it must also make this information available to the non-accredited investors as well);

- be available to answer questions from prospective purchasers who are non-accredited investors; and

- provide the same financial statement information as required under Rule 505.

Rule 506(c). To implement Section 201(a) of the JOBS Act, the SEC promulgated Rule 506(c) to eliminate the prohibition on using general solicitation under Rule 506 where all purchasers of the securities are accredited investors and the issuer takes reasonable steps to verify that the purchasers are accredited investors.

Under Rule 506(c), issuers may offer securities through means of general solicitation, provided that:

- all purchasers in the offering are accredited investors,
- the issuer takes reasonable steps to verify their accredited investor status, and
- certain other conditions in Regulation D are satisfied.

An "accredited investor" is:

- a bank, insurance company, registered investment company, business development company, or small business investment company;
- an employee benefit plan (within the meaning of the Employee Retirement Income Security Act) if a bank, insurance company, or registered investment adviser makes the investment decisions, or if the plan has total assets in excess of $5 million;
- a tax exempt charitable organization, corporation or partnership with assets in excess of $5 million;
- a director, executive officer, or general partner of the company selling the securities;
- an enterprise in which all the equity owners are accredited investors;
- an individual with a net worth of at least $1 million, not including the value of his or her primary residence;
- an individual with income exceeding $200,000 in each of the two most recent calendar years or joint income with a spouse exceeding $300,000 for those years and a reasonable expectation of the same income level in the current year; or
- a trust with assets of at least $5 million, not formed only to acquire the securities offered, and whose purchases are directed by a person who meets the legal standard of having sufficient knowledge and experience in financial and business matters to be capable of evaluating the merits and risks of the prospective investment.

Purchasers receive "restricted securities" in a Rule 506 offering. Therefore, they may not freely trade the securities after the offering, as explained below under the heading "Resales of restricted securities.

[Other exemptions that this textbook does not address in detail are the following:]

Regulation A

Regulation A is an exemption for public offerings not exceeding $5 million in any 12-month period.

Accredited Investor Exemption—Section 4(a)(5)

Section 4(a)(5) of the Securities Act exempts from registration offers and sales of securities to accredited investors when the total offering price is less than $5 million.

Intrastate Offering Exemption

Section 3(a)(11) of the Securities Act is generally known as the "intrastate offering exemption." This exemption facilitates the financing of local business operations.

What Are the New Exemptions Mandated by the JOBS Act?

The Jumpstart Our Business Startups Act (or JOBS Act), enacted in 2012, is intended, among other things, to reduce barriers to capital formation, particularly for smaller companies. Among other things, the JOBS Act requires the SEC to adopt rules amending existing exemptions and creating new exemptions that permit companies to raise capital without SEC registration.

Crowdfunding

The JOBS Act requires the SEC to develop new rules permitting capital raising by "crowdfunding." Crowdfunding is a means to raise money by attracting relatively small individual contributions from a large number of people.

Expansion of Regulation A

The JOBS Act requires the SEC to develop rules for a new exemption similar to existing Regulation A, which will permit offerings of up to $50 million a year without SEC registration (Regulation A currently has a limit of $5 million).

Resales of Restricted Securities

"Restricted securities" are previously-issued securities held by security holders that are not freely tradable because the sale transaction from the issuer to the security holders was a private transaction. After such a private transaction, the security holders can only resell the securities into the market by using an "effective" registration statement under the Securities Act or a valid exemption from the registration requirements of the Securities Act for the resale, such as Rule 144 under the Securities Act.

If holders of restricted securities want to resell using an effective registration statement, the issuing company can provide a registration statement for them to make sales in a public offering by following the process discussed above for registering a public offering of securities.

Alternatively, a holder of restricted securities can resell using an exemption. For example, Securities Act Rule 144 provides an exemption that permits the resale of restricted securities if a number of conditions are met, including holding the securities for six months or one year, depending on whether the issuer has been filing reports under the Exchange Act. Rule 144 may limit the amount of securities that can be sold at one time and may restrict the manner of sale, depending on whether the security holder is an affiliate. An affiliate of a company is a person that, directly, or indirectly through one or more intermediaries controls, or is controlled by, or is under common control with, the company.

Do State Law Requirements Apply in Addition to Federal Requirements?

Yes. State governments have their own securities laws and regulations. If your company is selling securities, it must comply with both federal regulations and state securities laws and regulations in the states where securities are offered and sold (typically, the states where offerees and investors are based). A particular offering exempt under the federal securities laws is not necessarily exempt from any state laws. Each state's securities laws have their own separate registration requirements and exemptions to registration requirements.

Historically, most state legislatures have followed one of two approaches in regulating public offerings of securities, or a combination of the two approaches. Some states review the securities offerings of small businesses to determine whether companies disclose to investors all information needed to make an informed investment decision. Other states also analyze the terms of public offerings using substantive standards to determine whether the structure of the offerings are fair to investors.

2. SECURITIES EXCHANGE ACT OF 1934

The Exchange Act requires companies that meet certain thresholds to report information regularly about their business operations, financial condition, and management. These companies must file periodic reports or other information with the SEC. In some cases, the company must deliver the information directly to investors. We discuss these obligations more fully below.

With this Act, Congress [also] created the Securities and Exchange Commission. The Act empowers the SEC with broad authority over all aspects of the securities industry. This includes the power to register, regulate, and oversee brokerage firms, transfer agents, and clearing agencies as well as the nation's securities self regulatory organizations (SROs). The various stock exchanges, such as the New York Stock Exchange, and American Stock Exchange are SROs. The Financial Industry Regulatory Authority, which operates the NASDAQ system, is also an SRO.

The Act also identifies and prohibits certain types of conduct in the markets and provides the Commission with disciplinary powers over regulated entities and persons associated with them.

Exchange Act Registration Requirements

Even if your company has not issued securities under a registration statement declared effective by the SEC staff, it could still become an SEC reporting company. In general, your company will be required to file a registration statement under Section 12 of the Exchange Act registering the pertinent class of securities if:

- it has more than $10 million in total assets and a class of equity securities, like common stock, that is held of record by either (1) 2,000 or more persons or (2) 500 or more persons who are not accredited investors; or

- it lists the securities on a U.S. exchange.

The information about the company required for an Exchange Act registration statement is similar to what is required for a registration statement under the Securities Act.

Exchange Act Reporting and Other Requirements

If your company files a registration statement under Section 12 of the Exchange Act, it becomes an SEC reporting company and subject to the same annual, quarterly, and current reporting obligations that result from Securities Act registration described above. In addition, the company's shareholders and management become subject to various requirements discussed below.

Proxy Rules

A company with Exchange Act-registered securities must comply with the SEC's proxy rules whenever its management submits proposals to shareholders that will be subject to a shareholder vote, usually at a shareholders' meeting. These rules get their name from the common practice of management asking shareholders to provide them with a document called a "proxy card" granting authority to vote the shareholders' shares at the meeting. The proxy rules require the company to provide certain disclosures in a proxy statement to its shareholders, together with a proxy card in a specified format, when soliciting authority to vote the shareholders' shares. Proxy statements describe matters up for shareholder vote, and include management and executive compensation information if the shareholders are voting for the election of directors.

If shareholders will take action on a matter but management is not soliciting proxies, the company must provide shareholders with an information statement that is similar to a proxy statement. The proxy rules also require the company to send an annual report to shareholders if the shareholders are voting for directors. The proxy rules also govern when your company must provide shareholder lists to investors and when it must include a proposal from a shareholder in its proxy statement or information statement.

Beneficial Ownership Reports

If your company has registered a class of its equity securities under the Exchange Act, shareholders who acquire more than 5% of the outstanding shares of that class must file beneficial owner reports on Schedule 13D or 13G until their holdings drop below 5%. These filings contain background information about the shareholders who file them as well as their investment intentions, providing investors and the company with information about accumulations of securities that may potentially change or influence company management and policies.

Tender Offers

The SEC's tender offer rules apply to transactions in which a public company faces a third-party tender offer or "takeover." The rules also apply if a public company makes a tender offer for its own securities. The filings required by these rules provide information to the holders of the securities about the person making the tender offer and the terms of the offer. The company that is the subject of a takeover must file its responses to the tender offer with the SEC. The rules also set minimum time periods for the tender offer and provide other protections to shareholders.

Listing Standards

If your company lists its securities on a securities exchange such as the Nasdaq or New York Stock Exchange, it will be subject to the rules or "listing standards" governing all companies listed on that exchange, including rules on corporate governance and audit committees. Companies whose securities are not listed on an exchange but are traded only through the facilities of the OTC Bulletin Board or OTC Markets Group's OTC Link typically are not subject to additional standards on corporate governance and audit committees.

B. SECURITIES FRAUD

The anti-fraud provisions of the Securities Exchange Act of 1934 make it unlawful to directly or indirectly use any measure to defraud, including making false statements or omitting relevant information, in relation to transactions involving the purchase or sale of stock and other securities.

1. AFFIRMATIVE FRAUD

DURA PHARMACEUTICALS, INC., et al., Petitioners,

v.

Michael BROUDO et al.

125 S.Ct. 1627 (2005)

Justice BREYER delivered the opinion of the Court.

Private federal securities fraud actions are based upon federal securities statutes and their implementing regulations. Section 10(b) of the Securities Exchange Act of 1934 forbids (1) the "use or employ[ment] … of any … deceptive device," (2) "in connection with the purchase or sale of any security," and (3) "in contravention of" Securities and Exchange Commission "rules and regulations." 15 U.S.C. § 78j(b). Commission Rule 10b–5 forbids, among other things, the making of any "untrue statement of a material fact" or the omission of any material fact "necessary in order to make the statements made … not misleading." 17 CFR § 240.10b–5 (2004).

The courts have implied from these statutes and Rule a private damages action, which resembles, but is not identical to, common-law tort actions for deceit and misrepresentation. See, *e.g., Blue Chip Stamps v. Manor Drug Stores*, 421 U.S. 723, 730, 744, 95 S.Ct. 1917, 44 L.Ed.2d 539 (1975); *Ernst & Ernst v. Hochfelder*, 425 U.S. 185, 196, 96 S.Ct. 1375, 47 L.Ed.2d 668 (1976). And Congress has imposed statutory requirements on that private action. *E.g.,* 15 U.S.C. § 78u–4(b)(4).

In cases involving publicly traded securities and purchases or sales in public securities markets, the action's basic elements include:

> *(1) a material misrepresentation (or omission),* see *Basic Inc. v. Levinson*, 485 U.S. 224, 231–232, 108 S.Ct. 978, 99 L.Ed.2d 194 (1988);

> *(2) scienter,* i.e., a wrongful state of mind, see *Ernst & Ernst*, supra, at 197, 199, 96 S.Ct. 1375;

> *(3) a connection with the purchase or sale of a security,* see *Blue Chip Stamps*, supra, at 730–731, 95 S.Ct. 1917;

> *(4) reliance,* often referred to in cases involving public securities markets (fraud-on-the-market cases) as "transaction causation," see *Basic*, supra, at 248–249, 108 S.Ct. 978 (nonconclusively presuming that the price of a publicly traded share reflects a material misrepresentation and that plaintiffs have relied upon that misrepresentation as long as they would not have bought the share in its absence);

Copyright in the Public Domain.

(5) economic loss, 15 U.S.C. § 78u–4(b)(4); and

(6) "loss causation," i.e., a causal connection between the material misrepresentation and the loss, *ibid.*; cf. T. Hazen, Law of Securities Regulation §§ 12.11[1], [3] (5th ed.2005).

2. INSIDER TRADING

"Insider trading" is a term that most investors have heard and usually associate with illegal conduct. But the term actually includes both legal and illegal conduct. The legal version is when corporate insiders—officers, directors, and employees—buy and sell stock in their own companies. When corporate insiders trade in their own securities, they must report their trades to the SEC.

Illegal insider trading refers generally to buying or selling a security, in breach of a fiduciary duty or other relationship of trust and confidence, while in possession of material, nonpublic information about the security. Insider trading violations may also include "tipping" such information, securities trading by the person "tipped," and securities trading by those who misappropriate such information.

Examples of insider trading cases that have been brought by the SEC are cases against:

- Corporate officers, directors, and employees who traded the corporation's securities after learning of significant, confidential corporate developments;

- Friends, business associates, family members, and other "tippees" of such officers, directors, and employees, who traded the securities after receiving such information;

- Employees of law, banking, brokerage and printing firms who were given such information to provide services to the corporation whose securities they traded;

- Government employees who learned of such information because of their employment by the government; and

- Other persons who misappropriated, and took advantage of, confidential information from their employers.

Because insider trading undermines investor confidence in the fairness and integrity of the securities markets, the SEC has treated the detection and prosecution of insider trading violations as one of its enforcement priorities.

Excerpt from *Insider Trading*, U.S. Securities and Exchange Commission (Jan. 15, 2013), https://www.sec.gov/fast-answers/answersinsiderhtm.html. Copyright in the Public Domain.

Speech by SEC Staff:

Insider Trading—A U.S. Perspective

Remarks by

Thomas C. Newkirk

Associate Director, Division of Enforcement

Melissa A. Robertson

Senior Counsel, Division of Enforcement
U.S. Securities & Exchange Commission

16th International Symposium on Economic Crime
Jesus College, Cambridge, England

September 19, 1998

I. Introduction

More Americans are investing in the stock market than ever before and Americans now have almost twice as much money invested in the stock market as in commercial banks. We believe this reflects Americans' trust and confidence in the American stock markets and that trust stems from a belief that our government relentlessly pursues its mandate to maintain the fairness and integrity of the stock markets. As Chairman Levitt of the United States Securities and Exchange Commission ("SEC" or "Commission") recently observed in an address to the legal and investment community:

> Our markets are a success precisely because they enjoy the world's highest level of confidence. Investors put their capital to work—and put their fortunes at risk—because they trust that the marketplace is honest. They know that our securities laws require free, fair, and open transactions.

An essential part of our regulation of the securities market is the vigorous enforcement of our laws against insider trading, an enforcement program, the Chairman noted, that "resonate[s] especially profoundly" among American investors. The enforcement program includes both civil and criminal prosecution of insider trading cases.

II. The Insider Trading Debate

"Insider trading" is a term subject to many definitions and connotations and it encompasses both legal and prohibited activity. Insider trading takes place legally every day, when corporate insiders—officers, directors or

Source: Thomas C. Newkirk & Melissa A. Robertson, Speech by SEC Staff: Insider Trading – A U.S. Perspective, U.S. Securities and Exchange Commission (Oct. 19, 1998), http://www.sec.gov/news/speech/speecharchive/1998/spch221.htm. Copyright in the Public Domain.

employees—buy or sell stock in their own companies within the confines of company policy and the regulations governing this trading.

The type of insider trading we discuss here is the illegal variety that most of us think of when we hear the term; the type of insider trading that achieved wide-spread notoriety in the 1980s with the SEC's civil cases and the United States Department of Justice's criminal cases against Michael Milken and Ivan Boesky and which inspired even Hollywood's imagination with the movie "Wall Street". It is the trading that takes place when those privileged with confidential information about important events use the special advantage of that knowledge to reap profits or avoid losses on the stock market, to the detriment of the source of the information and to the typical investors who buy or sell their stock without the advantage of "inside" information.

The American notion that insider trading is wrong was well-established long before the passage of the federal securities laws. In 1909, the United States Supreme Court held that a director of a corporation who knew that the value of the stock of his company was about to skyrocket committed fraud when he bought company stock from an outsider without disclosing what he knew. But this condemnation is not universal, even in the United States.

III. INSIDER TRADING LAW IN THE UNITED STATES

Rooted in the common law tradition of England, on which our legal system is based, we have relied largely on our courts to develop the law prohibiting insider trading. While Congress gave us the mandate to protect investors and keep our markets free from fraud, it has been our jurists, albeit at the urging of the Commission and the United States Department of Justice, who have played the largest role in defining the law of insider trading.

After the United States stock market crash of 1929, Congress enacted the Securities Act of 1933 and the Securities Exchange Act of 1934, aimed at controlling the abuses believed to have contributed to the crash. The 1934 Act addressed insider trading directly through Section 16(b) and indirectly through Section 10(b).

Section 10(b) of the Securities and Exchange Act of 1934 makes it unlawful for any person "to use or employ, in connection with the purchase or sale of any security registered on a national securities exchange or any security not so registered, any manipulative or deceptive device or contrivance in contravention of such rules and regulations as the [SEC] may prescribe." To implement Section 10(b), the SEC adopted Rule 10b–5, which provides, in relevant part:

It shall be unlawful for any person, directly or indirectly ... ,

c.   to employ any device, scheme, or artifice to defraud,

a.   d. to make any untrue statement of a material fact or omit to state a material fact necessary in order to make the statements made, in light of the circumstances under which they were made, not misleading, or

e.   to engage in any act, practice, or course of business which operates or would operate as a fraud or deceit upon any person, in connection with the purchase or sale of a security.

These broad anti-fraud provisions, make it unlawful to engage in fraud or misrepresentation in connection with the purchase or sale of a security. While they do not speak expressly to insider trading, here is where the courts have exercised the authority that has led to the most important developments in insider trading law in the United States.

The anti-fraud provisions were relatively easy to apply to the corporate insider who secretly traded in his own company's stock while in possession of inside information because such behavior fit within traditional notions of fraud. Far less clear was whether Section 10(b) and Rule 10b–5 prohibited insider trading by a corporate "outsider." In 1961, in the case of *In re Cady Roberts & Co.*, the Securities and Exchange Commission, applying a broad construction of the provisions, held that they do. The Commission held that the duty or obligations of the corporate insider could attach to those outside the insiders' realm in certain circumstances. The Commission reasoned in language worth quoting:

> Analytically, the obligation [not to engage in insider trading] rests on two principal elements: first, the existence of a relationship giving access, directly or indirectly, to information intended to be available only for a corporate purpose and not for the personal benefit of anyone, and second, the inherent unfairness involved where a party takes advantage of such information knowing it is unavailable to those with whom he is dealing. In considering these elements under the broad language of the anti-fraud provisions we are not to be circumscribed by fine distinctions and rigid classifications. Thus, it is our task here to identify those persons who are in a special relationship with a company and privy to its internal affairs, and thereby suffer correlative duties in trading in its securities. Intimacy demands restraint lest the uninformed be exploited.

Based on this reasoning, the Commission held that a broker who traded while in possession of nonpublic information he received from a company director violated Rule 10b–5. The Commission adopted the "disclose or abstain rule": insiders, and those who would come to be known as "temporary" or "constructive" insiders, who possess material nonpublic information, must disclose it before trading or abstain from trading until the information is publicly disseminated.

Several years later in the case of *SEC v. Texas Gulf Sulphur Co.*, a federal circuit court supported the Commission's ruling in *Cady*, stating that anyone in possession of inside information is required either to disclose the information publicly or refrain from trading. The court expressed the view that no one should be allowed to trade with the benefit of inside information because it operates as a fraud all other buyers and sellers in the market. This was the broadest formulation of prohibited insider trading.

The 1980s were an extraordinary time in this country's economic history, marked by a frenzy of corporate takeovers and mergers involving what then were dazzling amounts of money. Insider trading reached new heights. Ironically, it is during this period that courts narrowed the scope of Section 10(b) and Rule 10b–5 in the insider trading context.

In the 1980 case of *Chiarella v. United States*, the United States Supreme Court reversed the criminal conviction of a financial printer who gleaned nonpublic information regarding tender offers and a merger from documents he was hired to print and bought stock in the target of the companies that hired him. The case was tried on the theory that the printer defrauded the persons who sold stock in the target to him. In reversing the conviction, the Supreme Court held that trading on material nonpublic information in itself was not enough to trigger liability under the anti-fraud provisions and because the printer owed target shareholders no duty, he did not defraud them. In what would prove to be a prophetic dissent, Chief Justice Burger opined that he would have upheld the conviction on the grounds that the defendant had "misappropriated" confidential information obtained from his employer and wrongfully used it for personal gain.

In response to the *Chiarella* decision, the Securities and Exchange Commission promulgated Rule 14e-3 under Section 14(e) of the Exchange Act, and made it illegal for anyone to trade on the basis of material nonpublic information regarding tender offers if they knew the information emanated from an insider. The purpose of the rule was to remove the *Chiarella* duty requirement in the tender offer context—where insider trading was most attractive and especially disruptive.

In 1981, the Second Circuit adopted the "misappropriation" theory, holding in the case of *United States v. Newman* that a person with no fiduciary relationship to an issuer nonetheless may be liable under Rule 10b–5 for trading in the securities of an issuer while in possession of information obtained in violation of a relationship of trust and confidence. Newman, a securities trader, traded based on material nonpublic information about corporate takeovers that he obtained from two investment bankers, who had misappropriated the information from their employers.

Three years later in *Dirks v. SEC*, the Supreme Court reversed the SEC's censure of a securities analyst who told his clients about the alleged fraud of an issuer he had learned from the inside before he made the facts public. *Dirks* was significant because it addressed the issue of trading liability of "tippees": those who receive information from the insider tipper. *Dirks* held that tippees are liable if they knew or had reason to believe that the tipper had breached a fiduciary duty in disclosing the confidential information and the tipper received a direct or indirect personal benefit from the disclosure. Because the original tipper in *Dirks* disclosed the information for the purpose of exposing a fraud and not for personal gain, his tippee escaped liability.

A significant aspect of the decision was contained in a footnote to the opinion, which has come to be known as "*Dirks* footnote 14." There, Justice Powell formulated the concept of the "constructive insiders"—outside lawyers, consultants, investment bankers or others—who legitimately receive confidential information from a corporation in the course of providing services to the corporation. These constructive insiders acquire the fiduciary duties of the true insider, provided the corporation expected the constructive insider to keep the information confidential.

The Second Circuit again addressed the misappropriation theory in the 1986 case of *United States v. Carpenter*. The case centered on a columnist for the Wall Street Journal, whose influential columns often affected the stock prices of companies about which he wrote. The columnist tipped information about his upcoming columns to a broker (among others) and shared in the profits the broker made by trading in advance of publication. In upholding the convictions of the columnist and the broker for securities fraud under Rule 10b–5 and mail and wire fraud, the Second Circuit rejected the defendants' argument that the misappropriation theory only applies when the information is misappropriated by corporate or constructive insiders, holding "[T]he misappropriation theory more broadly proscribes the conversion by insiders' or others of material non-public information in connection with the purchase or sale of securities."

The case was appealed to the Supreme Court. The Supreme Court unanimously agreed that Carpenter engaged in fraud, but divided evenly on whether he engaged in securities fraud. But in unanimously affirming the mail and wire fraud convictions, the Court quoted an earlier New York decision that ruled: "It is well established, as a general proposition, that a person who acquires special knowledge or information by virtue of a confidential or fiduciary relationship with another is not free to exploit that knowledge or information for his own personal benefit but must account to his principle for any profits derived therefrom."

Over the next nine years, the misappropriation theory gained acceptance in federal courts. Then in 1995 and 1996, two federal circuit courts rejected the misappropriation theory on the grounds that the theory "requires neither misrepresentation nor nondisclosure" and that "the misappropriation theory is not moored [in] [section] 10(b)'s requirement that the fraud be "in connection with the purchase or sale of any security.""

Last year, in a landmark victory for the SEC, the Supreme Court reversed one of these decisions and explicitly adopted the misappropriation theory of insider trading in the case of *United States v. O'Hagan*. O'Hagan was a partner in a law firm retained to represent a corporation, Grand Met, in a potential tender offer for the common stock of the Pillsbury Company. When O'Hagan learned of the potential deal, he began acquiring options in Pillsbury stock, which he sold after the tender offer for a profit of over $4 million. O'Hagan argued, essentially, that because neither he nor his firm owed any fiduciary duty to Pillsbury, he did not commit fraud by purchasing Pillsbury stock on the basis of material, nonpublic information.

The Court rejected O'Hagan's arguments and upheld his conviction. The Court held, significantly, that O'Hagan committed fraud in connection with his purchase of Pillsbury options, thus violating Rule10b–5, based on the misappropriation theory. In the Court's words:

> The "misappropriation theory" holds that a person commits fraud "in connection with" a securities transaction, and thereby violates 10(b) and Rule 10b–5, when he misappropriates confidential information for securities trading purposes, in breach of a duty owed to the source of the information. Under this theory, a fiduciary's undisclosed, self-serving use of a principal's information to purchase or sell securities, in breach of a duty of loyalty and confidentiality, defrauds the principal of the exclusive use of the information. In lieu of premising liability on a fiduciary relationship between company insider and purchaser or seller of the company's stock, the misappropriation theory premises liability on a fiduciary-turned-trader's deception of those who entrusted him with access to confidential information

Although the law of insider trading in the United States is continuing to evolve, the decision in *O'Hagan* is a significant milestone in defining the scope of Rule 10b–5 insider trading prohibitions.

* * *

Final Rule: Selective Disclosure and Insider Trading
SECURITIES AND EXCHANGE COMMISSION
17 CFR Parts 240, 243, and 249
Release Nos. 33–7881, 34–43154, IC–24599, File No. S7–31–99
RIN 3235–AH82

III. INSIDER TRADING RULES

B. Rule 10b5–2: Duties of Trust or Confidence in Misappropriation Insider Trading Cases

Excerpts from *Final Rule: Selective Disclosure and Insider Trading*, U.S. Securities and Exchange Commission. https://www.sec.gov/rules/final/33-7881.htm (Aug. 21, 2000). Copyright in the Public Domain.

1. Background

As discussed more fully in the Proposing Release, an unsettled issue in insider trading law has been under what circumstances certain non-business relationships, such as family and personal relationships, may provide the duty of trust or confidence required under the misappropriation theory. Case law has produced the following anomalous result. A family member who receives a "tip" (within the meaning of <u>Dirks</u>) and then trades violates Rule 10b–5. A family member who trades in breach of an express promise of confidentiality also violates Rule 10b–5. A family member who trades in breach of a reasonable expectation of confidentiality, however, does not necessarily violate Rule 10b–5.

As discussed more fully in the Proposing Release, we think that this anomalous result harms investor confidence in the integrity and fairness of the nation's securities markets. The family member's trading has the same impact on the market and investor confidence in the third example as it does in the first two examples. In all three examples, the trader's informational advantage stems from "contrivance, not luck," and the informational disadvantage to other investors "cannot be overcome with research or skill." Additionally, the need to distinguish among the three types of cases may require an unduly intrusive examination of the details of particular family relationships. Accordingly, we believe there is good reason for the broader approach we adopt today for determining when family or personal relationships create "duties of trust or confidence" under the misappropriation theory.

2. Provisions of Rule 10b5–2

We are adopting Rule 10b5–2 substantially as proposed. The rule sets forth a non-exclusive list of three situations in which a person has a duty of trust or confidence for purposes of the "misappropriation" theory of the Exchange Act and Rule 10b–5 thereunder.

* * *

§240.10b5–2 Duties of trust or confidence in misappropriation insider trading cases.

Preliminary Note to §240.10b5–2: This section provides a non-exclusive definition of circumstances in which a person has a duty of trust or confidence for purposes of the "misappropriation" theory of insider trading under Section 10(b) of the Act and Rule 10b–5. The law of insider trading is otherwise defined by judicial opinions construing Rule 10b–5, and Rule 10b5–2 does not modify the scope of insider trading law in any other respect.

(a) *Scope of Rule.* This section shall apply to any violation of Section 10(b) of the Act (15 U.S.C. 78j(b)) and §240.10b–5 thereunder that is based on the purchase or sale of securities on the basis of, or the communication of, material nonpublic information misappropriated in breach of a duty of trust or confidence.

(b) *Enumerated "duties of trust or confidence."* For purposes of this section, a "duty of trust or confidence" exists in the following circumstances, among others:

(1) Whenever a person agrees to maintain information in confidence;

(2) Whenever the person communicating the material nonpublic information and the person to whom it is communicated have a history, pattern, or practice of sharing confidences, such that the recipient of the information knows or reasonably should know that the person communicating the material nonpublic information expects that the recipient will maintain its confidentiality; or

(3) Whenever a person receives or obtains material nonpublic information from his or her spouse, parent, child, or sibling; *provided,* however, that the person receiving or obtaining the information may demonstrate that no duty of trust or confidence existed with respect to the information, by establishing that he or she neither knew nor reasonably should have known that the person who was the source of the information expected that the person would keep the information confidential, because of the parties' history, pattern, or practice of sharing and maintaining confidences, and because there was no agreement or understanding to maintain the confidentiality of the information.

CHAPTER 21

TRANSFORMING THE CORPORATION

While a corporation's board of directors can make most decisions for a corporation, certain decisions, deemed "fundamental changes," require the approval of shareholders. This chapter will discuss events that are considered fundamental changes and what shareholder approval they require.

A. AMENDMENT OF ARTICLES

§ 10.01. Authority To Amend

(a) A corporation may amend its articles of incorporation at any time to add or change a provision that is required or permitted in the articles of incorporation as of the effective date of the amendment or to delete a provision that is not required to be contained in the articles of incorporation.

(b) A shareholder of the corporation does not have a vested property right resulting from any provision in the articles of incorporation, including provisions relating to management, control, capital structure, dividend entitlement, or purpose or duration of the corporation.

Official Comment

Under section 10.01(a), the sole test for the permissibility of an amendment to the corporation's articles of incorporation is whether the provision could lawfully have been included in (or in the case of a deletion, omitted from) the articles of incorporation on the effective date of the amendment. The articles of incorporation need not make any reference to, or reserve, the express power to amend the articles of incorporation. Under the Act, a provision in the articles of incorporation is subject to amendment under section 10.01 even though the provision is described, referred to, or stated in a share

Source: Model Bus. Corp. Act §§ 10.01, 10.03–06 (2016). Copyright © 2016 by American Bar Association. Reprinted with permission.

certificate, a written information statement, or other document issued by the corporation that reflects provisions of the articles of incorporation. Section 10.01 does not override contracts by a corporation outside of its articles of incorporation. For example, a corporation might contract with a shareholder or a third party that it would not make particular amendments to its articles. If the corporation made such an amendment, it would be in breach of the contract even if the amendment were otherwise permitted by this section. A shareholder may also obtain protection against amendments by establishing procedures in the articles of incorporation or bylaws that limit the power of amendment without that shareholder's consent.

Section 10.01(b) expressly rejects the concept that an otherwise lawful amendment to the articles of incorporation might be restricted or invalidated because it modified particular rights conferred on shareholders by the original or prior version of the articles of incorporation.

§ 10.03. Amendment By Board Of Directors And Shareholders

If a corporation has issued shares, an amendment to the articles of incorporation shall be adopted in the following manner:

(a) The proposed amendment shall first be adopted by the board of directors.

(b) Except as provided in sections 10.05, 10.07, and 10.08, the amendment shall then be approved by the shareholders. In submitting the proposed amendment to the shareholders for approval, the board of directors shall recommend that the shareholders approve the amendment, unless (i) the board of directors makes a determination that because of conflicts of interest or other special circumstances it should not make such a recommendation, or (ii) section 8.26 applies. If either (i) or (ii) applies, the board must inform the shareholders of the basis for its so proceeding.

(c) The board of directors may set conditions for the approval of the amendment by the shareholders or the effectiveness of the amendment.

(d) If the amendment is required to be approved by the shareholders, and the approval is to be given at a meeting, the corporation shall notify each shareholder, regardless of whether entitled to vote, of the meeting of shareholders at which the amendment is to be submitted for approval.

(e) Unless the articles of incorporation, or the board of directors acting pursuant to subsection (c), require a greater vote or a greater quorum, approval of the amendment requires the approval of the shareholders at a meeting at which a quorum consisting of a majority of the votes entitled to be cast on the amendment exists, and, if any class or series of shares is entitled to vote as a separate group on the amendment, except as provided in section 10.04(c), the approval of each such separate voting group at a meeting at which a quorum of the voting group exists consisting of a majority of the votes entitled to be cast on the amendment by that voting group.

Official Comment

Section 10.03 governs amendments to the articles of incorporation after shares have been issued. Most such amendments will require a shareholder vote. When submitting an amendment to the articles of incorporation to shareholders, the board of directors must recommend the amendment, subject to two exceptions in section 10.03(b). The board might exercise the exception under clause (i) where the number of directors having a conflicting interest makes it inadvisable for the board to recommend the amendment or where the board is evenly divided as to the merits of the amendment but is able to agree that shareholders should be permitted to consider it. Alternatively, the board of directors might exercise the exception under clause (ii), which recognizes that, under section 8.26, a board of directors may agree to submit an amendment to a vote of shareholders even if, after approving the amendment, the board of directors determines that it no longer recommends the amendment.

Section 10.03(c) permits the board of directors to set conditions for its submission of an amendment to the shareholders or effectiveness of an amendment. Examples of conditions that a board might impose are that the amendment will not be deemed approved (i) unless it is approved by a specified vote of the shareholders, or by one or more specified classes or series of shares, voting as a separate voting group, or by a specified percentage of votes of disinterested shareholders, or (ii) if shareholders holding more than a specified number or percentage of outstanding shares assert appraisal rights.

Section 10.03(e) specifies quorum and voting requirements applicable to a shareholder vote to approve an amendment to the articles of incorporation. If the prescribed quorum exists, then under sections 7.25 and 7.26 the amendment will be approved if more votes are cast in favor of the amendment than against it by the voting group or separate voting groups entitled to vote on the amendment, unless the articles of incorporation or the board of directors acting pursuant to section 10.03(c) require a greater vote.

§ 10.04. Voting On Amendments By Voting Groups

(a) The holders of the outstanding shares of a class are entitled to vote as a separate voting group (if shareholder voting is otherwise required by this Act) on a proposed amendment to the articles of incorporation if the amendment would:

    (1) effect an exchange or reclassification of all or part of the shares of the class into shares of another class;

    (2) effect an exchange or reclassification, or create the right of exchange, of all or part of the shares of another class into shares of the class;

    (3) change the rights, preferences, or limitations of all or part of the shares of the class;

    (4) change the shares of all or part of the class into a different number of shares of the same class;

    (5) create a new class of shares having rights or preferences with respect to distributions that are prior or superior to the shares of the class;

    (6) increase the rights, preferences, or number of authorized shares of any class that, after giving effect to the amendment, have rights or preferences with respect to distributions that are prior or superior to the shares of the class;

    (7) limit or deny an existing preemptive right of all or part of the shares of the class; or

    (8) cancel or otherwise affect rights to distributions that have accumulated but not yet been authorized on all or part of the shares of the class.

(b) If a proposed amendment would affect a series of a class of shares in one or more of the ways described in subsection (a), the holders of shares of that series are entitled to vote as a separate voting group on the proposed amendment.

(c) If a proposed amendment that entitles the holders of two or more classes or series of shares to vote as separate voting groups under this section would affect those two or more classes or series in the same or a substantially similar way, the holders of shares of all the classes or series so affected shall vote together as a single voting group on the proposed amendment, unless otherwise provided in the articles of incorporation or added as a condition by the board of directors pursuant to section 10.03(c).

(d) A class or series of shares is entitled to the voting rights granted by this section even if the articles of incorporation provide that the shares are nonvoting shares.

Official Comment

Section 10.04(a) requires separate approval by voting groups for certain types of amendments to the articles of incorporation where the corporation has more than one class or series of shares outstanding. Even if a class or series of shares is described as "nonvoting" or the articles purport to make that class or series nonvoting "for all purposes," that class or series nonetheless has the voting rights provided by this section. Likewise, shares are entitled to vote as separate voting groups under this section even though the articles of incorporation purport to allow other classes or series of shares to vote as part of the same voting group. However, an amendment that does not require shareholder approval does not trigger the right to vote by voting groups under this section. This would include a determination by the board, pursuant to authority granted in the articles of incorporation, of the rights, preferences and limitations of any class before the issuance of any shares of that class, or of one or more series within a class before the issuance of any shares of that series.

The right to vote as a separate voting group provides a major protection for classes or series of shares with preferential rights, or classes or series of limited or nonvoting shares, against amendments that affect that class or series. This section, however, does not make the right to vote by a separate voting group dependent on an evaluation of whether the amendment is detrimental to that class or series; if the amendment is one of those described in section 10.04(a), the class or series is automatically entitled to vote as a separate voting group on the amendment.

Sections 7.25 and 7.26 set forth the mechanics of voting by multiple voting groups. Section 10.04(b) extends the privilege of voting as a separate voting group to a series of a class of shares if the series is affected in one or more of the ways described in subsection (a). Any distinguishing feature of a series, which an amendment affects or alters, should trigger the right of voting as a separate voting group for that series. However, if a proposed amendment that affects two or more classes or series of shares in the same or a substantially similar way, under subsection (c), the shares of all the class or series so affected must vote together, as a single voting group, unless otherwise provided in the articles of incorporation or a condition set by the board of directors pursuant to section 10.03(c).

The application of sections 10.04(b) and (c) may best be illustrated by the following examples, all of which assume there is no provision in the articles of incorporation providing otherwise and that the board has not set an additional voting condition.

First, assume there is a class of shares comprised of three series, each with different preferential dividend rights. A proposed amendment would reduce the rate of dividend applicable to the "Series A" shares and would change the dividend right of the "Series B" shares from a cumulative to a noncumulative right. The amendment would not affect the preferential dividend right of the "Series C" shares. Both Series A and B would be entitled to vote as separate voting groups on the proposed amendment; the holders of the Series C shares, not directly affected by the amendment, would not be entitled to vote unless the Series C shares are voting shares under the articles of incorporation, in which case the Series C shares would not vote as a separate voting group but would vote in the voting group consisting of all shares in the class, as well as in the voting group consisting of all shares with general voting rights under the articles of incorporation.

Second, if the proposed amendment would reduce the dividend right of Series A and change the dividend right of both Series B and C from a cumulative to a noncumulative right, the holders of Series A would be entitled to vote as a single voting group, and the holders of Series B and C would be required to vote together as a single, separate voting group.

Third, assume that a corporation has common stock and two classes of preferred stock. A proposed amendment would create a new class of senior preferred that would have priority in distribution rights over both the common stock and the existing classes of preferred stock. Because the creation of the new senior preferred would affect all three classes of stock in the same or a substantially similar way, all three classes would vote together as a single voting group on the proposed amendment.

§ 10.05. Amendment By Board Of Directors

Unless the articles of incorporation provide otherwise, a corporation's board of directors may adopt amendments to the corporation's articles of incorporation without shareholder approval:

(a)　to extend the duration of the corporation if it was incorporated at a time when limited duration was required by law;

(b)　to delete the names and addresses of the initial directors;

(c)　to delete the name and address of the initial registered agent or registered office, if a statement of change is on file with the secretary of state;

(d)　if the corporation has only one class of shares outstanding:

　　(1)　to change each issued and unissued authorized share of the class into a greater number of whole shares of that class; or

　　(2)　to increase the number of authorized shares of the class to the extent necessary to permit the issuance of shares as a share dividend;

(e)　to change the corporate name by substituting the word "corporation," "incorporated," "company," "limited," or the abbreviation "corp.," "inc.," "co.," or "ltd.," for a similar word or abbreviation in the name, or by adding, deleting, or changing a geographical attribution for the name;

(f)　to reflect a reduction in authorized shares, as a result of the operation of section 6.31(b), when the corporation has acquired its own shares and the articles of incorporation prohibit the reissue of the acquired shares;

(g)　to delete a class of shares from the articles of incorporation, as a result of the operation of section 6.31(b), when there are no remaining shares of the class because the corporation has acquired all shares of the class and the articles of incorporation prohibit the reissue of the acquired shares; or

(h)　to make any change expressly permitted by section 6.02(a) or (b) to be made without shareholder approval.

Official Comment

The amendments described in subsections (a) through (h) are so routine and ministerial in nature as not to require approval by shareholders. None affects the substantive rights of shareholders in any meaningful way. Although the board of directors' designation of the preferences, rights and limitations of a new class or series of shares under section 6.02 may have substantive effects, amendments of the articles of incorporation to set forth the terms of a new class or series are already permitted by section 6.02(c).

§ 10.06. Articles Of Amendment

(a) After an amendment to the articles of incorporation has been adopted and approved in the manner required by this Act and by the articles of incorporation, the corporation shall deliver to the secretary of state for filing articles of amendment, […].

B. Amendment of Bylaws

§ 10.20. Authority To Amend

(a) A corporation's shareholders may amend or repeal the corporation's bylaws.

(b) A corporation's board of directors may amend or repeal the corporation's bylaws, unless:

   (1) the articles of incorporation, section 10.21 or, if applicable, section 10.22 reserve that power exclusively to the shareholders in whole or part; or

   (2) except as provided in section 2.06(d), the shareholders in amending, repealing, or adopting a bylaw expressly provide that the board of directors may not amend, repeal, or adopt that bylaw.

(c) A shareholder of the corporation does not have a vested property right resulting from any provision in the bylaws.

Official Comment

The power to amend or repeal bylaws is shared by the board of directors and the shareholders, unless that power is reserved exclusively to the shareholders by an appropriate provision in the articles of incorporation. Section 10.20(b)(1) permits the reservation of amendment power to the shareholders to be limited to specific articles or sections of the bylaws or to specific subjects or topics addressed in the bylaws.

The authority granted to the shareholders in section 10.20(b)(2) to prevent the board of directors from further changing a bylaw which the shareholders have amended, repealed, or adopted is expressly subject to section 2.06(d), which limits the authority of shareholders to restrict board action on bylaws with regard to procedures or conditions set forth in certain bylaws regulating the election of directors.

Source: Model Bus. Corp. Act §§ 10.20, 10.21 (2016). Copyright © 2016 by American Bar Association. Reprinted with permission.

§ 10.21. Bylaw Increasing Quorum or Voting Requirement for Directors

(a) A bylaw that increases a quorum or voting requirement for the board of directors may be amended or repealed:

    (1) if originally adopted by the shareholders, only by the shareholders, unless the bylaw otherwise provides; or

    (2) if adopted by the board of directors, either by the shareholders or by the board of directors.

(b) A bylaw adopted or amended by the shareholders that increases a quorum or voting requirement for the board of directors may provide that it can be amended or repealed only by a specified vote of either the shareholders or the board of directors.

(c) Action by the board of directors under subsection (a) to amend or repeal a bylaw that changes a quorum or voting requirement for the board of directors shall meet the same quorum requirement and be adopted by the same vote required to take action under the quorum and voting requirement then in effect or proposed to be adopted, whichever is greater.

Official Comment

The bylaws may increase a quorum or voting requirement for the board over the requirement that would otherwise apply under the Act ("supermajority requirements"). These requirements may be amended or repealed by the board of directors or shareholders as provided in section 10.21.

C. Mergers

§ 11.02. Merger or Share Exchange

(a) By complying with this chapter:

    (1) one or more domestic business corporations may merge with one or more domestic or foreign business corporations or eligible entities pursuant to a plan of merger, resulting in a survivor; and

    (2) two or more foreign business corporations or domestic or foreign eligible entities may merge, resulting in a survivor that is a domestic business corporation created in the merger.

(b) [...]

(c) [...]

(d) The plan of merger must include:

Source: Model Bus. Corp. Act §§ 11.02, 11.04, 11.06, 11.07 (2016). Copyright © 2016 by American Bar Association. Reprinted with permission.

(1) as to each party to the merger, its name, jurisdiction of formation, and type of entity;

(2) the survivor's name, jurisdiction of formation, and type of entity, and, if the survivor is to be created in the merger, a statement to that effect;

(3) the terms and conditions of the merger;

(4) the manner and basis of converting the shares of each merging domestic or foreign business corporation and eligible interests of each merging domestic or foreign eligible entity into shares or other securities, eligible interests, obligations, rights to acquire shares, other securities or eligible interests, cash, other property, or any combination of the foregoing;

(5) the articles of incorporation of any domestic or foreign business or nonprofit corporation, or the public organic record of any domestic or foreign unincorporated entity, to be created by the merger, or if a new domestic or foreign business or nonprofit corporation or unincorporated entity is not to be created by the merger, any amendments to the survivor's articles of incorporation or other public organic record; and

(6) any other provisions required by the laws under which any party to the merger is organized or by which it is governed, or by the articles of incorporation or organic rules of any such party.

(e) In addition to the requirements of subsection (d), a plan of merger may contain any other provision not prohibited by law.

Official Comment

Section 11.02 authorizes domestic corporations to merge with each other. It also authorizes one or more domestic corporations to merge with one or more foreign corporations or domestic or foreign eligible entities (such as limited liability companies or partnerships). In addition, it provides for the merger of two or more foreign corporations or foreign or domestic eligible entities, even if no domestic business corporation is a party to the merger, but only if the survivor is a domestic business corporation created by the merger.

§ 11.04. Action on a Plan of Merger of Share Exchange

In the case of a domestic corporation that is a party to a merger or the acquired entity in a share exchange, the plan of merger or share exchange shall be adopted in the following manner:

(a) The plan of merger or share exchange shall first be adopted by the board of directors.

(b) Except as provided in subsections (h), (j) and (l) and in section 11.05, the plan of merger or share exchange shall then be approved by the shareholders. In submitting the plan of merger or share exchange to the shareholders for approval, the board of directors shall recommend that the shareholders approve the plan or, in the case of an offer referred to in subsection (j)(2), that the shareholders tender their shares to the offeror in response to the offer, unless (i) the board of directors makes a determination that because of conflicts of interest or other special circumstances it should not make such a recommendation or (ii) section 8.26 applies. If either (i) or (ii) applies, the board shall inform the shareholders of the basis for its so proceeding.

(c) The board of directors may set conditions for the approval of the plan of merger or share exchange by the shareholders or the effectiveness of the plan of merger or share exchange.

(d) If the plan of merger or share exchange is required to be approved by the shareholders, and if the approval is to be given at a meeting, the corporation shall notify each shareholder, regardless of whether entitled to vote, of the meeting of shareholders at which the plan is to be submitted for approval.

(e) Unless the articles of incorporation, or the board of directors acting pursuant to subsection (c), require a greater vote or a greater quorum, approval of the plan of merger or share exchange requires the approval of the shareholders at a meeting at which a quorum exists consisting of a majority of the votes entitled to be cast on the plan, and, if any class or series of shares is entitled to vote as a separate group on the plan of merger or share exchange, the approval of each such separate voting group at a meeting at which a quorum of the voting group is present consisting of a majority of the votes entitled to be cast on the merger or share exchange by that voting group.

Official Comment

Submission to the Shareholders

When submitting a plan of merger or share exchange to shareholders, the board of directors must recommend the transaction, subject to two exceptions in section 11.04(b). The board might exercise the exception under clause (i) where the number of directors having a conflicting interest makes it inadvisable for them to recommend the transaction or where the board is evenly divided as to the merits of the transaction but is able to agree that shareholders should be permitted to consider the transaction. Alternatively, the board of directors might exercise the exception in clause (ii), which recognizes that, under section 8.26, a board of directors may include a "force the vote" clause in a plan of merger or share exchange, agreeing to submit the plan to shareholders even if, after approving the plan, the board of directors determines that it no longer recommends the plan. Section 11.04(c) permits the board of directors to condition its submission of a plan of merger or share exchange to the shareholders or the effectiveness of a plan of merger or share exchange. Among the conditions that a board of directors might impose are that the plan will not be deemed approved (i) unless it is approved by a specified vote of the shareholders, or by one or more specified classes or series of shares, voting as a separate voting group, or by a specified percentage of disinterested shareholders or (ii) if shareholders holding more than a specified fraction of the outstanding shares assert appraisal rights.

Quorum and Voting

Section 11.04(e) sets forth quorum and voting requirements applicable to a shareholder vote to approve a plan of merger or share exchange. If a quorum is present, and subject to any greater vote required by the articles of incorporation or the board of directors pursuant to section 11.04(c), under sections 7.25 and 7.26 the plan will be approved if more votes are cast in favor of the plan than against it by the voting group or each separate voting group, as the case may be, entitled to vote on the plan.

§ 11.06. Articles Of Merger Or Share Exchange

(a) After (i) a plan of merger has been adopted and approved as required by this Act, or (ii) if the merger is being effected under section 11.02(a)(2), the merger has been approved as required by the organic law governing the parties to the merger, then articles of merger shall be signed by each party to the merger except as provided in section 11.05(a). The articles must set forth:

   (1) the name, jurisdiction of formation, and type of entity of each party to the merger;

   (2) the name, jurisdiction of formation, and type of entity of the survivor;

   (3) if the survivor of the merger is a domestic corporation and its articles of incorporation are amended, or if a new domestic corporation is created as a result of the merger:

      (i) the amendments to the survivor's articles of incorporation; or

      (ii) the articles of incorporation of the new corporation;

   (4) if the survivor of the merger is a domestic eligible entity and its public organic record is amended, or if a new domestic eligible entity is created as a result of the merger:

      (i) the amendments to the public organic record of the survivor; or

      (ii) the public organic record of the new eligible entity;

   (5) if the plan of merger required approval by the shareholders of a domestic corporation that is a party to the merger, a statement

that the plan was duly approved by the shareholders and, if voting by any separate voting group was required, by each such separate voting group, in the manner required by this Act and the articles of incorporation;

(6) if the plan of merger or share exchange did not require approval by the shareholders of a domestic corporation that is a party to the merger, a statement to that effect;

(7) as to each foreign corporation that is a party to the merger, a statement that the participation of the foreign corporation was duly authorized as required by its organic law;

(8) as to each domestic or foreign eligible entity that is a party to the merger, a statement that the merger was approved in accordance with its organic law or section 11.02(c); and

(9) if the survivor is created by the merger and is a domestic limited liability partnership, the filing required to become a limited liability partnership, as an attachment.

Official Comment

The filing of articles of merger or share exchange makes the transaction a matter of public record.

§ 11.07. Effect of Merger or Share Exchange

(a) When a merger becomes effective:

(1) the domestic or foreign corporation or eligible entity that is designated in the plan of merger as the survivor continues or comes into existence, as the case may be;

(2) the separate existence of every domestic or foreign corporation or eligible entity that is a party to the merger, other than the survivor, ceases;

(3) all property owned by, and every contract right possessed by, each domestic or foreign corporation or eligible entity that is a party to the merger, other than the survivor, are the property and contract rights of the survivor without transfer, reversion or impairment;

(4) all debts, obligations and other liabilities of each domestic or foreign corporation or eligible entity that is a party to the merger, other than the survivor, are debts, obligations or liabilities of the survivor;

(5) the name of the survivor may, but need not be, substituted in any pending proceeding for the name of any party to the merger whose separate existence ceased in the merger;

(6) if the survivor is a domestic entity, the articles of incorporation and bylaws or the organic rules of the survivor are amended to the extent provided in the plan of merger;

(7) the articles of incorporation and bylaws or the organic rules of a survivor that is a domestic entity and is created by the merger become effective;

(8) the shares of each domestic or foreign corporation that is a party to the merger, and the eligible interests in an eligible entity that is a party to a merger, that are to be converted in accordance with the terms of the merger into shares or other securities, eligible interests, obligations, rights to acquire shares, other securities, or eligible interests, cash, other property, or any combination of the foregoing, are converted, and the former holders of such shares or eligible interests are entitled only to the rights provided to them by those terms or to any rights they may have under chapter 13 or the organic law governing the eligible entity or foreign corporation;

(9) except as provided by law or the terms of the merger, all the rights, privileges, franchises, and immunities of each entity that is a party to the merger, other than the survivor, are the rights, privileges, franchises, and immunities of the survivor; and

(10) if the survivor exists before the merger:

(i) all the property and contract rights of the survivor remain its property and contract rights without transfer, reversion, or impairment;

(ii) the survivor remains subject to all its debts, obligations, and other liabilities; and

(iii) except as provided by law or the plan of merger, the survivor continues to hold all of its rights, privileges, franchises, and immunities.

Official Comment

Under section 11.07(a), in a merger the parties that merge become one. The survivor automatically becomes the owner of all real and personal property and becomes subject to all the liabilities, actual or contingent, of each other party to the merger. A merger is not a conveyance, transfer, or assignment. It does not give rise to claims of reverter or impairment of title based on a prohibited conveyance, transfer, or assignment. It does not give rise to a claim that a contract with a party to the merger is no longer in effect on the ground of nonassignability, unless the contract specifically addresses that issue. All pending proceedings involving either the survivor or a party whose separate existence ceased as a result of the merger are continued.

D. ASSET SALES

§ 12.01. Disposition Of Assets Not Requiring Shareholder Approval

No approval of the shareholders is required, unless the articles of incorporation otherwise provide:

(a) to sell, lease, exchange, or otherwise dispose of any or all of the corporation's assets in the usual and regular course of business;

(b) to mortgage, pledge, dedicate to the repayment of indebtedness (whether with or without recourse), or otherwise encumber any or all of the corporation's assets, regardless of whether in the usual and regular course of business;

(c) to transfer any or all of the corporation's assets to one or more domestic or foreign corporations or other entities all of the shares or interests of which are owned by the corporation; or

(d) to distribute assets pro rata to the holders of one or more classes or series of the corporation's shares.

Official Comment

Section 12.01 specifies dispositions for which shareholder approval is not required, and section 12.02 specifies dispositions requiring shareholder approval.

Examples of dispositions in the usual and regular course of business under section 12.01(a) include the sale of a building that was the corporation's only major asset where the corporation was formed for the purpose of constructing and selling that building, the sale by a corporation of its only major business where the corporation was formed to buy and sell businesses and the proceeds of the sale are to be reinvested in the purchase of a new business, or sales of assets by an open- or closed-end investment company the portfolio of which turns over many times in short periods.

No shareholder approval is required for a transaction involving a pro rata distribution because it comes within section 12.01(d). An example is a spin-off in which shares of a subsidiary are distributed pro rata to the holders of one or more classes or series of shares. On the other hand, a non pro rata distribution—for example, a split-off in which shares of a subsidiary are distributed only to some shareholders in exchange for some or all of their shares—would require shareholder approval under section 12.02(a) if the disposition would leave the corporation without a significant continuing business activity. When the transaction involves a distribution in liquidation—for example, when two or more subsidiaries (whether they have existed previously or are newly

Source: Model Bus. Corp. Act §§ 12.01, 12.02 (2016). Copyright © 2016 by American Bar Association. Reprinted with permission.

formed) representing all of a dissolved corporation's business activities are distributed to shareholders (sometimes referred to as a split-up)—the transaction will be governed by chapter 14 (dissolution), not by chapter 12.

§ 12.02. Shareholder Approval Of Certain Dispositions

(a) A sale, lease, exchange, or other disposition of assets, other than a disposition described in section 12.01, requires approval of the corporation's shareholders if the disposition would leave the corporation without a significant continuing business activity. A corporation will conclusively be deemed to have retained a significant continuing business activity if it retains a business activity that represented, for the corporation and its subsidiaries on a consolidated basis, at least (i) 25% of total assets at the end of the most recently completed fiscal year, and (ii) either 25% of either income from continuing operations before taxes or 25% of revenues from continuing operations, in each case for the most recently completed fiscal year.

(b) To obtain the approval of the shareholders under subsection (a) the board of directors shall first adopt a resolution authorizing the disposition. The disposition shall then be approved by the shareholders. In submitting the disposition to the shareholders for approval, the board of directors shall recommend that the shareholders approve the disposition, unless (i) the board of directors makes a determination that because of conflicts of interest or other special circumstances it should not make such a recommendation, or (ii) section 8.26 applies. If either (i) or (ii) applies, the board shall inform the shareholders of the basis for its so proceeding.

(c) The board of directors may set conditions for the approval by the shareholders of a disposition or the effectiveness of the disposition.

(d) If a disposition is required to be approved by the shareholders under subsection (a), and if the approval is to be given at a meeting, the corporation shall notify each shareholder, regardless of whether entitled to vote, of the meeting of shareholders at which the disposition is to be submitted for approval.

(e) Unless the articles of incorporation or the board of directors acting pursuant to subsection (c) require a greater vote or a greater quorum, the approval of a disposition by the shareholders shall require the approval of the shareholders at a meeting at which a quorum exists consisting of a majority of the votes entitled to be cast on the disposition.

(f) [...]

(g) A disposition of assets in the course of dissolution under chapter 14 is not governed by this section.

(h) The assets of a direct or indirect consolidated subsidiary shall be deemed to be the assets of the parent corporation for the purposes of this section.

Official Comment

In General

Section 12.02(a) requires shareholder approval for a sale, lease, exchange or other disposition of assets by a corporation that would leave the corporation without a significant continuing business activity, other than as provided in section 12.01. Whether a disposition leaves a corporation with a significant continuing business activity, within the meaning of section 12.02(a), depends on whether the corporation's remaining business activity is significant when compared to the corporation's business before the disposition. The 25% safe harbor provides a measure of certainty in making this determination. The safe-harbor test is applied to assets and to revenue or income for the fiscal year ended immediately before the decision by the board of directors to make the disposition in question.

If a corporation disposes of assets for the purpose of reinvesting the proceeds of the disposition in substantially the same business in a somewhat different form (for example, by selling the corporation's only plant for the purpose of buying or building a replacement plant), the disposition and reinvestment should be treated together, so that the transaction should not be deemed to leave the corporation without a significant continuing business activity.

In determining whether a disposition would leave a corporation without a significant continuing business activity, the test combines a parent corporation with subsidiaries that are or should be consolidated with it under applicable accounting principles. For example, if a corporation's only significant business is owned by a consolidated subsidiary, a sale of that business requires approval of the parent's shareholders under section 12.02. Correspondingly, if a corporation owns one significant business directly, and several other significant businesses through one or more wholly or almost wholly owned subsidiaries, a sale by the corporation of the single business it owns directly does not require shareholder approval under section 12.02 (for example, the 25% retention tests of section 12.02(a) are met).

If all or a large part of a corporation's assets are held for investment, the corporation actively manages those assets, and it has no other significant business, for purposes of chapter 12 the corporation should be considered to be in the business of investing in assets, so that a sale of most of those assets without a reinvestment should be considered a sale that would leave the corporation without a significant continuing business activity. In applying the 25% tests of section 12.02(a), an issue could arise if a corporation had more than one business activity, one or more of which might be traditional operating activities, such as manufacturing or distribution, and another of which might be considered managing investments in other securities or enterprises. If the activity constituting the management of investments is to be a continuing business activity as a result of the active engagement of the management of the corporation in that process and the 25% retention tests were met upon the disposition of the other businesses, shareholder approval would not be required.

A board of directors may determine that a retained continuing business falls within the 25% bright-line tests of the safe harbor in section 12.02(a) based either on accounting principles and practices that are reasonable in the circumstances or (in applying the asset test) on a fair valuation or other method that is reasonable in the circumstances in a manner similar to that described in section 6.40(d) and the Official Comment 4 to that section.

The use of the term "significant" and the specific 25% safe harbor test for purposes of this section do not imply a standard for the test of significance or materiality for any other purposes under the Act or otherwise.

Submission to Shareholders

Section 12.02(c) permits the board of directors to condition its submission to the shareholders of a proposal for a disposition of assets or the effectiveness of the disposition. Among the conditions that a board of directors might impose are that the proposal will not be deemed approved: (i) unless it is approved by a specified percentage of the shareholders, or by one or more specified classes or series of shares, voting as a separate voting group, or by a specified percentage of disinterested shareholders; or (ii) if shareholders holding more than a specified fraction of the outstanding shares exercise appraisal rights.

CHAPTER 22

ENDING THE CORPORATION

§ 14.02. Dissolution By Board Of Directors And Shareholders

(a) The board of directors may propose dissolution for submission to the shareholders by first adopting a resolution authorizing the dissolution.

(b) For a proposal to dissolve to be adopted, it shall then be approved by the shareholders. In submitting the proposal to dissolve to the shareholders for approval, the board of directors shall recommend that the shareholders approve the dissolution, unless (i) the board of directors determines that because of conflict of interest or other special circumstances it should make no recommendation or (ii) section 8.26 applies. If either (i) or (ii) applies, the board shall inform the shareholders of the basis for its so proceeding.

(c) The board of directors may set conditions for the approval of the proposal for dissolution by shareholders or the effectiveness of the dissolution.

(d) If the approval of the shareholders is to be given at a meeting, the corporation shall notify each shareholder, regardless of whether entitled to vote, of the meeting of shareholders at which the dissolution is to be submitted for approval.

(e) (Unless the articles of incorporation or the board of directors acting pursuant to subsection (c) require a greater vote, a greater quorum, or a vote by voting groups, adoption of the proposal to dissolve shall require the approval of the shareholders at a meeting at which a quorum exists consisting of a majority of the votes entitled to be cast on the proposal to dissolve.

Source: Model Bus. Corp. Act §§ 14.02, 14.03, 14.05, 14.20, 14.30, 14.34 (2016). Copyright © 2016 by American Bar Association. Reprinted with permission.

Official Comment

When submitting a proposal to dissolve to shareholders, the board of directors must recommend the dissolution, subject to two exceptions in section 14.02(b). The board might exercise the exception under clause (i) where the number of directors having a conflicting interest makes it inadvisable for the board to recommend the proposal or where the board is evenly divided as to the merits of the proposal but is able to agree that shareholders should be permitted to consider it. Alternatively, the board of directors might exercise the exception under clause (ii), which recognizes that, under section 8.26, a board of directors may agree to submit a proposal to dissolve to a vote of shareholders even if, after approving the proposal, the board of directors determines that it no longer recommends the proposal.

Section 14.02(c) permits the board of directors to condition its submission to the shareholders of a proposal for dissolution or the effectiveness of the dissolution. Among the conditions that a board might impose are that the proposal will not be deemed approved unless it is approved by a specified percentage of the shareholders, or by one or more specified classes or series of shares, voting as a separate voting group, or by a specified percentage of disinterested shareholders.

§ 14.03. Articles of Dissolution

(a) At any time after dissolution is authorized, the corporation may dissolve by delivering to the secretary of state for filing articles of dissolution [...].

(b) The articles of dissolution shall take effect at the effective date determined in accordance with section 1.23. A corporation is dissolved upon the effective date of its articles of dissolution.

Official Comment

Filing the articles of dissolution makes the decision to dissolve a matter of public record and establishes the time when the corporation must begin the process of winding up and cease carrying on its business except to the extent necessary for winding up. Under the Act, articles of dissolution may be filed at the commencement of winding up or at any time thereafter. This is the only filing required for voluntary dissolution; no filing is required to mark the completion of winding up as the existence of the corporation continues for certain purposes even after the business is wound up and the assets remaining after satisfaction of all creditors are distributed to the shareholders. No time limit for filing the articles of dissolution is specified, although filing must precede making distributions to shareholders unless there is compliance with section 6.40.

§ 14.05. Effect of Dissolution

(a) A corporation that has dissolved continues its corporate existence but the dissolved corporation may not carry on any business except that appropriate to wind up and liquidate its business and affairs, including:

(1) collecting its assets;

(2) disposing of its properties that will not be distributed in kind to its shareholders;

(3) discharging or making provision for discharging its liabilities;

(4) making distributions of its remaining assets among its shareholders according to their interests; and

(5) doing every other act necessary to wind up and liquidate its business and affairs.

(b) Dissolution of a corporation does not:

(1) transfer title to the corporation's property;

(2) prevent transfer of its shares or securities;

(3) subject its directors or officers to standards of conduct different from those prescribed in chapter 8;

(4) change (i) quorum or voting requirements for its board of directors or shareholders; (ii) provisions for selection, resignation, or removal of its directors or officers or both; or (iii) provisions for amending its bylaws;

(5) prevent commencement of a proceeding by or against the corporation in its corporate name;

(6) abate or suspend a proceeding pending by or against the corporation on the effective date of dissolution; or

(7) terminate the authority of the registered agent of the corporation.

(c) A distribution in liquidation under this section may only be made by a dissolved corporation.

Official Comment

Although section 14.05(a) provides that dissolution does not terminate the corporate existence, it does require the corporation to wind up its affairs and liquidate its assets. After dissolution, the corporation may not carry on its business except as may be appropriate for winding up.

§ 14.20. Grounds For Administrative Dissolution

The secretary of state may commence a proceeding under section 14.21 to dissolve a corporation administratively if:

(a) the corporation does not pay within 60 days after they are due any fees, taxes, interest or penalties imposed by this Act or other laws of this state;

(b) the corporation does not deliver its annual report to the secretary of state within 60 days after it is due;

(c) the corporation is without a registered agent or registered office in this state for 60 days or more;

(d) the secretary of state has not been notified within 60 days that the corporation's registered agent or registered office has been changed, that its registered agent has resigned, or that its registered office has been discontinued; or

(e) the corporation's period of duration stated in its articles of incorporation expires.

Official Comment

Under the Act, actual or threatened administrative dissolution is an effective enforcement mechanism for a variety of statutory obligations. The advantages of administrative dissolution in the circumstances outlined in this section are compelling: it not only reduces the number of records maintained by the secretary of state, but also avoids futile attempts to compel compliance by abandoned corporations and returns corporate names promptly to the status of available names. It is also less costly and requires fewer legal resources than judicial dissolution.

§ 14.30. Grounds For Judicial Dissolution

(a) The [name or describe court or courts] may dissolve a corporation:

(1) in a proceeding by the attorney general if it is established that:

(i) the corporation obtained its articles of incorporation through fraud; or

(ii) the corporation has continued to exceed or abuse the authority conferred upon it by law;

(2) in a proceeding by a shareholder if it is established that:

(i) the directors are deadlocked in the management of the corporate affairs, the shareholders are unable to break the deadlock, and irreparable injury to the corporation is threatened or being suffered, or the business and affairs of the corporation can no longer be conducted to the advantage of the shareholders generally, because of the deadlock;

    (ii) the directors or those in control of the corporation have acted, are acting, or will act in a manner that is illegal, oppressive, or fraudulent;

    (iii) the shareholders are deadlocked in voting power and have failed, for a period that includes at least two consecutive annual meeting dates, to elect successors to directors whose terms have expired; or

    (iv) the corporate assets are being misapplied or wasted;

(3) in a proceeding by a creditor if it is established that:

    (i) the creditor's claim has been reduced to judgment, the execution on the judgment returned unsatisfied, and the corporation is insolvent; or

    (ii) the corporation has admitted in writing that the creditor's claim is due and owing and the corporation is insolvent;

(4) in a proceeding by the corporation to have its voluntary dissolution continued under court supervision; or

(5) in a proceeding by a shareholder if the corporation has abandoned its business and has failed within a reasonable time to liquidate and distribute its assets and dissolve.

(b) Subsection (a)(2) shall not apply in the case of a corporation that, on the date of the filing of the proceeding, has a class or series of shares which is:

(1) a covered security under section 18(b)(1)(A) or (B) of the Securities Act of 1933; or

(2) not a covered security, but is held by at least 300 shareholders and the shares outstanding have a market value of at least $20 million (exclusive of the value of such shares held by the corporation's subsidiaries, senior executives, directors and beneficial shareholders and voting trust beneficial owners owning more than 10% of such shares).

Official Comment

Section 14.30 provides grounds for the judicial dissolution of a corporation at the request of the state, a shareholder, a creditor, or when a corporation that has commenced voluntary dissolution seeks judicial oversight. Judicial oversight may be useful to protect the corporation from suits by creditors or shareholders. Under this section, the court has discretion as to whether dissolution is appropriate even though the specified grounds for judicial dissolution exist.

Involuntary Dissolution by State

Section 14.30(a)(1) provides a means by which the state may ensure compliance with the fundamentals of corporate existence and prevent abuse. That section limits the power of the state in this regard to grounds that are reasonably related to this objective.

Involuntary Dissolution by Shareholders

Section 14.30(a)(2) provides for involuntary dissolution at the request of a shareholder under circumstances involving deadlock or significant abuse of power by controlling shareholders or directors. The remedy of judicial dissolution is available only for shareholders of corporations that do not meet the tests in section 14.30(b). Even for those corporations to which section 14.30(a)(2) applies, however, the court can take into account the number of shareholders and the nature of the trading market for the shares in deciding whether to exercise its discretion to order dissolution. Shareholders of corporations that meet the tests of section 14.30(b) may often have the ability to sell their shares if they are dissatisfied with current management or may seek other remedies under the Act.

Section 14.30(a)(5) provides a basis for a shareholder to obtain involuntary dissolution in the event the corporation has abandoned its business, but those in control of the corporation have delayed unreasonably in either liquidating and distributing its assets or completing the necessary procedures to dissolve the corporation

Involuntary Dissolution by Creditors

Creditors may obtain involuntary dissolution only when the corporation is insolvent and only in the limited circumstances set forth in section 14.30(a)(3). Typically, a proceeding under the federal bankruptcy laws is an alternative in these situations.

Judicial Supervision of Dissolution

A corporation that has commenced voluntary dissolution may petition a court to supervise its dissolution. Such an action may be appropriate to permit the orderly liquidation of the corporate assets and to protect the corporation from a multitude of creditors' suits or suits by dissatisfied shareholders.

§ 14.34. Election To Purchase In Lieu Of Dissolution

(a) In a proceeding under section 14.30(a)(2) to dissolve a corporation, the corporation may elect or, if it fails to elect, one or more shareholders may elect to purchase all shares owned by the petitioning shareholder at the fair value of the shares. An election pursuant to this section shall be irrevocable unless the court determines that it is equitable to set aside or modify the election.

Official Comment

It is not always necessary to dissolve a corporation and liquidate its assets to provide relief for the situations covered in section 14.30(a)(2). Section 14.34 provides an alternative by means of which a dissolution proceeding under section 14.30(a)(2) can be terminated upon payment of the fair value of the petitioner's shares, allowing the corporation to continue in existence for the benefit of the remaining shareholders.

PART 5

Hybrid Entities

CHAPTER 23

LIMITED LIABILITY PARTNERSHIPS

Limited Liability Partnerships (LLPs) are an attempt to capture the upsides of both corporations and partnerships. LLPs provide partners with limited liability. State laws governing LLPs often reserve LLP status for certain groups of professionals (i.e., doctors, attorneys, and architects).

REVISED UNIFORM PARTNERSHIP ACT (1994)

Section 101. Definitions.

In this [Act]:

(5) "Limited liability partnership" means a partnership that has filed a statement of qualification under Section 1001 and does not have a similar statement in effect in any other jurisdiction.

Comment

The definition of a "limited liability partnership" makes clear that a partnership may adopt the special liability shield characteristics of a limited liability partnership simply by filing a statement of qualification under Section 1001. A partnership may file the statement in this State regardless of where formed. When coupled with the governing law provisions of Section 106(b), this definition simplifies the choice of law issues applicable to partnerships with multi-state activities and contacts. Once a statement of qualification is filed, a partnership's internal affairs and the liability of its partners are determined by the law of the State where the statement is filed. The partnership may not vary this particular requirement. See Section 103(b)(9).

Source: Rev. Unif. Partnership Act §§ 101, 106, 306, 1001, 1002 (1994). Copyright © 1994 by National Conference of Commissioners on Uniform State Laws. Reprinted with permission.

Section 1001. Statement of Qualification.

(a) A partnership may become a limited liability partnership pursuant to this section.

(b) The terms and conditions on which a partnership becomes a limited liability partnership must be approved by the vote necessary to amend the partnership agreement except, in the case of a partnership agreement that expressly considers obligations to contribute to the partnership, the vote necessary to amend those provisions.

(c) After the approval required by subsection (b), a partnership may become a limited liability partnership by filing a statement of qualification. The statement must contain:

    (1) the name of the partnership;

    (2) the street address of the partnership's chief executive office and, if different, the street address of an office in this State, if any;

    (3) if the partnership does not have an office in this State, the name and street address of the partnership's agent for service of process;

    (4) a statement that the partnership elects to be a limited liability partnership; and

    (5) a deferred effective date, if any.

(d) The agent of a limited liability partnership for service of process must be an individual who is a resident of this State or other person authorized to do business in this State.

(e) The status of a partnership as a limited liability partnership is effective on the later of the filing of the statement or a date specified in the statement. The status remains effective, regardless of changes in the partnership, until it is canceled pursuant to Section 105(d) or revoked pursuant to Section 1003.

(f) The status of a partnership as a limited liability partnership and the liability of its partners is not affected by errors or later changes in the information required to be contained in the statement of qualification under subsection (c).

(g) The filing of a statement of qualification establishes that a partnership has satisfied all conditions precedent to the qualification of the partnership as a limited liability partnership.

(h) An amendment or cancellation of a statement of qualification is effective when it is filed or on a deferred effective date specified in the amendment or cancellation.

Comment

Any partnership may become a limited liability partnership by filing a statement of qualification. Section 1001 sets forth the required contents of a statement of qualification. The section also sets forth requirements for the approval of a statement of qualification, establishes the effective date of the filing (and any amendments) which remains effective until canceled or revoked, and provides that the liability of the partners of a limited liability partnership is not affected by errors or later changes in the statement information.

Subsection (b) provides that the terms and conditions on which a partnership becomes a limited liability partnership must be generally be approved by the vote necessary to amend the partnership agreement. This means that the act of becoming a limited liability partnership is equivalent to an amendment of the partnership agreement. Where the partnership agreement is silent as to how it may be amended, the subsection (b) vote requires the approval of every partner.

The unanimous vote default rule reflects the significance of a partnership becoming a limited liability partnership. In general, upon such a filing each partner is released from the personal contribution obligation imposed under this Act in exchange for relinquishing the right to enforce the contribution obligations of other partners under this Act. The wisdom of this bargain will depend on many factors including the relative risks of the partners' duties and the assets of the partnership.

Subsection (c) sets forth the information required in a statement of qualification. [The statement] must include the name of the partnership which must comply with Section 1002 to identify the partnership as a limited liability partnership. The statement must also include the address of the partnership's chief executive office and, if different, the street address of any other office in this State. A statement must include the name and street address of an agent for service of process only if it does not have any office in this State.

As with other statements, a statement of qualification must be filed in the office of the Secretary of State.

Subsection (d) makes clear that once a statement is filed and effective, the status of the partnership as a limited liability partnership remains effective until the partnership status is either canceled or revoked "regardless of changes in the partnership." Accordingly, a partnership that dissolves but whose business is continued under a business continuation agreement retains its status as a limited liability partnership without the need to refile a new statement. Also, limited liability partnership status remains even though a partnership may be dissolved, wound up, and terminated. Even after the termination of the partnership, the former partners of a terminated partnership would not be personally liable for partnership obligations incurred while the partnership was a limited liability partnership.

Subsection (d) also makes clear that limited liability partnership status remains effective until actual cancellation under Section 1003 or revocation under Section 105(d).

Subsection (f) provides that once a statement of qualification is executed and filed under subsection (c) and Section 105, the partnership assumes the status of a limited liability partnership. This status is intended to be conclusive with regard to third parties dealing with the partnership. It is not intended to affect the rights of partners. For example, a properly executed and filed statement of qualification conclusively establishes the limited liability shield described in Section 306(c). If the partners executing and filing the statement exceed their authority, the internal abuse of authority has no effect on the liability shield with regard to third parties. Partners may challenge the abuse of authority for purposes of establishing the liability of the culpable partners but may not effect the liability shield as to third parties. Likewise, third parties may not challenge the existence of the liability shield because the decision to file the statement lacked the proper vote. As a result, the filing of the statement creates the liability shield even when the required subsection (b) vote is not obtained.

Section 1002. Name.

The name of a limited liability partnership must end with "Registered Limited Liability Partnership", "Limited Liability Partnership", "R.L.L.P.", "L.L.P.", "RLLP," or "LLP".

Comment

The name provisions are intended to alert persons dealing with a limited liability partnership of the presence of the liability shield. Because many jurisdictions have adopted the naming concept of a "registered" limited liability partnership, this aspect has been retained. These name requirements also distinguish limited partnerships and general partnerships that become limited liability partnerships because the new name must be at the end of and in addition to the general or limited partnership's regular name. Since the name identification rules of this section do not alter the regular name of the partnership, they do not disturb historic notions of apparent authority of partners in both general and limited partnerships.

Section 106. Governing Law.

(a) Except as otherwise provided in subsection (b), the law of the jurisdiction in which a partnership has its chief executive office governs relations among the partners and between the partners and the partnership.

(b) The law of this State governs relations among the partners and between the partners and the partnership and the liability of partners for an obligation of a limited liability partnership.

Comment

Contrasted with the variable choice-of-law rule provided by subsection (a), the law of the State where a limited liability partnership files its statement of qualification applies to such a partnership and may not be varied by the agreement of the partners. Also, a partnership that files a statement of qualification in another State is not defined as a limited liability partnership in this State. Unlike a general partnership which may be formed without any filing, a partnership may only become a limited liability partnership by filing a statement of qualification. Therefore, the situs of its organization is clear. Because it is often unclear where a general partnership is actually formed, the decision to file a statement of qualification in a particular State constitutes a choice of-law for the partnership which cannot be altered by the partnership agreement. If the partnership agreement of an existing partnership specifies the law of a particular State as its governing law, and the partnership thereafter files a statement of qualification in another State, the partnership agreement choice is no longer controlling. In such cases, the filing of a statement of qualification "amends" the partnership agreement on this limited matter. Accordingly, if a statement of qualification is revoked or canceled for a limited liability partnership, the law of the State of filing would continue to apply unless the partnership agreement thereafter altered the applicable law rule.

Section 306. Partner's Liability.

(c) An obligation of a partnership incurred while the partnership is a limited liability partnership, whether arising in contract, tort, or otherwise, is solely the obligation of the partnership. A partner is not personally liable, directly or indirectly, by way of contribution or otherwise, for such an obligation solely by reason of being or so acting as a partner. This subsection applies notwithstanding anything inconsistent in the partnership agreement that existed immediately before the vote required to become a limited liability partnership under Section 1001(b).

Comment

Subsection (c) alters classic joint and several liability of general partners for obligations of a partnership that is a limited liability partnership. Like shareholders of a corporation and members of a limited liability company, partners of a limited liability partnership are not personally liable for partnership obligations incurred while the partnership liability shield is in place solely because they are partners. As with shareholders of a corporation and members of a limited liability company, partners remain personally liable for their personal misconduct.

In cases of partner misconduct, Section 401(c) sets forth a partnership's obligation to indemnify the culpable partner where the partner's liability was incurred in the ordinary course of the partnership's business. When indemnification occurs, the assets of both the partnership and the culpable partner are available to a creditor. However, Sections 306(c), 401(b), and

807(b) make clear that a partner who is not otherwise liable under Section 306(c) is not obligated to contribute assets to the partnership in excess of agreed contributions to share the loss with the culpable partner. Accordingly, Section 306(c) makes clear that an innocent partner is not personally liable for specified partnership obligations, directly or indirectly, by way of contribution or otherwise.

Although the liability shield protections of Section 306(c) may be modified in part or in full in a partnership agreement (and by way of private contractual guarantees), the modifications must constitute an intentional waiver of the liability protections. Since the mere act of filing a statement of qualification reflects the assumption that the partners intend to modify the otherwise applicable partner liability rules, the final sentence of subsection (c) makes clear that the filing negates inconsistent aspects of the partnership agreement that existed immediately before the vote to approve becoming a limited liability partnership. The negation only applies to a partner's personal liability for future partnership obligations. The filing however has no effect as to previously created partner obligations to the partnership in the form of specific capital contribution requirements.

Inter se contribution agreements may erode part or all of the effects of the liability shield. For example, Section 807(f) provides that an assignee for the benefit of creditors of a partnership or a partner may enforce a partner's obligation to contribute to the partnership. The ultimate effect of such contribution obligations may make each partner jointly and severally liable for all partnership obligations—even those incurred while the partnership is a limited liability partnership. Although the final sentence of subsection (c) negates such provisions existing before a statement of qualification is filed, it will have no effect on any amendments to the partnership agreement after the statement is filed.

The connection between partner status and personal liability for partnership obligations is severed only with respect to obligations incurred while the partnership is a limited liability partnership. Partnership obligations incurred before a partnership becomes a limited liability partnership or incurred after limited liability partnership status is revoked or canceled are treated as obligations of an ordinary partnership.

When an obligation is incurred is determined by other law. Under that law, and for the limited purpose of determining when partnership contract obligations are incurred, the reasonable expectations of creditors and the partners are paramount. Therefore, partnership obligations under or relating to a note, contract, or other agreement generally are incurred when the note, contract, or other agreement is made. Also, an amendment, modification, extension, or renewal of a note, contract, or other agreement should not affect or otherwise reset the time at which a partnership obligation under or relating to that note, contract, or other agreement is incurred, even as to a claim that relates to the subject matter of the amendment, modification, extension, or renewal. A note, contract, or other agreement may expressly modify these rules and fix the time a partnership obligation is incurred thereunder.

For the limited purpose of determining when partnership tort obligations are incurred, a distinction is intended between injury and the conduct causing that injury. The purpose of the distinction is to prevent unjust results. Partnership obligations under or relating to a tort generally are incurred when the tort conduct occurs rather than at the time of the actual injury or harm. This interpretation prevents a culpable partnership from engaging in wrongful conduct and then filing a statement of qualification to sever the vicarious responsibility of its partners for future injury or harm caused by conduct that occurred prior to the filing.

CHAPTER 24

LIMITED PARTNERSHIPS

L imited partnerships are formed by two or more people, with at least one person acting as the general partner who has management authority and personal liability, and at least one person in the role of limited partner, who generally is a passive investor with no management authority.

THE UNIFORM LIMITED PARTNERSHIP ACT (2001)

The Uniform Limited Partnership Act (ULPA) was promulgated originally in 1916, and, with the Uniform Partnership Act (UPA), has been the basic law governing partnerships in the United States. The first revision of ULPA after 1916 occurred in 1976. There were further amendments in 1985. However, changes in modern business practices made it necessary to update and modernize the ULPA beyond the 1976 and 1985 revisions. Thus, the National Conference of Commissioners on Uniform State Laws (NCCUSL) has adopted a new, more flexible version of the Uniform Limited Partnership Act (ULPA 2001).

The previous Act, the Revised Uniform Limited Partnership Act (RULPA), set guidelines for the organization of limited partnerships, defined the rights and liabilities of both limited and general partners and provided rules for the registration of the partnership in the state of origin. The new Act does not change the basic structure of limited partnerships as defined in the original Act. But it does improve the capacity of limited partnerships both to do business and serve the best interests of partners and third parties conducting business with the partnership.

The new ULPA reflects modern business practices and represents a greater refinement of the scope and uses for limited partnerships. Modern businesses require ever-greater sophistication from the legal forms governing their

Source: Limited Partnership Act Summary, Unif. Law Comm'n, http://www.uniformlaws.org/ ActSummary.aspx?title=Limited%20Partnership%20Act (last visited June 9, 2013),. Copyright © by National Conference of Commissioners on Uniform State Laws. Reprinted with permission.

practices. The new ULPA recognizes modern day uses of limited partnerships by providing greater flexibility and protection to sophisticated groups seeking strongly entrenched, centralized management and persons requiring passive limited partners with little control over the partnership.

The 2001 ULPA is a stand-alone Act, de-linked from both the original general partnership act (UPA) and the Revised Uniform Partnership Act (RUPA). Thus the ULPA 2001 incorporates many provisions from RUPA and some from the Uniform Limited Liability Company Act (ULLCA). As a result, the new ULPA is more complex and substantively longer than its predecessor.

The new Act has been drafted for a world in which limited liability partnerships (LLPs) and limited liability companies (LLCs) can meet many of the needs formerly met by limited partnerships. Therefore, the new ULPA targets two types of enterprises that are largely beyond the scope of LLPs and LLCs.

First, the ULPA 2001 includes provisions to meet the needs of sophisticated, manager-entrenched commercial deals whose participants commit for the long term. Second, the ULPA 2001 addresses the modern needs of estate planning arrangements, so-called "family limited partnerships." In addressing these concerns, this Act assumes that people utilizing it will want both strong centralized, entrenched management, and passive investors or limited partners with little capacity to exit the entity. As a result, the Act's rules, and particularly its default rules, have been designed to reflect those assumptions.

A fundamental change from RULPA involves the liability of limited partners and general partners for the partnership debts. Under RULPA, a limited partner could be held liable for the entity's debts if he participated in the control of the business and the third party transacted business with the partnership with the reasonable belief that the limited partner was a general partner. Under the new Act, a limited partner cannot be held liable for the partnership debts even if he participates in the management and control of the limited partnership. Concerning general partners, under RULPA, liability was complete, automatic and formally inescapable. Under this Act, limited liability limited partnership (LLLP) status is expressly available to provide a full liability shield to all general partners.

Another important change concerns a limited partner's right to disassociate from the partnership. Under RULPA a limited partner could theoretically withdraw from the partnership on six months notice unless the partnership agreement specified the withdrawal events for a limited partner. Due to estate planning concerns, the new ULPA default rule affords no right to disassociate as a limited partner before the termination of the limited partnership. The power to disassociate is expressly recognized, but may be exercised only through the partnership agreement or those events listed in section 601(b) of this Act.

Further, under RULPA the dissolution of the partnership entity required the unanimous, written consent of all the partners. Under this Act, dissolution of the partnership only requires the consent of all the general partners and of the limited partners owning a majority of the rights to receive distributions as limited partners at the time the consent is to be effective.

RULPA has served well as the backbone of the law on limited partnerships. However, as usages change, new problems arise, and modern business practices require the law to reflect these new developments. The new ULPA now comes forward as a response to the changes that have occurred. It is the same organization, but with characteristics for today's business and estate planning conditions. Adoption of ULPA (2001) will enhance a state's business climate by adding another distinct, specific purpose entity to the list of entities available for business and estate planning purposes. It maximizes opportunity and gives more choices with economic benefit.

CHAPTER 25

LIMITED LIABILITY COMPANIES

A limited liability company is a newer form of business entity. It has advantages over corporations and partnerships. The LLC's main advantage over a partnership is that, like the owners (shareholders) of a corporation, the liability of the owners (members) of an LLC for debts and obligations of the LLC is limited to their financial investment. However, like a general partnership, members of an LLC have the right to participate in management of the LLC, unless the LLC's articles of organization and operating agreement provide that the LLC is to be managed by managers.

LIMITED LIABILITY COMPANY (REVISED) SUMMARY

The Uniform Limited Liability Company Act gestated from 1994 to 1996 when it was finally promulgated by the Uniform Law Commission. By that time the majority of the states had legislation that provided for limited liability companies. Therefore, the 1996 Uniform Act has been enacted in only nine states by 2006. The limited liability company as a distinct form of business organization has a very recent history. The first legislation in Wyoming in 1977 introduced the concept. A limited liability company is generally characterized as a business organization which looks like a partnership or limited partnership in terms of internal structure and relationships between members, or members and managers, but with the additional characteristic of a liability shield from vicarious liability for members and managers.

A limited liability company has members who primarily contribute capital to the company and who share in the profits or losses. It may have managers who do the business of the company. A member may be a manager, but non-member managers are also allowed. If there are no designated managers, members run the company as general partners in a general partnership would.

Source: Limited Liability Company (Revised) Summary, Unif. Law Comm'n, http://www.uniformlaws.org/ActSummary.aspx?title=Limited%20Liability%20Company%20%28Revised%29 (last visited Oct. 31, 2014). Copyright © by National Conference of Commissioners on Uniform State Laws. Reprinted with permission.

A limited liability company statute has certain key features: a means of creating the company, usually by filing a certificate; a liability shield provision; rules governing the relations between members, and between members and any managers; rules governing distributions of profits or losses to members and a member's creditor's rights; rules governing a member's exit rights from the company; rules on dissolution of the company, and rules governing mergers and conversions. A limited liability company is usually governed by an operating agreement that almost always supersedes and overcomes the statutory rules.

The limited liability company originated in the desire to have a full liability shield while retaining the so-called "pass-through" qualities of a partnership. This means that the company itself pays no federal income tax, leaving any tax liability to members receiving taxable distributions from the company. Before limited liability companies, full limitation of liability was available only for corporation shareholders. Corporations, however, are taxed as individuals on their income, but shareholders are also taxed on corporate distributions made to them. The ability to obtain pass-through status, then, provided very substantial incentive for states to enact limited liability company statutes. They did this, but did not do so with anything like coherent uniformity. The great wave of statutes preceded the promulgation of the 1996 Uniform Act.

Limited liability companies have other qualities than pass-through status that make them desirable as a business organization. A limited liability company may be tailored specifically to the business or objective of the members because its structure mainly depends upon the agreement between members and managers (if there are managers). This means a kind of flexibility coupled with the liability shield that makes the limited liability company a more efficient kind of organization than the corporation (specifically) or any of the other unincorporated business organizations for many purposes. The limited liability company kind of structure lends itself to nonprofit organizations, and many states (and the successive Uniform Acts) do not require a for-profit reason for organization. The limited liability company form has been adapted to allow a single member company to be formed. A single person may not form a partnership or limited partnership. Forming a corporation raises the tax issue and the complexities of maintaining a corporation for a single shareholder. A single-member limited liability company resolves these problems, and makes it an efficient way for a single individual to have a vicarious liability shield.

Because of its utility, the law of limited liability companies is very dynamic. New ideas and features seem to appear yearly with the objective of enhancing this form of business organization. The many developments since 1996 have led the Uniform Law Commission to reconsider the Uniform Act. The result is the 2006 Uniform Limited Liability Company Act.

A. FORMATION

Section 104. Nature, Purpose, and Duration of Limited Liability Company.

(a) A limited liability company is an entity distinct from its members.

(b) A limited liability company may have any lawful purpose, regardless of whether for profit.

(c) A limited liability company has perpetual duration.

Comment

Subsection (a)—The "separate entity" characteristic is fundamental to a limited liability company and is inextricably connected to both the liability shield, Section 304, and the charging order provision, Section 503.

Subsection (b)—The phrase "any lawful purpose, regardless of whether for profit" means that: (i) a limited liability company need not have any business purpose; and (ii) the issue of profit vel non is irrelevant to the question of whether a limited liability company has been validly formed. Although some LLC statutes continue to require a business purpose, this Act follows the current trend and takes a more expansive approach.

Subsection (c)—In this context, the word "perpetual" is a misnomer, albeit one commonplace in LLC statutes. Like all current LLC statutes, this Act provides several consent-based avenues to override perpetuity: a term specified in the operating agreement; an event specified in the operating agreement; member consent. Section 701 (events causing dissolution). In this context, "perpetuity" actually means that the Act does not require a definite term and creates no nexus between the dissociation of a member and the dissolution of the entity.

Section 105. Powers.

A limited liability company has the capacity to sue and be sued in its own name and the power to do all things necessary or convenient to carry on its activities.

Comment

The capacity to sue and be sued is mentioned specifically so that Section 110(c)(1) can prohibit the operating agreement from varying that capacity.

Source: Rev. Unif. Ltd. Liab. Co. Act §§ 102, 104–108, 110, 201 (2006). Copyright © 2006 by National Conference of Commissioners on Uniform State Laws. Reprinted with permission.

Section 106. Governing Law.

The law of this state governs:

> (1) the internal affairs of a limited liability company; and

> (2) the liability of a member as member and a manager as manager for the debts, obligations, or other liabilities of a limited liability company.

Comment

Paragraph (1)—Like any other legal concept, "internal affairs" may be indeterminate at its edges. However, the concept certainly includes interpretation and enforcement of the operating agreement, relations among the members as members; relations between the limited liability company and a member as a member, relations between a manager-managed limited liability company and a manager, and relations between a manager of a manager-managed limited liability company and the members as members.

Paragraph (2)—This paragraph certainly encompasses Section 304 (the liability shield) but does not necessarily encompass a claim that a member or manager is liable to a third party for (i) having purported to bind a limited liability company to the third party; or (ii) having committed a tort against the third party while acting on the limited liability company's behalf or in the course of the company's business. That liability is not by status (i.e., not "as member … [or] as manager") but rather results from function or conduct.

This paragraph is stated separately from Paragraph (1), because it can be argued that the liability of members and managers to third parties is not an internal affair. In any event, the rule stated in this paragraph is correct. All sensible authorities agree that, except in extraordinary circumstances, "shield-related" issues should be determined according to the law of the state of organization.

Section 107. Supplemental Principles of Law.

Unless displaced by particular provisions of this [act], the principles of law and equity supplement this [act].

Section 108. Name.

(a) The name of a limited liability company must contain the words "limited liability company" or "limited company" or the abbreviation "L.L.C.", "LLC", "L.C.", or "LC". "Limited" may be abbreviated as "Ltd.", and "company" may be abbreviated as "Co.".

Section 201. Formation of Limited Liability Company; Certificate of Organization.

(a) One or more persons may act as organizers to form a limited liability company by signing and delivering to the [Secretary of State] for filing a certificate of organization.

(b) A certificate of organization must state:

(1) the name of the limited liability company, which must comply with Section 108;

(2) the street and mailing addresses of the initial designated office and the name and street and mailing addresses of the initial agent for service of process of the company; and

(3) if the company will have no members when the [Secretary of State] files the certificate, a statement to that effect.

(c) Subject to Section 112(c), a certificate of organization may also contain statements as to matters other than those required by subsection (b).

Comment

Subsection (b)—This Act does not require the certificate of organization to designate whether the limited liability company is manager-managed or member-managed. Under this Act, those characterizations pertain principally to inter se relations, and the Act therefore looks to the operating agreement to make the characterization.

Section 102. Definitions in this [Act]:

(9) "Manager" means a person that under the operating agreement of a manager-managed limited liability company is responsible, alone or in concert with others, for performing the management functions stated in Section 407(c).

(11) "Member" means a person that has become a member of a limited liability company under Section 401 and has not dissociated under Section 602.

(13) "Operating agreement" means the agreement, whether or not referred to as an operating agreement and whether oral, in a record, implied, or in any combination thereof, of all the members of a limited liability company, including a sole member, concerning the matters described in Section 110(a). The term includes the agreement as amended or restated.

Comment

Paragraph (9) [Manager]—The Act uses the word "manager" as a term of art, whose applicability is confined to manager-managed LLCs. The phrase "manager-managed" is itself a 11 term of art, referring only to an LLC whose operating agreement refers to the LLC as such. Thus, for purposes of this

Act, if the members of a member-managed LLC delegate plenipotentiary management authority to one person (whether or not a member), this Act's references to "manager" do not apply to that person.

This approach does have the potential for confusion, but confusion around the term "manager" is common to almost all LLC statutes. The confusion stems from the choice to define "manager" as a term of art in a way that can be at odds with other, common usages of the word. For example, a member-managed LLC might well have an "office manager" or a "property manager." Moreover, in a manager-managed LLC, the "property manager" is not likely to be a manager as the term is used in many LLC statutes.

Under this Act, the category of "person" is not limited to individuals. Therefore, a "manager" need not be a natural person.

Paragraph (13) [Operating Agreement]—An operating agreement is a contract, and therefore all statutory language pertaining to the operating agreement must be understood in the context of the law of contracts.

Section 110. Operating Agreement; Scope, Function, and Limitations.

(a) Except as otherwise provided in subsections (b) and (c), the operating agreement governs:

   (1) relations among the members as members and between the members and the limited liability company;

   (2) the rights and duties under this [act] of a person in the capacity of manager;

   (3) the activities of the company and the conduct of those activities; and

   (4) the means and conditions for amending the operating agreement.

(b) To the extent the operating agreement does not otherwise provide for a matter described in subsection (a), this [act] governs the matter.

(c) An operating agreement may not:

   (1) vary a limited liability company's capacity under Section 105 to sue and be sued in its own name;

   (2) vary the law applicable under Section 106;

   (3) [...];

   (4) subject to subsections (d) through (g), eliminate the duty of loyalty, the duty of care, or any other fiduciary duty;

   (5) subject to subsections (d) through (g), eliminate the contractual obligation of good faith and fair dealing under Section 409(d);

   (6) unreasonably restrict the duties and rights stated in Section 410;

(7) vary the power of a court to decree dissolution in the circumstances specified in Section 701(a)(4) and (5);

(8) vary the requirement to wind up a limited liability company's business as specified in Section 702(a) and (b)(1);

(9) [...];

(10) [...]; or

(11) restrict the rights under this [act] of a person other than a member or manager.

(d) If not manifestly unreasonable, the operating agreement may:

(1) restrict or eliminate the duty:

(A) as required in Section 409(b)(1) and (g), to account to the limited liability company and to hold as trustee for it any property, profit, or benefit derived by the member in the conduct or winding up of the company's business, from a use by the member of the company's property, or from the appropriation of a limited liability company opportunity;

(B) as required in Section 409(b)(2) and (g), to refrain from dealing with the company in the conduct or winding up of the company's business as or on behalf of a party having an interest adverse to the company; and

(C) as required by Section 409(b)(3) and (g), to refrain from competing with the company in the conduct of the company's business before the dissolution of the company;

(2) identify specific types or categories of activities that do not violate the duty of loyalty;

(3) alter the duty of care, except to authorize intentional misconduct or knowing violation of law;

(4) alter any other fiduciary duty, including eliminating particular aspects of that duty; and

(5) prescribe the standards by which to measure the performance of the contractual obligation of good faith and fair dealing under Section 409(d).

(e) The operating agreement may specify the method by which a specific act or transaction that would otherwise violate the duty of loyalty may be authorized or ratified by one or more disinterested and independent persons after full disclosure of all material facts.

(f) [...].

(g) The operating agreement may alter or eliminate the indemnification for a member or manager provided by Section 408(a) and may eliminate or limit a member or manager's liability to the limited liability company and members for money damages, except for:

(1) breach of the duty of loyalty;

(2) a financial benefit received by the member or manager to which the member or manager is not entitled;

(3) a breach of a duty under Section 406;

(4) intentional infliction of harm on the company or a member; or

(5) an intentional violation of criminal law.

(h) The court shall decide any claim under subsection (d) that a term of an operating agreement is manifestly unreasonable. The court:

(1) shall make its determination as of the time the challenged term became part of the operating agreement and by considering only circumstances existing at that time; and

(2) may invalidate the term only if, in light of the purposes and activities of the limited liability company, it is readily apparent that:

(A) the objective of the term is unreasonable; or

(B) the term is an unreasonable means to achieve the provision's objective.

Comment

The operating agreement is pivotal to a limited liability company.

A limited liability company is as much a creature of contract as of statute, and Section 102(13) delineates a very broad scope for "operating agreement." As a result, once an LLC comes into existence and has a member, the LLC necessarily has an operating agreement.

This phrasing should not, however, be read to require a limited liability company or its members to take any formal action to adopt an operating agreement. *Compare* CAL. CORP. CODE § 17050(a) (West 2006) ("In order to form a limited liability company, one or more persons shall execute and file articles of organization with, and on a form prescribed by, the Secretary of State and, either before or after the filing of articles of organization, the members shall have entered into an operating agreement.")

The operating agreement is the exclusive consensual process for modifying this Act's various default rules pertaining to relationships *inter se* the members and between the members and the limited liability company.

Subsection (a)—This section describes the very broad scope of a limited liability company's operating agreement, which includes all matters constituting "internal affairs." This broad grant of authority is subject to the restrictions stated in subsection (c), including the broad restriction stated in paragraph (c)(11) (concerning the rights under this Act of third parties).

Subsection (a)(1)—Under this Act, a limited liability company is emphatically an entity, and the members lack the power to alter that characteristic.

Subsection (a)(2)—Under this paragraph, the operating agreement has the power to affect the rights and duties of managers (including non-member managers). Power is not the same as right, however, and exercising the power provided by this paragraph might constitute a breach of a separate contract between the LLC and the manager.

Subsection (a)(4)—If the operating agreement does not address this matter, under subsection (b) this Act provides the rule. The rule appears in Section 407(b)(5) and 407(c)(4)(D) (unanimous consent).

Subsection (c)—If a person claims that a term of the operating agreement violates this subsection, as a matter of ordinary procedural law the burden is on the person making the claim.

Subsection (c)(4)—This limitation is less powerful than might first appear, because subsections (d) through (g) specifically authorize significantly alterations to fiduciary duty. The reference to "or any other fiduciary duty" is necessary because the Act has "un-cabined" fiduciary duty. *See* Comment to Section 409.

Subsection (c)(11)—This limitation pertains only to "the rights under this [act] of" third parties. The extent to which an operating agreement can affect other rights of third parties is a question for other law, particularly the law of contracts.

Subsection (d)—Delaware recently amended its LLC statute to permit an operating agreement to fully "eliminate" fiduciary duty within an LLC. This Act rejects the ultra-contractarian notion that fiduciary duty within a business organization is merely a set of default rule and seeks instead to balance the virtues of "freedom of contract" against the dangers that inescapably exist when some have power over the interests of others. As one source has explained:

> The open-ended nature of fiduciary duty reflects the law's long-standing recognition that devious people can smell a loophole a mile away. For centuries, the law has assumed that (1) power creates opportunities for abuse and (2) the devious creativity of those in power may outstrip the prescience of those trying, through ex ante contract drafting, to constrain that combination of power and creativity. CARTER G. BISHOP AND DANIEL S. KLEINBERGER, LIMITED LIABILITY COMPANIES: TAX AND BUSINESS LAW, ¶ 14.05[4][a][ii]

Subsection (d)(1)—Subject to the "not manifestly unreasonable" standard, this paragraph empowers the operating agreement to eliminate all aspects of the duty of loyalty listed in Section 409. The contractual obligation of good faith would remain, see subsections(c)(5) and (d)(5), as would any other, uncodified aspects of the duty of loyalty.

Duty	Extent of operating agreement's power to restrict the duty (subject to the "manifestly unreasonable" standard) Section 110(d)(1), (3) and (4)	Power of the operating agreement to provide indemnity or exculpation w/r/t breach of the duty Section 110(g)
Loyalty	Restrict or completely eliminate	None
Care	Alter, but not eliminate; specifically may not authorize intentional misconduct or knowing violation of law	Complete
Other fiduciary duties, not codified in the statute	Restrict or completely eliminate Section 110(4)	Complete

Subsection (d)(3)—The operating agreement's power to affect this Act's duty of care both parallels and differs from the agreement's power to affect this Act's duty of loyalty as well as any other fiduciary duties not codified in the statute. With regard to all fiduciary duties, the operating agreement is subject to the "manifestly unreasonable" standard. The differences concern: (i) the extent of the operating agreement's power to restrict the duty; and (ii) the power of the operating agreement to provide indemnity or exculpation for persons subject to the duty.

Subsection (e)—Section 409(f) states the Act's default rule for authorization or ratification—unanimous consent. This subsection specifically empowers the operating agreement to provide alternate mechanisms but, in doing so, imposes significant restrictions—namely, any alternate mechanism must involve full disclosure to, and the disinterestedness and independence of, the decision makers. These restrictions are consonant with ordinary notions of authorization and ratification.

Subsection (g)—This subsection specifically empowers the operating agreement to address matters of indemnification and exculpation but subjects that power to stated limitations.

Those limitations are drawn from the raft of exculpatory provisions that sprung up in corporate statutes in response to *Smith v. Van Gorkum*, 488 A.2d 858 (Del. 1985). Delaware led the response with DEL. CODE ANN. tit. 8, § 102(b)(7) (2006), and a number of LLC statutes have similar provisions.

Subsection (g)(4)—Due to this paragraph, an exculpatory provision cannot shield against a member's claim of oppression.

Subsection (h)—The "not manifestly unreasonable standard" became part of uniform business entity statutes when RUPA imported the concept from the Uniform Commercial Code. This subsection provides rules for applying that standard, which are necessary because:

- Determining unreasonableness *inter se* owners of an organization is a different task than doing so in a commercial context, where concepts like "usages of trade" are available to inform the analysis. Each business organization must be understood in its own terms and context.

- If loosely applied, the standard would permit a court to rewrite the members' agreement, which would destroy the balance this Act seeks to establish between freedom of contract and fiduciary duty.

- Case law research indicates that courts have tended to disregard the significance of the word "manifestly."

- Some decisions have considered reasonableness as of the time of the complaint, which means that a prospectively reasonable allocation of risk could be overturned because it functioned as agreed.

B. How Is an L.L.C. Managed and Controlled?

Section 407. Management of Limited Liability Company.

(a) A limited liability company is a member-managed limited liability company unless the operating agreement:

    (1) expressly provides that:

        (A) the company is or will be "manager-managed";

        (B) the company is or will be "managed by managers"; or

        (C) management of the company is or will be "vested in managers"; or

    (2) includes words of similar import.

(b) In a member-managed limited liability company, the following rules apply:

    (1) The management and conduct of the company are vested in the members.

    (2) Each member has equal rights in the management and conduct of the company's activities.

    (3) A difference arising among members as to a matter in the ordinary course of the activities of the company may be decided by a majority of the members.

    (4) An act outside the ordinary course of the activities of the company may be undertaken only with the consent of all members.

    (5) The operating agreement may be amended only with the consent of all members.

(c) In a manager-managed limited liability company, the following rules apply:

Source: Rev. Unif. Ltd. Liab. Co. Act § 407 (2006). Copyright © 2006 by National Conference of Commissioners on Uniform State Laws. Reprinted with permission.

(1) Except as otherwise expressly provided in this [act], any matter relating to the activities of the company is decided exclusively by the managers.

(2) Each manager has equal rights in the management and conduct of the activities of the company.

(3) A difference arising among managers as to a matter in the ordinary course of the activities of the company may be decided by a majority of the managers.

(4) The consent of all members is required to:

(A) sell, lease, exchange, or otherwise dispose of all, or substantially all, of the company's property, with or without the good will, outside the ordinary course of the company's activities;

(B) approve a merger, conversion, or domestication under [Article] 10;

(C) undertake any other act outside the ordinary course of the company's activities; and

(D) amend the operating agreement.

(5) A manager may be chosen at any time by the consent of a majority of the members and remains a manager until a successor has been chosen, unless the manager at an earlier time resigns, is removed, or dies, or, in the case of a manager that is not an individual, terminates. A manager may be removed at any time by the consent of a majority of the members without notice or cause.

(6) A person need not be a member to be a manager, but the dissociation of a member that is also a manager removes the person as a manager. If a person that is both a manager and a member ceases to be a manager, that cessation does not by itself dissociate the person as a member.

(d) An action requiring the consent of members under this [act] may be taken without a meeting, and a member may appoint a proxy or other agent to consent or otherwise act for the member by signing an appointing record, personally or by the member's agent.

(e) [...]

(f) This [act] does not entitle a member to remuneration for services performed for a member-managed limited liability company, except for reasonable compensation for services rendered in winding up the activities of the company.

Comment

Subsection (a)—This subsection follows implicitly from the definitions of "manager-managed" and "member-managed" limited liability companies, Section 102(10) and (12), but is included here for the sake of clarity. Although this Act has eliminated the link between management structure and statutory apparent authority, Section 301, the Act retains the manager-managed and member-managed constructs as options for members to use to structure their *inter se* relationship.

Subsection (b)—The subsection states default rules that, under Section 110, are subject to the operating agreement.

Subsection (c)—Like subsection (b), this subsection states default rules that, under Section 110, are subject to the operating agreement. For example, a limited liability company's operating agreement might state "This company is manager-managed," Section 102(10)(i), while providing that managers must submit specified ordinary matters for review by the members.

The actual authority of an LLC's manager or managers is a question of agency law and depends fundamentally on the contents of the operating agreement and any separate management contract between the LLC and its manager or managers. These agreements are the primary source of the manifestations of the LLC (as principal) from which a manager (as agent) will form the reasonable beliefs that delimit the scope of the manager's actual authority. RESTATEMENT (THIRD) OF AGENCY § 3.01 (2006).

If (i) an LLC's operating agreement merely states that the LLC is manager-managed and does not further specify the managerial responsibilities, and (ii) the LLC has only one manager, the actual authority analysis is simple. In that situation, this subsection:

- serves as "gap filler" to the operating agreement; and thereby

- constitutes the LLC's manifestation to the manager as to the scope of the manager's authority; and thereby

- delimits the manager's actual authority, subject to whatever subsequent manifestations the LLC may make to the manager (e.g., by a vote of the members, or an amendment of the operating agreement).

If the operating agreement states only that the LLC is manager-managed and the LLC has more than one manager, the question of actual authority has an additional aspect. It is necessary to determine what actual authority any one manager has to act alone.

Paragraphs (c)(2), (3), and (4) combine to provide the answer. A single manager of a multi-manager LLC:

- has no actual authority to commit the LLC to any matter "outside the ordinary course of the activities of the company," paragraph (c)(4)(C), or any matter encompassed in paragraph (c)(4); and

- has the actual authority to commit the LLC to any matter "in the ordinary course of the activities of the company," paragraph (c)(3), unless the manager has reason to know that other managers might disagree or the manager has some other reason to know that consultation with fellow managers is appropriate.

The first point follows self-evidently from the language of paragraphs (c)(3) and (c)(4). In light of that language, no manager could reasonably believe to the contrary (unless the operating agreement provided otherwise).

The second point follows because:

- Subsection (c) serves as the gap-filler manifestation from the LLC to its managers, and subsection (c) does not require managers of a multi-manager LLC to act only in concert or after consultation.

- To the contrary, subject to the operating agreement:

- paragraph (c)(2) expressly provides that "each manager has equal rights in the management and conduct of the activities of the company," and

- paragraph (c)(3) suggests that several (as well as joint) activity is appropriate on ordinary matters, so long as the manager acting in the matter has no reason to believe that the matter will be controversial among the managers and therefore requires a decision under paragraph (c)(3).

While the individual members of a corporate board of directors lack actual authority to bind the corporation, subsection (c) does not describe "board" management. Instead, subsection (c) provides management rules derived from those that govern the members of a general partnership and multiple general partners of a limited partnership.

The common law of agency will also determine the apparent authority of an LLC's manager or managers, and in that analysis what the particular third party knows or has reason to know about the management structure and business practices of the particular LLC will always be relevant. could reasonably believe that a [manager] is authorized to commit the organization to a particular transaction.").

As a general matter, however—i.e., as to the apparent authority of the position of LLC manager under this Act—courts may view the position as clothing its occupants with the apparent authority to take actions that reasonably appear within the ordinary course of the company's business. The actual authority analysis stated above supports that proposition; absent a reason to believe to the contrary, a third party could reasonably believe a manager to possess the authority contemplated by the gap-fillers of the statute.

Subsection (c)(5)—An LLC does not cease to be "manager-managed" simply because no managers are in place. In that situation, absent additional facts, the LLC is manager-managed and the manager position is vacant. Non-manager members who exercise managerial functions during the vacancy (or at any other time) will have duties as determined by other law, most particularly the law of agency.

Source: Rev. Unif. Ltd. Liab. Co. Act §§ 301, 304 (2006). Copyright © 2006 by National Conference of Commissioners on Uniform State Laws. Reprinted with permission.

Subsection (f)—This Act does not provide for remuneration to a manager of a manager-managed LLC. That issue is for the operating agreement, or a separate agreement between the LLC and the manager.

C. WHO MAY BE LIABLE IN AN L.L.C.?

Section 301. No Agency Power of Member as Member.

(a) A member is not an agent of a limited liability company solely by reason of being a member.

(b) A person's status as a member does not prevent or restrict law other than this [act] from imposing liability on a limited liability company because of the person's conduct.

Comment

Subsection (a)—Most LLC statutes, including the original ULLCA, provide for what might be termed "statutory apparent authority" for members in a member-managed limited liability company and managers in a manager-managed limited liability company. This approach codifies the common law notion of apparent authority by position and dates back at least to the original, 1914 Uniform Partnership Act. UPA, § 9 provided that "the act of every partner … for apparently carrying on in the usual way the business of the partnership … binds the partnership," and that formulation has been essentially followed by RUPA, § 301, ULLCA, § 301, ULPA (2001), § 402, and myriad state LLC statutes.

This Act rejects the statutory apparent authority approach, for reasons summarized in a "Progress Report on the Revised Uniform Limited Liability Company Act," published in the March 2006 issue of the newsletter of the ABA Committee on Partnerships and Unincorporated Business Organizations:

> The concept [of statutory apparent authority] still makes sense both for general and limited partnerships. A third party dealing with either type of partnership can know by the formal name of the entity and by a person's status as general or limited partner whether the person has the power to bind the entity.
>
> Most LLC statutes have attempted to use the same approach but with a fundamentally important (and problematic) distinction. An LLC's status as member-managed or manager-managed determines whether members or managers have the statutory power to bind. But an LLC's status as member- or manager-managed is not apparent from the LLC's name. A third party must check the public record, which may reveal that the LLC is manager-managed, which in turn means a member as member has no power to bind the LLC. As a result, a provision that originated in 1914 as a protection

for third parties can, in the LLC context, easily function as a trap for the unwary. The problem is exacerbated by the almost infinite variety of management structures permissible in and used by LLCs.

The new Act cuts through this problem by simply eliminating statutory apparent authority.

PUBOGRAM, Vol. XXIII, no. 2 at 9–10.

Codifying power to bind according to position makes sense only for organizations that have well-defined, well-known, and almost paradigmatic management structures. Because:

- flexibility of management structure is a hallmark of the limited liability company; and
- an LLC's name gives no signal as to the organization's structure,

it makes no sense to:

- require each LLC to publicly select between two statutorily preordained structures (i.e., manager-managed/member-managed); and then
- link a "statutory power to bind" to each of those two structures.

Under this Act, other law—most especially the law of agency—will handle power-to-bind questions.

This subsection does not address the power to bind of a manager in a manager-managed LLC, although this Act does consider a manager's management responsibilities. For a discussion of how agency law will approach the actual and apparent authority of managers, see Section 407(c), cmt.

Subsection (b)—As the "flip side" to subsection (a), this subsection expressly preserves the power of other law to hold an LLC directly or vicariously liable on account of conduct by a person who happens to be a member. For example, given the proper set of circumstances: (i) a member might have actual or apparent authority to bind an LLC to a contract; (ii) the doctrine of *respondeat superior* might make an LLC liable for the tortious conduct of a member (i.e., in some circumstances a member acts as a "servant" of the LLC); and (iii) an LLC might be liable for negligently supervising a member who is acting on behalf of the LLC. A person's status as a member does not weigh against these or any other relevant theories of law.

Moreover, subsection (a) does not prevent member status from being relevant to one or more elements of an "other law" theory. The most categorical example concerns the authority of a non-manager member of a manager-managed LLC.

> EXAMPLE: A vendor knows that an LLC is manager-managed but chooses to accept the signature of a person whom the vendor knows is merely a member of the LLC. Assuring the vendor that the LLC will stand by the member's commitment, the member states, "It's

such a simple matter; no one will mind." The member genuinely believes the statement, and the vendor accepts the assurance.

The person's status as a mere member will undermine a claim of apparent authority. RESTATEMENT (THIRD) OF AGENCY § 2.03, cmt. d (2006) (explaining the "reasonable belief" element of a claim of apparent authority, and role played by context, custom, and the supposed agent's position in an organization). Likewise, the member will have no actual authority. Absent additional facts, section 407(c)(1) (vesting all management authority in the managers) renders the member's belief unreasonable. RESTATEMENT (THIRD) OF AGENCY § 2.01, cmt. c (2006) (explaining the "reasonable belief" element of a claim of actual authority).

In general, a member's actual authority to act for an LLC will depend fundamentally on the operating agreement.

EXAMPLE: Rachael and Sam, who have known each other for years, decide to go into business arranging musical tours. They fill out and electronically sign a one page form available on the website of the Secretary of State and become the organizers of MMT, LLC. They are the only members of the LLC, and their understanding of who will do what in managing the enterprise is based on several lengthy, late-night conversations that preceded the LLC's formation. Sam is to "get the acts," and Rachael is to manage the tour logistics. There is no written operating agreement.

In the terminology of this Act, MMT, LLC is member-managed, Section 407(a), and the understanding reached in the late night conversations has become part of the LLC's operating agreement. Section 111(c). In agency law terms, the operating agreement constitutes a manifestation by the LLC to Rachael and Sam concerning the scope of their respective authority to act on behalf of the LLC. RESTATEMENT (THIRD) OF AGENCY § 2.01, cmt. c (2006) (explaining that a person's actual authority depends first on some manifestation attributable to the principal and stating: "Actual authority is a consequence of a principal's expressive conduct toward an agent, through which the principal manifests assent to be affected by the agent's action, and the agent's reasonable understanding of the principal's manifestation.")

Circumstances outside the operating agreement can also be relevant to determining the scope of a member's actual authority.

EXAMPLE: Homeworks, LLC is a manager-managed LLC with three members. The LLC's written operating agreement:

- specifies in considerable detail the management responsibilities of Margaret, the LLC's manager-member, and also states that Margaret is responsible for "the day-to-day operations" of the company;

- puts Garrett, a non-manager member, in charge of the LLC's transportation department; and

- specifies no management role for Brooksley, the third member.

When the LLC's chief financial officer quits suddenly, Margaret asks Brooksley, a CPA, to "step in until we can hire a replacement."

Under the operating agreement, Margaret's request to Brooksley is within Margaret's actual authority and is a manifestation attributable to the LLC. If Brooksley manifests assent to Margaret's request, Brooksley will have the actual authority to act as the LLC's CFO.

In the unlikely event that two or more people form a member-managed LLC without any understanding of how to allocate management responsibility between or among them, agency law, operating in the context the Act's "gap fillers" on management responsibility, will produce the following result:

A single member of a multi-member, member-managed LLC:

- has no actual authority to commit the LLC to any matter "outside the ordinary course of the activities of the company," section 407(b)(3); and

- has the actual authority to commit the LLC to any matter "in the ordinary course of the activities of the company," section 407(b)(2), unless the member has reason to know that other members might disagree

- or the member has some other reason to know that consultation with fellow members is appropriate.

For an explanation of this result, see Section 407(c), cmt., which provides a detailed agency law analysis in the context of a multi-manager, manager-managed LLC whose operating agreement is silent on the analogous question.

The common law of agency will also determine the apparent authority of a member of a member-managed LLC, and in that analysis what the particular third party knows or has reason to know about the management structure and business practices of the particular LLC will always be relevant. RESTATEMENT (THIRD) OF AGENCY § 3.03, cmt. b (2006) ("A principal may also make a manifestation by placing an agent in a defined position in an organization. ... Third parties who interact with the principal through the agent will naturally and reasonably assume that the agent has authority to do acts consistent with the agent's position ... unless they have notice of facts suggesting that this may not be so.").

Under section 301(a), however, the mere fact that a person is a member of a member-managed limited liability company cannot *by itself* establish apparent authority by position. A course of dealing, however, may easily change the analysis:

EXAMPLE: David is a one of two members of DS, LLC, a member-managed LLC. David orders paper clips on behalf of the

LLC, signing the purchase agreement, "David, as a member of DS, LLC." The vendor accepts the order, sends an invoice to the LLC's address, and in due course receives a check drawn on the LLC's bank account. When David next places an order with the vendor, the LLC's payment of the first order is a manifestation that the vendor may use in establishing David's apparent authority to place the second order.

Section 304. Liability of Members and Managers.

(a) The debts, obligations, or other liabilities of a limited liability company, whether arising in contract, tort, or otherwise:

   (1) are solely the debts, obligations, or other liabilities of the company; and

   (2) do not become the debts, obligations, or other liabilities of a member or manager solely by reason of the member acting as a member or manager acting as a manager.

(b) The failure of a limited liability company to observe any particular formalities relating to the exercise of its powers or management of its activities is not a ground for imposing liability on the members or managers for the debts, obligations, or other liabilities of the company.

Comment

Subsection (a)(2)—This paragraph shields members and managers only against the debts, obligations and liabilities of the limited liability company and is irrelevant to claims seeking to hold a member or manager directly liable on account of the member's or manager's own conduct.

> EXAMPLE: A manager personally guarantees a debt of a limited liability company. Subsection (a)(2) is irrelevant to the manager's liability as guarantor.

> EXAMPLE: A member purports to bind a limited liability company while lacking any agency law power to do so. The limited liability company is not bound, but the member is liable for having breached the "warranty of authority" (an agency law doctrine). Subsection (a)(2) does not apply. The liability is not *for* a "debt[], obligation[], [or] liabilit[y] of a limited liability company," but rather is the member's direct liability resulting because the limited liability company is *not* indebted, obligated or liable. RESTATEMENT (THIRD) OF AGENCY § 6.10 (2006).

> EXAMPLE: A manager of a limited liability company defames a third party in circumstances that render the limited liability company vicariously liable under agency law. Under subsection (a)(2), the third party cannot hold the manager accountable for the *company's* liability, but that protection is immaterial. The manager is the tortfeasor and in that role is directly liable to the third party.

Subsection (a)(2) pertains only to claims by third parties and is irrelevant to claims by a limited liability company against a member or manager and *vice versa*.

Subsection (b)—This subsection pertains to the equitable doctrine of "piercing the veil"—i.e., conflating an entity and its owners to hold one liable for the obligations of the other. The doctrine of "piercing the corporate veil" is well-established, and courts regularly (and sometimes almost reflexively) apply that doctrine to limited liability companies. In the corporate realm, "disregard of corporate formalities" is a key factor in the piercing analysis. In the realm of LLCs, that factor is inappropriate, because informality of organization and operation is both common and desired.

This subsection does not preclude consideration of another key piercing factor—disregard by an entity's owners of the entity's economic separateness from the owners.

> EXAMPLE: The operating agreement of a three-member, member-managed limited liability company requires formal monthly meetings of the members. Each of the members works in the LLC's business, and they consult each other regularly. They have forgotten or ignore the requirement of monthly meetings. Under subsection (b), that fact is irrelevant to a piercing claim.

> EXAMPLE: The sole owner of a limited liability company uses a car titled in the company's name for personal purposes and writes checks on the company's account to pay for personal expenses. These facts are relevant to a piercing claim; they pertain to economic separateness, not subsection (b) formalities.

D. WHAT FIDUCIARY DUTIES DO MEMBERS AND MANGERS HAVE?

Section 409. Standards of Conduct for Members and Managers.

(a) A member of a member-managed limited liability company owes to the company and the other members the fiduciary duties of loyalty and care stated in subsections (b) and (c).

(b) The duty of loyalty of a member in a member-managed limited liability company includes the duties:

  (1) to account to the company and to hold as trustee for it any property, profit, or benefit derived by the member:
    (A) in the conduct or winding up of the company's activities;
    (B) from a use by the member of the company's property; or

Source: Rev. Unif. Ltd. Liab. Co. Act § 409 (2006). Copyright © 2006 by National Conference of Commissioners on Uniform State Laws. Reprinted with permission.

(C) from the appropriation of a limited liability company opportunity;

(2) to refrain from dealing with the company in the conduct or winding up of the company's activities as or on behalf of a person having an interest adverse to the company; and

(3) to refrain from competing with the company in the conduct of the company's activities before the dissolution of the company.

(c) Subject to the business judgment rule, the duty of care of a member of a member-managed limited liability company in the conduct and winding up of the company's activities is to act with the care that a person in a like position would reasonably exercise under similar circumstances and in a manner the member reasonably believes to be in the best interests of the company. In discharging this duty, a member may rely in good faith upon opinions, reports, statements, or other information provided by another person that the member reasonably believes is a competent and reliable source for the information.

(d) A member in a member-managed limited liability company or a manager-managed limited liability company shall discharge the duties under this [act] or under the operating agreement and exercise any rights consistently with the contractual obligation of good faith and fair dealing.

(e) It is a defense to a claim under subsection (b)(2) and any comparable claim in equity or at common law that the transaction was fair to the limited liability company.

(f) All of the members of a member-managed limited liability company or a manager-managed limited liability company may authorize or ratify, after full disclosure of all material facts, a specific act or transaction that otherwise would violate the duty of loyalty.

(g) In a manager-managed limited liability company, the following rules apply:

(1) Subsections (a), (b), (c), and (e) apply to the manager or managers and not the members.

(2) The duty stated under subsection (b)(3) continues until winding up is completed.

(3) Subsection (d) applies to the members and managers.

(4) Subsection (f) applies only to the members.

(5) A member does not have any fiduciary duty to the company or to any other member solely by reason of being a member.

Comment

This section follows the structure of many LLC acts, first stating the duties of members in a member-managed limited liability company and then using that statement and a "switching" mechanism, subsection (g), to allocate duties in a manager-managed company. The duties stated in this section are subject to the operating agreement, but Section 110 contains important limitations on the power of the operating agreement to affect fiduciary duties and the obligation of good faith.

The standards, duties, and obligations of this Section are subject to delineation, restriction, and, to some extent, elimination by the operating agreement.

Subsections (a) and (b)—Until the promulgation of RUPA, it was almost axiomatic that: (i) fiduciary duties reflect judge-made law; and (ii) statutory formulations can express some of that law but do not exhaustively codify it. The original UPA was a prime example of this approach.

In an effort to respect freedom of contract, bolster predictability, and protect partnership agreements from second-guessing, the Conference decided that RUPA should fence or "cabin in" all fiduciary duties within a statutory formulation. That decision was followed without re-consideration in ULLCA and ULPA (2001).

This Act takes a different approach. After lengthy discussion in the drafting committee and on the floor of the 2006 Annual Meeting, the Conference decided that: (i) the "corral" created by RUPA does not fit in the very complex and variegated world of LLCs; and (ii) it is impracticable to cabin all LLC-related fiduciary duties within a statutory formulation.

As a result, this Act: (i) eschews "only" and "limited to"—the words RUPA used in an effort to exhaustively codify fiduciary duty; (ii) codifies the core of the fiduciary duty of loyalty; but (iii) does not purport to discern every possible category of overreaching. One important consequence is to allow courts to continue to use fiduciary duty concepts to police disclosure obligations in member-to-member and member-LLC transactions.

Subsection (c)—Although ULLCA § 409(c) followed RUPA § 404(c) and provided a gross negligence standard of care, at least a plurality of LLC statutes use an ordinary care standard.

In some circumstances, an unadorned standard of ordinary care is appropriate for those in charge of a business organization or similar, non-business enterprise. In others, the proper application of the duty of care must take into account the difficulties inherent in establishing an enterprise's most fundamental policies, supervising the enterprise's overall activities, or making complex business judgments. Corporate law subdivides circumstances somewhat according to the formal role exercised by the person whose conduct is later challenged (e.g., distinguishing the duties of directors from the duties of officers). LLC law cannot follow that approach, because a hallmark of the LLC entity is its structural flexibility.

This subsection, therefore, seeks "the best of both worlds"—stating a standard of ordinary care but subjecting that standard to the business judgment rule to the extent circumstances warrant. The content and force of the business judgment rule vary across jurisdictions, and therefore the meaning of this subsection may vary from jurisdiction to jurisdiction.

That result is intended. In any jurisdiction, the business judgment rule's application will vary depending on the nature of the challenged conduct. There is, for example, very little (if any) judgment involved when a person with managerial power acts (or fails to act) on an essentially ministerial matter. Moreover, under the law of many jurisdictions, the business judgment rule applies similarly across the range of business organizations. That is, the doctrine is sufficiently broad and conceptual so that the formality of organizational choice is less important in shaping the application of the rule than are the nature of the challenged conduct and the responsibilities and authority of the person whose conduct is being challenged.

Subsection (d)—This subsection refers to the "*contractual* obligation of good faith and fair dealing" to emphasize that the obligation is not an invitation to re-write agreements among the members. As explained in the Comment to ULPA (2001), § 305(b):

> The obligation of good faith and fair dealing is not a fiduciary duty, does not command altruism or self-abnegation, and does not prevent a partner from acting in the partner's own self-interest.
>
> Courts should not use the obligation to change ex post facto the parties' or this Act's allocation of risk and power. To the contrary, in light of the nature of a limited partnership, the obligation should be used only to protect agreed-upon arrangements from conduct that is manifestly beyond what a reasonable person could have contemplated when the arrangements were made…. In sum, the purpose of the obligation of good faith and fair dealing is to protect the arrangement the partners have chosen for themselves, not to restructure that arrangement under the guise of safeguarding it.

At first glance, it may seem strange to apply a contractual obligation to statutory duties and rights—i.e., duties and rights "under this [act]." However, for the most part those duties and rights apply to relationships *inter se* the members and the LLC and function only to the extent not displaced by the operating agreement. In the contract-based organization that is an LLC, those statutory default rules are intended to function like a contract. Therefore, applying the contractual notion of good faith makes sense.

Subsection (e)—Section 409 omits a noteworthy provision, which, beginning with RUPA, has been standard in the uniform business entity acts. RUPA, ULLCA, ULPA (2001) each placed the following language in the subsection following the formulation of the obligation of good faith:

> A member … does not violate a duty or obligation under this [act] or under the operating agreement merely because the member's conduct furthers the member's own interest.

This language is inappropriate in the complex and variegated world of LLCs. As a proposition of contract law, the language is axiomatic and therefore unnecessary. In the context of fiduciary duty, the language is at best incomplete, at worst wrong, and in any event confusing.

This Act's subsection (e) takes a very different approach, stating a well-established principle of judge-made law. Despite Section 107, the statement is not surplusage. Given this Act's very detailed treatment of fiduciary duties and especially the Act's very detailed treatment of the power of the operating agreement to modify fiduciary duties, the statement is important because its absence might be confusing. (An *ex post* fairness justification is not the same as an *ex ante* agreement to modify, but the topics are sufficiently close for a danger of the affirmative pregnant.)

Subsection (f)—The operating agreement can provide additional or different methods of authorization or ratification, subject to the strictures of Section 110(e).

Subsection (g)—This is the "switching" mechanism, referred to in the introduction to this Comment.

Subsection (g)(2)—On the assumption that the members of a manager-managed LLC are dependent on the manager, this paragraph extends the duty longer than in a member-managed LLC.

Subsection (g)(5)—This paragraph merely negates a claim of fiduciary duty that is exclusively status-based and does not immunize misconduct.

E. What Are the Financial Rights of an L.L.C.?

Section 102. Definitions in this [Act]:

(2) "Contribution" means any benefit provided by a person to a limited liability company:
   (A) in order to become a member upon formation of the company and in accordance with an agreement between or among the persons that have agreed to become the initial members of the company;

   (B) in order to become a member after formation of the company and in accordance with an agreement between the person and the company; or

   (C) in the person's capacity as a member and in accordance with the operating agreement or an agreement between the member and the company.

Source: Rev. Unif. Ltd. Liab. Co. Act §§ 102, 402, 404, 405 (2006). Copyright © 2006 by National Conference of Commissioners on Uniform State Laws. Reprinted with permission.

(5) "Distribution" means a transfer of money or other property from a limited liability company to another person on account of a transferable interest

Section 402. Form of Contribution.

A contribution may consist of tangible or intangible property or other benefit to a limited liability company, including money, services performed, promissory notes, other agreements to contribute money or property, and contracts for services to be performed.

Section 404. Sharing of and Right to Distributions before Dissolution.

(a) Any distributions made by a limited liability company before its dissolution and winding up must be in equal shares among members and dissociated members, except to the extent necessary to comply with any transfer effective under Section 502.

(b) A person has a right to a distribution before the dissolution and winding up of a limited liability company only if the company decides to make an interim distribution. A person's dissociation does not entitle the person to a distribution.

(c) A person does not have a right to demand or receive a distribution from a limited liability company in any form other than money. Except as otherwise provided in Section 708(c), a limited liability company may distribute an asset in kind if each part of the asset is fungible with each other part and each person receives a percentage of the asset equal in value to the person's share of distributions.

(d) If a member or transferee becomes entitled to receive a distribution, the member or transferee has the status of, and is entitled to all remedies available to, a creditor of the limited liability company with respect to the distribution.

Comment

This Act follows both the original ULLCA and ULPA (2001) in omitting any default rule for allocation of losses. The Comment to ULPA (2001), § 503 explains that omission as follows:

> This Act has no provision allocating profits and losses among the partners. Instead, the Act directly apportions the right to receive distributions. Nearly all limited partnerships will choose to allocate profits and losses in order to comply with applicable tax, accounting and other regulatory requirements. Those requirements, rather than this Act, are the proper source of guidance for that profit and loss allocation.

Subsection (b)—The second sentence of this subsection accords with Section 603(a)(3)—upon dissociation a person is treated as a mere transferee of its own transferable interest. Like most *inter se* rules in this Act, this one is subject to the operating agreement.

Section 405. Limitations on Distribution.

(a) A limited liability company may not make a distribution if after the distribution:

    (1) the company would not be able to pay its debts as they become due in the ordinary course of the company's activities; or

    (2) the company's total assets would be less than the sum of its total liabilities plus the amount that would be needed, if the company were to be dissolved, wound up, and terminated at the time of the distribution, to satisfy the preferential rights upon dissolution, winding up, and termination of members whose preferential rights are superior to those of persons receiving the distribution.

(b) A limited liability company may base a determination that a distribution is not prohibited under subsection (a) on financial statements prepared on the basis of accounting practices and principles that are reasonable in the circumstances or on a fair valuation or other method that is reasonable under the circumstances.

F. WHAT ARE INFORMATIONAL RIGHTS OF MEMBERS AND MANAGERS?

Section 410. Rights of Members, Managers and Dissociated Members to Information.

(a) In a member-managed limited liability company, the following rules apply:

    (1) On reasonable notice, a member may inspect and copy during regular business hours, at a reasonable location specified by the company, any record maintained by the company regarding the company's activities, financial condition, and other circumstances, to the extent the information is material to the member's rights and duties under the operating agreement or this [act].

    (2) The company shall furnish to each member:

        (A) without demand, any information concerning the company's activities, financial condition, and other circumstances which

Source: Rev. Unif. Ltd. Liab. Co. Act §§ 410 (2006). Copyright © 2006 by National Conference of Commissioners on Uniform State Laws. Reprinted with permission.

the company knows and is material to the proper exercise of the member's rights and duties under the operating agreement or this [act], except to the extent the company can establish that it reasonably believes the member already knows the information; and

(B) on demand, any other information concerning the company's activities, financial condition, and other circumstances, except to the extent the demand or information demanded is unreasonable or otherwise improper under the circumstances.

(3) The duty to furnish information under paragraph (2) also applies to each member to the extent the member knows any of the information described in paragraph (2).

(b) In a manager-managed limited liability company, the following rules apply:

(1) The informational rights stated in subsection (a) and the duty stated in subsection (a)(3) apply to the managers and not the members.

(2) During regular business hours and at a reasonable location specified by the company, a member may obtain from the company and inspect and copy full information regarding the activities, financial condition, and other circumstances of the company as is just and reasonable if:

(A) the member seeks the information for a purpose material to the member's interest as a member;

(B) the member makes a demand in a record received by the company, describing with reasonable particularity the information sought and the purpose for seeking the information; and

(C) the information sought is directly connected to the member's purpose.

(3) Within 10 days after receiving a demand pursuant to paragraph (2)(B), the company shall in a record inform the member that made the demand:

(A) of the information that the company will provide in response to the demand and when and where the company will provide the information; and

(B) if the company declines to provide any demanded information, the company's reasons for declining.

(4) Whenever this [act] or an operating agreement provides for a member to give or withhold consent to a matter, before the consent is given or withheld, the company shall, without demand, provide the member with all information that is known to the company and is material to the member's decision.

[…]

(f) The rights under this section do not extend to a person as transferee.

(g) In addition to any restriction or condition stated in its operating agreement, a limited liability company, as a matter within the ordinary course of its activities, may impose reasonable restrictions and conditions on access to and use of information to be furnished under this section, including designating information confidential and imposing nondisclosure and safeguarding obligations on the recipient. In a dispute concerning the reasonableness of a restriction under this subsection, the company has the burden of proving reasonableness.

Comment

The rules stated here are what might be termed "quasi-default rules"— subject to some change by the operating agreement. Section 110(c)(6) (prohibiting unreasonable restrictions on the information rights stated in this section).

Although the rights and duties stated in this section are extensive, they may not necessarily be exhaustive. In some situations, some courts have seen owners' information rights as reflecting a fiduciary duty of those with management power.

Subsection (a)—Paragraph 1 states the rule pertaining to information memorialized in "records maintained by the company." Paragraph 2 applies to information not in such a record. Appropriately, paragraph (2) sets a more demanding standard for those seeking information.

Subsection (a)(2) and (3)—In appropriate circumstances, violation of either or both of these provisions might cause a court to enjoin or even rescind action taken by the LLC, especially when the violation has interfered with an approval or veto mechanism involving member consent. E.g. Blue Chip Emerald LLC v. Allied Partners Inc., 299 A.D.2d 278, 279-280 (N.Y. App. Div. 2002) (invoking partnership law precedent as reflecting a duty of full disclosure and holding that "[a]bsent such full disclosure, the transaction is voidable).

Subsection (a)(2)—Violation of this paragraph could give rise to a claim for damages against a member or manager [see subsection (b)(1)] who breaches the duties stated in Section 409 in causing or suffering the LLC to violate this paragraph.

Subsection (a)(3)—A member's violation of this paragraph is actionable in damages without need to show a violation of a duty stated in Section 409.

Subsection (b)(1)—This is a switching provision. A manager's violation of the duty stated in subsection (a)(3) is actionable in damages without need to show a violation of a duty stated in Section 409.

Subsection (b)(2)—This paragraph refers to "information" rather than "records maintained by the company"—compare subsection (a)—so in some circumstances the company might have an obligation to memorialize information. Such circumstances will likely be rare or at least unusual. Section 410 generally concerns providing existing information, not creating it. In any event, a member does not trigger the company's obligation under this paragraph merely by satisfying subparagraphs (A) through (C). The member must also satisfy the "just and reasonable" requirement.

Subsection (g)—The phrase "as a matter within the ordinary course of its activities" means that a mere majority consent is needed to impose a restriction or condition. This approach is necessary, lest a requesting member (or manager-member) have the power to block imposition of a reasonable restriction or condition needed to prevent the requestor from abusing the LLC.

G. WHAT ARE THE PROPERTY RIGHTS OF MEMBERS?

Section 102. Definitions in this [Act]:

(20) "Transfer" includes an assignment, conveyance, deed, bill of sale, lease, mortgage, security interest, encumbrance, gift, and transfer by operation of law.

(21) "Transferable interest" means the right, as originally associated with a person's capacity as a member, to receive distributions from a limited liability company in accordance with the operating agreement, whether or not the person remains a member or continues to own any part of the right.

(22) "Transferee" means a person to which all or part of a transferable interest has been transferred, whether or not the transferor is a member.

Section 501. Nature of Transferable Interest.

A transferable interest is personal property.

Section 502. Transfer of Transferable Interest.

(a) A transfer, in whole or in part, of a transferable interest:

　　(1) is permissible;

　　(2) does not by itself cause a member's dissociation or a dissolution and winding up of the limited liability company's activities; and

　　(3) [...] does not entitle the transferee to:

　　　　(A) participate in the management or conduct of the company's activities; or

　　　　(B) [...] have access to records or other information concerning the company's activities.

Source: Rev. Unif. Ltd. Liab. Co. Act §§ 102, 501, 502 (2006). Copyright © 2006 by National Conference of Commissioners on Uniform State Laws. Reprinted with permission.

(b) A transferee has the right to receive, in accordance with the transfer, distributions to which the transferor would otherwise be entitled.

Comment

One of the most fundamental characteristics of LLC law is its fidelity to the "pick your partner" principle. This section is the core of the Act's provisions reflecting and protecting that principle.

A member's rights in a limited liability company are bifurcated into economic rights (the transferable interest) and governance rights (including management rights, consent rights, rights to information, rights to seek judicial intervention). Unless the operating agreement otherwise provides, a member acting without the consent of all other members lacks both the power and the right to: (i) bestow membership on a non-member, Section 401(d); or (ii) transfer to a non-member anything other than some or all of the member's transferable interest. Section 502(a)(3). However, consistent with current law, a member may transfer governance rights to another member without obtaining consent from the other members. Thus, this Act does not itself protect members from control shifts that result from transfers among members (as distinguished from transfers to non-members who seek thereby to become members).

Subsection (a)—The definition of "transfer," Section 102(20), and this subsection's reference to "in whole or in part" combine to mean that this section encompasses not only unconditional, permanent, and complete transfers but also temporary, contingent, and partial ones as well. Thus, for example, a charging order under Section 504 effects a transfer of part of the judgment debtor's transferable interest, as does the pledge of a transferable interest as collateral for a loan and the gift of a life-interest in a member's rights to distribution.

Subsection (a)(2)—Section 602(4)(B) creates a risk of dissociation via expulsion when a member transfers all of the member's transferable interest.

Subsection (a)(3)—Mere transferees have no right to intrude as the members carry on their activities as members.

Subsection (b)—Amounts due under this subsection are of course subject to offset for any amount owed to the limited liability company by the member or dissociated member on whose account the distribution is made.

H. How Do You Exit an L.L.C.?

Section 601. Member's Power to Dissociate; Wrongful Dissociation.

(a) A person has the power to dissociate as a member at any time, rightfully or wrongfully, by withdrawing as a member by express will under Section 602(1).

Source: Rev. Unif. Ltd. Liab. Co. Act §§ 601–603, 701, 702 (2006). Copyright © 2006 by National Conference of Commissioners on Uniform State Laws. Reprinted with permission.

(b) A person's dissociation from a limited liability company is wrongful only if the dissociation:

  (1) is in breach of an express provision of the operating agreement; or

  (2) occurs before the termination of the company and:

    (A) the person withdraws as a member by express will;

    (B) the person is expelled as a member by judicial order under Section 602(5);

    (C) the person is dissociated under Section 602(7)(A) by becoming a debtor in bankruptcy; or

    (D) in the case of a person that is not a trust other than a business trust, an estate, or an individual, the person is expelled or otherwise dissociated as a member because it willfully dissolved or terminated.

(c) A person that wrongfully dissociates as a member is liable to the limited liability company and to the other members for damages caused by the dissociation. The liability is in addition to any other debt, obligation, or other liability of the member to the company or the other members.

Section 602. Events Causing Dissociation.

A person is dissociated as a member from a limited liability company when:

(1) the company has notice of the person's express will to withdraw as a member;

(2) an event stated in the operating agreement as causing the person's dissociation occurs;

(3) the person is expelled as a member pursuant to the operating agreement;

(4) the person is expelled as a member by the unanimous consent of the other members if:

  (A) it is unlawful to carry on the company's activities with the person as a member;

  (B) there has been a transfer of all of the person's transferable interest in the company, other than:

    (i) a transfer for security purposes;

  (C) the person is a corporation and, within 90 days after the company notifies the person that it will be expelled as a member because the person has filed a certificate of dissolution or the equivalent, its charter has been revoked, or its right to conduct business has been suspended by the jurisdiction of its incorporation, the certificate of dissolution has not been revoked or its charter or right to conduct business has not been reinstated; or

(D) the person is a limited liability company or partnership that has been dissolved and whose business is being wound up;

(5) on application by the company, the person is expelled as a member by judicial order because the person:

(A) has engaged, or is engaging, in wrongful conduct that has adversely and materially affected, or will adversely and materially affect, the company's activities;

(B) has willfully or persistently committed, or is willfully and persistently committing, a material breach of the operating agreement or the person's duties or obligations under Section 409; or

(C) has engaged in, or is engaging, in conduct relating to the company's activities which makes it not reasonably practicable to carry on the activities with the person as a member;

(6) in the case of a person who is an individual:

(A) the person dies;

(7) in a member-managed limited liability company, the person:

(A) becomes a debtor in bankruptcy;

(B) executes an assignment for the benefit of creditors; or

(C) seeks, consents to, or acquiesces in the appointment of a trustee, receiver, or liquidator of the person or of all or substantially all of the person's property;

[...]

(10) in the case of a member that is not an individual, partnership, limited liability company, corporation, trust, or estate, the termination of the member;

[...]

(14) the company terminates.

Section 603. Effect of Person's Dissociation As Member.

(a) When a person is dissociated as a member of a limited liability company:

(1) the person's right to participate as a member in the management and conduct of the company's activities terminates;

(2) if the company is member-managed, the person's fiduciary duties as a member end with regard to matters arising and events occurring after the person's dissociation; and

(3) any transferable interest owned by the person immediately before dissociation in the person's capacity as a member is owned by the person solely as a transferee.

(b) A person's dissociation as a member of a limited liability company does not of itself discharge the person from any debt, obligation, or other liability to the company or the other members which the person incurred while a member.

Comment

Subsection (a)(2)—This provision applies only when the limited liability company is member-managed, because in a manager-managed LLC these duties do not apply to a member qua member.

Subsection (a)(3)—This paragraph accords with Section 404(b)—dissociation does not entitle a person to any distribution. Like most inter se rules in this Act, this one is subject to the operating agreement. For example, the operating agreement has the power to provide for the buy out of a person's transferable interest in connection with the person's dissociation.

Subsection (b)—In a member-managed limited liability company, the obligation to safeguard trade secrets and other confidential or proprietary information is incurred when a person is a member. A subsequent dissociation does not entitle the person to usurp the information or use it to the prejudice of the LLC after the dissociation. (In a manager-managed LLC, any obligations of a non-manager member viz a viz proprietary information would be a matter for the operating agreement, the obligation of good faith, or other law.)

Section 701. Events Causing Dissolution.

(a) A limited liability company is dissolved, and its activities must be wound up, upon the occurrence of any of the following:

(1) an event or circumstance that the operating agreement states causes dissolution;

(2) the consent of all the members;

(3) the passage of 90 consecutive days during which the company has no members;

(4) on application by a member, the entry by [appropriate court] of an order dissolving the company on the grounds that:
(A) the conduct of all or substantially all of the company's activities is unlawful; or

(B) it is not reasonably practicable to carry on the company's activities in conformity with the certificate of organization and the operating agreement; or

(5) on application by a member, the entry by [appropriate court] of an order dissolving the company on the grounds that the managers or those members in control of the company:

(A) have acted, are acting, or will act in a manner that is illegal or fraudulent; or

(B) have acted or are acting in a manner that is oppressive and was, is, or will be directly harmful to the applicant.

(b) In a proceeding brought under subsection (a)(5), the court may order a remedy other than dissolution.

Comment

Subsection (a)(5)—This provision's reference to "those members in control of the company" implies that such members have a duty to avoid acting oppressively toward fellow members. Subsection (a)(5) is non-waivable.

Subsection (b)—In the close corporation context, many courts have reached this position without express statutory authority, most often with regard to court-ordered buyouts of oppressed shareholders. This subsection saves courts and litigants the trouble of re-inventing that wheel in the LLC context. However, unlike, subsection (a)(4) and (5), subsection (b) can be overridden by the operating agreement. Thus, the members may agree to a restrict or eliminate a court's power to craft a lesser remedy, even to the extent of confining the court (and themselves) to the all-or-nothing remedy of dissolution.

Section 702. Winding Up.

(a) A dissolved limited liability company shall wind up its activities, and the company continues after dissolution only for the purpose of winding up.

(b) In winding up its activities, a limited liability company:

(1) shall discharge the company's debts, obligations, or other liabilities, settle and close the company's activities, and marshal and distribute the assets of the company; and

(2) may:

(A) deliver to the [Secretary of State] for filing a statement of dissolution stating the name of the company and that the company is dissolved; reasonable time;

(B) preserve the company activities and property as a going concern for a reasonable time;

(C) prosecute and defend actions and proceedings, whether civil, criminal, or administrative;

(D) transfer the company's property;

(E) settle disputes by mediation or arbitration;

(F) deliver to the [Secretary of State] for filing a statement of termination stating the name of the company and that the company is terminated; and

(G) perform other acts necessary or appropriate to the winding up.

PART 6

Taxation

CHAPTER 26

THE CHOICE OF BUSINESS ENTITY: CORPORATE, PASS-THROUGH, AND DISREGARDED ENTITIES

When starting a business, there are many important choices that must be made, from the hiring of key personnel to the choice of a business model. One choice that can have far-reaching effects on the success of any business is the legal form through which it will operate and interact with the rest of the business community. Not only does the choice of a legal form have important federal income tax implications, but it can also affect a business owner's administrative workload, the manner in which he runs his day-to-day operations, his ability to transfer his ownership interest, and how he can compensate his employees. This technical note focuses on common business entities: sole proprietorships, general partnerships (GPs), limited partnerships (LPs), limited liability partnerships (LLPs), limited liability companies (LLCs), S corporations, and C corporations and offers insights into the basic factors to consider when choosing one of these entities.[1]

FEDERAL INCOME TAX: DISREGARDED ENTITIES, TAXABLE ENTITIES, AND PASS-THROUGH ENTITIES

For federal income tax purposes, there are three general types of entities: disregarded entities, taxable entities, and pass-through entities. Among the pass-through entities, the federal tax code also distinguishes between entities taxed as partnerships and entities taxed as S corporations **(Figure 26.1).**

---

1 The discussion of the factors in this note is far from exhaustive. For example, it addresses only federal income taxation. State and international taxation is also important, but the existence of 50 state tax systems and an even greater number of foreign tax systems makes these subjects beyond the scope of this note.

Mary Margaret Frank, Melissa Garza, and Alexander Holtan, *The Choice of Business Entity: Corporate, Pass-Through, and Disregarded Entities*, pp. 1, 14–28. Copyright © 2010 by Darden Business Publishing. Reprinted with permission.

Figure 26.1 Tax returns by entity type, 2003.

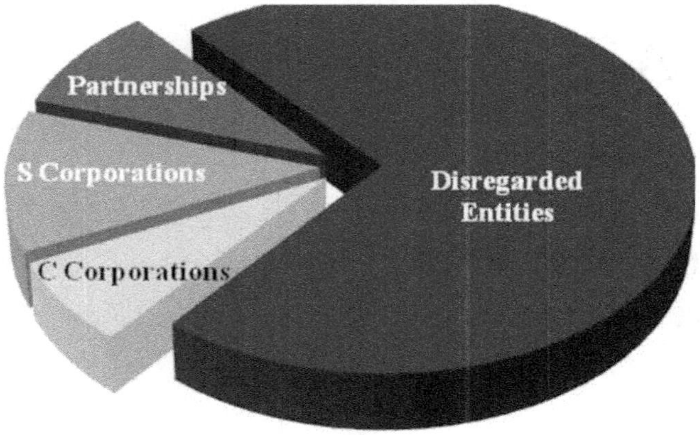

Source: Joint Committee on Taxation.[2]

Because state law and federal tax code are generally independent of one another, the state law form of a business does not necessarily dictate how an entity is treated from a federal income tax perspective. For example, an LLC can be treated as a disregarded entity, a taxable entity, or a pass-through entity. Under the check-the-box regulations issued by the IRS,[3] any form of partnership or LLC can choose to be taxed as a partnership (pass-through) or as a corporation (taxable). In addition, any corporation or entity choosing to be taxed as a corporation can also elect to be treated as an S corporation (pass-through) if they meet the eligibility requirements discussed above. The differences in the taxation of these entities affect the *allocation of profits and losses* to the owners, *distributions* to owners, and the *basis of the investment* that the owners have in the entity (stock, partnership interest, etc.). The basis of an investment is the amount of after-tax dollars the owner has invested in the business and is used to calculate any gains or losses upon sale of an owner's interest in a business.

Disregarded Entities: Sole Proprietorship and Single Member LLC

A *disregarded entity* is an entity that is ignored for federal income tax purposes. Sole proprietorships are automatically disregarded entities, and single-member LLCs are typically treated as such. A disregarded entity is treated as nonexistent under the tax code and does not have to file its own tax return with the IRS. The income of the business is the income of the owner, so all profits

---

2   In 2003, this was the breakdown of business income tax returns: disregarded entities, 19,710,079; C corporations, 2,059,631; S corporations, 3,341,606; partnerships, 2,375,375. See Joint Committee on Taxation, JCX-41-06, September 19, 2006.

3   See IRS Reg. 301.7701–1 through 301.7701–3. See also Allen, 77 for a discussion of the effect of the regulations. Previous IRS regulations provided that an entity would be taxed as a corporation of it possessed three or more of the following four corporate characteristics: (1) limited liability, (2) centralized management, (3) freely transferable ownership interests, and (4) continuity of life.

and losses flow directly to the owner. The owner of the business reports any income or loss on his own individual tax return.[4] Because a sole proprietorship is functionally inseparable from its owner, for tax purposes, distributions from the business to an owner are ignored. In addition, an owner has a basis not in the business but in the assets and liabilities of the company, so when the owner sells the company, he actually sells the individual assets and liabilities and not his interest. Any gain or loss in the transaction is determined using the owner's basis in the assets of the business.

Taxable Entities: C Corporations

A *taxable entity* is one that is taxable at the entity level (e.g., a corporate tax). Taxable income or loss is computed at the entity level and is attributed to the business and not its owners, and the business pays income tax on that income. Owners of entities, which are taxed as C corporations, pay income tax only when the corporation makes a distribution to them or they sell their ownership interest (shareholder tax). C corporations cannot pass their net operating losses (NOLs) or their capital losses from the sale of capital assets through to their shareholders. The losses are the property of the corporation and can be transferred to another business through some types of restructuring strategies, but their use by the acquiring company is limited.[5]

There are two ways that a C corporation can make distributions to its owners. First, a corporation can make a distribution to an owner in the form of a dividend. If a shareholder is an individual, dividends are currently taxed at the same rate as long-term capital gains.[6] If the shareholder is another corporation, the effective tax rate on the dividend depends on the corporate shareholder's level of ownership of the distributing corporation.[7] Dividends are not tax deductible to the issuing corporation. Second, a corporation can make a distribution to an owner through a transaction called a *redemption*, in which the corporation purchases an owner's stock. The gain or loss to the owner from a redemption is typically treated as capital in character,[8] and the amount of gain or loss recognized is the difference between the redemption price paid by the corporation and the owner's basis in the stock. An owner's basis in his interest in the corporation is equal to the amount he originally paid for the share plus any fees incurred. If he purchases a share of stock in a corporation for $50 and a $5 transaction fee, his basis in the share is $55. His basis in that share remains the same, regardless of whether the market value

---

4   Income and expenses from the business are reported on Schedule C of the individual's tax return.

5   See *The Value of Net Operating Losses* (UVA-C-2256) for further information.

6   Historically, dividends have not enjoyed such favorable tax treatment. Prior to the Economic Recovery Tax Act of 1981, the top tax rate on dividends was 70%, and the top tax rate on ordinary income was 50%.

7   See IRC Section 243.

8   Redemptions can be treated as extraordinary dividends in certain cases; see IRC 1059 (e).

of the share changes or if the corporation pays cash dividends. When he sells the share for $60, his gain is $60 – $55 = $5.

Fiduciary duty requirements limit a corporation's ability to distribute a disproportionate share of income to one owner or group of owners through a dividend; however, such distributions are permissible when different classes of stock have different rights to dividends and differing priority upon dissolution. It may also be possible to give an owner an unequal share of the company's profits by redeeming his or her shares at a premium, but the fiduciary duties of a board of directors to the other shareholders limits a corporation's ability to do so. To engage in such a transaction, the board must have at least a legitimate business purpose for favoring one owner over another.[9]

Pass-through Entities: Partnerships and S Corporations

For tax purposes, there are two primary types of pass-through entities: partnerships and S corporations. Every entity other than a corporation, sole proprietorship, or single member LLC (e.g., LP, multimember LLC, etc.) can elect to be treated as a partnership for tax purposes.[10] Entities that meet the strict qualification requirements discussed above can elect to be an S corporation.

Pass-through entities are entities that are acknowledged under federal tax law but do not incur any tax liability at the entity level. Pass-through entities file informational tax returns with the federal government but do not have to pay federal income tax. Instead, the income and losses are "passed-through" to the business's owners, who are responsible for paying tax on their income from the business, whether or not any cash is actually distributed to them by the business. The character of the income or loss that is attributed to owners of pass-through businesses is also determined at the entity level.

For example, consider a situation where a loss is an ordinary loss to the business but would be a capital loss if the owner engaged in the same transaction as an individual. The character of the loss is determined at the entity level, and therefore an ordinary loss passes through to the owner.[11] For pass-through

---

9   An example of this was greenmail paid to corporate raiders in the 1980s in order to prevent hostile takeovers. The existence of unwanted takeover advances gave boards the business purpose required to favor the hostile party over the other shareholders and buy their shares back at a large premium. It was essentially a payoff in exchange for a corporate raider's abandonment of its bid. Corporate governance reforms, advanced takeover defenses, and a 50% federal excise tax on greenmail proceeds has all but eliminated greenmail.

10   In addition, many foreign entities can elect partnership treatment for U.S. tax purposes through the check-the-box regulations; see IRS Reg. 301.7701–2b.

11   There are limitations on this general rule. In the case of a partnership, any assets contributed to the partnership by its partners retain the character it had in the hands of the contributor. Among other things, this prevents partners who are real estate dealers, and consequently must characterize income from the sale of real estate as ordinary, from being able to contribute real estate to a partnership, which would characterize the same gain as capital; see IRC Section 724. S corporations also have regulations in place to prevent the similar kinds of tax avoidance; see IRS Reg. 1.1366–1(b).

entities, distributions from the business to the owners are not taxable events. Instead, the distributions are treated as return of capital because the income has already been subject to taxation. The goal of the pass-through structure is to allow centralized oversight and accounting, as in the case of a C corporation, while avoiding double taxation at the entity and owner level. To ensure that pass-through entities avoid the entity-level tax but do not avoid taxation altogether, the rules concerning the allocation of income and losses across owners, the distributions to owners, and the basis of owners' interests are interrelated and more complicated than the rules pertaining to disregarded and taxable entities.

While the partnership and S corporation tax laws both offer pass-through taxation, entities taxed as partnerships have more flexibility in determining the allocation of income and loss among their owners than do S corporations. As discussed above, the S corporation's one class of stock rule requires that the allocation of income and losses among owners be pro rata. But while the default rule for partnerships is pro rata distribution of income and losses, partnerships are free, with some limitation, to assign income and loss in a non-pro rata manner.[12] Partnerships can even distribute disproportionate amounts of loss and income over time to the same partner. For example, a partnership can structure its distributions to distribute all the losses to A, who is a 75% owner of a business worth $100,000 and who also receives the first $75,000 of income to recover his or her initial investment and then 40% of profit thereafter, while his or her partner B is allocated none of the losses and 60% of the profit after A recoups his or her investment.

Tracking the owner's basis in a pass-through entity is more complex than with a C corporation; however, it is the basis calculation that allows an owner of a pass-through entity to avoid double taxation. Consistent with a C corporation, an owner's basis in a pass-through entity reflects the amount of capital invested into the business over time after *owner-level* taxes. The initial investment into the pass-through entity is the starting point for the owner's basis, similar to a C corporation. But an owner's basis in a pass-through entity fluctuates annually because the income and losses from the entity pass through and are taxed at the owner's level every year, whereas the basis in a C corporation is static. Contributions (distributions) also increase (decrease) an owner's basis in the pass-through entity. Upon the sale of the interest in the business, an owner subtracts his basis from the sale price to determine the total gain or loss on his investment.

Consider the following example: XYZ LLC is owned by A and B, who each contributed $1,000 to found the business. They each have an initial basis

---

12   Non-pro rata distributions of income or losses must have "economic effect." To have economic effect, partners must: (1) maintain their capital accounts; (2) make liquidating distributions in accordance with capital accounts; and (3) make up any negative capital accounts (the actual application of this rule varies for general and limited partners); see IRS Reg. 1.704–1(b) (2).

of $1,000 in their 50% interest in XYZ. In Year 1, the business has a net profit of $5,000 and does not make a distribution. In Year 2, XYZ breaks even and distributes $1,000 to each member. In Year 3, XYZ suffers a loss of $3,000 and does not make a distribution. In Year 4, XYZ makes a $1,500 distribution to A with B's consent **(Table 26.1).**

Table 26.1 XYZ, LLC.

	YEAR 0	YEAR 1	YEAR 2	YEAR 3	YEAR 4
Contributions by A	$1,000				
Contributions by B	$1,000				
XYZ Income to A		$2,500		($1,500)	
XYZ Income to B		$2,500		($1,500)	
Distributions to A			$1,000		$1,500
Distributions to B			$1,000		
A's Basis	$1,000	$3,500	$2,500	$1,000	($500)
B's Basis	$1,000	$3,500	$2,500	$1,000	$1,000
A's Taxable income/gain (loss)		$2,500		($1,500)	$500
B's Taxable income/gain (loss)		$2,500		($1,500)	

Source: Created by case writer.

Year 1: A and B must pay income tax on their shares of XYZ's income, $2,500, even though the company does not distribute any cash to them. Both A and B increase their respective basis in their interest in XYZ by $2,500, their individual shares of the income. Each owner has a basis of $3,500 at the end of the year.

Year 2: A and B's basis is reduced by the amount of their respective distributions, $1,000, to $2,500. Distributions are not taxable events. The owners of XYZ are simply extracting income on which they have already paid taxes. Therefore, taxing the distribution would be double taxation. In other words, A and B reinvested the $5,000 of income into their business and are currently extracting a portion of their invested capital.

If the basis was not reduced by a distribution, the owners could avoid paying taxes when they sold their business. Assume A and B were able to sell their business for $7,000 after Year 2. Economically, each owner made a profit of $1,000 ($3,500 – $2,500). But their taxable income on the sale would be zero if the basis was not reduced by distributions ($3,500 less a basis of $3,500), and they would avoid paying taxes on $1,000 of gain. To remedy this issue, the basis is reduced by distributions to ensure gains or losses on sales are properly determined.

Year 3: The business's losses reduce A's and B's basis by $1,500 each. A and B can apply this loss to offset income from other sources subject to limitations...[13] At the end of Year 3, each owner has a basis of $1,000 in their interest in XYZ.

Year 4: A takes a $1,500 distribution, which exceeds A's basis in the company by $500. The first $1,000 of the distribution reduces his basis to zero. The remaining $500, the distribution in excess of basis, is most likely taxed as capital gain.[14]

Conclusion

This note highlights the major factors that founders of businesses should consider before choosing their forms. Choices regarding the level of liability protection, pass-through or double taxation, the allocation of profits and losses, and the transferability of ownership are important and shape the future of a business. This note highlights the major choices and tradeoffs that confront a business owner; however, many more complexities exist to the factors discussed and other factors also affect the entity-choice decision.

---

13   If either A or B were unable to take advantage of the loss in the current period, the loss could be carried forward. Carry-forwards are addressed briefly later in this note.
14   For the effects on A's ownership interest relative to B, see the discussion on capital accounts later in this

INDEX

CPSIA information can be obtained
at www.ICGtesting.com
Printed in the USA
LVHW022035080119
603185LV00001B/3/P

9 781516 513635